# SOME UNHOLY WAR

# TERENCE STRONG

# SOME UNHOLY WAR

## SIMON &
## SCHUSTER

London · New York · Sydney · Toronto · New Delhi

A CBS COMPANY

First published in Great Britain by Simon & Schuster, 2013
An imprint of Simon & Schuster UK
A CBS company

1 3 5 7 9 10 8 6 4 2

Simon & Schuster UK Ltd
1st Floor
222 Gray's Inn Road
London WC1X 8HB

www.simonandschuster.co.uk

Simon & Schuster Australia, Sydney
Simon & Schuster India, New Delhi

A CIP catalogue record for this book is available from the British Library

Hardback ISBN: 978-0-74328-565-0
Trade Paperback ISBN: 978-0-74328-566-7
Ebook ISBN: 978-0-85720-683-1

Typeset by Hewer Text UK Ltd, Edinburgh
Printed and bound in Great Britain by CPI Group (UK) Ltd, Croydon, CR0 4YY

FOR VIXEN
with love

# SOME UNHOLY WAR

# One

So the rumour was true. He was back in town.

I'd heard it mentioned a couple of days earlier, when I'd been having a few Saturday evening pints with some of my old army mates. It was a rare chance for me to unwind at our favourite Hereford watering hole.

Big Brian Duffy, my former Troop sergeant in 22 SAS, had let it slip. When he realised what he'd said, he'd looked decidedly embarrassed. The cheeks of his grey-bearded face reddened deeply.

'Sorry, boss,' he said in his thick Dorset accent, whilst studiously avoiding my gaze. 'Just summat someone said. Expect it's just the usual tittle-tattle, you knows.'

I noticed that our mutual companions were shifting a little uneasily. They all knew my marriage was over, that I was out of work and that my life was in freefall. And they were equally aware that it was Sally's affair with the brash young Family Officer that had proved to be the final catalyst. An army regiment is like a village and the jungle drums appear to beat faster than the speed of light.

Everyone seemed to have known what had been going on except me, and no one had felt it his place to interfere or give me the bad news. Duffy was a good friend and the best comrade-in-arms you could hope for. It had been him who had saved my life during that final ambush in Afghanistan. So I certainly didn't want to make him feel bad for letting this proverbial cat out of the bag.

To defuse the sudden tension, I forced a smile. 'I'm not the *boss* any more, Brian,' I reminded. Duffy had been pensioned off at the age of forty-five and I'd been invalided out.

He shrugged and the powder-blue eyes finally met mine, realising I was letting him know it was all right. 'I knows,' he said. 'But old habits dies hard. Don't them – *boss*?' The gentle giant's shoulders shook as he laughed.

Everyone in our group had then moved the conversation on with artificial haste, but I had thought of nothing else for the rest of the evening.

On the Sunday I'd phoned the adjutant's office at Stirling Lines barracks and spoke to an old pal, known as 'Banger' Cumberland, who was on the duty desk.

But he was cagey. 'Sorry, Dave old son. More than my life's worth to tell you if he's back in the country. And certainly not to give you an address.'

I understood. 'In case I murder the bastard?' I suggested.

'Something like that.' Cumberland hesitated for a moment, obviously deciding how much he could say. 'Tell you what though, Dave, I *can* tell you he is due to be "returned to unit". It would have happened sooner, only you know how stretched we've been. His face never really fitted and, after the business with Sally became public, no one wanted to know him.' He added, 'Hope that makes you feel better.'

It hadn't, but on the Monday morning I suddenly *did* feel better. Because that was when I saw Lieutenant Luke Hartley with my own eyes. As I was leaving the front door of the dilapidated building, where I rented a single room with mildewed walls and a worn carpet, Hartley was walking by on the opposite pavement.

He was in civvies: smart cords, a tweed hacking jacket and brogues. He was every inch the toff with that old-fashioned yet timeless classic look the landed gentry go for, carrying it off with a slightly arrogant, easy swagger.

I pulled back into a shop doorway so that he wouldn't spot me. As I did so, I caught sight of my reflection in the window glass.

I couldn't help noticing the comparison, me in scruffy jeans, trainers and a leather bomber jacket; his face smooth and tanned, mine drawn and unshaven, haggard from too little sleep and too much booze. At thirty-six he wasn't even ten years younger than me, but I thought I looked old enough to be his father. My own cold blue eyes stared back at me, tired and weary eyes that had seen too much. I ran my fingers through my thinning fair hair, absently thinking that if I really wanted to land a job I ought to get it cut.

But now my planned visit to the Job Centre was out the window anyway. I had Luke Hartley in my sights and I was damned if he was going to get away. As he strode towards the town centre, I stepped out of the doorway, shoulders hunched and head bowed, following at a discreet distance. I kept him in view through the gaps in the passing traffic, confident that he wouldn't notice me.

I had been back in Hereford a year now, following eleven months at Birmingham Selly Oak Hospital, where they'd glued me back together again, and then a remorseless rehab course at Headley Court in Surrey.

It was there that I learned that Hartley had been sent on overseas assignments with the SAS, having completed his short stint as Family Officer. That role is sometimes considered to be rather like that of a tea boy in the commercial sector, part of the rites of passage for a young captain. In retrospect I wondered if he'd been sent away sharpish because the Regiment hierarchy had wind of his affair with my wife. The Regiment likes to look after its own. After all, I was an experienced WO1 – warrant officer, first class – who'd been in the Regiment since 1991 and Hartley had only just passed 'Selection' from the Intelligence Corps to do his first three-year SAS tour as a junior 'Rupert'. Rumours of him and Sally were never going to be good for unit morale.

As I followed him down the street, I had absolutely no clear plan or idea what I was going to do. Confront him, I suppose. Demand why the hell he thought he could play fast and loose with my wife in our house while I was in hospital, recovering from wounds that had almost cost me my life? Why had he no conscience about shagging her on the sofa while my young daughter Daisy was in bed upstairs? It was something that Sally had admitted to me once in a flood of tears.

Then again, I thought, what was the point in challenging him? His fling with Sally was long over and, as far as I was aware, wasn't likely to start up again. Perhaps I should just punch his lights out for the hell of it.

Ahead of Hartley, the sidelights of a BMW convertible, parked at a meter, suddenly blinked. It took a moment for me to realise that the vehicle was his. Damn, I thought, as I stopped and stared. I didn't want to confront him in a busy street. So now what was I going to do? My mind raced. He was already in the car, had started the engine and was nosing the vehicle out into the stream of traffic. At that very moment a taxi drove up behind me. I waved frantically and just caught the driver's eye as he passed.

He hit the brakes. I opened the rear passenger door and dived in.

I grinned at the driver as he turned round. 'I've always wanted to say this. Follow that car, will you?'

Irritatingly, the man was unfazed, as if people said that to him every day of the week. 'Which car's that then, guv?'

'The BMW convertible,' I replied. 'Just spotted an old friend of mine. Not sure where he lives now.'

That brought a chuckle from the driver. 'Then I hope he hasn't moved to London, guv,' he said dryly. 'Could be an expensive ride.'

In fact Luke Hartley hadn't moved far at all. Fifteen minutes later, I discovered he had a neat but very expensive-looking townhouse in a small new development on the edge of town.

As the BMW pulled into the short drive, I leaned forward to the cabby. 'Just drop me here, will you. I'd like this to be a surprise for him.'

After I paid the driver off, I stood on the pavement and stared down at the loose change in my palm. Just four pound coins. The sudden realisation hit me that it was all the money I had left in the world.

A lorry driver on the main road hit his air horns as my taxi suddenly pulled out in front of him. I jumped, nearly dropping my precious remaining change.

Abrupt noises did that to me now. Doors slamming, exhausts backfiring, car wheels on gravel sounding like machine-gun fire, a glass or plate dropped in a pub . . . it didn't take much to trigger my frayed and shredded nerves. Even silence was no protection, because I just had to see a sudden movement from the corner of my eye . . . and I was back on the streets of Iraq or Afghanistan. It hardly mattered which. And . . . people. I couldn't stand crowds or busy places, any more. I never felt safe, constantly on alert.

It didn't seem to matter that I was back in England, my brain seemed to overlook that simple fact. My eyes would be scanning, flashing up images in vivid psychedelic colours, my hearing so fine-tuned that its high pitch and resonance almost hurt my eardrums. I was still always searching for the man or woman in the crowd who was a suicide bomber. Or praying that I, or one of my patrol members, would be sharp enough to spot the hidden roadside bomb.

I shut my eyes momentarily and inhaled a deep lungful of air. For God's sake, I told myself, get a bloody grip.

After a minute or so I felt my heartbeat slow and the adrenalin surge at last begin to ebb. I took another deep breath to clear my head of the fading mental pictures, then I continued along the pavement towards the house with the

BMW. There was a small front garden behind some low railings. I rang the bell and waited.

When it opened, Hartley didn't recognise me at first. 'Can I help you . . . ?' He sounded hesitant and when I didn't reply immediately he squinted uncertainly. I was unshaven and looked pretty scruffy. 'Aston? It is, isn't it? Dave Aston.'

I was aware of a sarcastic smile on my lips. 'The very same.'

Hartley shuffled awkwardly, almost imperceptibly starting to edge the door shut. I saw the cloud of concern pass behind his eyes. 'It's been a while,' he commented, trying to find something to say.

I ignored that. 'Aren't you going to invite me in?'

'What do you want?'

'To talk.'

'A bit difficult, actually. I was just going out.'

'You've only just got in,' I said.

The gap between the door and the jamb was still narrowing. I placed my foot in the way. Hartley forced a smile. 'Will it take long?'

'I shouldn't think so.'

He swallowed hard and reluctantly backed off, allowing the door to swing open and me to step in. I was shown into the front lounge. It was tastefully and expensively decorated: shag pile carpet, dark leather armchairs and settee, with a huge plasma TV and a Bose home entertainment system, which took up most of one wall.

I was still glancing around when a woman entered from the adjoining dining room. She seemed to go with Hartley, a long blonde, dressed in suede and chiffon with heels that were too high to be wearing around the home.

Her nose wrinkled a fraction as she noticed me. 'Who's this, Luke?'

Hartley hesitated. 'An old army acquaintance. Dave.' He turned to me. 'This is Tara, my fiancée.'

She made no attempt to smile or offer me her hand. 'Please don't be long, Luke. I want to get the packing finished before lunch.'

Turning briskly on her spikes, she disappeared again and closed the door. 'We're getting married tomorrow,' Hartley explained. I think it was his nerves that made him keep on talking. 'Chelsea Registry Office with family and friends. Then a honeymoon in Goa. A lot to do and think about . . . so Tara's a little wound-up just now.'

I smiled faintly. 'So I see. Known her long?'

'Since we were kids . . .' His words trailed off. 'Oh, I see what you mean . . . No, we weren't engaged when . . .'

I helped him out. 'When you were humping my wife.'

He looked awkward. 'Look, Aston, I'm sorry about that. It was never intentional.'

'It just happened?' I suggested.

His eyes narrowed with a distinct look of contempt. 'As a matter of fact it did. And it was Sally who made the move on me.'

'You were our Family Officer,' I said in a low voice. 'I was badly wounded and it was your job to help us through that bad patch. Not make things worse.'

Hartley's chest swelled with indignation. 'I didn't have to make things worse. Sally was already at her wits' end with you. Your drinking, your gambling, your short temper . . . She told me how you nearly hit her in a drunken rage.'

Anger flashed in my head like red lightning. 'Hit her? *Nearly!* I deflected the blow to the wall beside her head and broke my bloody fingers!' I glared at him. 'I can't believe she left that bit out . . . And you know what happened to us since, don't you?'

The man sighed. 'Of course, everyone does. You lost it. You turned down a desk job at Hereford HQ. Then you couldn't handle civilian life. You hit the bottle, you gambled money you didn't have . . . Then you assaulted the boss in your new job—'

'The car wash.'

'It was still a job.'

The anger flashed again. '*Because* he made some snide comment about Sally having an affair. Even he'd heard it on the grapevine – *outside* the army. I'm told you were always boasting about your *conquest* when you'd had a few.'

'That's not true,' he countered. Then he shrugged. 'Anyway, if you'd treated Sally properly . . . if you hadn't been so bloody proud and taken the advice on offer to you, you wouldn't be in this mess right now.'

I felt my blood pressure rising, like a tumultuous volcanic power growing from deep within the core of me. Calmly I said, 'You mean if I'd taken the advice from my friendly Family Officer.'

There was a hint of a sneer on his face. 'Despite every-thing, it was excellent advice I gave you back then.'

He didn't see it coming, or if he did he left it too late to evade the straight right jab to his face. It was so hard I actually heard the snap of bone and saw a tooth spin across the room. Hartley tried to follow his tooth, flying backwards over an armchair, tripping and crashing to the carpet. I heard the thud as his head hit the floor. Then blood from his nose began pumping over the shag pile.

I rubbed the sore knuckles of my right hand with the palm of my left as I looked down at him. He just lay there, motion-less with his eyes shut, his jaw dropped open at an odd angle where it had been dislocated. I wondered if he'd also cracked his skull. But at that moment I just didn't care.

The adjoining door flew open and Tara stepped in. 'What's going on . . . ?'

She froze, staring down at Hartley. 'Oh, Luke!' She dropped to one knee, putting her hand to his cheek. More blood began trickling from his mouth. Then she glared up at me. 'What the hell have you done?'

I said quietly, 'Just settled an old score.'

He didn't respond, out for the count. Tara looked up again. 'You bastard! You've killed him!'

'Just call an ambulance,' I replied helpfully. 'Sorry to have spoiled your big day.'

I turned and slowly walked out of the room and out of his house. On the pavement I paused.

That, I thought to myself, had been a bloody stupid thing to do. I was already subject to a suspended sentence for grievous bodily harm to my one and only boss in Civvy Street. Now I'd almost certainly be doing time behind bars.

But did that or *anything* matter any more? After all, being in jail would solve the immediate problem of having nowhere to live and no money. Then again, it was just postponing the problems I would eventually have to face.

Then I heard her voice through the open window. 'My husband's dead!' She was almost screaming on the telephone. 'The man's just killed him!'

Shit, I suddenly thought. I haven't, have I?

He wasn't moving when I left him and I hadn't checked he was still breathing. What was the matter with me? I should have checked his airways were clear, checked he wasn't choking on his own blood or vomit. Checked he hadn't had a seizure. I was a fucking trained medic for God's sake; I'd done time in hospital A & E departments on Regiment programmes.

On impulse I turned back and banged on the front door, hard. I saw her at the window with a telephone handset clamped to her ear. 'Oh, it's him! He's back! He's trying to break in!' Her voice level took off into the stratosphere.

I stepped back. This was hopeless, she'd never let me back in and who could blame her?

I tried to tell myself she was wrong. Luke Hartley would survive, of course he would, even if he needed a set of false teeth. Of course he would. Bastards like him always bloody survived. Officers like him sent their men to die, but they always survived.

Don't shed any tears over that bastard, I scolded myself. He'll be all right. Turning sharply on my heel, I strode off back towards the centre of town.

Only minutes after setting off, a police car passed me going the other way, its blue lights flashing eagerly, like some mechanical dog on a scent.

I ducked into a side street and took a more circuitous route back to my digs. By the time I got there my right leg was really playing up.

I'd almost lost it back in Afghanistan. I was told the bone was badly shattered and it was only held together by shredded muscle and sinew – and my body's obstinate determination to stay in one piece. It had been touch and go whether or not I lost it at the field hospital in Camp Bastion before I was casevaced back to Britain. At Selly Oak Hospital the senior orthopaedic surgeon had no doubt that he should amputate. It was only the pleading of a new junior surgeon to let him try to save it – because he wanted some practice – that persuaded him to change his mind. Ironically he was from Pakistan, the very country where so many elements in its government supported the Taliban.

Anyway, I was grateful for his youthful enthusiasm and, for once, refusal to accept conventional wisdom and experience. My leg could throb and ache sometimes, keeping me awake at night, but at other times I hardly knew there was anything wrong with it, except that I walked with a slight limp. Somehow I'd lost the best part of an inch off that leg.

At last I reached my digs and collected my one holdall. In it I had one suit that was twenty years old, reserved for job interviews. Then there were two ties; three white and two casual shirts, and a change of socks and underwear. I stuffed my toilet bag on top of the pile and snapped the lid shut. I'd already paid my rent up to the end of that week, but there was no point hanging around, waiting to be arrested. I returned to the street and caught a bus to the house that had formerly been my own.

I alighted at the stop on the main road and took the next turning to the neat street of 1930s semis with their carefully tended front gardens. There was no car parked on the short tarmac drive. I glanced at my watch. Just gone twelve thirty. Perfect timing, Sally would be back for her lunch break at any moment. I barely had time to smoke a rollie, when the old family Discovery came into view at the end of the road.

It pulled in beside me and Sally clambered down. I thought how good she looked for a woman in her late thirties. She was only around five-four tall with a slim but solidly built body that showed off the jodhpurs and well-cut tweed hacking jacket nicely. As usual she wore only the scantest of make-up, yet that just seemed to accentuate those beautiful, bright-blue eyes more than ever.

She broke into a smile, a hand brushing the wave of short blonde hair from her eyes. 'Dave! What a lovely surprise!'

I smiled back hesitantly. 'Still working at the stables, I see.'

Sally did the admin and accounts there, when she wasn't sneaking a crafty ride. We'd always joked she'd loved horses more than me. A pity she hadn't stuck to four-legged critters, I thought in a flash of savage anger.

'I'm still there for the moment,' she replied. 'But they think they may have to lay some people off. Business is tough.'

I nodded. 'Hopefully it won't be you. Expect you're indispensable.'

'Hopefully I am,' she said. 'And you, Dave? How's my rough diamond?' It had been her pet name for me since our earliest days together. She frowned, then added hesitantly, 'You're looking a bit . . . ?'

'Rough?' I said helpfully.

'Are you eating properly?'

'Yes,' I lied.

She tilted her head to one side in an expression of mild disapproval. 'And drinking properly as well, no doubt.'

I shrugged. 'I do my best.' Quickly I changed the subject. 'How's Daisy?'

'Missing you a lot.' She sighed wearily. 'And so what do I owe this unexpected pleasure?'

'I wondered if I could collect a few things?'

Sally moved towards the front door, extracting a key from her shoulder bag. 'Of course, Dave. It's your house.'

'Not any more.'

'Only because you gave it to me.'

I ignored that. I said, 'I've done something stupid.'

As the door swung open, she turned back. 'Again?'

'I bumped into Luke Hartley.'

Her face paled. 'Oh.'

'I'm afraid I hit him. And a bit harder than I intended.'

There was a sadness in her eyes. 'Oh, Dave, that was so pointless. You know it's all long over between him and me.'

I nodded. 'I know. But it made me feel better.' The words were out before I realised that it hadn't made me feel better at all. Quite the opposite, in fact.

'But it's *you* who'll get hurt, and you've been hurt enough already.' She stepped aside to let me in. 'He's bound to call the police.'

I didn't want to go into any more detail, didn't want to tell her I thought I'd killed him. 'That's why I'm here. To collect a few things.'

'Making yourself scarce?'

'Thought I'd leave town for a bit.'

She shut the front door behind us. 'Just as well. That room you've been renting sounded awful.'

I didn't tell her that was better than what I was likely to be facing from now on. A wanted murderer, on the run with nowhere to hide.

I shrugged. 'I didn't have an option, Sally. An out-of-work soldier with a criminal record doesn't seem that high up on the council's list of housing priorities.'

Sally looked pained. 'You could stay here for a bit. Until you find your feet. I could soon clear out the spare room.'

I shook my head. 'We're divorced, Sal. Best not to look back. The cops could be here any minute. I need to get away.'

She shrugged. 'OK, if that's what you think. Do you know where you're going?'

'Not yet.'

'D'you want to go upstairs and get your stuff? It's still all there in the wardrobe.'

It was strange going back to the bedroom that I'd shared with Sally for so many years. The same curtains, carpet, duvet cover . . . so familiar, like an indelible photograph imprinted in my mind, a room I'd conjured up so many times during a lonely night in some far-off war zone. And there was that soft and floral feminine smell of the place. It was hard to know if it was perfume, air-freshener or just clean laundry. But it was unmistakably home.

I went to my side of the louvred-door wardrobe and opened it. On the floor was my old, huge DPM camo bergen, alongside all the kit I used to keep together, ready to pack at a moment's notice – if and when a call came. A lot was army-issue, but much was private purchase to ensure the very best.

Carefully I began spreading it all out on the floor beside the double bed. Main equipment including a camouflaged Gore-Tex bivvy bag, a basha sheet, arctic sleeping bag, Jetboil stove and mess tins. Clothing was a mix of army DPM and plain olive drab. I decided the thick Norwegian Army shirts would be especially useful, along with a lightweight, fibre-filled top made in dark-green Pertex.

Adding boots and Gore-Tex gaiters to the top of the bergen, I zipped up the lid.

I'd barely done that when I heard Sally's voice from downstairs. 'Dave! The police have arrived! A car's just pulled up!'

I shoved my empty holdall into the wardrobe, shouldered the bergen, and headed for the stairs. Sally was waiting on the ground floor, indicating for me to go through the kitchen at the rear. 'Quick,' she said. 'I'll stall them. You go out the back way. The Fosdykes will be out at work.'

I nodded. 'Thanks, Sal.'

I wasn't expecting the quick kiss to my cheek. 'Now go,' she said. 'Keep in touch.'

Two figures were outlined in the front-door windows as I slipped away through the back to the kitchen. Once in the garden, I crossed the lawn, scrambled onto the disused coal-bunker and jumped the neighbours' fence. I crossed their lawn and slipped down the side of the house and into the next street.

Until I'd put a mile or so between the house and me, I didn't slow. It was a mild late-summer day, the sun was out and I was perspiring under my heavy load. I was painfully aware that I was nowhere like as fit and agile as in my army days. I found a roadside bench and sat down. I had to think things through, come up with some sort of plan.

After an hour or so, I made my decision. First I needed to say goodbye to my daughter, Daisy, explain that I loved her and she would see me again before too long. Mind you, that could mean visiting me in prison while I was on remand for murder. I wouldn't want that.

I pushed the thought from my mind. After talking to Daisy, I'd make my way to Brian Duffy's place.

Since he'd left the Regiment, Duffy had been making use of his HGV licence and doing a fair amount of work for a local haulier. When I'd been drinking with him on Saturday, he'd mentioned that he was due to be heading off to France tonight. At least it would be free transport if I could hitch a lift, because I wasn't going to go anywhere fast on four quid.

I took my time making the journey to Daisy's school and waited for her opposite the gate as the exodus of teenagers exploded across the playground in a sea of uniform colour. My fourteen-year-old daughter was quite easy to spot. She'd inherited my height and, luckily, her mother's fair good looks. Those looks weren't enhanced by her sloppy weekday dress style. Her blouse was half hanging out of the waistband of her skirt, and her socks had collapsed around the ankles of her long, white and painfully thin legs.

'Dad!' she called, suddenly recognising me and leaving her group of friends to cross the road.

'Hello, sweetheart. How you doing?'

She smiled broadly. 'Fine, Dad. But how are *you* doing? Are you coming home?'

That hurt. 'You know I can't come home. Mum and I are divorced now.'

'You could try.' Her head bowed slightly, but her mother's beautiful eyes still looked up at me coquettishly. 'I'm sure she wouldn't mind really.'

I didn't want to tell her there was no hope. 'Maybe one day, sweetheart. But we really need our own space for now.' It was the opportunity I needed to break it to her. 'In fact that's why I wanted to see you. To tell you, I'm going away.'

Her brow fractured into a frown. 'Why?'

'Looking for work,' I replied. 'There doesn't seem to be anything around here.'

The corners of her mouth down turned. 'So I won't see you at all . . .'

'Not for a while.'

'Where are you going?'

'I'm not sure yet.'

'To friends?'

'I don't know. I'll be OK.'

'Are you going for weeks, for months?' she pressed. 'Will you come and see us at Christmas?'

God, was this daughter of mine deliberately trying to break my heart? 'I hope so,' I replied, 'but that's still a long way off yet.'

She forced a smile. 'It's not. Time flies, you know.' Another thought occurred to her. 'It's only a year before I leave school.'

I frowned with mild disapproval. 'Unless you do your A-levels and go to university.'

Daisy straightened her back and suddenly looked very grown up. 'You mean land myself with a huge student loan to pay back . . . for a degree that employers say are ten a penny.'

'I don't know about that . . .' I began, somewhat defensively.

'It's true, Dad. Most degrees nowadays aren't worth the paper they're printed on. And jobs are drying up all over the place. That's what the sixth-formers are saying.'

'It'll get better,' I said with more optimism than I felt. 'Recessions don't go on for ever.'

She smiled, realising I was trying to cheer her up, and put her hand on mine. 'I know, Dad . . . Anyway, I can always join the army.'

'Don't you even . . . !' I blurted, even before I realised she was teasing.

Her laughing eyes looked into mine. 'I'd better go now. Promise me you will take care?'

I nodded. 'I love you, little lady.'

'I love you, too,' she replied, turned and scurried off to catch up with her friends.

Feeling not a little saddened, I watched her go. Then, taking a deep breath, I set off on my own journey across town to where 'Big Brian' Duffy lived.

Late summer sun filled the landscape with a mellow and dusty light as the shadows lengthened. Walking along a country lane, the bergen weighing on my back, I was reminded momentarily of the magical desert light of Afghanistan where Duffy and I had last served together.

I remembered clearly the day when it had marked the beginning of the end for the both of us.

# Two

The palms of my hands had been slick with sweat, and I knew it wasn't down to the oppressive Afghan heat. Somehow the sweat of fear feels and smells different.

Besides, it was late in the day. The temperature was actually waning as our four-vehicle column of sand-coloured 'Snatch' Land Rovers waited in the shade of a compound mud wall. The vehicles, designed for grabbing troublemakers off the streets of Northern Ireland, had received a lot of criticism in the media as lacking any meaningful protection. But sometimes they suited our purposes. They were small, fast and relatively inconspicuous. And to be inconspicuous was exactly what we wanted on this and many other missions.

I shifted uneasily in the driver's seat, aware of the increasing tempo of my heartbeat. I didn't know why; I wasn't used to that happening. Andy Smith, the youngest member of our team and not long out of selection, sat next to me and I hoped he hadn't noticed the slight tremor of my hands on the wheel.

No one had known we were coming. So why did I suddenly have this ridiculous notion that we might be parked beside an IED planted in the roadside ditch? I tightened my fists until the knuckles showed white.

As the sun lowered in the sky, a sulphurous yellow haze of dust painted the mud-brick houses of the village, the air heavy with the conflicting smells of open drains and pots of cooking food. Yet there was not a woman in sight, anywhere. I still hadn't properly got used to it – as though they had all been abducted by aliens, just like in one of those awful 1950s sci-fi horror movies.

At least my frayed nerves should have been comforted by the fact that Duffy was behind us in the back of our custom-modified Land Rover, standing up in the hatch and nursing a mounted general-purpose machine gun. His use of that weapon was legendary, sometimes using it almost as a sniper rifle. It was said – only half in jest – that he could blow the balls off a mosquito at a hundred metres. Modestly, Duffy himself claimed that would only be possible on his second attempt.

Suddenly young Andy nodded his head. He indicated the compound gate on the opposite side of the track. 'Here's Abdullah now,' he observed.

A small group of Afghan men, some carrying old Soviet Kalashnikovs, milled around by the gate. They watched warily as our 25-year-old liaison agent emerged from the villa compound and crossed over the track to us.

'He doesn't look too pleased,' I murmured.

Another voice joined the conversation from the rear of our Land Rover. 'I'm really not too sure how good Abdullah is, you know.'

The silky urbane voice belonged to Charles Houseman. He was a field officer with SIS, the Secret Intelligence Service, more generally known to the public as MI6. A real-life

James Bond, but without any 'licence to kill'. From my experience, people like him were more likely to have a licence to cock things up.

His words irritated me. 'Well, Chas,' I muttered. 'Abdullah's all we've got. And he's shown a lot of balls helping us.'

We all knew what would happen to him if ever he fell into the hands of the Taliban. Not only he himself, but his entire extended family could expect to pay a horrible price.

Abdullah was a schoolteacher and regularly acted as an interpreter for us and as an unofficial liaison officer with the local tribal elders. Those village elders and religious leaders were today holding a *shura*, or meeting, in the house opposite.

Abdullah opened the rear door and slid in to sit beside Houseman. The teacher wore baggy black trousers and a loose pullover shirt. He rarely smiled and his eyes were dark and serious.

'No luck?' Houseman asked.

'Why you say that?'

'You don't look happy,' the SIS man replied a little awkwardly.

Abdullah shrugged. 'For me there is nothing to be so happy about . . . You have heard it said. Helmand is the place where Allah comes to cry.'

The teacher seemed satisfied that he'd made his point. In my rear-view mirror, I could see Houseman looking a little uncomfortable. Whatever we kidded ourselves we were achieving in this place, as far as ordinary Afghans were concerned we still had a long way to go.

Abdullah added, 'In fact, some of the elders have agreed to grant a short audience when their meeting is over. They are talking about this year's opium crop, and they are concerned at what you might have to say.'

'Ah, Abdullah, that's perfect,' Houseman congratulated. 'You've done well.'

I don't know how Houseman always managed to look so smug. Maybe it was the permatanned face, the lazy Hollywood smile or that perfect coiffure of crinkly dark-blond hair. Always immaculately presented, he also seemed ahead of the game whenever I'd seen him operate. That was probably just as well in a place as dangerous as Afghanistan.

'And they understand that Chas will have armed protection?' I asked.

Abdullah nodded, a hint of amusement in his eyes. 'Of course,' he replied. We all knew how easy it was for a simple misunderstanding to spiral out of control.

I spoke to the rest of the team, who were deployed in the other two Land Rovers. Our bespoke short-range radio kit linked each individual member via a mike and earpiece. 'Zulu Two to Red and Blue Two. You are cleared to deploy, over.'

'*OK that*,' replied the other two team-leaders in unison.

I added, 'Green Two remain in support.'

'*OK that*,' confirmed the third team leader. '*Out.*'

Instantly the doors of the two Land Rovers behind us flew open and a total of eight SAS troopers stepped out. They carried a lethal mix of weaponry between them, from Canadian-made Diemaco C8 carbines and grenade launchers to automatic pistols. But they were 'dressed down' in military terms, with no helmets and a mix-and-match selection of DPM military clothing over their body armour that was not all instantly recognisable as official British Army issue. It helped reinforce the concept that this was a peace mission, and not an active military operation that might raise alarm amongst innocent locals.

The troopers fanned out quietly and purposefully from our column of vehicles, moving to predetermined points surrounding the villa opposite, from which they would have clear fields of fire in the event of any trouble.

The group of Pashtun tribesmen continued to watch from outside the gate of the villa. Some began to finger their weapons nervously. They were there to protect the village elders, who were attending the *shura*, from any vengeance attacks by Taliban fundamentalists. It was clear that the villagers recognised our team as friendly, but they would also have been keenly aware that our very presence could attract unwanted – and lethal – attention.

'Right,' Houseman said, 'let's go.'

A small contingent of our men, including Duffy on the general-purpose machine gun, stayed with the column to protect the vehicles and to offer any additional backup if things went pear-shaped.

Meanwhile I climbed out of my seat, joining Houseman and Abdullah as they started to cross the street. This cracked and potholed strip of paving was the main drag of the village and off it fed a labyrinth of interlinking alleys and passageways. They ran between the mud walls in a confusion of low, primitive mud-brick houses and compounds, dusty backyards and dead ends. The entire residential complex was dilapidated, its tired buildings merging in the mellow dusk light with the desiccated and dun-coloured landscape.

It was difficult to believe that in the 1950s and 1960s, according to Houseman, the Americans had poured in millions of dollars in aid to develop a 1,600-kilometre irrigation system in Helmand. The province had flourished, with neat new homes flanking freshly paved, tree-shaded streets, and farmers prospered from the growth of wheat, fruit and vegetables.

The burgeoning heroin boom in Western cultures and the invasion of the Soviet Union in 1979 changed all that. Before then few poppies had been grown by the Pashtun, who are naturally a very reserved people.

Ironically it was the encouragement of the United States that persuaded the farmers to switch to poppy production, in order to raise funds to fight the Soviets – by buying American arms. The United States also backed one particular military leader of the Afghan mujahedin. His name was Osama bin Laden.

But when the Soviets finally gave up the fight and left the country in 1989, the farmers did not give up the poppy. And the reason was simple economics. The poppy harvest fetched ten times the equivalent income of wheat. It was no contest. During that period of instability, civil war and political infighting followed, in which a number of vicious drug barons emerged to control the opium industry in a patchwork of fiefdoms around the country.

It was only when one section of the warring mujahedin, the fundamentalist Taliban, emerged as a cohesive and united

entity that things changed. Their forces took Kabul and
formed the government in 1996, their devout leadership
imposing a strict ban on the growing of the poppy. By the
time of the American-led invasion of Afghanistan in 2001,
following 9/11, the opium crop had all but been eradicated.

However, five years later everything had turned full circle.
The Taliban was at first driven back to the border wastelands
of Pakistan by American and British forces. But, over time,
its fighters regrouped and gradually returned, adopting classic guerrilla warfare techniques – sniping, ambushing and,
increasingly, using deadly roadside bombs. These are known
in the military as 'improvised explosive devices', or IEDs.
Often they utilised leftover artillery rounds or mines from the
previous Soviet occupation.

Meanwhile, during the temporary absence of the Taliban,
Afghan farmers had, hardly surprisingly, gone back to growing the lucrative poppy crop. But now, when the holy warriors
returned, they linked up with local drug barons to *encourage*
the heroin trade in order to fund their insurgent fight against
NATO troops.

As my small SAS team approached the villa, it was high
summer and the harvest time for the opium crop was fast
approaching. That was the reason this *shura* had been called.
Everyone in the region was anxious, not just the farmers. The
wealth created by the annual crop affected everybody, in one
way or another. Each year there had been the threat of its
eradication by the Kabul government or NATO forces. So
far it hadn't happened, but all the locals were twitchy. This
time it might. Each group would be represented at the *shura*

– local leaders, farmers and drug lords – and this was when deals were done.

With so much at stake, it was hardly surprising that I could almost sense the tension in the baked afternoon air, and hardly surprising that my palms were still sweating as the three of us approached the group of armed tribesmen guarding the front gate. Houseman and I were tooled up, but only with 9mm SIG Sauer automatic pistols. If anything went wrong, we'd be hard-pressed to escape from a scrap without injury.

Abdullah smiled nervously at the Afghans and indicated the two of us. I didn't need any translation as he said, 'These are the gentlemen I was telling you about. They are expected.'

Houseman was looking as suave as ever in a white-and-blue check shirt, chinos and lightweight travel vest. He smiled one of his winning lazy smiles. '*As-salaam-aleikum*,' he greeted with one of his limited Pashto phrases. '*Allahu Akbar.*'

A tall man with a wispy black beard and a flat pancake hat regarded him sullenly and nodded. '*Allahu Akbar*,' he replied without enthusiasm. 'Follow me,' he added in his own language.

He shuffled towards the villa, disturbed dust swirling around the hems of his baggy pantaloons. Pushing open the sun-rotted timber gate, he led the way into a grassless courtyard. Its central and only feature was an ancient mulberry tree, a gnarled canopy of branches providing shade for the low table and scattering of empty chairs arranged beneath it.

The walls of the villa formed three sides of the dusty square. It was a well-appointed building by Afghan standards and belonged to a tribal elder. I could see through a set of open double doors into a spacious reception room. Despite its size, the place was crowded with the great and the good of the region, all engaged in heated and sweaty debate.

Our chaperone jabbed a thumb towards the chairs beneath the tree and muttered something.

'He says to wait here,' Abdullah translated. 'The meeting is nearly over.'

We helped ourselves to seats and waited for the voices of irritation and anger to diminish slowly as each argument ran its course. Finally the farmers, traders and dealers began to spill out into the comparative cool of the courtyard. They made their way in small groups to the front gate, still fiercely debating matters between themselves.

At last the room was empty, apart from three austere-looking men. The meeting now over, the village leaders stepped out into the waning afternoon sunshine. Each was bearded and wore a turban and a long, coloured dishdasha shirt.

Abdullah was the first to jump to his feet. With a quick, respectful little bow of his head, he addressed the tallest of the Afghans, talking quickly in Pashto. I could pretty much follow it as he said, 'Mr Mayor, this is the gentleman from England who wants to speak with you. He is Mr Houseman.'

Anthracite eyes regarded the Englishman's extended hand as though it might be part of some elaborate hoax.

In the brief moment of hesitation, Abdullah said quickly in English, 'This is our mayor, and these two other gentlemen are the leader of our local council of trade and our oldest-serving mullah.'

Then Houseman's hand was grasped in a powerful grip. '*Tha tsanga ye?*' the Englishman asked.

To my surprise, the mayor replied, 'I am well, thank you.' Then he added, 'Do you speak Pashto?'

Houseman shook his head. 'I've done a course, but languages are not really my thing.'

A faint and reluctant smile passed fleetingly across the mayor's lips. 'Then you will perhaps endure my equally poor English? I am Aryan Ameer.'

'A pleasure to meet you, Mr Mayor,' Houseman replied.

'Please call me Aryan.'

'Very well,' Houseman replied and turned to me. 'This is Dave. He is with the soldiers who are looking after me.'

Aryan's eyes narrowed as his hand grasped mine in a grip like a steel vice. I winced inwardly, but tried not to show the pain. It was a test of wills. His voice was quiet and even, giving no indication that he was crushing the small bones of my hand deliberately, as he said, 'I believe you and your team arrived in Camp Bastion only just recently.'

I nodded as he finally relieved the pressure, but I was unsettled that he should have any information about me, or my team. I said cautiously, 'You are very well informed, Aryan.'

'It is my job to be, Mr Dave.' There was a hint of mirth in his eyes at my evident surprise. He was enjoying the game. 'Direct from Iraq, I understand. At a time when, I believe, you had been expecting some well-earned leave?'

I think my silence rather confirmed what he clearly already knew. He continued, 'Therefore, looking after Mr Houseman must be considered a job of great value by your British government.'

I smiled at that. 'Oh, he's a very important person all right,' I said with just a hint of sarcasm for Houseman's benefit.

The SIS field officer glanced sideways at me with disapproval. Then he returned his attention to Aryan. 'I have been sent by Her Majesty's Government to discuss this year's poppy harvest.'

The expression on the mayor's face froze. Then the moment passed and he smiled. But I noticed that the warmth failed to reach his eyes. 'In that case,' the man said, 'we must discuss the matter over some refreshments.'

That seemed to break the ice somewhat. We selected our chairs and dragged them into a rough circle while Aryan called for one of his young houseboys to bring black tea and sweetmeats.

The mayor came quickly to the point. 'Each year you threaten us with eradication of our poppy crop,' he said as he poured the tea from a gleaming copper pot.

Houseman accepted his cup. 'That is just our government's *public* position. In order to encourage your farmers to grow other crops.'

As the exchange continued, Abdullah translated their conversation for the benefit of the other two Afghans. The leader of the local trade council interrupted, protesting heatedly.

'He says there are no other options, but no one will admit it,' Abdullah explained. 'If your Western governments were willing to pay a higher price for wheat or cotton, then my farmer members would willingly give up the poppy.'

Houseman raised an eyebrow. 'Despite the Taliban?' he asked.

That hit home. The trade council leader may not have understood much English, but he understood one word all too well. Taliban. He fell silent, exchanging concerned glances with Aryan and the head mullah.

'Don't worry, I understand,' Houseman said. 'The British Army also understands, and they are here as friends of the Afghan people.'

Aryan nodded slowly. 'You came with the Americans because the Taliban government gave safe haven to the al-Qaeda fighters. You drove them back into the Pakistan borderlands. And you promised us many things. Roads, bridges, schools, clinics, wells and irrigation . . . we've have not seen many of these things . . .'

'Yes, yes,' Houseman said, a little irritably. 'That is because the Taliban are back and the security situation is such that aid and construction workers, your *own* and those from abroad, are afraid to come here. Many have been intimidated or even murdered by the Taliban.'

Aryan nodded his acknowledgement.

I could tell that Houseman felt he was successfully making his point. He added, 'Likewise farmers who refuse to cooperate and cultivate the poppy. They, too, have been butchered. That is why, despite any official position, the British Army commanders have no intention of eradicating your crop.'

Of course, what Houseman didn't mention was that many farmers, local businessmen, traders and drug barons had no problem with the Taliban methods, because they were doing very nicely out of the trade. According to army intelligence, Mayor Aryan was one of them.

Abdullah gabbled off his translation and the expression lightened on the faces of all three Afghans. 'We are most relieved to hear that,' the mayor said at length. 'It is good that you understand our problems.'

'And I hope, in return,' Houseman said, 'that you will try to understand ours.'

'But of course.'

'As you well know, Mayor Aryan, our soldiers are taking a real hammering in Helmand province. A member of the Parachute Regiment and another soldier in the Royal Irish have been killed in the past few days.'

Aryan's eyes narrowed. 'And *they* have been killing many Taliban. Also many civilians with their aircraft and bombs.'

Houseman didn't deny it. 'That is why it is time to talk.'

The mayor looked surprised. 'You wish to talk to the Taliban?'

'Yes, the local leadership.'

'They may not want to talk to you, Mr Houseman.'

'Persuade them, Aryan, and I will guarantee that the question of eradication here will be put on hold for at least another year.'

The mayor's eyes met with Houseman's, each man sizing up the other.

Finally Aryan said quietly, 'I shall see what I can do. More tea?'

# Three

Two hours later, we returned to Camp Bastion, our main base in Helmand province.

The vast and primitive tented city rested in the parched flatlands to the north of the provincial capital of Lashkar Gah. Chaotic patterns of khaki-coloured tents stretched across the dust bowl. If ever the military planners had hoped to bring a sense of order to the shifting sands, they had failed miserably. The place had grown into a huge maze of a squatter camp.

Each day the eddying dust and grit just refused to be tamed – almost a metaphor for Afghanistan itself, I thought idly, as our lead Snatch Land Rover drove through the compound gates.

At least the latrine and ablution blocks were properly operational now, and there was decent scoff to be had in the mess tents, dominating the site like giant brown polytunnels. Logistically the Afghanistan operation had been and continued to be a nightmare, absolutely everything needed to fight the campaign having to be flown in or shipped in via Pakistan.

Since the beginning of anti-al-Qaeda operations in Afghanistan, covert and clandestine operations had been mostly handled by our rivals of the Special Boat Service, the elite of the Royal Marines, because we in the SAS had been fully deployed in Iraq. However, it was clear that all 'special operations' on both fronts were under such huge pressure that a few SAS units were needed to reinforce the smaller numbers of SBS troops operating in Afghanistan.

My own SAS contingent had a couple of tents close to Joint Operational Command HQ, which was adorned with a complex array of different radio antennae, aerials and satellite dishes. We had only recently been plucked out of Basra in Iraq and brought straight to Helmand, apparently to babysit a number of intelligence wallahs on a mission to sleep with the enemy. British and allied casualties had been getting unacceptably high and Whitehall felt it was time to try to talk with the Taliban.

At least that was the story. But true or not, none of us was too pleased. The 'Sabre' squadron, of which my sixteen-man Troop was part, was long overdue some rotational leave. Everyone was painfully aware that the entire British Army was seriously overstretched, but that had an even greater significance for a small specialist regiment like 22 SAS.

It was made up of just four Squadrons, each of those comprising four sixteen-man Troops, providing a total of sixty-four fighting soldiers. Each Troop has developed a speciality in behind-the-lines 'insertion' skills, as in Air Troop, Boat Troop, Mobility Troop and Mountain Troop. In turn, each Troop is divided into an individual, self-sufficient fighting unit, the four-man patrol or 'brick'.

Our specialist services were wanted on two major battlefronts at the same time. That was before other commitments were taken into consideration. So it was hardly surprising that all this neatly planned structure and pattern of deployment had recently been falling apart. Individual Troops and 'bricks' were increasingly a mix-and-match patchwork of whoever was available.

Holes in manning levels caused by death, injury or lack of qualified new recruits were increasingly being plugged by civilians co-opted from the two SAS Territorial Army regiments, or members of L Detachment, who were former full-timers. Either way, many soldiers were not pleased with the depth of these developments and the effect on morale of even the regular professionals was becoming disturbingly noticeable.

Even I was getting cheesed off with the relentless pace of operations and cancelled leave. When a scheduled period of leave started, it wasn't uncommon for us to be sitting around at airports for days waiting for seats on flights back to the UK.

None of us had joined the SAS for the easy life, and regular moaners were not popular. Put up or shut up was the attitude and an unspoken rule amongst us. But cracks were starting to show in some of the guys' personal lives. Separations and divorces were increasing, as were reports of domestic violence. All were signs of the unsustainable mental strain that some of the men were under.

Perhaps I should have noticed the telltale little changes in my own attitude and behaviour, but I didn't.

The last time I'd been on leave – nine months earlier – my wife Sally had pointed out how irritable I'd become. Of course, I snapped back at her, explained that I was having trouble sleeping with all the bad dreams. Even Daisy noticed it and asked why I couldn't sit still for five minutes to watch *EastEnders* with her. I'd become nervous, twitchy, and liked to be constantly on the move.

When I wasn't, I started getting my kicks from online gambling. It was like an adrenalin buzz without anyone trying to kill me. So nothing *dangerous*, I had it all under control.

Then there were the long walks, even in the middle of the night, when the whisky hadn't done its job.

Thankfully, when the leave was over and I returned to operational theatre in Iraq, a lot of those symptoms ebbed away. I guess that was because I was confronting my demons face-to-face again.

Now, a new period of leave was well overdue.

Before this current deployment in Afghanistan, which we were promised would be very short, my Troop had been operating in Iraq alongside US Delta Force and other specialist US units as part of a clandestine formation known colloquially as 'Task Force Black'. Others called it 'Knight'.

Running alongside US General David Petraeus's well-advertised 'Surge Offensive' – pouring thousands of extra American troops into no-go areas held by enemy Sunni and Shia factions – Task Force Knight had fought a deadly and dangerous covert war.

Based on communications intercepts, plus new and often risky close-up intelligence techniques on the streets, the Force's objective was to go after the actual Islamic terrorists who were planning or carrying out the suicide bombings that had created such hideous carnage. Task Force Knight used meticulous planning to carry out surgical strikes, often taking out terrorists actually on their way to a planned attack. They could be car bombers or on foot wearing belts full of explosives and nails.

Immediate follow-up sweeps would often take out the terrorists' support teams: the armed escorts, plotters and explosive technicians behind these evil operations that had killed and maimed thousands of innocent Iraqis.

As a result, over time, bombers became harder to recruit and the eventual huge loss of terrorist support expertise led to a falling away of the mass murder campaigns. I'd learned recently that by last year the Force had taken out some four thousand Islamic terrorist bombers and their masters – an incredible toll. And a degree of peace, safety and normality had returned to most towns and cities as a result.

But the triumph had come at a cost. Overall, the Force itself had suffered some twenty per cent of its number killed or injured. There was another casualty, too. Often unseen, undetected and insidious. Combat stress.

All warfare is bad, but deniable 'black ops' are the worst. They are always a messy business, with too much innocent life lost. The collateral damage of war, they call it. But it's not just the dead and injured, it's the killers too. No one is immune. People don't realise how rare it is to kill your fellow man face to face. Most casualties are caused at long distance, by artillery or mortar rounds, air strikes or even rifle fire. When killing is close up and personal, it becomes a different game altogether.

I'm not sure exactly when it happened, when I had begun to sicken of all the death, maiming and utter destruction of it all. When that little trip-switch blew in my head.

For whatever reason, I failed to see it coming. After all, I'd been with the 'hooligans from Hereford' – as we liked to call ourselves – for some sixteen years. There wasn't much I hadn't done and seen. Of course, not all of it had been pleasant, but mostly I'd had a great time. I'd worked with some great characters and we'd all taken a pride in our achievements and professionalism.

I certainly don't think I'd appreciated I was cracking up as I drove the Land Rover up to our tents and applied the handbrake.

Duffy was out of the front passenger seat in a trice. 'I'm parched,' he announced unnecessarily. 'Big Bri' was always parched and ready for a drink. 'Can I get you anything, boss?'

I grinned. 'Is bin Laden a Muslim? You bet.'

'Me, too,' added young Andy.

'Ginger beer it is then!' Duffy guffawed.

The plastic bottles contained local home-brew labelled ginger beer in felt-tip pen. Indeed it was a type of beer, but there was certainly no bloody ginger in it.

As the giant of a man ambled off, Chas Houseman and Abdullah were alighting from the rear of my Land Rover.

Houseman restrained the Afghan by the arm. 'I must ask you, Abdullah, how does Mayor Aryan know so much about what is going on in this camp?'

I could see the look of alarm flash momentarily in Abdullah's eyes, but he covered it well with a quick shrug of his shoulders. Andy looked surprised and, at hearing the challenge, glanced in my direction. I shook my head. It wasn't our business, we were just the babysitters.

Abdullah replied, 'Many locals are working here in the camp. They all see things, like to gossip.'

Houseman nodded in my direction. 'But they wouldn't have known about Dave here. Or his team. You are the only one who has dealings with us.'

Another shrug. 'Word gets around.'

'Please don't lie to me, Abdullah,' Houseman replied flatly. 'We must have trust between us. Especially in matters of security.'

Abdullah glowered at the Englishman with dark, angry eyes. 'Trust is exactly what Mayor Aryan needs, too. All he has is a lot of empty promises. The clinics don't come, the clean water doesn't come, the schools don't come . . .'

Houseman raised his hand. 'That's because of the poor security situation.'

'That's what you say, but the locals don't always see it like that.' Abdullah took a deep breath. 'That's *how* I try to build bridge between them and you. By making trust, by exchanging informations. He tells me when he learns something about the Taliban, so I can tell you. If there is something of interest here, I tell him. It is a fair trade.'

'So he can tell the Taliban?' Houseman accused.

'No, so that he knows what is going on all around him. He is the top man, but mostly he is ignored by those in military authority.'

Houseman retaliated. 'How do you know information you give him isn't passed straight on to the Taliban?'

'Why should he?' Abdullah shook his head, clearly not seeing why Houseman couldn't understand. 'The mayor hates the Taliban – they killed his brother over ten years ago just because he belonged to another faction of the mujahedin. His daughter's education and career was ruined because they closed schools for women. He hates them, but he still has to deal with them. They are part of his reality. But he does not hate me. He likes me, likes me because I try to help him. That is why he agreed to see you, why I think he will help you.'

I had to hand it to him. Abdullah had a thankless – not to say dangerous – task. He was one brave and selfless man who was doing what he knew to be right. Apart from a little cash in hand, there was nothing in it for him.

Maybe Houseman was starting to recognise this because he smiled and extended his hand. 'I'm sorry, Abdullah, I didn't mean to go off at you. I'm just worried about the security situation just now. Too many lives being lost.'

The Afghan shook the offered hand with a little reluctance. 'I would do nothing to endanger the life of my English friends here in Bastion,' he said firmly.

'I know,' Houseman replied and watched as our negotiator turned and walked away.

When he was out of earshot, I said, 'Cross a Pashtun and you've an unforgiving enemy. Help him and you've a friend for life. I think Abdullah's a very honest man, Chas.'

'Yeah,' he agreed reluctantly. 'As honest as you're likely to get from any Afghan. Trouble with them is they tend to sway with whichever way the wind is blowing.'

That rankled, especially in the case of Abdullah. 'Different culture, Chas, wasn't that ever explained to you?'

He gave a half smile. 'Sure.' After a pause, he added, 'Thanks for your help, Dave. See you around.'

With that he turned and walked away to one of the nearby tents that was home to the camp's intelligence community. Mostly they comprised members of the Intelligence Corps and the recently formed Special Reconnaissance Regiment. It had obviously been felt by those above that Houseman was best billeted with his own kind.

As I was about to enter my own tent, I came face to face with my second-in-command, Sergeant Major Eddie Crisp.

'Ah, there you are, Dave!' he said, looking down at me.

I was five-eleven in height, but Crisp was skyscraper tall. He was also strong and wiry, turned out in immaculately ironed desert DPMs. 'Wondered where you'd got to. How'd it go?'

'Promising,' I replied. 'Abdullah got us a meeting with the mayor.'

'He's a good lad.'

'And the mayor promised to get in touch with the local Taliban.'

'Houseman will be pleased. Personally I wouldn't want to have anything to do with the little scrotes.'

I scratched at the stubble on my chin. 'I'm afraid, Eddie, I think we'll have to one day. Meanwhile, roll on next month. I can't wait to get home.'

'Ah,' Crisp said, clearly more aware of what my future held than I was. There was a smug little smile on that freckled face with its thin strip of ginger moustache. 'Dreaming of long cool beers, watching cricket and long lie-ins with the missus, are we?'

'More like redecorating the living room and hall,' I replied. 'Sally will have a list as long as your arm. Always does.'

Crisp said, 'Think this time she might have to get a man in.' He enjoyed a good wind-up. 'You won't have heard, of course.'

'Heard what?'

'Leave's been postponed. Our tour here's been extended for at least another month.' He smiled thinly. 'Overstretch.'

Everybody's heart in the Troop had sunk after that little item of news.

Once the initial expletives and cusses had subsided, no one really said anything, but everyone knew what everyone else was thinking. Is all this really worth the candle? Should we be leaving, joining a private outfit and getting paid a small fortune to do similar work to what we were doing now? The dip in morale was almost palpable in the atmosphere around our part of the camp.

Two weeks later we got news from the mayor. In the gentle warmth of the cooling afternoon sun, Sergeant Major Crisp and Duffy and I were outside our tent relaxing on some old car seats while we played cards.

The long shadow of Chas Houseman passed over the upturned plastic crate that served as our table. There were two people by his side. One was Abdullah and the other was a tall, slightly built soldier who I'd only recently got to know.

The swarthy Ravi Azoor was in his mid-thirties and a member of the newly formed Special Reconnaissance Regiment. That unit was an expanded version of the small covert anti-terrorist unit known generally as 14 Int or the 'Det'. It had operated under changing names in Northern Ireland for years and had earned a fearsome reputation. Its members specialised in very close reconnaissance work, deep inside enemy territory.

Ravi and I had hit it off instantly. We learned quite a lot about each other. That in itself was quite remarkable given his secretive intelligence background and my special forces' paranoia about giving away anything to anyone about personal matters.

It transpired that Ravi was of Sri Lankan descent, but had actually been born in Britain to the wife of an eminent eye surgeon. Ravi clearly had a razor sharp wit and intellect. So it was hardly surprising to learn he'd studied law at university, where he also got his first taste of army life as a cadet in the attached Officer Training Corps. He went on to join a big firm of solicitors in the Midlands. Even now, when he was thinking out loud, he had the unnerving habit of speaking as if he was dictating a letter or a client's defence strategy.

To his parents' horror, Ravi had one day just decided he'd had enough of his promising legal career and joined the army. It wasn't long before he'd been spotted by the Intelligence Corps. Selection for 14 Int soon followed. I gathered he had done especially well in Northern Ireland, given his distinct and darkly handsome Asian looks. A Pakistani businessman was the last person Ulster terrorists suspected of working for army intelligence.

I didn't mind the interruption of Ravi's arrival with Houseman and Abdullah. I'd been dealt a lousy hand of cards and was happy to throw it in.

'Abdullah's got some news,' Houseman announced.

'The mayor?' I asked.

The Afghan nodded. 'He has persuaded Dr Zam-Zama to meet with Mr Houseman.'

I raised an eyebrow. That was really something. Zam-Zama's ugly mug featured prominently in our rogues' gallery of faces pinned to the board in our ops room. He had a particularly vicious reputation and his men controlled large swathes of Helmand. Not a lot was known about him as everyone was too scared to talk for fear of the consequences.

'The bastard's bloody influential in this neck of the woods,' Houseman said. 'So it'll be a real coup if we can get some dialogue going with him.'

Ravi nodded. 'Rumour has it that not only is he a warlord with a pretty big following within the Taliban, but that now he's a drug baron in his own right.'

Houseman glanced at Abdullah. 'Did Mayor Aryan tell you that?'

The Afghan's serious expression cracked for the first time. 'You joke with me! The mayor looks very, very nervous when he speaks of Zam-Zama. He knows if anything goes wrong with your meeting, he and his family are likely to suffer for having set it up.' His smile slipped away as quickly as it had appeared. 'But it is common knowledge. Zam-Zama is a doctor of theology and very highly placed in the Taliban hierarchy. When they were in power, he was very draconian, ruling without mercy. Many men and women were executed, often stoned to death. Anyone caught farming opium was made to watch as his crop and home was destroyed.

Sometimes other members of his family might also be killed before the farmer too was murdered.'

'Nice man,' I murmured.

Abdullah said, 'But since he has come back into the area, he appears to have changed his mind. Now he encourages the poppy to be grown; he finds pleasure in the power it buys. And, of course, the money buys weapons for the Taliban.'

'Where and when is this meeting taking place?' I asked.

Houseman said, 'I asked Abdullah to give us as much notice as possible . . . We've got agreement for a meet in five days' time. At a property Zam-Zama owns. It's a smart house, in the hills north of Now Zad.'

I winced. That was bandit country, the front line. The British were trying to hold the Taliban up there in the north so that they couldn't swoop down to seize Highway One, the strategic main road through southern Afghanistan. Because if they ever managed that, it was reckoned they'd be able to grab Helmand's provincial capital of Lashkar Gah, together with its airfield, and have our main camp at Bastion surrounded in short order.

I said, 'That'll really be putting your head in the lion's mouth, Chas.'

Houseman gave an uncomfortable smile. 'Hell, Dave, someone's got to do it. We can't keep on taking casualties at this rate. Better jaw jaw, than war war, as the saying goes.'

I agreed with him, of course. I just wished it wasn't my crew and me who had to go into the lion's cage with him. I had this increasingly nagging feeling that my luck could run out sometime soon.

Ravi, however, seemed to have no such concerns. 'Five days is manageable for my people,' he said lightly. 'From what we know, Zam-Zama doesn't live at the house normally. He keeps on the move, from one secret location to another. Usually just a housekeeper and a few Taliban henchmen at the place. Should be easy enough for a close recce. Maybe even get some surveillance or bugging equipment in place.'

I said, 'Then the sooner we get an initial plan in place the better.' I glanced at Sergeant Major Crisp. 'Eddie, can you liaise with JOC and set up a meeting with 3 Para for sometime tomorrow.'

Houseman stepped forward. 'Actually, Dave, I need to keep this as low-key as possible, strictly need-to-know.'

I frowned. 'Don't you think, Chas, that Joint Operation Command *needs* to know?' I asked sarcastically.

I saw both Crisp and Duffy give me a concerned sideways glance.

'I have my instructions from London,' Houseman replied tartly. 'We'll keep the exact nature of this mission between your Troop and Ravi's people. That way we'll have absolute security, plus be fast and light on our feet. Don't really want the whole of 3 Para battle group all over Now Zad. in their size elevens, do we?'

I should have realised then that this was a disaster waiting to happen. I should have contacted my OC, Major Malone, who was still back at Basra in Iraq, and run it past him. Or made my own decision and refused point-blank to agree to the mission without clearing it first with the JOC.

Houseman smiled and tapped the side of his nose. 'You can just see some self-important bugger in Brigade HQ getting in a flap and having this mission vetoed. Half the time, I don't think those at Kandahar understand the reality on the ground.'

Of course, the truth was it was probably Houseman who didn't understand that grim reality.

# Four

It had just turned five when I arrived at Duffy's house. It took me a moment or two to drag myself back from my memories of that last ill-fated mission.

I think it was the first time I'd allowed myself to recall the events in such detail, and doing so had left me in a sort of trance. I could barely remember anything about the long walk from Daisy's school.

I was at the edge of an estate of basic, low-cost homes run by a local housing association. The tired-looking buildings were in need of some attention and a lick of paint, and the grass verges were littered with lager cans and takeaway cartons. On the street corner, a gathering of hoodies and other teenagers wearing baseball caps with pushbikes watched me sullenly as I passed. Most were smoking or drinking from tins of Red Bull.

Seeing the camouflaged bergen on my back, one called out. 'Hello, soldier boy! Bang-bang, you're dead!' Another mimicked a burst of machine-gun fire.

They giggled together, safe in having let some distance pass between us. Then another felt brave enough to shout: 'Killed any babies lately?!'

Instinctively my pace slowed, my hackles rising. My

knuckles tightened. There'd been some half-baked story about the Afghan war in one of the tabloids. As was often their practice, Taliban fighters had forced their way into the home of an innocent family before opening fire on a British patrol. When the squaddies fought back, shooting at the house, a baby inside was accidentally killed in its cot by a ricocheting round. The resulting media coverage had grown like a rolling snowball. There was a lot of hype, hysteria and ill-informed insinuation.

I took a deep breath and forced myself to walk on. Ignorant scrotes like those hanging around on the street corner weren't worth it. Besides, I was in big enough trouble as it was.

After turning the corner, I found myself in the little cul-de-sac where Brian Duffy lived. His was a former two-bedroom council semi. He lived there with his mother, Constance, a delightful and frail woman in her seventies. She'd been widowed at an early age when her professional soldier husband died in action during the Malaysia conflict with Indonesia.

Brian was the only child from that apparently deeply affectionate marriage. He once told me how he'd always wanted to have that sort of closeness in a relationship with a woman in his life, but it was never quite to be. Brian himself had got through a couple of wives, and it had resulted in quite a tribe of children and now grandchildren. But by his own admission he'd been difficult to live with.

The army had been like a very indiscreet and demanding mistress. To avoid the stress of family and job he could become withdrawn and morose. Typically of Brian, it was he who had ended his marital relationships on the basis that he thought it was in the kids' best interests. I knew he loved them dearly, but he would deliberately keep out of their lives except for a short visit at Christmas and a phone call on their birthdays.

Now he lodged with his ageing mother and did what he could to look out for her.

I pushed open the wooden gate onto a small garden given over to vegetables, the usual lawn replaced by neatly regimented lines of late summer crops. Duffy himself was just replacing some tools in the small shed I knew he had built himself from scratch. There seemed hardly anything practical he couldn't turn his hand to.

His head turned as he heard the gate scrape on the flagstone path. He frowned and squinted in my direction. 'That you, boss?'

'Hi, Bri,' I replied. 'Thought I'd drop by.'

He shut the shed door. 'Well, if you's come round to help me do the weedin',' he blustered, shutting the shed door, 'you's too late. I've just finished!'

I grinned. 'Shame.'

The smile dropped from the bearded, florid face and he regarded me closely with those penetrating blue eyes. It was easy to be fooled by Duffy's good-hearted and sometimes exuberant way of speaking. He was in fact very astute with a quick mind. I could tell that he'd already deduced that something was wrong.

He indicated my bergen. 'Goin' back to the army, are we? Or off on our holidays?'

'Just going away for a while,' I replied. 'Seem to have got myself in a bit of bother.'

He shook his head in disapproval. 'Again, boss? How you goin' to manage in Civvy Street without your old sergeant to look after you?' The smile suddenly returned. 'C'mon in and have a cuppa tea. Have to see what we can't sort out.'

I followed as he led the way to the back of the house, his long arms swinging. Inside, the kitchen was very clean, neat and tidy with recently varnished pine units.

It was a bit of contradiction with Duffy that when he was working he was one of the scruffiest individuals imaginable. This was because he would throw himself into whatever task he faced with unstoppable determination and complete abandon, regardless of any obstacles in his way. On the battlefield he had only one focus, to destroy the enemy. Severe discomfort, even pain, meant nothing to him. You would never want for a better man at your side in a firefight. When he was in a garden – I knew he helped out a lot of pensioners who struggled to keep on top of things – it was the turn of brambles to become his sworn enemy.

More than once I'd met him at the pub for a lunchtime drink and he'd turn up with his trousers splattered in mud and his shirt torn and bloodstained after a morning's battling in the borders.

Yet on most other matters in his life, Duffy was meticulously tidy, with a place for everything and everything in its place. As a young recruit he'd have been a drill-sergeant's nightmare – there'd never be anything to pick on. And when needed, even his uniform would be presented to the required perfection.

His mother Constance sat in a wheelchair at the table putting freshly boiled and peeled eggs into a couple of pickling jars. I knew they were one of Duffy's favourite treats.

'Got a friend come to visit, Mother.'

Constance looked up, peering over the top of her wire-rimmed glasses. She seemed to shrink a little more each time I met her, a tiny woman in an old-fashioned floral dress with slender shoulders and a shock of curly white hair. But mostly you noticed the winning smile and could see immediately that Brian was her son.

'Goodness me, if it isn't that nice Mr Aston!' she exclaimed.

'Hello, Mrs Duffy,' I said, then saw that she was struggling to stand up. 'No, no please.'

'Bah,' she said irritably. 'It's horrid when your legs don't work proper. Don't you go getting old, Mr Aston, it isn't much fun.' She smiled. 'Oh, and you can calls me Connie.'

'Only if you call me Dave,' I replied, as Duffy poured water into an electric kettle. 'And how are you keeping, Connie?'

'Mustn't grumble. Won't help if I do. At least I haves someone to get me up in the mornings and going to bed.'

'Huh!' Duffy grunted. 'Can't have a lie-in in your own house though. Have to get up when the carer comes. And how would you like to go to bed at seven whether you like it or not – because, again, that's when the carer is scheduled to come?'

Constance turned and hit her son lightly on his leg. 'Oh, don't goes on so, Brian. We should be thankful for small mercies.'

'Yeah,' Duffy agreed sarcastically. 'Small mercies like if theys turn up at all in the school holidays! A real worry if I'm away on the road. The other week mother was stuck in bed all day because the carer didn't turn up. Led to all manner of problems—'

'That's enough, dear,' she scolded.

'Social services don't really care or have the resources,' he added quickly as he put teabags and hot water into three mugs and placed them on the table.

Constance said, 'Tell you what, why don't you boys go in the sitting room. I wants to get this finished, and I'm sure you've got lots to talk about.'

'OK, Mother,' Duffy said and led the way into the adjoining room with its red, floral-patterned carpet, chintzy sofa and chairs and a huge bookcase overflowing with paperbacks of all types and subjects.

He indicated for me to take a seat. 'So, boss, what mischief has yous been up to?'

'I caught up with Luke Hartley.'

'Oh,' he said simply, holding me with his mesmerising stare. Duffy was only some three or four years older than me, but he'd always had the knack of coming across like a father figure. The prematurely grey hair and beard helped.

I said, 'I'm afraid I decked him.'

'Badly?'

'Christ, Brian, I think I might have killed him.'

'What?' He stared at me, disbelieving.

'I hit him harder than I meant to.' I took a deep breath. 'He just went down and didn't move. There was blood everywhere.'

'You sure he was dead?' Duffy pressed.

'No, I just don't know. His fiancée certainly thought he was.'

'That don't mean anything. Radio news was on just now. Nothing on there.'

'Probably too soon,' I replied. 'I *know* the police are looking for me.'

Duffy's eyes gave nothing away. 'So there's a price on your head? I'll give them a call.'

'For God's sake, Brian, this is no joking matter.'

He grinned at his own wind-up. 'Where you stayin'? Still at that dosshouse in town.'

I shook my head. 'I'm out of funds, and the council doesn't reckon I qualify for housing.'

'Stay here if you wants,' Duffy said quickly. 'This sofa's comfy enough.'

'Kind offer,' I said gratefully. 'I'd be in the way, and it'll only be a matter of time before the cops come here.'

'Then maybe I could lends you some cash?'

I smiled at his kindness. 'Maybe you could give me a lift. On Saturday you mentioned you were taking a truck to France.'

He nodded and with a poker-straight face said, 'Is that wise? Expect Interpol and all them gendarmes will be out lookin' for you, too.'

I wasn't in the mood. 'I was thinking somewhere closer to home. Haven't managed to get a job round here, so I'd have no chance over there with my French. Which way you going?'

Duffy considered for a moment. 'Probably to Gloucester, down the M5, pick up the M4 eastward, then head south for the Poole ferry.'

A thought occurred to me. 'Would that take you anywhere near Swinthorpe?'

He shrugged. 'It could do. Why Swinthorpe?'

I grinned. 'Just happens to be my birth town. Maybe I'll get lucky there.'

Constance invited me to join them for tea. It was simple but delicious: local free-range ham and salad stuff from Duffy's garden. But I had no appetite. I kept thinking about Luke Hartley lying in a pool of his own blood. Again, I cursed my own stupidity, my outrageous anger. Half of me screamed to just give myself up to the police. Another part of me was just eager to get away. Somewhere, anywhere I could take stock and work out what the hell was the best thing to do.

I had a huge sense of relief when Duffy and I finally set off in his car for the haulier's depot.

I waited outside the wire, just in case management objected to an unauthorised passenger, and waited for Duffy to pull up his massive articulated truck beside me.

'What's the load?' I asked.

'A million English frog legs and a squillion snails!'

I settled down to try to relax on the journey through some of England's finest rolling landscape, all bathed in a soft late-summer glow.

'I suppose I can't smoke?' I asked.

'Catch fire to youself as far as I'm concerned,' Duffy replied amiably, swinging the steering wheel in big extravagant movements. 'But more than my life's worth if you's caught! Smokers is treated worse than criminals nowadays. Lunatics is running the asylum here now.'

Duffy, a man who had once decided he couldn't afford to both smoke and drink, said suddenly: ''Ave you heard from that Indian bloke, er, Ravi Azoor? He was that half-decent sneaky-beaky wallah on our last Afghanistan jaunt.'

'I remember him,' I said. 'Actually, Brian, he's British with Sri Lankan parents. Got to know him a bit on the ward at Selly Oak. His family didn't live far away and he visited me a few times, smuggled me out for a pint. Said we'd keep in touch, but we didn't.'

'Had a postcard from him, anyway,' Duffy continued. 'Left the army now. Wants to set up a reunion bash.'

'Nice idea,' I said.

Duffy shook his head. I knew he didn't do God, medals or going back in life. 'Not for me,' he said. 'I like to keep moving on.'

My ex-sergeant had also told me once he believed in *something*, but wasn't yet sure what. I couldn't help but wonder that if there were more wise men in the world like him, it would be a much saner – and safer – place.

As we drove south towards the coast, mesmerised by soporific easy-listening numbers from the radio, I found myself hovering on the edge of sleep, my mind drifting back to that five-day 'window' intelligence had before the promised meeting with Dr Zam-Zama.

I remembered with amusement Ravi Azoor's infectious enthusiasm for making the most of the time available.

# Five

As far as Joint Operational Command was aware, this was just a low-key reconnaissance operation run by Ravi's intelligence unit – with hard backup from us.

Chas Houseman put it forward to the JOC as exploratory surveillance in order to glean more information on the powerful Dr Zam-Zama. It was an open secret that he was suspected of being well connected with local – if not central – government figures, the Taliban, the drug barons, and even dodgy elements of Pakistani intelligence.

The lieutenant colonel of 3 Para expressed approval at the subject for investigation. But then I also noticed his look of mild surprise when Houseman waved aside the offer of additional support from his men.

'Thanks, but I want this to be very low-key.'

'It might not be your choice to make,' the colonel replied a little frostily. He threw a glance at me. 'If the Taliban become alerted to your presence, it'll be they who call the shots. Literally.'

Nevertheless our plan went ahead. Ravi's team of eight comprised six men and two women. I understood that they were all born in the United Kingdom, but were all of Asian descent. They had been recruited from various units of the armed forces and, after selection and specialist training, had been thoroughly schooled in Pashto at the Defence School of Languages in Beaconsfield. With a carefully developed cover story, two men, one of whom was Ravi himself, and one woman descended on the nearest village to Zam-Zama's house. The men dressed in long dishdasha robes and she in a burka; they drove a beat-up old car and posed as a husband and wife and husband's brother, supposedly passing through on their way to visit relations further north. Unfortunately the car broke down, it seemed.

The fault was simplicity itself. Ravi lifted up the bonnet, removed the distributor cap and replaced the rotor arm with a dud. It took mere seconds before the original was secreted in his pocket. Immediately villagers gathered around to see who the strangers were. Mechanics were summoned. The fault was identified. A replacement rotor arm was not available. Ravi declared that he would have to send for a spare part, which would take time to locate and deliver.

As it was late in the day, in the true tradition of Pashtun hospitality, the strangers were invited to eat and stay overnight with the family of one of the village elders. After the meal, the male visitors and men of the family sat separately from the women. Through a relaxing haze of opium smoke, to which many of the villagers were clearly addicted, the men started to laugh and joke a little more, relaxing their guard.

Tea was passed around. There were many digs at the expense of the British and Americans, but even spikier jibes at President Karzai and his government. They were clearly regarded as corrupt and the villagers repeatedly asked each other where all the international aid money had gone? They had, it was declared, seen none of it.

No one actually mentioned the Taliban until Ravi and the other SRR soldier casually began talking about the political situation in the town where they claimed to live. Ravi told me that their comments were carefully pitched to neither praise nor condemn the fundamentalists.

There was a moment of tense silence as the guests were scrutinised by their hosts. But the opium was taking effect, a joke was made, and the tribesmen eventually forgot their caution and lowered their guard. They seemed to have a mixed view of the Taliban. They were thought to be harsh and unforgiving, but at least they were not as corrupt as the elected government, of which the villagers had once had such high hopes. Then the name of Dr Zam-Zama drifted into the conversation.

'An important local dignitary,' one man said. 'Very powerful. He has many connections. Some say he is a senior Taliban commander, but no one knows for sure. He has a reputation for being kind, of helping local people . . . But never, ever cross him. He is unforgiving.'

'And he is rich,' said another, a timid little man called Reza. 'Very rich. He has a fabulous house up in the hills near here. I work there as his gardener and general helper. My wife is hired to cook for him when he is at home.'

Ravi, who was playing the husband, said, 'I should *so* like to see such a house. You know, from the inside. I hear stories, sometimes I see pictures in magazines.'

Reza, who it transpired understood and spoke a little English, smiled widely. 'I wonder if I could show you.'

Immediately he appeared to regret his offer, but Ravi pounced. 'That is so kind of you!' he proclaimed. 'What a nice gesture! You are a really good man. May Allah always smile upon you and your family . . . But might you get into trouble for showing me?'

Reza thought for a moment, clearly trying to persuade himself. 'Well, the doctor is away until next week. Why should anyone know? It will only take a few minutes. After all, what harm could it do? It would be my pleasure to show you.'

In the next room, the female SRR soldier, Laura, was making equally good progress. Although not relaxing on opium, the women of the village were less guarded than the men and happy to gossip. There was an increasing accumulation of small detail information on Zam-Zama, his habits and lifestyle and his visitors, that would be added to the file back at HQ.

Next morning, while they awaited the arrival of the spare part for their car, the family of three were shown around the doctor's home.

The village couple who worked there, Reza and his wife Asifa, beamed with pride at the delight of their guests who had never seen such luxury before. The local gunman who was paid to guard the villa took little persuasion to turn a blind eye for a few moments in return for a bag of Asifa's home-baked biscuits. The housekeeping couple also happily posed for photographs taken on Ravi's mobile phone in different rooms in the building.

'Worked like a charm,' Laura said at the intelligence debriefing the following day. She had played the wife, although she had actually been born in Pinner, North London, to Indian parents. Now dressed in desert DPM, she was darkly attractive and in her late twenties.

'We got some fairly good photographic coverage, too,' she added. 'Once we'd snapped the couple, Anba, who played my brother, started filming and videoing all over the place. He'd show the village couple what he'd taken. Of course, they were thrilled to see it on film themselves. A novelty to them.'

I said, 'And I gather you managed to plant a couple of bugs?'

Ravi nodded. 'Apparently there are two rooms where Zam-Zama likes to entertain or do business deals. We were told that by Reza and his wife Asifa. They really are a lovely couple, speak a little English . . . Anyway, with a small diversion my fictitious brother managed to slip back and place a transceiver in each room. They're not *very* secure, it had to be done so quickly. But the doctor's people should have no reason to think the house could or might have been wired.'

I wasn't sure I shared Ravi's confidence about that, but we just had to trust his judgement.

In the meantime, twelve members of my Troop had been infiltrated into the target area under cover of darkness by a dedicated special forces twin-rotor Chinook helicopter.

Two four-man bricks were dropped off with their surveillance and sophisticated communications equipment, as well as C8 rifles and grenade launchers, to the west of

Zam-Zama's house. They made their way silently on foot, wearing night-vision goggles, through the hills for several miles until they were overlooking the target. The remaining four soldiers were landed separately in hills to the east beyond Now Zad.

By the time the first soft eddies of light began to illuminate the landscape, two invisible observation posts had been established. Each overlooked the home of Dr Zam-Zama from a different direction.

Our intelligence dossier on the doctor was growing. According to Chas Houseman, GCHQ had managed to intercept calls from his satellite telephone and his emails. It was clear that he was a much bigger player than any of us had first realised. His influence stretched to the offices of administration in Afghanistan's capital of Kabul and also the military hierarchy in neighbouring Pakistan. He was also well connected to elements within the government of Iran.

Apart from the house in Now Zad, the doctor was now known for certain to have a house in Kandahar and a luxury apartment in Kabul, with yet another across the Pakistan border in Islamabad. It had been reported that he hoped to be able to buy himself a luxury yacht one day. Meanwhile, he was thought to own even more properties through his construction and development companies. They were part of a commercial group that also covered transport, moneylending and agricultural banking. It was hardly surprising that Zam-Zama also had important personal contacts with government and business leaders in China and the other neighbouring countries to the north.

Houseman told me that Zam-Zama was not only an influential Taliban leader, but was able to smuggle in arms from other countries, some of which was paid for by aid money he'd siphoned off through his construction companies.

As the day of the meeting approached, I was becoming increasingly agitated, and I wasn't sure why. The night before, the OPs had reported the arrival at the house of a couple of pickup trucks filled with armed men. This entourage was hardly part of Zam-Zama's domestic staff. It was clear by the number of black turbans – a favourite Taliban look – and the preponderance of Kalashnikovs and rocket launchers that these mean-looking foreign fighters were his personal bodyguard.

Houseman had heard via GCHQ that the man himself was reportedly on the move, heading towards the Now Zad region. He didn't say *how* they knew.

My initial plan had been to infill to the target area by Chinook, taking with us a mix of quad bikes and Land Rovers. But Houseman still insisted on keeping JOC out of the loop, which meant that use of a helicopter was a non-starter. So instead we were to travel overland by night.

I tried to get some sleep the previous afternoon, but it was probably stupid to have even tried. I ended up spending a few hours just tossing and turning in my cot, bathed in sweat. With the thankful arrival of sunset and a drop in temperature, I made my way to the mess where I'd arranged to meet the rest of our team and the intelligence boys, who we would be protecting. We had tea and a light meal and a final run-through of the plan.

When that was finished, a silence fell over our table. No one was in much of a mood to talk. As I looked at their faces I became aware of how utterly tired and haunted my friends Eddie, young Andy and Duffy had become. Even the banter and gallows humour, the oil that kept our spirits going in adversity, was drying up.

After one final mug of strong, sweet tea, I led our little group back to the tents to pick up all our kit and weapons. Then, dressed like a bunch of desert pirates in a pick 'n' mix of army cargo trousers, civilian jackets and boots, and Arab *shamag* headscarves, we headed off to the vehicle park.

This time, rather than using Snatch Land Rovers, or the new two and a half ton Pinzgauer troop carriers that had started arriving in theatre, we opted for a couple of locally converted Toyota pickup trucks and a battered and ageing Shogun. Our pals in REME had done some special modifications for us. Not out of kindness. I recall that the substantial bribe involved elements of alcohol.

The vehicles offered no protection whatsoever but, in accordance with Chas Houseman's wishes, were as inconspicuous and light as possible. At the time Eddie and I agreed with him, probably clinging to the prevalent SAS notion that we were pretty much invincible. Duffy was unusually quiet on the matter, I noticed.

When we'd finished loading, I pulled on my night-vision goggles, fired up my Shogun and led our little patrol out of Camp Bastion and into the velvety desert night. Chas Houseman was with me in the first vehicle, followed by Eddie Crisp with young Andy and Ravi Azoor. Brian Duffy took the rear, with our translator Abdullah as his passenger in a Toyota. The idea was, if everything went tits-up, just one surviving pickup would be enough to carry us all back.

We'd selected a route along tracks that avoided most villages. It was always exciting and somewhat precarious driving without any lights, being able to see without being seen. There were few people about in the dark and even fewer vehicles. No civilian would choose to bump into the Taliban at night, as their actions and reactions were always danger-ously unpredictable. Even fewer would want to risk being mistaken *for* the Taliban and accidentally bring down the full wrath of a NATO air strike.

Taking it slow and steady, like marauding phantoms, we crept along the unmade roads in the direction of Now Zad. Orchards, crop plantations and poppy fields slid by on either side.

Chas Houseman soon became bored, being unable to see the landscape without goggles, and began talking about Zam-Zama and how much more had been found out about him recently.

'If he's such a big noise and troublemaker,' I said, 'why don't we do everyone a favour, and just take him out?'

'Doesn't work like that,' Houseman replied. 'Take out one tribal chief or warlord and he'll be replaced by another. And you're back to square one. We need consistency. Get to know them, each one.'

I knew where he was coming from. 'And try to influence them?'

'Everyone has a price. Even evil little bastards like Zama.'

'Sounds like he's got all the money he needs,' I said.

'It's never enough for people like him. Besides, it's not *just* wealth that turns his type on. They get off on power and of being feared by lesser mortals.'

'Respect,' I mused. 'Power without responsibility. The way with his type around the world.'

'Pretty much,' he agreed.

I said, 'So us, the British, asking to see him, appeals to his vanity?'

'Sure,' he acknowledged. 'The powerful infidel invader, going to him cap in hand, seeking his advice for a way out of the current military impasse.'

'Well, I wish you luck,' I said with a slight edge of sarcasm to my voice.

Houseman picked up on my tone. 'Luck doesn't enter into it, Dave. There'll be something he hasn't got, something he wants badly. I've just got to find out what it is.'

Personally, the only thing I'd have given Zam-Zama was a double-tap to the back of his head with a 9mm SIG automatic. But then I was a bit non-PC like that.

Finally we arrived at a high pass between two rocky hills. It overlooked a small fertile depression through which ran a wide stream and that was where the Afghan oligarch had built his house. Once we'd parked up line abreast, I got on the radio to one of the OPs.

'No sign of chummy?' I asked.

'*Not yet, boss,*' came the reply. '*But his gang at the house are very much on the alert. Sentries posted on the compound walls and at points in the surrounding terrain. My guess is, he'll pitch up in the morning once his gunmen are satisfied this isn't some sort of trap.*'

That made sense. I said, 'OK that. Meanwhile we're remaining in our lying-up position until it's time to move in tomorrow at 1100 hours. Obviously call if anything changes. Out.'

Eddie and young Andy, and Duffy and I made our way to two different rocky outcrops, keeping watch in case any Taliban members accidentally stumbled across our positions. That left the two spooks, Houseman and Ravi, with Abdullah on their own with the vehicles to discuss their side of the mission.

The hours dragged by. There was little radio traffic from Camp Bastion and in the quiet, hot night it was hard to believe that in daylight, frequently without warning, this place could suddenly become hell on earth. Within seconds, an often unseen and unknown enemy would fill the air full of hot lead, each bullet seemingly with your name engraved on it.

Yet before the dawn you could almost feel becalmed, wrapped in the cocoon of warm, tranquil night air, the only noises the strangely comforting call of cicadas and the distant chime of a goat's bell.

Despite the gentle sunrise, I felt the fear return. It was almost imperceptible: a slight quickening of my pulse, a sudden dryness in my mouth, and that little niggling worm of worry at the back of my mind starting to eat away at it again.

A buttery wash of light spread over the dun-coloured hills, into the fertile hollow below us, the plantations surprisingly green considering there was little water in the river at this time of year.

The first sunbeam reached Zam-Zama's house, hitting it in a dazzling display of colour and refracted light. These garish and fanciful structures were popular with warlords and drug barons and were called by lesser mortals, who nevertheless had more taste, as 'Pakistani wedding cakes': they were brightly painted in a carnival of shades reflected by the liberal architectural use of twinkling mirrors. If it wasn't for the sinister origins of these houses, they might have been a charming invention of tellers of fairy tales.

I took out my Zeiss pocket binoculars. Zam-Zama's house was bigger than most others I'd seen, three storeys of sugar-pink stucco with ornate iron balconies outside the numerous bedroom windows. There was a proper, cultivated garden with palm trees between it and the compound walls, which were capped with fancy stonework. Half a dozen of his henchmen wandered out of the house, yawning and stretch-ing as though they'd just woken. Some were drinking tea, others munching on breakfast, probably dates or nuts or figs.

The leader amongst them was waving his arms, shouting, urging them to get a move on. Within minutes they were arming themselves with rifles and wandering out onto the dirt road to relieve their comrades who had been on guard throughout the night.

I watched as a few of them walked in our direction for a couple of hundred metres before setting up a roadblock. It was a makeshift affair using the bone-white branch of a long-dead tree and some sheets of rusty corrugated iron.

In the surrounding countryside below me, scattered hamlets were coming to life. There were rare glimpses of women in their backyards, preparing food within the compound walls. A trader led his heavily laden three camels out of their corral, farmers walked and chatted together on their way to the fields, and a goatherd drove his charges along a track for another day in the hills.

The time dragged by while each member of our team breakfasted alone on oatmeal biscuits and cold water. Finally, at around nine thirty, one of the OPs called over our radio net that there were vehicles approaching from the far side of Zam-Zama's house.

I swung the binoculars up to my eyes and was just able to pick up the tornado of dust swirling in from the far distance. It just had to be the arrival of the man that Houseman was so desperate to meet.

# Six

As the vehicles came closer I was able to identify a smart BMW X3 four-by-four with smoked-glass windows. It was sandwiched between two pickup trucks. Each of these was manned by armed guards and boasted a mounted heavy machine gun.

Even from that distance I could distinguish their lavish array of weaponry. Apart from the ubiquitous AK-47s and RPG-7s, I was really surprised to see a couple of tribesmen toting what looked like shoulder-fired Chinese HN-5s. These were lightweight anti-aircraft missiles, similar to the Russian Strela-2. They might not be heavy-duty kit, but in the right hands could take out helicopters or even a low-flying jet.

If this sort of equipment was finding its way to the Taliban fighters, then any hope we had of a quick victory over them was looking increasingly bleak. And Dr Zam-Zama clearly had no intention of being taken out by his NATO enemies from either land or sky.

As the little convoy reached the compound and the gates opened in welcome, I beckoned to Eddie, Andy and Duffy to join me back at our own vehicles. When we reached them, we found that Houseman and Ravi had set up the satellite phone, which Abdullah was about to use.

Moments later he was through to one of Zam-Zama's aides. They had a slightly heated conversation that lasted several minutes. At last our interpreter replaced the handset.

Houseman frowned. 'What's the problem?'

Abdullah smiled thinly and shook his head. 'No real problem. They're just trying to lay down rules, make conditions . . . who can enter the doctor's house, who can't, whether they are armed or not. I have settled it with them.'

'And?' I pressed.

'No more than four persons,' Abdullah explained. 'He said unarmed, but I said that was unreasonable given all of Dr Zam-Zama's bodyguards. So he conceded a handgun for each man, but it must be holstered.'

'I suppose that's better than nothing,' Houseman said. He turned to me. 'I'll need Abdullah and Ravi, Dave. So you'd better make up the numbers. If it goes tits-up, you'll be good in a scrap.'

From the corner of my eye I saw the expressions on the faces of Eddie, Duffy and even young Andy. I knew exactly what they were all thinking.

Suddenly I wished to hell I wasn't there, trusting on the spook's interpretation of the Taliban chief's psyche. If he'd got that wrong, the four of us could be taken hostage and held for ransom, armed or not. Because, in reality, we wouldn't have stood a chance.

Following the instructions that had been given to Abdullah, we drove our three vehicles towards the roadblock that had been set up by the doctor's henchmen. The two pickups, manned by Eddie and Duffy, held back some hundred metres distant, while the remaining four of us proceeded forward in our Shogun.

As we approached, the tribesmen waved us down at gunpoint and dragged aside the tree branch. One man in a dark turban and sporting a ragged beard scrambled onto the footplate of my driver's door and shouted at me to drive on.

The house may have been a 'narco-palace', but its compound was still surrounded by the usual moat of a drainage ditch, full of litter and a stinking, watery green sludge.

The tall timber doors of the entrance yawned open, allowing us to drive straight in. The garden was mostly paved in cobbled mosaic tiles, set off by a few beds of exotic flowering shrubs, which appeared to be thriving in the dappled shade of half-a-dozen palm trees. A number of gunmen, who wore the cold and emotionless expression of seasoned fighters, stood around, fingering AK-47s and viewing us with undisguised hostility.

The man on the footplate of my Shogun jumped down and opened my door, gabbling something at me as I switched off the engine.

'He says his name is Masood Babur,' Abdullah translated. 'He claims that he is Zam-Zama's top man. We must go with him. And we must keep our hands well away from our gun holsters, otherwise we are shot dead, no question.'

'Can't put it plainer than that,' I murmured, and climbed out, nodding and smiling at the sullen faces of the gathered tribesmen. No one smiled back. This clearly wasn't going to be a great day for winning hearts and minds.

Houseman joined me, carrying his laptop computer in a padded case, followed by Ravi and Abdullah. Babur led the way up some terracotta steps beneath an ornate portico. A high gloss, spray-painted red door stood open, allowing us to pass straight into an impressive, marble-floored hallway.

As I tried to take in my surroundings, I was aware of a plethora of gilt mirrors glaring back at me from every direction. Huge, ostentatious chandeliers hung from the domed ceiling high above me. It all screamed immense wealth – and incredibly bad taste.

Babur led us straight into a marble-floored reception room, this one containing a large circle of ornate faux-antique carved chairs which had been upholstered in the sort of bright red velour you might have found in a nineteenth-century brothel.

Abdullah looked impressed. 'I imagine,' he said quietly, 'this is where Dr Zam-Zama holds his meetings with other men of power.'

Jerking his thumb towards the chairs, Babur indicated for us to sit. As we did, I noticed a large pair of double doors, with gold handles, apparently leading to another reception room.

Idly I wondered just exactly where Ravi's colleagues had planted their listening devices.

At that moment, those double doors were thrown open by two armed tribesmen and Dr Zam-Zama walked through. His appearance struck me as somewhat theatrical as he stood there with his legs astride and arms folded across his chest like some huge pantomime genie.

He must have stood six-four tall, the voluminous dishdasha and colourful embroidered waistcoat struggling to contain his large torso. From beneath his traditional pancake hat sprouted ringlets of greasy black hair, which matched his long and wild black beard. For a moment he stood there in silence, glowering at us with dark emotionless eyes.

In his shadow were a slightly built man and woman. As she was covered from head to toe in a burka, it was impossible to read any expression on her face, but the man, who I took to be her husband, looked decidedly nervous. I saw him cast a quick, puzzled glance in Ravi's direction. His mouth dropped momentarily in recognition, then quickly closed again.

Zam-Zama took two steps forward into the room, his armed henchmen urging the couple to follow him into our room. Meanwhile we all rose from our seats in an expression of common courtesy.

However, the doctor ignored Abdullah, Ravi and me, and instead focused directly on Houseman.

'*Ze-ma num dai Dr Zama,*' he announced in a voice so deep and resonant that I could almost have believed the building had trembled. '*S-ta num t-se dai?*'

'He asks your name—' Abdullah began.

'Enough!' the doctor boomed, turning on him. 'Your services will not be needed.' Having delivered the sentence in perfect English, he turned his attention back to Houseman. 'Do you think that all Afghans are fools? Is it not a courtesy to find out if a man you visit speaks your language, before you treat him as a village idiot?'

'Forgive me,' Houseman said, smiling uneasily. 'But we could find out very little about you. No one suggested that you spoke English.'

'I studied in England. Went to your very own Oxford University.'

Houseman's jaw fell with surprise.

Zam-Zama's eyes narrowed. 'And you are?'

'Houseman. Chas Houseman.' He extended his hand. 'From the British Foreign Office.'

Reluctantly, the Afghan unfolded his arms and shook the offered hand. 'Let us sit down.'

Zam-Zama took the centre seat with the arrogant posture of some feudal monarch holding court. 'I received a request from Mayor Aryan that you wish to speak with me.'

Houseman nodded. 'Yes, doctor. Too many people are dying. Your people and our people.'

'That is true,' Zam-Zama conceded. 'And it is easily remedied. Your people leave our country.'

A half-smile played on Houseman's lips. 'Ah, if only it was that simple. And it is not, as you are well aware. But both you and your people, and me and my people, we both want what only the other party can offer.'

It was my turn for a sardonic smile as I recognised the start of the typical Arab barter. In fact I found my lips moving silently to Houseman's words: 'If only we can put our differences to one side for a moment. For long enough to discuss what the other wants.'

Zam-Zama stroked his beard, caressingly, tickling it as though it was a cat. 'British military losses are running high just now,' he said. 'Very high. So I'm thinking . . . an opium harvest gathered in, in return for a ceasefire . . . Is that the idea?'

'It is something we should both consider,' Houseman replied calmly.

The warlord almost smiled. 'I think such a trade-off is unlikely, Mr Houseman, but then who knows?' He paused for dramatic effect. 'Firstly we have to know whether or not we can *trust* each other.'

'Oh, I'm sure we can,' Houseman replied silkily.

The doctor gave a throaty chuckle and reached into the pocket of his waistcoat. He extracted a small round microphone hanging on a coil of wire. 'Are you familiar with this, Mr Houseman?'

My heart sank like a lift in a shaft, ending with a sick feeling in the pit of my stomach. I wasn't familiar with the exact type, but it was clearly some sort of listening and transmitting device. I glanced sideways at Ravi, whose face had paled noticeably.

Houseman played it cool. 'I think it is what's called a bug, doctor.'

'Then I *know* how much I can *trust* you,' retorted Zam-Zama. 'That famous English expression – as far as I can throw you.'

'It was not planted on my orders,' Houseman countered. Technically, I suppose, that was just about true.

Zam-Zama's cheeks reddened. 'Well, I did not place bugs, as you call them, to spy on myself, Mr Houseman!'

He paused and turned in his chair, beckoning his two henchmen to bring the couple a few paces forward. The woman began to resist, and immediately had her arm forced up into the small of her back. She yelped in pain.

The doctor added, 'A very elaborate scheme was used by

you infidel English to get into my house. These are two of my housekeepers. Reza and his wife Asifa.'

I wasn't exactly sure how this was developing, but I didn't like the signs. I tried to defuse the situation. I cleared my throat and said, 'Doctor, may I assure you this couple has had nothing at all to do with the British Army.'

Zam-Zama seemed to notice me for the first time. 'Ah, yes. You are a recent arrival at Camp Bastion. Special forces, maybe SAS. You may even be commander of that small contingent. By the name of Aston.'

That took the wind out of my sails. I just could not believe that he knew my name. Somewhere in our military chain of command between the UK, Iraq and Afghanistan, highly classified information was leaking like a sieve. Of course, Abdullah had to be the immediate suspect.

I ignored the warlord's comments. 'I know nothing about these bugs,' I lied. 'Or your housekeepers.'

Zam-Zama stroked his beard. 'Well, someone in the British Army does. Perhaps it is those new army spies, the Special Reconnaissance Regiment.'

From the corner of my eye I could see that Ravi was remaining utterly poker-faced. The doctor seemed vaguely amused. 'No matter. The fact is that using trickery, British Army spies duped this simple man of mine and his wife into letting them into my house. They then planted listening devices.' He glanced up at the couple. 'They must now be duly punished for their stupidity and breach of trust.'

The woman must have understood. She began to protest:

'No—!' Her words were abruptly halted as her captor tightened his grip until it was clearly hurting her.

'Take off her headdress.' Abdullah translated Zam-Zama's order in a quiet aside to us. 'Let's see her shame!'

'Please!' protested her pale-faced husband, trying to resist.

But the man was firmly restrained by the tribesman behind him. His wife's guard yanked the blue burka hood from her head in one violent, fluid movement. I was momentarily taken aback by the young woman's stunning beauty. She was barely in her twenties, I thought. Her honey-skinned almond face, with its startlingly blue eyes, was set off by a frame of silky, raven's wing hair. I could see that she was trembling. There was a patina of sweat on her brow.

'Asifa,' Zam-Zama growled.

Abdullah continued his whispered translation to us.

'Master?' the woman replied. Her reply was barely audible as she hung her head, avoiding eye contact with everyone else in the room.

'Your name means clean, pure . . . does it not?'

Asifa nodded. Another whisper: 'Master,' she acknowledged.

'Yet you and your husband betrayed my trust, did you not?' He did not wait for a response. 'You tell me it was not your husband, but *you* who wanted to show off my house to total strangers. Yet you know that is strictly against my rules.'

'Yes, Master,' Asifa replied, a tremor in her voice.

Zam-Zama turned to his two henchmen. 'Take them out to the garden. I shall deal with them later.'

The tribesmen obeyed immediately, pushing the hapless couple before them and out of the room.

Now the warlord turned his attention back to us, and focused on Houseman. 'Again, the British treat us like fools. We, the Taliban, agree to have a secret meeting with our sworn infidel enemies . . . and your people assume we are too stupid to do a security sweep for listening devices! Despite the fact they know we have many friends within the Pakistani and Iranian communities – with access to sophisticated expertise.' He paused for effect. 'You have to ask who are the real fools amongst us?'

Houseman swallowed his pride. 'I for one shall never underestimate you, doctor, you may be sure of that.'

Zam-Zama stood up. 'That is very wise. Now just you and I shall go next door to talk in private.' He turned to Ravi, Abdullah and me. 'You, gentlemen, will remain here with Babur.'

Houseman picked up his laptop case, rose to his feet and followed the doctor through the double doors. Babur closed the doors firmly, then crossed the room to the internal phone. 'I shall call down for refreshments,' he announced.

Five minutes later a teenage houseboy arrived. Babur smiled fondly at him as he entered the room.

He was carrying a tray laden with a large, ornate brass teapot and cups, together with some snacks. As time passed while we drank and ate fresh figs and *bolannee*, tasty little potato and leek wraps, Babur became gradually less sullen. He even talked with us in his limited broken English.

When he realised we weren't being hostile to him, he became a little more friendly. Suddenly he blurted out, 'I do not mind you Englishers. It is the American aeroplanes that kill my cousin and her family. That is bad.'

'I am sorry to hear that,' I said.

He gave a tight smile, wrinkled his nose, and shrugged. 'Thank you. But you Englishers should not be here. We defeat you before – in history – and Russian soldiers too. Many dead. You not defeat Afghanistan.'

I thought I might as well try to build a bridge. 'We're trying to help Afghanistan, not defeat it.'

Babur shook his head. 'You make us do things your way. Impose president and do not talk to Taliban. You want to win, you talk with Taliban.' He jabbed his thumb in the direction of the double doors. 'Your friend wants to talk. Wise man. Then he can win *with* Taliban, not against us.'

We ended up talking with him for quite some time. I was just starting to wonder how much longer Houseman was going to be with Zam-Zama, when the doors reopened and the two men reappeared. Houseman was at his side, carrying his laptop case. I was surprised to see the hint of a smile on the Afghan warlord's face, light from the window catching on one of his gold fillings.

He paused in front of us and turned to the British intelligence officer. 'What you say has been of interest to me, Mr Houseman. I and others shall consider it.' He extended his hand and Houseman shook it with considerable enthusiasm. It was the only clue that he, too, was pleased with the outcome, because his face remained impassive.

'We shall meet again,' he added. 'At last your government may have started to understand that they will never find peace here until you talk with us. Because we will always be here. In the hills, in the sunlight where you can see us, and in the shadows where you can't.'

Babur had already risen to his feet and the rest of us followed his example, starting to move towards the door.

'Wait,' Zam-Zama ordered suddenly. 'I wish you to observe something before you go. Please, come with me.'

He led the way across the marble floor and out onto a raised patio with an ornate iron balustrade. It overlooked the garden in which his two henchmen waited in the shade of a mulberry tree with Reza and Asifa. Other followers stood around, some squinting through the camera viewfinders of their mobile phones.

In a booming voice, Zam-Zama called across to the young woman. 'Hey, Asifa! Stand aside from your husband and answer my question.'

Abdullah again began translating for our benefit.

As Asifa obeyed the warlord's command, Zam-Zama added, 'Is it true what I have heard? That in your spare time you have been helping aid-workers at the new school?'

She nodded.

'Helping the infidel enemy – an unforgivable sin in the eyes of Allah. There must be a lesson to others.' Zam-Zama looked to one of his henchmen. 'Hakim, take out your hand-gun.'

Immediately the man called Hakim fumbled under his long shirt and extracted a revolver that looked like a modern Ruger.

'Take out the bullets, leaving just one remaining,' the warlord commanded. 'Spin the chamber. Then hand the weapon to Reza.'

Hakim didn't look happy about that, yet he still obeyed

with an obvious reluctance. Reza was clearly petrified, accepting the butt of the offered gun with a trembling hand.

Zam-Zama turned his attention back to the girl. 'On your knees, Asifa . . .' As she refused to move and glared back at him, defiant, he snapped, 'Now!'

The second henchman jerked his knee into the back of her legs and she dropped unceremoniously to the ground.

'Well, Reza,' Zam-Zama said in a low voice, 'this is to be a lesson to any others who disobey me or other Taliban commanders. You will now place the barrel of the gun behind your wife's neck – and pull the trigger!'

'NO!' the man protested.

I glanced sideways at Abdullah, scarcely believing his rapid translation. Houseman remained stony-faced, staring straight ahead.

'You have two children,' the warlord reminded. 'They will lose their mother. Disobey me and they will be without both a father and a mother. You have five seconds to decide. One . . .'

I turned to Houseman. 'We can't let this happen—'

'Shut up, Dave!' he snapped from the corner of his mouth.

'Two . . . Three . . .'

Asifa looked up at her husband with pleading eyes. 'Be brave, Reza, do it. Our children cannot be without us both.'

'I can't!'

'Four . . .'

'You must.'

The first henchman pushed Reza into position behind his wife as she bowed her head. The man's shaking hand was guided until the revolver barrel was pressed against her neck.

Zam-Zama paused for the rapt audience of onlookers. Their cameras on mobile phones began to click and whirr, witness to this deadly game of Russian roulette.

Involuntarily my hand moved towards my holster. From the corner of my eye I saw Houseman give a small, terse shake of his head. My fingers closed around thin air. Of course, he was right. It would have been suicidal to try anything. I suddenly became aware of the dark stain spreading across the white material of Reza's baggy pantaloons and the puddle expanding out from his sandals to soak into the dust.

'NOW!' Zam-Zama snapped suddenly. The word was followed by a flurry of phone camera shutters.

We were aware of the metallic click of the gun hammer as it fell onto an empty chamber.

Reza's face was quite pale as he dropped the gun and rocked unsteadily on his feet. Asifa pitched forward onto her elbows, her body heaving as she began to sob. Some of the onlookers began to laugh and joke with each other.

'Get her up!' Zam-Zama ordered.

When the couple were both standing in front of him, he said, 'You are lucky. Today Allah is merciful. And so am I. But defy me again and you will both be dead, and so will your children. And your extended family. Your salaries will now be halved for the next year.'

The doctor turned around to face us. 'That is one example of why you will never defeat us. The Taliban rules its peoples with the blessing of Allah, in a manner that is fair – but unforgiving, if it is disobeyed.'

'Of course,' Houseman murmured.

I thought how Zam-Zama was just showing off his power, how he controlled by terror and the fear of awful reprisals. The same recipe had been used by rulers, governments and their opponents throughout history. Zam-Zama was nobody special, he hadn't invented it.

I said, 'I think we'd better go now.'

As we all turned to leave, Zam-Zama positioned himself directly in front of Abdullah. 'Hello. We haven't spoken directly, have we?'

Our interpreter shook his head. 'No, doctor.'

A twist of a smile appeared on the warlord's face. 'No, indeed. Yet I do believe I know who you are. Not only do you translate for our infidel enemy, but you teach at their schools. In the past, when we were in government, you also illegally taught young women.'

Abdullah paled and hesitated for a moment before replying. Then he took a deep breath, drew himself up to his full height, and stared Zam-Zama directly in the face. 'Yes, doctor, I did and I am proud of it.'

The thin smile of the other man's face twitched fractionally. 'Then, Abdullah, I do hope Allah remains in his forgiving mood today.'

I took hold of Abdullah's shoulder and urged him towards the door. 'OK, guys,' I said. 'It's time to leave.'

It was a relief to get outside. The air was hot and fetid, but at least it felt clean compared to the uneasy atmosphere in Zam-Zama's house and his own menacing personal presence.

Houseman was marching briskly, almost angrily by my side, swinging his laptop case like some City businessman.

'Can you believe that, Dave? The bastard was actually educated at Oxford University and our cretins in London couldn't even find that out.'

'Maybe he used a different name at the time,' I suggested, 'or perhaps this one isn't his real one now.'

'You don't get the point, Dave. It doesn't matter *why*! It's our people's job to find out these things. If we can't manage something as simple as that, how the hell are we supposed to win this frigging war?'

I said, 'Of course, maybe Zam-Zama's just lying about his education.' Houseman just stared at me. I decided it best to change the subject. 'Anyway, Chas, how did the meeting go?'

Houseman shrugged. 'So-so. Each set out his stall,' he said wearily. 'We each made our initial demands, stated our positions, jockeyed for position at the first hurdle. Usual bollocks.' He reached into his pocket. 'By the way, keep this with you till we're safely back at Bastion. An extra copy, just in case of accidents. A record of the meeting.'

I glanced down at the computer memory stick in my palm. 'Sure,' I said, and dropped it into a secure pocket in my cargo trousers.

Crisp and Andy were waiting anxiously for us beside our three parked vehicles, Duffy manning a roof-mounted GPMG on one of the pickups.

'You're OK, boss!' he confirmed. 'Ain't no bastards following you!'

'Good,' I replied, 'then let's get the hell out of here.'

Houseman said quickly, 'Take Abdullah with you in the Shogun, Dave. I need a debrief with Ravi on the way back.'

I thought that could have waited, but shrugged. 'Whatever makes you happy, Chas.'

So, playing musical chairs, I scrambled into the lead Shogun with Abdullah. Meanwhile Andy rode shotgun on the pickup driven by Duffy. In the rear Houseman and Ravi sat in their private little conference room in the open back of the last truck with Eddie Crisp at the wheel.

I fired up the engine and led the way from Zam-Zama's palace into the hills, returning along the route we had used before.

It was a relief that the meeting appeared to have gone well, because it meant that we shouldn't have any trouble on the return leg of our journey. But then this was Afghanistan, and you could never take anything for granted.

Nevertheless, I think my guard had dropped. After all, the main job was done. Houseman seemed to have a result and there was actually a light breeze this morning, which cooled the sultry air quite pleasantly. I was even enjoying the stark beauty of the rugged and desiccated landscape.

Abdullah might have been reading my thoughts. 'Such a beautiful land, Mr Dave. So magnificent, yet full of such stupid peoples. And worse, evil people like Dr Zam-Zama.'

I grunted. 'Can't say I can disagree with you there, Abdullah. Many beautiful lands are run by evil people – and ugly regimes.' He didn't reply, he couldn't.

The impact of the bullet smashed into his forehead and threw him back hard in his seat.

# Seven

Because he wasn't wearing a seatbelt, the impetus of the bullet rocked Abdullah forward again, slamming his head into the dashboard.

Above the noise of the engine and moving shale beneath the wheels, I had not heard the sniper round as it punched a neat hole in the glass before entering Abdullah's skull. I just felt the warm spray of blood on the side of my face from the horrific exit wound at the base of his neck.

I was totally stunned, finding myself muttering some expletive as I gathered my senses. A hail of heavy machine-gun fire sent dust clouds dancing across the track in front of me.

Finally I found my voice. 'AMBUSH!' I screamed into the radio mike, and threw the steering wheel hard to my right to throw off any attacker's aim.

Then came another torrent of fire, this time creating a spiralling cloud of dust between my Shogun and the first pickup behind me. In the rear-view mirror, I just glimpsed the look of horror on Brian Duffy's face behind the wind-screen before it disappeared from view in the maelstrom.

I spun the wheel back to the left through my palms, feeling the suspension pick up the iron-hard ruts of the track, then the tyres bite into crushed rubble as I continued to veer in the opposite direction.

Thank God, I thought, the other attackers were not marksmen like the man who had taken out Abdullah with a single shot.

I was suddenly aware of the deep stammer of the GPMG opening up from the truck behind me. In the mirror, I glimpsed the hunched figure of young Andy, his Arab headdress flapping in the slipstream, as he began emptying the belt of cartridges up into the hillside.

In an ambush situation, it's a natural instinct to dive for cover. But that's exactly what your enemy wants you to do, so he can cut you to shreds in a withering crossfire, with you caught in a position from which there is no escape.

I knew that our Taliban attackers would be firing from ahead of us and from at least one of our flanks. Most likely they had already installed a stop-group behind us, in case we were able to turn and run back the way we had come. Perversely the enemy's weakest point is usually dead ahead. The last thing he expects is for his victim to run pell-mell into the face of the attack.

All this flashed through my mind in a split second. The reaction is deeply embedded by training into the mind's military matrix. My foot pushed the accelerator to the floor as I heard my voice yelling into the mike: 'ALL UNITS! STRAIGHT AHEAD, MAX SPEED!'

As I felt the powerful forward thrust of the engine, my view was instantly blocked by the fog of dust from endless incoming rounds. The whole vehicle was swallowed up, as the intensity of fire increased. It was like a sudden hailstorm. I instinctively crouched slightly lower behind the wheel, trying in vain to offer a smaller target. Rounds slammed into the ground all around us or pinged off the surrounding rocks.

Then, as quickly as it had begun, it was over. The eye of the storm had passed, the swirling curtains of dust beginning to drift. I wondered vaguely why they had stopped.

In the rear-view mirror I could see young Andy, still hammering away on the GPMG at distant muzzle flashes in the hills. I felt my adrenalin rush begin to ebb, thankful that I'd got away with it one more time.

That was a bit premature, because I suddenly I heard the noise of a ricochet off a crag at the side of the Shogun. I swung the steering wheel to send the vehicle careering off to the right, leaving the track again. Glancing to my left I saw the enemy machine-gun rounds chewing up the ground where we had been a split-second before.

That's when it happened.

I only heard the horrendous roar of sound for a nanosecond before my eardrums burst. My vision disappeared in a blinding, scalding flux of dazzling pure whiteness. Momentarily I was aware that I was moving, flying. Whether upwards, sideways or backwards, I had no idea. There was a wicked sharp pain in my right leg, a feeling of steel slicing into my leg, scraping along the bone of my thigh. The floating sensation ended with an explosion of force as my body slammed into the hard, unforgiving ground of sun-hot shale. My face was dragged across the stone, the skin of my cheek shredding and flaking with the friction, a tooth shattering.

Then the dazzling whiteness in my eyes began to fade, darkness closing in rapidly. It was the arrival of death to commit the final act of life. I was aware of a brief fluttering of my heartbeat, then everything went blank as I passed out.

I don't think it can have been for long, probably less than a minute, yet it seemed like an eternity. I felt like I was lying at the edge of a tide, drifting in and out of consciousness on its ebb and flow. I was deaf, straining to hear even the most muted of noises. There was a distant chatter of gunfire, sounding foggy and unreal, like it came from another planet. Voices shouted, close yet far away.

My vision was blurred and unfocused. I rubbed my eyes with the back of my hand, and blood came away on my finger-tips. It was my blood, and it was moist. I blinked hard, trying to clear whatever it was that was interfering with my sight. Slowly the focus began to sharpen. In fact it sharpened so crisply and suddenly that the brightness seemed to scorch my retinas, as my sight zoomed in on the sun-bright landscape.

My Shogun was lying on its side, a smouldering carcass protruding from a deep hole in the earth. Twenty feet away there was a large blackened shape from which some white linen flapped. I just knew it was what remained of Abdullah. God, had I been lucky!

*'Dave!'*

I knew the voice was screaming at me, but it sounded like it was a million miles away.

Looking past the wreck of my vehicle, I saw the two pickup trucks and my colleagues gathered around, outlined momen-tarily, a shock-frozen tableaux of figures. Then I recognised young Andy as he started to move, the first to break free of the mental paralysis.

He was running, heading straight for me.

Even with my head reeling, my thoughts tumbling over each other to find sense and reason, I knew it was wrong.

'NO, ANDY!' I screamed at the top of my voice, yet hearing nothing in my own ears. 'ANDY, STOP!'

Taliban fighters planted IEDs in the makeshift roads, dug in or buried beside them. Our Shogun had been well off the track when it was blown up. It was a penny to a pound I'd driven into an old minefield, left over from the earlier Soviet occupation.

Those mines could be everywhere and anywhere around me.

'STOP, ANDY!' I yelled, raising my right hand to wave him away.

Later, in retrospect, I realised he probably thought I was waving him on to help me. He didn't hear, or refused to listen, or just plain misunderstood. He just kept on coming.

I watched, mesmerised, as he loomed closer and closer. My God, I thought, the luck of the devil is with him. He's going to make it, he really is.

Then came the pulsing flux of light and the rush of displaced air. I covered my eyes with my forearm, felt the patter of small stones and dry earth falling on my back and legs as the second mine went off.

As the reverberating sound gradually melted away, I slowly opened my eyes. There was fresh blood and tiny pieces of body matter glistening and matted into the hair of my forearms. I felt the bile rising in my gut and fought to hold it back.

There was not one remaining part of Andy. There was the larger mass of scorched torso, wrapped in desert camo, with its head detached. One of his arms and both of his legs were all in separate locations.

After what seemed like several minutes, I heard a voice whispering in the earpiece of my radio. *'Dave, can you hear me? Over.'* It was Eddie Crisp.

My mouth was parched, so dry I could hardly move my tongue or lips in order to form some words. 'Just, Eddie. I'm afraid Andy's copped it. Over.'

*'We could see. What about you? Over.'*

'I'm alive,' I replied, stupidly trying to make a joke of it. 'One of my legs is shit. Over.'

*'Hold on, Dave,'* Crisp said. *'Thank God the ragheads seem to have stopped firing. Can't think why. Anyway, I'm calling up JOC for a helo evacuation. Over.'*

I said quietly, beginning to feel faint from blood loss and the heat, 'Don't let 'em land here, Eddie. Reckon I'm sitting in an old Soviet minefield.'

Crisp acknowledged me, then got on the radio to HQ. He understood that the last thing I needed was a huge twin-rotor Chinook helicopter coming down beside me with its massive forty-ton downdraught. The light from the exploding mines would have been seen all the way to Kabul.

As it was, the casualty evacuation Chinook wasn't going to be coming any time soon. There were only six serviceable helicopters working that day and, as always, all were fully committed. And this was an unauthorised mission.

First Eddie Crisp got it in the neck from a furious young Para OC, then it was Chas Houseman's turn as he tried to pour his smarmy oil on troubled waters. It didn't wash, and it certainly wasn't going to get a rescue helicopter to us any quicker.

I had started to slip in and out of consciousness again, aware suddenly of big Brian Duffy's voice in my earpiece. *'Hey, boss, you look like you's noddin' off. You keep awake now. I'm goin' to come and see to you. Over.'*

His words jolted me awake. I worked up saliva into my mouth. 'No, Bri,' I croaked. 'It's too dangerous. Mines everywhere . . .'

*'Andy nearly got to you. I'll use his footsteps. It'll be OK . . .'*

'No, Bri,' I began.

*'You just keep talkin', boss, keep awake. Sing me a song.'*

'For fuck's sake—'

He began singing in a voice as flat as his size twelve feet. *'Roll out the barrel . . . come on now, boss,'* he urged.

I knew he was right. I tried to force some air from my lungs to my mouth, but it just came out in a dry, rasping whisper. 'Roll out the barrel . . .'

I squeezed my eyes shut for a moment, then tried to focus. If only I could concentrate, keep awake. Thirty metres away I could see Duffy's giant body flailing up the slope towards me, taking ungainly huge steps as he tried to discern Andy's footprints in the dust. But typical of Duffy, he wasn't taking his time, instead going at the task head on, defying fate to do its worst.

My heart fluttered as he passed the spot where the youngster had perished just moments before. Now he was on his
own, trusting only in his personal guardian angel.

Again I was starting to fade, my vision going when I felt
Duffy's huge hand shaking me vigorously. He'd made it.
'Hey, boss, you keep awake now!'

I was vaguely aware of him ripping the plastic syrette from
the chain around his neck, his hands rubbing my arm, forcing up a vein. My leg was throbbing so badly that the stab of
the needle going in barely registered. Duffy was no nurse
when it came to the niceties of medicine. He dug a permanent marker from his first-aid pack and scrawled a large M
for morphine on my forehead. Then he began to tie bandages
around my blood-sodden leg.

As I began to pass out again, I was just vaguely aware of
him lifting me up effortlessly from the ground and throwing
me across his shoulders, carrying me back down the hillside.
I remember little after that. For the rest of the day I sat
propped in the shade of one of the pickups with Houseman
and Ravi, while Duffy and Crisp stood guard in case of any
further attack. It was late afternoon before my companions
eventually heard the approach of the Chinook coming in for
our evacuation. By that time I was oblivious to everything,
dead to the world, and holding on to my leg and my life by
only a thread.

# Eight

'Penny for them, boss?' Duffy asked, still studying the road. 'You've hardly said a word since we left Hereford.'

The large articulated truck was swallowing up the miles as we headed south, basking in the gentle light of the setting sun.

Duffy's voice, slightly accusing, had suddenly boomed over the 1960s retro track on the radio as I sat beside him in the cab. 'Sorry, Bri,' I said, 'I was miles away.'

'Yeah?' He glanced at me sideways. 'And where's that then?'

'Now Zad. My final op.'

'Oh, that.' Dismissive.

'I owe you my life.'

Duffy wrinkled his nose. 'Right, then I'll send you the bill.'

I grinned. 'You really should have got that gong. It *was* put forward, you know.'

He nodded. 'I know. MOD turned it down. Unauthorised op.' The huge shoulders shrugged. 'Don't bother me none.'

'You still *deserved* it, Bri, you of all people.'

'Can't pay for care for me old mum with a medal,' he said, staring ahead at the road. 'If I *had* got it, you know where it would be now? Sitting in a drawer at home, still in the box it came in.' Even in profile I could see he felt embarrassed.

I dropped the subject and looked out at the rural land-scape that was becoming rapidly smothered with tight little modern housing estates. All cloned buildings with white plastic windows and bargeboards and claustrophobically small gardens that had little or no room for trees.

'Swinthorpe coming up,' Brian announced.

I was genuinely surprised at just how far the outskirts of the town had spread since I'd last been here. I wouldn't have been surprised to learn that the population had more than doubled.

'We'll soon be at the ring road,' Brian said. 'Where'd you want dropping, the market square?'

I shook my head. 'You don't want to take this wagon down some of those medieval streets. I've seen artics get stuck many a time.'

Duffy shrugged. 'Will the Abbey roundabout be all right?'

'Excellent,' I confirmed, reaching behind the seats for my bergen. 'I really appreciate this, Bri.'

Signalling, Duffy pulled into a bus stop lay-by and halted with a hiss of air brakes. 'You take care now, boss. Don't you hesitate to phone me, if . . . you know.'

I shook the outstretched hand, scrambled down and pulled the bergen out after me. Hauling it onto my shoulders, I slammed the cab door shut. To the strident blast of twin air horns, Duffy swung his mighty charge back out onto the road.

For a moment I watched as his vehicle merged into the steady stream of traffic on the road that would take him on his way to the ferry port.

As the lorry vanished from sight, I suddenly felt very alone. An evening breeze had picked up and, momentarily, I shivered in the cool air.

Yet it wasn't cold. Previously, on missions, I'd felt an inexplicable chill feeling. Maybe it was some secret, unrecognised fear I felt, or some sixth sense warning me that all was not right. Such sensations had rarely been wrong during operations. But this was a new world for me now, uncharted territory. Yet, although it could hardly be simpler – living like every other citizen in the land – I was aware that I'd already made a complete hash of it.

For God's sake, I scolded myself, stop wallowing in self-pity.

I took a deep breath, stabilised the bergen straps on my shoulders, and set off along the pavement. It ran alongside the lichen-encrusted, eighteen-foot medieval walls of the vast grounds of Swinthorpe Abbey. The street led towards the central market square. It was a Monday evening and there were few pedestrians about. Traffic was light.

This was the one night of the week that the Chinese restaurant I passed stayed closed. Seeing it reminded me of my predicament. No money for food or lodging, or anything else for that matter. I did have one small trick up my sleeve. Two large boil-in-the-bag sachet meals and a little gas stove.

Whilst technically I might now be a down-and-out, I was determined not to become a complete tramp and a wino. Things were bad enough, and I didn't want them getting worse. I *had* to lay off the booze. If I was going to get through this period of my life, I needed to hold my nerve, take the

time necessary to try to rebuild my life from the bottom up
– brick by bloody brick if necessary.

I reached the first inner crossroads of the market town, the
four corners marked by an upmarket family hotel, recently
taken over and ruined by a chain, a sixteenth-century pub, an
insurance office and the magistrates' court. Beyond that was
the market square itself. Surrounded by mottle-barked plane
trees, it was given over to car parking on non-market days. To
one side, next to the closed steel gates of a shopping arcade,
there was an ornate fountain and some benches.

As always, such places act as a magnet for alcoholics,
tramps and disaffected youth. I could see it was no different
here as I paused for a moment to survey the scene.

A trio comprising two older men and one bag lady were
occupying two facing benches, smoking and drinking from a
large, shared bottle of cider. The men were both shabbily
dressed and unshaven, their hair long and unwashed. The
woman wore a headscarf and was huddled in a moth-eaten
winter overcoat. All her worldly possessions were loaded
beside her in a Tesco shopping trolley.

The adjoining two benches had been commandeered by a
gaggle of sink estate teenagers. They weren't exactly in
conversation with the down-and-outs, but were exchanging
insults and sniping at them with derogatory comments.

Although it was summer, most of the boys sported woollen beanie hats, and thought they looked cool with their
boxers hanging out of the back of their designer-torn jeans.
They swigged from tins of supermarket lager and laughed
raucously, swearing and spitting like footballers. A couple of

them were clattering around noisily on skateboards, trying to impress the girls.

For their part, the girls pretended not to notice them. Wearing sprayed-on pussy pelmets for skirts, they smoked rollies, sent texts or chatted on their mobile phones, and tried to blag free drinks from their opposite numbers.

'A swig for a snog,' suggested one spotty-faced male. 'That fair?'

'In your dreams, mate,' came the retort. 'I'd rather kiss a dog turd.'

I moved forward, skirting around the youngsters, in an attempt to reach the older group. One of the skateboarders noticed my approach. Quickly he accelerated in my direction, throwing himself into an impressive semicircular sweep that brought him to a halt right in front of me, forcing me to a stop.

It was a half-baked act of intimidation. My eyes narrowed but I said nothing.

He looked me up and down, taking in my olive drab anorak and the DPM bergen strapped to my shoulders. The slack, gormless mouth formed into a sort of smile. 'New 'ere, ain't yer?'

I just said, 'Born here, actually.'

That surprised him. 'Ain't seen yer.'

'Been away a long time.'

He indicated my bergen. 'In the army?'

'Not any longer.' I smiled thinly, and added, 'So now they're one man down. You should try it. Make up the numbers.'

That really amused him, and he turned to one of his mates who'd started to listen. 'You must be fucken jokin'!' he replied, turning back to me, then jabbed his thumb in the direction of the vagrants at the adjoining benches. 'Half that lot in this town is fucken ex-army. Bloody barkin', they are, the lot of 'em. That's what the fucken army does to you.'

One of the vagrants rose to his feet. He was a very tall, thin man with long, dark hair and a matching beard that curled all the way down to his chest. He wore a woollen hat and what looked like an old naval topcoat that still retained a few of its original brass buttons.

The loud voice had lost little of its harsh Glaswegian accent. 'Aaron, you muppet, leave the poor man alone! Canna you see, you're boring him to death?!'

The skateboarder turned his head. 'Piss off, Jock! Mind your own business.'

The Scotsman waved to me. 'Pay no heed to the wee lad. Thinks he's a hard case – doesn't realise he's just a nut case.'

He paused for a moment, flinty grey eyes appraising me across the short distance. 'Saw you walk over here – no t'other way. Most people cross the street to avoid us.' He stepped closer and pushed his face closer to mine. I could smell the alcohol on his breath as he glared at me. 'So what you want? Lookin' for someone in particular?' he demanded, his words slightly slurred.

I took a backward step. 'No. I've just arrived. Just looking around.'

'For a place to stay? A few pubs do rooms. And there's the Abbey Hotel, of course.'

'I wish,' I replied. 'Low on funds.'

The Scotsman appraised me for a moment. 'Ah, *low on funds* are we?' His accent and drunken delivery made it hard to tell if he was being aggressive and sarcastic, or neither. After a pause, he said, 'Then you should consider joining this highly selective club. Being *low on funds* is a prime qualification for membership, don't ya know.'

He waved his hand. 'We don't own these benches. If you need to sit down . . .'

That was unnerving. Just because I said I was short of cash, his attitude seemed to have undergone a mercurial change. Maybe it was just the drink at work.

I got the feeling the man seemed to know, just by looking at me, that I was one of them. Was it some signal I gave off, in my body language perhaps? I wasn't sure I wanted to get involved with these tramps, but it seemed churlish to reject the Scotsman's wary offer of hospitality.

'Thanks,' I replied flatly. I walked around Aaron and swung the bergen down from my shoulders.

'Nice bit of kit,' the Scotsman observed. 'Recent issue, isn't it? Seen a bit of wear.'

I smiled thinly. 'It's been around a bit.'

A long, gnarled hand extended in my direction as he introduced himself. 'Mahoney,' he said. 'Known as Jock round here. Can't think why.'

I frowned. 'You ex-army, Jock?' I asked.

'A pongo, me?' He threw back his head and laughed. 'No way. Tha' idjit Aaron thinks everyone from the forces is a brown job. Don't think he's ever heard of the Royal Navy.

Don't suppose he's a clue about Francis Drake and the Armada, or Nelson. Not his fault, ignorant little bugger. It's how they teach 'em nowadays.' Mahoney paused and looked at his two scruffy companions. 'Girls first. This is Lady Penelope.'

Watery blue eyes looked up from under the old woman's floral headscarf and glanced daggers sideways at Mahoney before focusing on me. 'Actually, young man, my real name is Edwina – as well Jock knows.' The voice was pure, cut-glass crystal. Well, it would have been if the finishing-school enunciation hadn't been roughened by too many years of heavy smoking and drinking.

Mahoney laughed. 'You'll always be Lady Penelope to us. An aristocrat fallen on hard times. It takes all sorts.'

A smile made it to the woman's crumpled face and the sunken eyes came alive for a moment with the light of mischief. 'Aw, Jock, y'know, you can be my Parker any day,' she laughed, referring to the classic TV puppet characters.

'Sure, woman,' the Scotsman replied lightly, 'it's the sporran and sight of my knobbly knees that gets you going!'

Edwina looked back at me and nodded. 'He's right, dear heart. Took to wearing a kilt round town earlier this summer, he did. Really quite a fine pair of legs on him – for an old fella.'

I glanced at the long naval officer's coat that covered a pair of trousers. 'But not now,' I observed.

A voice said, 'Got too much aggro from the local yobs.'

I turned to look at the third vagrant. The man, with straggly ginger hair, was probably ten years younger than Mahoney and Edwina, both of whom, I guessed, were in their late fifties or early sixties.

While none of them looked in the best of health, this younger man looked decidedly unwell. He had deeply sunken eyes and an emaciated face that wouldn't have looked out of place in a photograph of Belsen concentration camp.

Mahoney said, 'This's Ginger, by the way, if you hadn't guessed his name. We're nothing if not original round here.'

Ginger didn't offer his hand, just a tic of a smile.

'Get much trouble from these local kids?' I asked.

'Aaron and his mates are OK,' Mahoney answered. 'Some of the older gang members can get a bit tiresome. Into drugs and stuff. See us as easy pickings, like to have a bit of fun at our expense.'

Ginger said, 'I do smack. Had a few problems with them.'

Edwina leaned forward and placed the palm of her hand reassuringly over the man's clenched fist. 'You *used* to do smack, dear heart. Remember that. Past tense.'

A grin cracked the man's face, his open mouth exposing bad and missing teeth. 'Sorry, forgot. I haven't shot up for five days. I'm clean.' He began to laugh, but the light sound of merriment caught in his throat and soon descended into a thick and chesty cough.

'Serves you right for being facetious!' Edwina scolded, then turned to me. 'Actually, Ginger's doing very well. Going through cold turkey on the streets is no fun. We're very proud of him.'

Ginger had gained some composure. 'Trouble with me is

I've got natural addictive disorder. Smack, tobacco, alcohol, chocolate, coffee . . .'

'Women,' Mahoney added.

'I wish,' Ginger rejoined.

Mahoney said, 'At least now you've a fellow pongo for company. Ginge was with the Cheshires in Bosnia.'

'I was Royal Wessex,' I said quickly, naming the original unit I'd joined the moment I was seventeen, way back in 1985. In fact, six years later, at the age of twenty-three, I'd passed selection for the Special Air Service and had never returned. But I didn't mention that; other members of the military can sometimes be a bit funny about special forces.

'So you were in Bosnia?' Ginger asked. I sensed the initial barrier between us starting to break down.

'I did some time there,' I answered truthfully, but not saying what my behind-the-lines roles entailed.

Ginger's eyes were a very pale powder-blue and seemed to be focused at some point in the distance, so that he appeared to look right through you. I noticed that the whites of his eyes were egged with yellow. 'Some very bad shit went down there.'

'It did,' I agreed.

'I saw some stuff,' he added bleakly, speaking slowly as he thought back. 'It blew me away. Not then, not at the time, but later. Gnawed away like some maggot in my head.'

'Now, now,' Edwina intervened. 'Don't let's get maudlin. We're forgetting our manners.' She picked up the large plastic bottle of strong cider and thrust it at me. 'Do have some.'

I didn't want any. I tried to think of an excuse.

It was embarrassing. I said, 'I've only got a pound.'

Mahoney said sternly, 'Did we ask for money? We share and share alike.' He glared at me. When he was satisfied that I realised I'd broken their code, he asked, 'You staying around?'

I shrugged. 'For a few days.'

'Then you buy us a bottle to share – *when* you can.'

I felt bad as I accepted the bottle from Edwina and took a swig. I wiped my mouth with the back of my hand. 'That's good,' I said, realising I was never likely to give up alcohol. 'I needed that.'

'You told Aaron this was your hometown, yeah?' Ginger asked.

I nodded. 'Left over twenty years ago. Never came back.' I glanced around. 'Bigger population, I guess. But nothing else seems to have changed much.'

'So why return now?' Mahoney asked.

I wasn't sure it was wise to talk to homeless people about this, but I took the honest approach. 'I was hoping maybe to get a small flat. Council or housing association, something like that.'

Mahoney was taking a swig of cider and almost blew a mouthful of the stuff over me. As he recovered from his fit of laughter, he said, 'Oh, yes, *right*! Fat chance!'

'Like that is it?' I asked.

'Fine if you're a single mother,' he replied, 'or an asylum-seeker. Top of the list for you.'

'That's just right-wing propaganda,' I said.

Edwina shook her head. 'It may be, but it's also true. Certainly is here in Swinthorpe, and a lot of other places. Not official, but *guidelines* to the housing office. I've been told by people who work there.'

Ginger added, 'Homeless pregnant teenagers and refugees make good newspaper headlines. The housing people don't want that sort of bad publicity. But no one gives a stuff about alcoholic old soldiers. Or druggies.'

'So you'll have to make do with a cardboard box,' Mahoney said with a laugh. 'You can get the best ones from Currys.'

Ginger indicated the rolled foam kip-mat strapped to the base of my bergen. 'Looks like our friend here will have all his own kit with him.'

'And what *is* our friend's name?' Edwina asked.

'I'm Dave,' I replied cautiously, shaking her hand.

Mahoney said, 'And you've got nowhere to stay?'

I sighed. 'From what you say, I'm not likely to have anywhere any time soon, either.' I glanced around the market square. 'Where's a good place to sleep?'

'Not here,' Mahoney answered quickly. 'Mondays are all right, usually quiet enough. But other nights, you get a lot of yobs around, especially in summer . . .' He stopped abruptly as something caught his eye in the direction from which I had just come. He inclined his head. 'Oh, yes, and our local friendly plod, of course.'

Ginger and Edwina looked up. The former soldier groaned, 'Oh, not the laughing bloody policeman. Just when I was starting to enjoy myself.'

Edwina put on a deep Germanic accent, pronouncing loudly, 'Enjoying yourself eez *against* zee law. Eet eez forboten. Ve have vays of making you miserable!'

The young police constable, in black shirtsleeve order, was very tall and reed thin, almost swamped by his stab vest that was weighed down with his radio and all the other gizmos of modern policing. I think someone had been having a laugh when they'd issued him a helmet a couple of sizes too big so that, with it sitting on top of his thin, pinched face, he began to resemble a novelty standard lamp.

But I couldn't see the funny side of it at that moment. At the sight of the uniform I was momentarily seized with fear. Crazy that, given the situations I'd been in with the SAS. Yet this was different. I was now wanted for a murder I hadn't meant to commit. I'd been lucky enough to get away from the crime scene. I'd got some distance, safe for now – or so I thought…Only to walk into this stupid situation. I'd have upped and run again, but my legs seemed to freeze. Instead I shrank into the corner of the bench, trying to make myself seem smaller. It was, of course, never going to work.

The police officer ambled along with a manner of studied arrogance, thumbs thrust into the armholes of his stab vest, it was clear he was unaware of the comical impression he made. He was obviously far too immersed in trying to make a good impression on the short, auburn-haired rookie WPC by his side.

'Blimey!' Aaron called out. 'If it's not PC Daddy Longlegs and his new girlfriend!'

A collective hoot of laughter rose from the group of teenagers.

# Nine

The constable tilted his chin and regarded the group of young-sters with disdain. He glanced sideways at the diminutive and chubby probationer, smirked and muttered something to her.

But the challenge from Aaron and his friends was half-hearted and they began to drift away before he got too close to them.

From the corner of his mouth Mahoney said, 'Constable Tiddy likes to stamp his authority on the place. Sad to see a tall man with short man syndrome.'

'Zealous little prat,' Edwina muttered under her breath. 'Do you for breathing air in a public place if he could.'

'Evening, Constable!' Mahoney called out. 'Nice to see the Blues and Twos out protecting us! Sleep safe in our beds tonight.'

Tiddy appeared to notice us for the first time and, head still held imperiously high, changed course towards us. The WPC trotted at his side, trying to keep up with her companion's long strides. 'Hello, Jock. You still around? We can hardly protect you unless you are tucked up in bed, now, can we?' The man's pale, pinched face looked up at the rustling canopy of leaves. 'Don't think that really counts as a roof over your head.'

'Here we go,' Ginger muttered under his breath.

Tiddy heard him. 'Indeed, old son. There *you* go. This is not a place of residence. You can't sleep here.'

'We're *not* planning to sleep here,' Edwina insisted.

'I don't know that,' the policeman retorted sharply.

'Yes you do, Constable, because we've just told you.'

Tiddy looked down at the plump young policewoman by his side. 'See, what we have to put up with.' She smiled awkwardly.

'And the young lady's name?' Mahoney asked.

She appeared pleased to have been noticed. 'I'm WPC Sharman,' she answered brightly.

Mahoney smiled as he nodded. 'Do you have a first name, sweetheart?'

I had the feeling she'd been trained to answer questions like that at Hendon. 'Just WPC Sharman to you, sir. It's best to keep things formal.'

'Bridey,' Ginger said suddenly. 'She looks like a Bridey to me.'

Mahoney shook his head. 'No, definitely an Elspeth.'

'Now, now,' Edwina scolded. 'Leave the poor lass alone. Let her keep her little secret if she thinks it helps to preserve her dignity.' She smiled and extended her hand. 'Hello, WPC Sharman, welcome to Swinthorpe.' The probationer looked uncomfortable as she accepted the grubby hand.

'And, for the record,' Edwina said, 'I'm known as Penelope, Lady Penelope. These two are Jock and Ginger.' She nodded in my direction. 'And this gentleman is called Dave.'

But PC Tiddy showed no interest in me. I felt my heartbeat slow. I'd got away with it again. The officer now had the look of someone who was starting to feel left out of things. 'Er, right, well, now we all know who we are, it's time for you lot to move on. I can't have you sleeping here.'

'I've already told you . . .' Edwina began. '*And* it's too early to go to bed.'

WPC Sharman looked up at her mentor. 'Penelope has a point, Ray. It's only just gone eight.'

Tiddy looked decidedly irritated. 'You'll learn, Sharon. Give these people an inch and they'll take a metre.' He turned to Mahoney. 'It may not be your bedtime, Jock, but it's not too early for you to create a breach of the peace.' He pointed a finger at the cider bottle in the Scotsman's hand. 'What's that you're drinking in a public place?'

'Oh, here we go,' Ginger muttered, again.

Tiddy indicated the little metal signs dotted around the benches on poles and rubbish bins. Outline drink glasses struck through with the forbidding red slash. 'You know the by-laws. Hand it over.'

Mahoney shook his head slowly and glanced down at the plastic bottle in his hands. It was almost empty. Nevertheless, in defiance, he lifted it to his lips and drained the contents, before handing it to Tiddy.

The officer considered for a moment, then made a decision not to make an issue of it. He crossed the pavement and shoved it into the overflowing rubbish bin.

'I don't need this,' Mahoney said, glancing around at the rest of us. 'You guys comin'?'

Edwina rose to her feet and reached for her supermarket trolley. 'I've got some things to get. See you all later.'

As Ginger shuffled to his feet, I said, 'Mind if I tag along?'

Realisation was dawning that living rough wasn't as easy as it might seem. I needed to learn the ropes.

'Sure,' Mahoney replied without enthusiasm.

I shouldered my bergen and fell into step alongside Ginger and Mahoney, as the Scotsman looked back. ''Night, Ray!' he called out. 'Sweet dreams, *Sharon*.'

We crossed the market square, now serving as a late-night car park. 'Tiddy's a bit of a plonker,' Mahoney said. 'Most of the other cops are all right, have a bit of an understanding of our situation. Helps that some of them are ex-forces.'

'That's what I should have done,' Ginger said, ruefully. 'Joined the cops. Nice salary. Good pension.'

'Nah,' Mahoney said, 'that would never have been for you, Ginge. Both your parents were hippies, you told me. It's in your blood.'

'True enough.' The man looked sheepish. 'I've got to score, Jock, sorry. Please don't tell Lady Penelope, but this is doing my head in.'

He held out his palms. I could see that they were slick with sweat and visibly trembling.

'How long did you use heroin?' I asked.

Ginger nodded. 'Nearly fifteen years. I did some for the first time when I was in Bosnia. Back in the UK the bad dreams started, the flashbacks and nightmares. There was plenty of stuff on the streets, and cheap. For a while it seemed to ease the pain . . . you know?'

Mahoney asked, 'Who you planning to buy from?'

A mouthful of bad teeth showed when Ginger smiled. 'Mmm, yes, I've got to be a bit careful there. I owe Aaron's brother a few quid.'

'Aaron?' I queried. 'The kid back in the market square?'

'Sure,' Mahoney said. 'His older brother Jak runs a drug gang in town.'

'The Chip Shop Boys,' Ginger added.

I grinned. 'Sounds like another boy band.'

Ginger shrugged. 'That's their base, so to speak. The chippie on Salisbury Street. They're always hanging around. Weed, smack, coke. Take your pick.'

'Nasty little shits though,' Mahoney said, 'despite their daft name. They beat up that busker back in the spring, the one who played by the Poultry Cross. Stamped on his fingers. He'll never play his guitar again.'

'Why'd they do that?' I asked.

Ginger looked at me as if I was stupid. 'Because he owed them money.'

Mahoney interjected. 'So you're going to buy from that other lot?'

Ginger nodded. 'Yeah, they'll be in Coronation Gardens. I thought that's where we're going.'

'It is,' Mahoney confirmed, 'but not to get you a fix. Thought I might show Dave a good place to spend the night.'

'Coronation Gardens,' I echoed, recalling the place from my childhood. It was an open park of lawns interspersed with flower beds and a wide variety of trees, originally imported from all around the former British Empire by the town's elders in Victorian times. A shallow tributary from the main river meandered lazily through the middle of the area, making it a favourite with paddling children and picnickers.

'A bit too blowy in winter,' Mahoney said. 'But lovely at night this time of year. Quiet and no cops.' He indicated the bergen on my back. 'You got a tent in there?'

I shook my head. 'No, just a bivvy bag and a basha sheet.'

'Aw sure, that'll be ideal,' Mahoney declared. 'A real home in the shrub beds. No one will even know you're there. Might think of doing that myself next year.'

'Where do you sleep?' I asked.

He looked up at the darkening night sky. 'In weather like this, just my favourite park bench. Overhung by a tree branch that keeps me amazingly dry – unless there's a real downpour.'

Ginger shook his head at Mahoney's rose-tinted description. 'Or the slightest wind blows and the raindrops shake off – like sleeping in a permanent shower.'

Mahoney shrugged. 'You can't have it all ways.'

We'd long left the market square, walking down a succession of picturesque medieval streets, now ruined by the brash and brazen signage of modern shops. Finally we crossed a low stone bridge that took us to the first flower bed that marked the outer perimeter of Coronation Gardens.

Ginger shuffled to a halt. 'That's them,' he said hoarsely. I detected a nervous edge to his voice.

In the ambient light of nearby street lamps, I could just determine the figures. They were gathered around a stone drinking fountain. I counted seven of them.

'You still planning to buy?' I asked.

Ginger swallowed hard and nodded.

I was curious. 'Where d'you get your cash?'

The man scowled at me. 'What the fuck's it to do with you? Let's just say I came by it.'

Mahoney said, 'I'm not sure this is a good idea.'

'They're OK,' Ginger assured with a voice that didn't carry too much conviction. 'As long as you don't cross them.'

'You know the stories . . .' Mahoney began.

'Everyone knows stories!' Ginger cut in irritably. 'They like to come across as important. It's all part of their game. That way people don't take advantage, don't try it on.'

'So these aren't the . . . what . . . Chip Shop Boys?' I asked.

Ginger shook his head. 'No, these are their big new rivals. An Asian gang, mostly Pakis. Call 'emselves Swords of Allah. Some like to think they're Islamist big shots, let their customers think they've got – you know, *connections*. In fact they're just a bunch of wankers from the Evinmore estate. Rosebury Street area.'

'Become a bit of a Muslim quarter in recent years,' Mahoney explained.

'The two gangs are at loggerheads,' Ginger added. 'Been fighting a bit of a turf war.'

I could hardly believe it of sleepy Swinthorpe. 'So drugs are even a big thing *here*?' I asked.

Ginger gave a snort of derision. 'Which planet you been living on, Dave? This whole country's swamped in drugs. We live in a total drug culture.'

Mahoney cut in. 'Anyway, I'll come with you.'

Ginger glared. 'Thanks, Jock, but I don't need no bloody babysitter!'

'Just a bit of moral support.' Mahoney glanced sideways at me. 'What d'you say, Dave?'

'Why not,' I replied. 'If this Asian gang's a bit unpredictable, then it's better safe than sorry.'

Ginger shifted uneasily. 'Promise you won't say anything, you'll keep your nose out of it?'

'Of course.'

The former Cheshire Regiment soldier grunted uncertainly, turned his head and began walking towards the group of Asians. Mahoney glanced at me, winked and indicated for me to join him, walking just a few paces behind as Ginger approached the gang.

Its members had already noticed us, their conversation dying away to become a hostile silence. They watched warily with sullen eyes. I became aware of an irritating background music beat from someone's smartphone.

I gauged that most of the group were in their late teens or early twenties. They shared the ubiquitous urban battledress of vulgar T-shirts, jogging pants and designer trainers. Most wore baseball caps or hooded tops, which I suspected were worn to disguise identities rather than as fashion statements.

One, however, didn't bother with either. He was, in fact, the tallest, topping six feet by a good few inches. But it was his confident demeanour that really marked him out as their leader, that and his swarthy good looks, with lush, curly black hair and a neatly trimmed goatee beard.

'Hello, Ginger,' he said as we got closer. 'Long time, no see.'

'Hi, Rashid,' our companion answered flatly.

'And to what do I owe the pleasure?' Rashid asked. I noticed the man's irises were so dark, almost black, that his eyes appeared to have no colour and no emotion.

Ginger shifted awkwardly. 'You know, I'd like to buy. Some gear, some smack.'

Rashid's thin lips curved in a lop-sided half smile. 'Yeah? You been buying elsewhere?'

'I've been trying to give it up.' His laugh came out as a nervous little croak. 'That's a joke. Not easy. Five days now and I'm crawling up the wall.'

The tall Asian tilted his head to one side in an expression of mock sympathy. 'Ah, poor you. Yet I do believe it's a lot longer than five days since we last met.' He glanced at one of his sidekicks, whose hood framed a gormless-looking face that was trying and failing to sprout a beard. 'More like five weeks, ain't that right, Amir?'

Amir dug in the pocket of his jacket, extracted a tatty note-book and thumbed the pages. 'Six weeks, actually, boss,' he said as he consulted his notes.

'Soo-oo,' Rashid said slowly and thoughtfully. 'Where is your customer loyalty, Mr Ginger? It couldn't be that you have been doing business with the Chip Shop Boys?' His eyes narrowed. 'You know how we feel about that, don't you?'

Ginger shifted uncomfortably. 'Er, I didn't have an option at the time, Rashid. You know you're *always* my *first* choice.'

Rashid's voice dropped an octave, now quietly menacing. 'You mean they were cheaper?'

'I-I was hard up at the time.' Ginger's voice was quavering. He repeated, 'I didn't have an option.'

'There's always an option.' Rashid's attempt at a smile became no more than a sneer. 'We appreciate customer loyalty.'

Ginger tried to make a joke of it. 'Well, I'm back now, Rashid. And, I promise, it won't happen again. Honest.'

There was a long pause from Rashid and a nervous shuffling of feet as the members of the gang glanced at each other in anticipation of their leader's response.

At last the man said, 'Are you coming to me, Mr Ginger, because you owe the Chip Shop Boys money and therefore cannot do business with them? The word on the street is it's over one hundred pounds.'

Ginger shrugged, unable to deny what was clearly common knowledge amongst the drug-dealing community. 'Around that, yeah, I'm afraid . . .' He added quickly, 'I'll pay up front with you.'

For a second Rashid's smile almost became real. 'Indeed you will.'

Mahoney was becoming impatient. 'So what's the going rate now?' he asked.

Rashid seemed to notice the two of us for the first time. 'And who are you?'

'I'm Jock. We're friends of Ginge.' He inclined his head towards me. 'This is Dave.'

Virtually ignoring us, Rashid directed his reply to Ginger. 'Normal current price, my friend, is forty pounds for one bag of smack. One gram.'

I could see the relief flood across Ginger's face as he scrabbled in the pocket of his jacket. 'Oh, thank God for that, Rashid.' He extracted two crumpled notes.

But Rashid ignored them. 'However, that is including my customer loyalty discount. To outsiders the price is fifty pounds.'

'What?' Ginger's face crumpled like a child's.

Without thinking I said, 'C'mon, Rashid, can't you see the poor man's desperate.'

The hard, cold eyes focused on me. 'And who are you, again?'

'I'm Dave,' I said, suddenly wishing I'd kept my mouth shut. 'Just a friend.'

'Well, *friend*, you are witnessing market forces at work. Yes, I can see Mr Ginger is desperate. But I am now his *only* supplier in town. So what was forty pounds is suddenly fifty.'

'That's not fair,' Ginger protested. 'Forty is all I've got. I've saved it especially. Haven't even got enough left over for a tea.'

'Then you'll have to earn some more,' Rashid replied offhandedly. 'Go sell more copies of the *Big Issue*, or however it is you get your money.'

'C'mon,' Mahoney pleaded. 'Give the guy a break.'

But Rashid was unmoved. 'Your friend now knows the price. Pay it and the goods are his. It really is that simple.'

Mahoney dug deep into the pocket of his old naval greatcoat and extracted a dirty, crumpled five-pound note. 'How about a compromise, it's all I have? Call it forty-five, what about it?'

I could tell that Rashid was really getting a kick out of showing off his power to his followers. 'It remains at fifty. Ginger can have his fix. But *you* will owe me five pounds. A deal?'

Ginger turned to Mahoney. 'Please, mate,' he implored.

The Scotsman ignored him and scowled at Rashid. 'Go on, then. Take it.'

He waved the note, but the gang leader waited for a moment before he finally plucked it from his fingers. 'Remember,' Rashid said, 'I shall hold you personally responsible for the debt.'

Rashid's sidekick, Amir, held out a little polythene sachet of powder and Ginger snatched it.

'Cheers, mate,' he said to Mahoney, then turned and began scurrying back towards the town centre.

Mahoney looked at me and shrugged. Amir began a slow handclap and the other members of the gang started joining in, laughing as they watched the pathetic receding figure of Ginger.

Rashid said, 'What's your name . . . Jock? I'll give you two days. Until Wednesday night. Bring the money to me here, without fail.'

Mahoney didn't reply. He just grunted and placed his hand on my shoulder. 'C'mon, Dave, let's get away from here. Away from the smell.'

We shuffled away across the lawn to a tarmac footpath that wound its way into the darkness. We were both aware of the hostile glare of Rashid and his gang following us as we disappeared from view.

'Nasty piece of work,' I muttered.

Mahoney nodded. 'Seems the country's full of them nowadays. No respect for anyone.'

'Including themselves,' I added. 'No self-respect.'

Mahoney's laugh coarsened and broke into a cough. 'And we're great examples to them, aren't we?'

I smiled at that. 'You're right. Maybe we're not the best.'

A ragged cluster of trees appeared ahead of us, outlined in the moonlight that showed through the fleeting high cloud. Beneath the branches, a bed of shrubs spread out over several metres.

'I thought you might want to camp in there,' Mahoney said, 'as you've all the kit you need. No one will disturb you, won't even know you're there.'

And he was right.

I had the best night's kip I'd had in months. Under the stars and breathing the fresh night air, my mind and brain seemed to switch off completely. I found myself plunged into a deep, deep slumber. For once there were no nightmares and no bad dreams. It was as though I'd been totally immersed in a soothing balm.

It was the distant, strident blast of a car's hooter that finally penetrated the protective cocoon that seemed to have been spun around me. I cranked open one eye, momentarily disorientated, aware only of the dripping rhododendron leaves and the rich smell of damp earth. It took a moment to recall that I was in the municipal gardens, hidden within a large bed of shrubs and trees.

I wriggled out of my sleeping bag which was within an outer waterproof DPM camouflage bivvy bag. It was an arrangement that would allow me to sleep happily through wind, rain or snow.

I glanced at my watch and was amazed to find that it was already seven thirty. The sky was blue and the sun shining. I was just pulling on my trainers and starting to wonder what I might be able to rustle up for breakfast when I heard the shrill, angry voice of a young male.

'DON'T GIVE ME THAT, SCOTTIE! YOU KNOW WHERE HE IS! YOU'RE FRIGGIN' MATES!'

# Ten

Standing up, I peered through a gap in the rhododendrons.

Jock Mahoney was sitting on his favourite bench, nursing a roll-up cigarette in cupped hands. Three young men stood directly in front of him, their backs to me. They were dressed in hooded tops, sports trousers and designer trainers. To one side of them, appearing in profile to me, was a shorter, younger teenager. I suddenly recognised him from the previous night. He was the lippy skateboarder called Aaron.

As I moved quietly to the edge of the shrubs, I could just make out Mahoney's voice. It was quiet and croaky, as though in desperate need of a morning cuppa. 'Look, lads, Ginger's a mate . . . But we're *not* brothers. I've *no* idea where he spent last night or where he is now.'

I took a couple of steps nearer, curious to find out what was going on.

The man in the middle of the three with their backs to me appeared to be the leader and was doing all the talking. 'Listen, Scottie, I don't like to be up this early just to sort out the likes of you and your fuckin' boyfriend. Understand me?' He lowered his voice, 'Now you were mates enough to pay for his fix last night. Pay them Muslim bastards.'

Mahoney shrugged. 'And who told you that?'

'They did! Thought it was a huge joke, knowing he already owed us! Made us look right fuckin' soft prats!'

I guessed then that the one giving Mahoney a hard time must be Aaron's older brother Jak, the one who dealt in drugs. What was that stupid name his gang was called? The Chip Shop Boys.

'Well,' Mahoney was saying, 'you do certainly seem to be sensitive souls, that's for sure.'

Aaron's brother didn't like that. 'You takin' the piss, Scottie? 'Cos if you are, I'll make sure you won't be takin' the piss again – with your dick missing!' The switchblade flashed momentarily in the sunlight.

Mahoney was unmoved, raising one eyebrow as he regarded the weapon that was inches from his face. 'Steady, son. No need to get excited.'

'Take me to Ginger, Scottie,' the youth spat back, 'or we do things the hard way.'

I was hidden from Mahoney's view behind the three lads. I decided it was time to let him know he wasn't alone.

Leaves rustled as I brushed past the bushes and out into the open, my trainers soundless on the dew-damp grass.

As I moved up behind him, the leader was saying, 'Well, Scottie, if you can pay Ginger's debt to them Paki bastards, then you can also pay what he owes me.'

'And how much might that be?'

'Hundred and twenty quid,' the youth snarled, '– plus interest!'

Mahoney almost spat out his roll-up as he laughed. *'Right!'*

Just then Aaron noticed me, and turned his head sharply. Mahoney looked up. As he did so, their leader froze, suddenly realising someone was behind him.

His companions on either side turned their heads as he spun round to face me. The switchblade was held in his right hand, his knuckles whitening as his grip tightened.

He stepped back as he saw me. 'And who the fuck are you?' he demanded.

Before I could respond, Aaron shouted, 'That's 'is mate, Jak! 'E's army!'

We regarded each other intently. He had a drawn face, sprinkled with acne spots, and sunken eyes. 'Army?' he said with a snigger. 'He's a fuckin' tramp like the others.'

He moved his right hand forward a fraction, tilting the switchblade upward. Light played along its razor edge.

Something snapped in my head. The last time a knife had been pointed at me had been some three years ago in Iraq.

It had been a night op, it always was a night op in the top-secret world of Task Force Knight – we in the SAS and the Americans' Delta Force working in deadly harness together. Night after night, relentless, catching the insurgent bombers and their planners when at their most vulnerable, in their deepest sleep. Turning *their* dreams into instant, living night-mares. Those not killed or injured were spirited away to secret Yankee 'intelligence centres' . . . and within hours we'd have the names and addresses for the next night's list of attacks.

The operations ran the enemy and us ragged, and it was very rough justice. You had to wonder how many just gave a name, any name, just to stop the endless 'water-boarding' and other tortures? Of course, officially we didn't know about the questioning techniques employed and the blatant defiance of the Geneva Convention. And no one bothered to ask. All that mattered was that it got results, good or bad. In the end, the bombs that had been exploding in market places, outside mosques, hotels and police stations finally stopped. Or, at least, they slowed to a trickle, and our job was done.

The kid was still flashing his blade, but suddenly I was back in that run-down Baghdad suburb. I was leaving the helicopter ramp with the others barely before it touched down outside the compound wall. We were phantoms, moving shadows beneath a nail-clip of a moon. Unseen but seeing everything ourselves through night-vision optics fitted to our helmets.

The armed watchman on the gate never woke from his sleep, just dropped slackly from his wooden stool with his throat cut. We'd breached the gate and were inside the building before the first waking voice was raised in alarm. There were shapes all around in the green-grey vision of our night sights, insurgents sleeping on sofas, on camp beds or curled up with blankets on the floor.

Our warnings were yelled as the bodies stirred. Those who stirred too fast never stirred again, quashed by the vicious *phut-phut* of silenced double-taps.

A sudden flashlight beam from my left side blinded me. I thrashed out with the padded gloved fist of my free hand. The torch flew from the insurgent's grasp and I could now see the huge blade glinting in his other hand. I remembered thinking, in the nanosecond of reaction time that I had, that this was no ordinary knife as I lifted my Heckler & Koch.

I saw the big wide brown eyes staring at me and fired straight between them.

The red mist closed in as I looked down at the boy on the floor, all of ten years old, and the ornamental scimitar sword he had taken down from the wall.

That boy had laid claim to my soul then – and now the red mist of anger and despair and self-loathing returned. A vivid negative image of the small body floated between me and the lout called Jak, as he brandished his switchblade.

Had that boy really died in his remote tribal homeland so that the likes of this man could live just how the hell he wanted?

I drew suddenly to my full height, filling my lungs with air. I threw my arms wide like the wings of an enraged, attacking swan. Jak and his two companions were taken by utter surprise, stepping back. As the almighty yell of a madman escaped my lips, I lunged forward. My arms came swooping down, closing on the neck of the lout called Jak and the head of the man next to him.

As my fingers felt the ears of each man, I threw their skulls together with as much force as I could muster. The crack of bone was quite distinct as they sank to their knees in unison, the switchblade spinning harmlessly away along the path. I swung my own left knee up hard under Jak's chin, snapping his jaw hard shut. He fell back into a whimpering heap, clutching at his broken face.

While the second man stayed on his knees, nursing his head in his hands, the third man was up for a fight. An earlier glance had told me only that he was maybe older than the other two. He had the cumbersome build of someone who had pumped far more iron than he needed to. Beneath the fine-shaven fuzz of hair, his face was horribly distorted with rage.

He rushed at me, hands extended, reaching for my throat. I grabbed his wrists with both hands and rolled backwards with him onto the grass, pushing my feet hard into his stomach so that he flew high up over my head. As I kicked up my legs, my mobile phone detached itself from my belt and spun across the path.

The man crashed head first onto the tarmac, yelping as the skin was scraped from his face.

'Bloody hell, Dave!' Mahoney cried out. 'For God's sake, *stop* before you bloody well *kill* someone!'

I stood with shoulders hunched and my legs astride, panting heavily as I waited for a renewed attack from any one of the three injured men.

But no one seemed to have the stomach for it. Each lay where he had fallen, too stunned to work out what had happened. I breathed deeply, filling my lungs with the cool morning air.

Slowly the red mist that had so quickly clouded my head began to clear. I was aware of my heart rate easing. Suddenly I noticed again birdsong and the soft touch of morning sunlight on my face.

A man and his dog gave me a wide berth. An elderly lady passed by on her mobility scooter and glared.

The man called Jak finally climbed shakily to his feet and glowered. He had difficulty in speaking and I could see that his jaw was clearly out of alignment. 'You're fuckin' dead, man!' he lisped painfully.

I kicked his fallen switchblade well out of the way. 'No stupid threats, Jak,' I warned quietly. 'Just get out of here. And don't give Jock or Ginger any trouble, ever again. Or you'll have me to answer to. Understand?'

His two other companions were now on their feet, backing away. Jak went to say something but winced with pain as his lips moved. Clutching his jaw in silence, he turned his back on me and joined the others.

It was at that moment that his young brother Aaron and I spotted my mobile telephone at the same time. It was lying at the edge of the path. He must have seen an opportunity to save some family pride. Being much closer to it than me, he dived forward and snatched it up.

As I went to follow him, Mahoney grabbed my arm. 'For God's sake, Dave, leave it! D'you want to break the wee kid's skull as well?'

I stopped and glared after the three men and the boy as they walked slowly away. Aaron waved my phone in the air with one hand and gave me a V-sign with the other.

I sighed and turned back to Mahoney. 'No, Jock, guess you're right.'

He gave a wry smile. 'God save us from posh dossers with mobile phones. You'll just have t' learn to live without one.'

After quickly packing up my temporary camp and stowing it away in my bergen, I joined Mahoney on the path that led to the town centre.

'And *do* you know where Ginger is?' I asked, falling into step beside him.

Mahoney shrugged. 'Probably. At any one of his four or so favourite places. As he scored big last night, he'll probably be away with the fairies, fast asleep. Not much company.'

I jerked a thumb over my shoulder. 'And that lot?'

He grinned. 'I think that might just extend his credit a little now, don't you?'

The footpath had reached the river, which ran beside the open main car park of the town. The grassy embankments were a home to a variety of ducks, coots and moorhens, as well as half a dozen swans, which patrolled with all the mean purpose of a naval flotilla. Large willows on the far bank hid the rows of shops and offices that backed onto the river as the water gathered speed towards the foaming millrace.

The medieval mill had long ago been converted into an unattractive theme pub and a row of modern shops had grown up alongside it, an artless contribution of 1960s archi-tecture. One of the outlets was a cafe with a scattering of aluminium tables and chairs outside, overlooking the river.

I turned to Mahoney. 'Fancy a coffee?'

The Scotsman shook his head. 'I'd better find Ginger.' He grinned broadly. 'Make sure he's OK.'

He left me sitting outside the cafe, rolling tobacco into a cigarette paper and examining the menu blackboard. I dug in my pocket and extracted my precious last two pound coins. That wouldn't quite get me a coffee and a bacon roll. Worse, with my mobile phone gone, I should really be using the money to phone Sally as I'd promised. Just to at least let her and Daisy know which town I was in should there be some emergency.

However the only phone kiosks I'd seen took cards or had been vandalised. So I weakened and decided breakfast should take priority.

A skinny blonde woman in her early twenties appeared from the cafe entrance, wearing a green uniform tabard over a short frock. Her hair was scraped back hard from her face and she wore no make-up.

'Sorry, sir, didn't notice you. We don't really open until eight.'

I glanced at my watch; it was five minutes to. 'That's all right, I'm in no hurry.'

She smiled a quick little smile that also lit up her lively, bright-blue eyes. 'No, I didn't mean that. I just didn't see you here. We're all pumped up and ready to go, as me boss would say. Shoot me for not spotting you.' She tilted her head back and laughed lightly as she drew a notepad and pen from her tabard. She mimicked her boss's Greek accent. '*Don't you know there's a recession on, girl! You'll be the ruin of me!*'

I smiled. 'Actually, I might need a couple of minutes to work out what I can afford.'

She noticed my solitary coin on the table. 'Ah, on a budget, are we?'

'Afraid so.'

'What were you thinking of?'

'Black coffee and a bacon roll.'

'Make that tea instead with the roll – *and* you get five pence change.'

Laughing, I said, 'The coffee bit's important. I'm a certi-
fied coffee junkie. Couldn't do me *half* a bacon roll instead,
could you?'

'That's possible . . .' She leaned down to me and dropped
her voice to a whisper. '. . . because *I'm* making all the sarnies
today. Our regular sandwich-maker has just buggered off
back to Poland without a word. But don't tell Andreas, he'll
do his nut.'

'Andreas?'

'He's the owner, my boss.'

A sudden thought occurred to me. 'Do you need any
special training to be a sandwich-maker?'

The girl looked thoughtful. 'Not much really.'

I said, 'I can cut a straight slice of bread. And I'm looking
for work.'

A look of realisation came to her face. 'Don't think me
rude, but have you just left the army?'

I glanced down at my issue bergen and DPM trousers. 'Bit
of a giveaway, I guess . . . er . . . ?'

'Gem,' she said quickly with a breathless giggle. 'Gemma
Wilkins.'

She accepted my offered hand a little hesitantly. 'Dave,' I
said.

It was strange, but after years in special forces it becomes
second nature to only ever offer the minimum amount of
personal information to anyone. 'Are you serious?' she asked.

'Never been more so.'

Gem regarded me carefully. 'Let me get your order. I'll ask
Andreas when he's free. He's making all the curries and

pastas for lunch just now. I won't get no sense out of him till that's done.'

She left then and, as good as her word, returned with a steaming mug of black coffee and an *entire* bacon roll. Over the next hour there was a constant flow of office and shop workers grabbing breakfast or a wrapped lunch snack on their way to work. Miraculously, my coffee mug was replenished every twenty minutes or so, delivered with a smile and a knowing wink.

At just gone nine thirty Gem came out with two mugs of coffee and dropped into the seat next to mine. 'Goes quiet now until twelve,' she said, pushing the mug of black coffee across to my side of the table. 'I've told Andreas someone wants to speak to him.' She smiled conspiratorially. 'He said to get you a coffee on the house. He'll be out in a minute.'

I grinned at her. 'I appreciate your help.'

She lit up a cheap brand of cigarette and inhaled deeply. 'Think nothin' of it. I'm from an army family meself. Me grandad died in Korea and me dad fought in the first Iraq war. Got that Gulf War syndrome thing. Did his head in and he left me and me mum.'

Her eyes had dulled and I could see the telltale moisture of unshed tears. I touched her forearm. 'I'm sorry,' I said. 'That can be tough.'

She winced suddenly and I pulled back in surprise. 'It's OK, Dave! Didn't mean to make you jump! It's a bit tender, that's all.'

It was only then that I noticed the early purpling bruise on her skin. 'Walked into a cupboard door,' she explained quickly with a light laugh.

At that moment a dumpy, middle-aged man emerged from the cafe. He was wearing a full-length striped chef's apron over black trousers and a short-sleeved shirt. I couldn't help thinking that Gem sounded relieved as she said, 'Ah, this is Andreas, my boss. Andreas Simitis.'

The man stopped in front of me, vigorously wiping his hands on his apron. Dark eyes regarded me warily from beneath angry black eyebrows and I somehow doubted that a chef's hat could ever have managed to tame the riot of curly white hair on his head.

'This is Dave,' Gem said helpfully.

Satisfied that his big hairy hands were now dry, Simitis offered the right one to me as I stood up to greet him. 'Hello, Andreas.'

The smile on the unshaven face flashed so briefly that if you'd blinked you would have missed it. 'I am pleased to meet you, Dave . . . You have another name, yes?'

'Jones,' I replied without much imagination. 'I believe there may be a job vacancy here?'

Simitis flashed an angry sideways glance at Gem. 'I am not thinking of sacking her – yet.'

Gem pulled a face. 'Sandwich-making, Andreas. I really can't do that *and* serve the customers at the same time.'

The Greek returned his attention to me. 'It is true I had this helper from Poland. He worked very hard, very good. Otherwise I cannot afford him. You understand? There is a recession and I am facing ruin. Every day it is harder, fewer customers.'

I nodded my understanding. 'I come cheap,' I said.

Those big eyebrows rose together in interest. 'It will be casual work . . . and I cannot afford this crazy national minimum blackmail stuff. I manage just five pounds an hour . . . otherwise there is no job.'

I pounced. 'When do I start?'

He blinked at the speed of my decision. 'OK, then. Tomorrow morning – starting at seven – to make sandwiches . . . You know how to make sandwiches?'

'I've eaten many in my life. I know a good one when I eat it.'

I wasn't sure he liked that. He said, 'But not too generous on the spread, eh? And watch portion control, you understand? Too much filling will be the ruin of me.'

'I understand,' I assured. 'So that will be two hours a day, at five pounds an hour. Yes?'

Simitis nodded as we shook hands again. 'That is agreed . . . A trial, *if* you work hard for your money.'

I said, 'I'll work hard.'

His parting words were, 'Tomorrow at seven,' as he turned back to his cafe.

'Well done,' Gem said. 'I think he liked you.'

I sat down again. 'Then I'd hate to be in his bad books.'

She giggled. 'He's a heart of gold really.'

I raised an eyebrow. 'Well, thanks anyway.'

Gem added, 'Actually you'll probably find you'll often get an extra hour of sandwich-making in the morning – when Andreas is forced to realise there's only sixty minutes in every hour.' She laughed. 'So you might clear fifteen quid.'

I said, 'What's the cheapest mobile phone you can get nowadays?'

'About thirty quid,' she replied. 'Pay-as-you-go. Why?'

'I – er – lost mine this morning. And I promised I'd make someone a call.'

She fumbled in the pocket of her tabard. 'You can use mine.'

'That's OK, thanks. It can wait a couple of days.' I shook my head and grinned. 'Dammit, what's wrong with a post-card?'

She frowned, looking at the last five-pence piece of change on the table. 'You can't *afford* a postcard – let alone a stamp.' She thrust her bright pink mobile phone at me. 'Please use mine,' she repeated.

I took it as she stood up and made her way across to a table where a couple of elderly women had just arrived.

Sometimes it can really lift your spirits in life when you discover there are still decent people in the world and the milk of human kindness hasn't completely dried up yet. I reckoned I should be able to catch Sally before she left for work. With a smile on my face, I tapped in my old home number.

'Hi, Sal,' I said as she picked up the phone.

'Dave?' she gasped. 'Gosh, how are you?'

'I'm fine.'

'So the police haven't caught you then?'

That was meant to be a joke, but I didn't find it funny. 'Not yet. What happened when I left? Did they give you any trouble?'

Sally laughed lightly. 'Not a lot. They asked if you were in. I just said you didn't live here any more and I didn't know where to find you.'

'Did they say how Luke Hartley was? Did they say if he was dead?'

'*Dead?*' she echoed. Her laugh was brittle. 'You didn't say you'd *murdered* him.'

I felt the huge surge of relief like an ebb tide begin. 'No, well, I just wanted to be sure he was OK.'

'Well, the police didn't mention Luke. Nothing about him, or anything else. And it didn't exactly *feel* like a murder inquiry.'

I laughed dryly. 'Good. I really *didn't* mean to kill the bastard.'

I could sense the tension in the brief silence that followed before Sally added, 'By the way, there's been someone else looking for you. He just turned up about half an hour ago, out of the blue. A man called Houseman, Charles House-man. Just knocked on the door. Said he was from the MOD.'

For a second I was shocked. I'd almost forgotten the exist-ence of the man. A sudden vision of the blue eyes and crinkly blond hair flashed across my mind, and I could almost hear the low, oily tone of his voice. The last time I'd seen House-man was just before the fateful ambush in Afghanistan when Abdullah had been shot and I drove over a mine.

'What did he want?' I asked.

'You. Said he needed to talk to you urgently about some-thing important.'

'There can't *be* anything important,' I thought aloud. And I really didn't need any reminders about Afghanistan just now. After all, I'd just had my first night without a bad dream.

Sally said, 'Well, he certainly seemed to think there is. He was pleasant enough, but he was clearly agitated about something, anxious.'

For some reason I started to panic. 'You didn't tell him where I am . . . ?'

There was a slight pause before Sally said, with a sarcastic edge to her voice, 'Couldn't really tell him that, Dave, now could I?'

I slapped my forehead with my left palm. 'Idiot! Of course, not . . . I'm in Swinthorpe.'

I'm not sure why Sally was surprised. 'Oh, really? Back to your roots, eh? Have you got a place to stay?'

'Not yet. I'm roughing it for a bit.' I added, 'But I'm warm and dry.'

'I could send you some money,' she offered. 'You know. Cash, a postal order.'

'Thanks, but I'm fine.'

'You wouldn't have to pay it back.'

'Really, Sal. I'm all right.'

She sighed lightly in exasperation. 'Well, you take care.'

I said, 'Sal, this is someone else's mobile phone – I lost mine. As soon as I've got a new one, I'll call you with the number.'

'Sure.'

'And tell Daisy I called. Give her my love.'

'Of course.'

Finally, I said, 'And if that man Houseman calls again, *don't* tell him where I am.'

Sally gave a small laugh. 'Can't really, I still don't really know myself. What is it, third cardboard box on the left under the railway arch?'

'Sal, I *mean* it.'

'It's OK, Dave. Your secret is safe with me.' She paused. 'I've got to leave for work now. Bye.'

There was a hint of exasperation in her voice as she hung up.

I felt better, a huge sense of relief. But then, although I didn't face a life sentence for murder, I still faced the likelihood of a long stretch for GBH.

# Eleven

'No sign of Ginger anywhere?' Jock Mahoney asked. He sounded really down.

It was nine thirty the next morning and I'd just sat down outside the cafe for a cigarette. Gem had been right. Such had been the demand for lunch-pack sandwiches and rolls that I'd worked for a full two and a half hours. I'd earned a *full* twelve pounds fifty pence from a grudging Andreas Simitis.

I looked up at Mahoney as he arrived with Edwina, who still had the fully laden supermarket trolley at her side.

'You said yourself,' I reminded. 'Now Ginger's scored, he's probably curled up somewhere, fast asleep.'

Edwina turned on him. 'Oh, no, Jock! You didn't tell me that.'

The Scotsman shrugged. 'Hell, Penelope, he's a hopeless case. You just can't help some people.'

'But I thought you were looking after him, Jock!'

Mahoney was getting annoyed. 'Look, I'm not his big brother and I'm not his father – any more than you're his mother or his nursemaid! Ginger is a big boy now!'

I intervened quickly. 'Hey, you two, sit down and let me get you a coffee and something to eat.'

Edwina's nostrils flared. 'No need to show off, young man, just 'cos *you've* got a job.'

I smiled. 'So is that a no, then?'

'It's most certainly a yes,' she replied, shuffling past Mahoney to get the seat next to me. 'I really didn't believe Jock when he told me you were working here.' She leaned across and gave me a cidery-smelling kiss on the cheek. 'Well done.'

Gem came out of the cafe as Mahoney took his seat. 'Hi, Jock. Hello, Lady P!'

It came as something of a surprise that they knew each other. 'And how's the new boy getting on, dear girl? Don't spare his blushes.'

'Well,' Gem replied, stifling a giggle, 'the boss thinks he's putting too much butter on the bread . . . right to the edges . . . and not counting the number of lettuce leaves accurately. Andreas reckons he'll be ruined in a week.'

'And what do you think, dear love?'

Gem smiled at me. 'I think Dave will do fine! Now, what can I get you all?'

When she'd finished scribbling down the orders for two pots of tea and a selection of my sandwiches, she asked suddenly, 'No Ginger today?'

Mahoney shook his head. 'Unless you've seen him, he's gone AWOL.'

'He hasn't been here today,' Gem confirmed.

Edwina sighed heavily. 'Apparently he's on the smack again.'

'Oh no. He seemed to be doing so well, too.' But I didn't

think Gem looked that surprised as she shook her head sadly and went back inside with our order.

'Terrible stuff heroin,' Edwina muttered. 'The dealers, the crime . . .'

Mahoney grunted. 'We're fine ones to talk. *Alcohol* hasn't done me any favours – or you.'

There was a moment's silence as she looked at him scornfully.

I said thoughtfully, 'I guess we all just want anything that helps deaden the pain. You know, the pain of life. All that stuff.'

Mahoney's eyes narrowed, the pupils small and hard. 'I'll drink to that, Dave. That's how it started for me. A wee dram to blot out the memory. Then another, and another. Before you know it, you need your first one before breakfast.'

It was something about the way he said it. I knew we'd been through something very similar. 'What happened to you, Jock?' I asked.

He looked at me curiously. I had a feeling not many people had ever asked him that directly. He hesitated, pursed his lips as if in thought, and pulled a tobacco tin from the pocket of his naval greatcoat.

Edwina regarded him closely, saw he was struggling to find the words, and placed her hand on his wrist. He glanced at her, smiled a tight, appreciative smile, and withdrew his hand.

He began to roll a cigarette. 'The Falklands,' he said stiffly. Then, after a pause, it seemed to come flooding back to him. '1982. Flight Deck Officer Mahoney, at your service! The Argies had invaded our islands and – like all of us – I was fired up and ready to go. Get our islands back come hell or high water! Of course, we never thought Maggie Thatcher would go through with it. Thought the fleet would be turned round by the time we reached Ascension. I was all of twenty-four years old, a supply officer, green as salad. A Supply Branch officer going to war on one of our mightiest and latest frigates!'

Edwina looked puzzled. 'What's a Supply Branch officer?'

Mahoney smiled. 'Not real salty dogs like the watch-keeping officers. We were basically admin, pen pushers. We'd look to specialise later in stores, pay, advocacy . . . I had a law degree . . . But to make us useful in times of conflict, we'd also been given some basic training at HMS *Osprey* down at Portland Naval Base. Directing aircraft on and off the flight deck, ensuring safety procedure was followed, and that we operated within weather limitations.'

'What flew off your frigate?' I asked. I'd been only fourteen at the time but also had had a boy's encyclopaedic knowledge of military aircraft and helicopters. 'A Lynx helicopter?'

Mahoney nodded. 'A flight of eight maintenance crew,' he confirmed, 'two pilots and an observer. And, as FDO, they were *my* responsibility.'

He finished rolling his cigarette and paused to light it. 'Well, the fleet *wasn't* called back at Ascension. We went all the way to the South Atlantic. It was a hell of a battle that we fought and won. I've gotta say, pretty much against all odds. Not least against the weather.

'The seas down there have to be seen to be believed. Waves as tall as tower blocks. Wind that brings rain in horizontal

– like the proverbial stair rods. Our Lynx got caught out one time, racing in too fast to land before a sudden squall hit us. The pilot was quite new. He misjudged the rise and fall of the flight deck, and slammed down hard – right on the edge. The pilot killed the engine and the crew scrambled out. Huge waves were washing over the deck but we managed to get a single securing line around the helicopter's landing gear.'

'Sounds precarious,' I observed.

'That was the problem,' Mahoney confirmed. 'A storm was brewing and the light had virtually gone. The securing line was never going to hold in that – and the fleet was desperately short of helicopters. I went to the bridge to see the skipper.

'He asked if I could save the helicopter if he altered course, steering a full three-sixty degree circle? That would give us approximately two seven-minute windows when the flight deck wasn't fully awash and not flattened by the howling wind.

'To my eternal regret, I said yes.'

'What happened?' Edwina asked.

'The skipper turned the frigate. In the first window the maintenance crew winched the Lynx fully on board. In the second window, it got securely lashed down.' Mahoney took a deep breath. 'Then one of the lashings snapped unexpectedly. It was like a giant bullwhip. It hit one of the maintenance crew around the neck, all but decapitating him. Young Jimmy Cox.' Mahoney sniffed. 'Nineteen years old. Had got married before we set sail, he'd just learned they had a bairn on the way.'

I understood. The image of young Andy Smith, racing to my rescue in Afghanistan, flashed unbidden into my head. The earnest, sweat-drenched face, the piercing blue eyes . . . all suddenly disappearing in the searing white flash of the explosion.

I said hoarsely, 'I'm sorry, Jock.'

Edwina nodded sagely. 'But it wasn't your fault, Jock.'

Mahoney looked at her. 'It was *my* decision. I told the skipper we could save the helicopter.'

'And you did?' she asked.

'Yes.'

'Jock, you were fighting a war,' she added.

Despite the gentle autumn sun, I felt suddenly chill. 'And that has haunted you ever since?' I asked.

Mahoney paused to take a deep drag on his spindly cigarette. Then he said softly, 'Of course, I was upset at the time. We all were. I thought I'd got over it. I did a few more years in the navy until I got out in eighty-five. Joined a firm of solicitors and did pretty well for myself. Then in ninety-two it all went wrong. It was the tenth anniversary of the Falklands and I started thinking about the Falklands more and more. More and more about young Coxy.

'How, by rights, he should have been twenty-nine by then. Happy with his family, more kids – almost certainly promoted. Maybe got a good aviation mechanics job in the private sector.

'But, he had *nothing*. And I didn't even know what had happened to his family. Yet I'd been responsible for his death – and I had it all! Happy family, healthy kids, regular holidays, money – and a future. How unfair was that?'

Edwina looked pained as she listened intently.

I said hoarsely, 'Life isn't fair, Jock, it never can be. And it *still* wasn't your fault.'

Mahoney didn't seem to hear me, or didn't want to. 'That year my wife Greta and I were passing Pangbourne College near Reading. There's a commemoration chapel there for the British fallen of the Falklands. It's quite a striking design, sort of resembles a ship's bows. Inside, the name of each of the dead is embroidered on individual prayer cushions along the pews. Just over two hundred and fifty names in all. Greta waited in the car while I popped inside for a few private moments. The place was empty. I knelt down and shut my eyes. It all came back to me like it was yesterday.

'That night, the wind and rain, the stricken Lynx. The skipper, his eyes boring into mine, asking if I could save it? Me, in dripping oilskins, saying yes. It was all so vivid.

'I opened my eyes, looking down at the prayer cushion beneath my knees . . . I could not believe it! Of all the names. James Cox.'

'Oh my God,' Edwina breathed. 'That must have really shocked you.'

Mahoney nodded and stubbed out his cigarette butt. 'That was the end for me. Well, the beginning of the end. The nightmares started, the sleepless nights, my drinking and fighting with Greta. Mistakes started happening at work, bottles of booze were found in my filing cabinet. Within five years it was all lost. My job, my marriage, my home.'

Edwina grabbed his wrist and squeezed it hard. So hard, it must have hurt. 'It wasn't your fault, Jock!' she repeated.

He didn't flinch, didn't seem to notice the pain in his wrist. 'You don't understand. Whatever anyone else says, little Jimmy Cox clearly thinks it was my fault. That is why he came back – to make me pay the price!'

I could tell there was no reasoning with Mahoney, how could there be?

'My, we're all looking glum!' Gem's cheery voice cut across the silence as she emerged from the cafe with a tray. 'This should put a smile on your faces. A pot of tea and a selection of Dave's sandwiches.'

Edwina peered closely at the plate. 'Are you sure they came from here? Looks like they come from the baker's. Very nice.'

Mahoney emerged slowly from his memories, seeming groggy, like someone waking from a deep sleep. Then he, too, peered at my handiwork. He sniffed heavily and took a deep breath. With some effort he said, 'Bless me, Gem, they're stuffed to bursting!' He winked at her. 'And that's just the sandwiches.'

She ignored his coarse joke and replied, 'Andreas isn't very happy. Ran out of fillings.'

I shrugged. 'Apparently I haven't got much idea about portion control.'

Edwina helped herself to a chicken and sweetcorn on whole-meal. 'Oh, that's excellent!' she declared with her mouth full. 'Not like the miserable sandwiches you usually get here.'

'Absolutely right,' Mahoney agreed, blinking heavily and wiping his eyes with the back of his hand. He helped himself to a beef and horseradish. 'These look the business.'

'Look the business?' Another voice joined us as Andreas Simitis came out of his cafe for a cigarette. 'Ruin the business, more like.'

I really was starting to feel a bit guilty. 'I learn fast, Andreas. I promise I'll get it right tomorrow.'

Simitis was about to reply, then stopped. Something had caught his attention, and I followed his gaze towards the riverside path. The tall, gangling figure of PC Ray Tiddy was walking slowly and imperiously towards us, his head swivelling steadily left and right as he scrutinised the steady stream of shoppers and office workers coming towards him. Little probationer WPC Sharman bobbed along at his side.

He caught sight of our little gathering outside the cafe, and his body automatically clicked into a new direction. WPC Sharman scurried to catch up as his stride lengthened.

''Allo, Raymond,' Simitis greeted. ''Ave you caught that couple who left without paying yet?'

'G'morning, Andreas,' the constable replied. 'But, no, I'm afraid not. Wasn't much of a description to go on.'

'They were Japanese,' Gem said. 'That must have been a bit of a clue.'

PC Tiddy's nostrils flared. 'Trouble is there were three coaches in town, visiting the Abbey yesterday.'

'There!' Simitis said triumphantly. 'You even know *where* to find the culprits!'

'Hardly "culprits", Andreas,' Tiddy said defensively. 'They probably just forgot to pay in their rush to catch their coach. Besides, it was hardly the crime of the century.'

Simitis's face reddened with so much fury it looked as though his cheeks might explode. 'Over *ten pounds* they stole from me! If that happened every day I'd soon be ruined . . . I am very disappointed in your great British police force. It is very bad.'

'We were very busy yesterday,' WPC Sharman chimed in.

'Yes, indeed,' Tiddy said with a nod of acknowledgement to his tiny probationer. 'There was an alleged altercation down here by the river yesterday morning. Around seven thirty. A serious assault. Apparently two older men attacked three young Caucasian males. I was wondering if any of you saw anything?'

Mahoney picked the escaped remnants of beef sandwich from his beard and popped them in his mouth. 'What happened?' he asked in a tone of studied disinterest.

Tiddy's eyes narrowed. 'Curiously enough, Jock, one of the older assailants rather matches *your* description.'

The Scotsman raised his eyebrows in mock amazement. 'Really?'

Tiddy's gaze switched to me. 'And the other, a remarkable similarity to this newcomer and friend of yours here! Whose name escapes me . . . ?'

I tried to emulate Mahoney's nonchalance. 'Dave,' I said and asked, 'what happened to the victims? Did they report the attack?'

'No, they didn't,' Tiddy replied. 'It was reported separately by two witnesses, members of the public. One lady was in a severe state of shock. On investigation, we found three youths in A & E at the district hospital. One had a severely broken jaw, another facial injuries and the other was awaiting X-rays for a suspected skull fracture.'

Edwina winced. 'And they hadn't reported the attack to the police themselves?'

'No. They aren't cooperating. Perhaps because the row was something to do with drugs.'

WPC Sharman said, 'Or perhaps they were just too scared.'

Mahoney began rolling another cigarette. 'I don't do drugs!'

'But your mate, Ginger . . . ?' Tiddy said sniffily. 'He does. Where is he?'

'Gone for a walk. I've no idea.'

Simitis shook his head as he stubbed out his cigarette. 'This country, she goes to the dogs! It is full of druggies, and thugs and Japanese peoples who do not pay for their cakes. I despair!'

Seeing that the owner was about to return inside his cafe, Tiddy asked quickly, 'Suppose there's not a chance of a cuppa for me and Sharon?'

'Huh, Raymond, I get no service, but you *still* want your policeman's free cuppa. It feels like a protection racket!'

'I'm still on the case, Andreas, I promise you. I even have the telephone numbers of the coach companies!'

The Greek's reply was interrupted by a squawking little voice on Tiddy's radio. The officer turned away, wandering towards the river to get a better reception. I watched him absently as he listened. Suddenly his body stiffened and his head bent towards the receiver pinned to his shoulder. It was as if he was having difficulty in catching every word being spoken. He paled noticeably and glanced back towards our table. He caught my eye and then turned away quickly, as though trying to avoid contact.

It was some minutes before he returned, by which time Simitis was back with a tray of tea for the police patrol.

PC Tiddy stood before us. 'Jock . . . Edwina . . . I'm afraid I've got bad news. It's your friend Ginger. He's been found.'

'Where?' Mahoney demanded.

'At the railway sidings, by the station.'

'I never looked there—'

'Is he all right . . . ?' Edwina began.

PC Tiddy took a deep breath. 'I'm afraid Ginger is dead.'

I shook my head. It didn't seem possible.

'It looks like a heart attack.' Tiddy looked uncomfortable. 'It's not official, you understand. Or he may have had some sort of stroke, a clot. We've had reports recently of a big batch of heroin cut with brick dust or some other muck. Chances are that's what killed him. We don't know yet. I'm so sorry.'

'My God,' Edwina said tearfully. 'I don't believe it. He was doing so well, too.'

Tiddy looked suddenly angry, as though for the first time in his life he had really grown up. 'Some people will do anything for money, Edwina.'

I felt shocked, utterly shocked and empty. I'd hardly known Ginger, but I had recognised his pain and his struggle. He'd been in Bosnia, as I had. He'd seen what I had seen. But it had got to him before it had got to me. Perhaps that made him a better human being? I was beginning to think so.

'The bastards,' Edwina murmured.

Still pale, PC Tiddy picked up his mug of tea and downed it in one. 'I may be needing to take some statements from some of you.'

There were nods of understanding around the table. Then he glanced down at his probationer. 'Time for us to go, Sharon.'

The girl looked awkward and tucked under his wing as he left us and headed back towards the police station.

Andreas Simitis moved towards the door of his cafe with Gem, and paused momentarily to whisper in her ear.

She looked uncomfortable as she returned and ushered me to one side. 'I am sorry, Dave, but Andreas is not happy that our friends come here. They are scruffy . . .' Her big blue eyes looked candidly into mine. '. . . And they do rather smell a bit. He says they are not really welcome here. And then the police, asking questions. He thinks they put off other customers. I am sorry.'

I opened my mouth to retort then shut it again. Of course the man was right. No one wants to sit amid a group of drunken tramps to have a snack or lunch. Simitis had a business to protect.

Mahoney stared at the feeble cigarette butt that was smouldering between his cupped fingers. 'Ginger . . . gone. I don't believe it.'

I said, 'Time to go, Jock. I'll see you and Edwina tonight. Maybe we can have a drink to Ginger. The cider will be on me.'

The Scotsman glared at me. 'Sure, on you.'

# Twelve

When I arrived at the cafe at seven the following morning the door was opened by Simitis's jovial wife, Lexi.

'No Gem?' I asked.

Lexi was short, dumpy and dressed in brightly coloured clothes and heavy gold jewellery. She gave a cheerful shrug. 'Gem phones in, being sick.' She raised one finely painted eyebrow. 'It must be serious. She is a good girl. Never swings the lead, as you English like to say. She is a hard little worker, like my own daughter.'

Actually from what I understood from Gem, Lexi's own daughter hated the cafe and any notion of hard work.

I said, 'I'd better get cracking.' Heading for the kitchen, I called back, 'And I promise I'll watch the fillings.'

Lexi laughed. 'Never mind that. You just do them like yesterday. I heard many compliments from customers about our new-look sandwiches!'

'Andreas didn't tell me that,' I replied, washing my hands.

'Well no, he wouldn't, would he?'

At least her words of encouragement cheered me up a little. The previous day had left me feeling down. I'd met Mahoney in the market square in the early evening with some plastic bottles of cider in a bag and leftover sandwiches from the cafe. But Mahoney was still in a morose, bad mood and Edwina just sat in a weepy kind of silence. It was really quite depressing. After an hour or so with them, I'd left to take a walk round the town before getting my head down for an early night in Coronation Gardens.

I delighted Lexi by finding my feet in the kitchen and making much shorter work of the sandwich preparation than on my first day.

'Andreas is at the veg market this morning,' she announced just before eight. 'I have to do the curries and bolognaise sauce. So maybe you can look after the customers?'

'Sure,' I agreed willingly.

'But not looking like that!' she retorted. 'At least wash your face and comb your hair. I'll get you some clothes.'

I must admit, I hadn't yet mastered the art of being a smart tramp. But after ten minutes in the cafe lavatory, I'd cleaned up and changed into a pair of worn but clean black trousers and a frayed white shirt that I imagine had belonged to my Polish predecessor.

At eight I was fielding my first punter and taking orders, doing my best to sell those little extras that boost the profits. To my amazement it seemed to work and several people also ordered extra sandwiches to have later for their lunch. I knew from Gem that this rarely happened at Simitis's cafe. Two customers actually commented that they thought our sandwiches had improved recently, although they didn't exactly say *how* recently. Either way, it seemed that either Gem or I might have made a difference.

When the main rush finished after nine thirty, I finished my shift and sat down for a coffee and a smoke.

'You skiving again, Dave?' It was Mahoney. 'Whenever I see you here, you've got a coffee and a fag on.'

'I've only just stopped.'

He nodded. 'I believe you, millions wouldn't.' He took a seat and squinted at me. 'Hardly recognised you without the beard.'

'Serving at table,' I explained. 'Gem's off sick.'

Again he nodded, then said, 'By the way, the funeral's next Monday, at the crem.'

'How do you know?'

'I called in at the cop shop. Spoke to Constable Tiddy. They'd been trying to trace relatives. Just found Ginger's dad, on some estate up north. Father and son fell out years ago. The old man doesn't want to know.'

'So it's just us?' I asked.

Mahoney nodded and smiled tersely. 'Any chance of a tea?'

I hesitated for a moment, remembering the ban that Simitis had announced the previous day. But then the Greek still wasn't back from the market and I thought what the hell! 'Just give me a minute,' I said.

A slice of home-made but out-of-date fruitcake completed Mahoney's breakfast and he looked a lot happier when he'd finished it. 'Doesn't matter how many people you know, does it?' he asked, wiping the crumbs from his moustache with a paper serviette. 'Or how many people love you?'

I frowned. 'What do you mean?'

'We still all die alone. Well, most of us. Horrible thought, that.'

He had a point. It was a point I dwelt on more now than when I'd been fighting fit on operations. I deliberately looked away, across the river where swans and ducks were gathering as tourists threw bread.

It was then that I saw him, and he saw us.

The lean, towering figure of Rashid was striding along the riverside promenade, forcing shoppers and bystanders to step aside as he led his gang of hooded stragglers into town. Fixing us with an angry, dark gaze, he changed direction sharply and veered over the river bridge towards the cafe.

'Trouble,' I said.

Mahoney looked up and saw the approaching gang. 'Oh God,' he mumbled under his breath.

Rashid's long shadow fell across the table in front of us. He ignored me. 'Well, Jock, where were you? We were waiting for you in Coronation Gardens last night.' His voice was very light, yet there was no mistaking the underlying tone of menace. 'Seems you stood me up.'

The Scotsman regarded the good-looking youngster with his goatee beard and pretty lashes with undisguised contempt. 'Afraid I had other things on my mind, Rashid. Like thinking about the funeral of my friend Ginger.'

A ghost of a smile played around the other man's lips. 'Sorry to hear about that, Jock. Very sad. But then if you mess with drugs . . .'

I was aware of Mahoney's fist clenching on the table, his knuckles whitening. I caught his eye, and shook my head imperceptibly. He returned his gaze to the gang leader. 'What did y'cut the stuff with, y'greedy scumbag? Brick dust or bloody builder's rubble?'

Rashid's gormless little sidekick, whose name I recalled was Amir, stepped forward. He tried to look mean and hard, but wasn't quite up to it.

'Language, Jock,' Rashid chided. 'It was very unfortunate. But you know how the business market works – buyer beware. Our mutual friend didn't have to buy from me – he chose to.' He hesitated and smiled very gently, very sweetly. 'And it seems to me now that you, likewise, think you can *choose* not to pay.'

'Faulty goods!' Jock snarled back. 'That's why.'

The sickly smile faded from Rashid's lips. He said very slowly, 'You owe me five pounds, Jock. Do not mess with me. You will be very, very sorry.'

Mahoney rose suddenly to his feet. 'Go fuck yourself!'

He turned sharply on his heel. Amir grabbed at his great-coat, but Mahoney shook his hand free and strode off. The gang of some nine yobbos seemed to react in unison, like some connected amoebic entity. Without a word being exchanged, backs stiffened and hands were withdrawn from pockets, eyes narrowed.

'Wait!' I said quickly.

'Who the hell—?' Rashid began.

'Dave,' I reminded. 'I was there with Jock and Ginger when you did the deal.'

He sneered at me. 'Oh, yeah, the other tramp.'

'Jock's upset,' I said quickly. 'And he's broke. But I'll get your money by tonight. As you can see, I've got a job now.' I looked him closely in the eyes. 'A deal?'

Rashid hesitated. 'Now there's interest. It will be ten pounds.'

I winced and nodded. 'After dark,' I said. 'Somewhere quiet. The cops are taking an unhealthy interest in me.'

Amir sniggered. 'AWOL, are we?'

I smiled at him. 'Something like that.'

Rashid said, 'The car park behind Tesco along the river. There is a yard for recycling bins. Amir will be there at nine o'clock tonight. Don't keep us waiting again.'

'I promise.'

He gave a sneer of a smile and turned away, his gang members stepping aside to let him pass through before dutifully following after him.

As I watched I saw Gem approaching, having to step out of their path as they marched by.

She said, 'That's the gang from Rosebury Street, I think. On the Evinmore estate.' She stared back at them. 'Real troublemakers. Drugs and all sorts.'

I looked up at her. 'And you? Are you OK? Lexi said you'd phoned in.'

Gem sat down and dumped her handbag on the table. 'Felt sick this morning. Couldn't stop retching. It was horrible.'

'But you're OK now?'

She fished a cigarette pack and plastic lighter from her bag. 'Fine. I've got an appointment with the doc this evening.' She drew deeply on her cigarette. 'Can you keep a secret?'

'I've spent my life keeping secrets.'

She looked directly at me with those big, bright-blue eyes. 'I'm late. Like seriously late.'

'Ah,' I said awkwardly, and added cautiously, 'is that a call for celebration? I hope.'

The instant smile with those cute, slightly rabbity teeth lit up her face. 'It is for me! Not so sure about Steve though.'

'Sorry . . . Steve?'

'My BF.' She noticed my bemused expression. 'BF . . . Text-speak . . . Steve's my boyfriend. At least I think he is.'

'You're an item?'

She nodded. 'Seems that way. We don't live together, not yet. He's got a place with some mates.'

'But you're not sure he's ready to be a dad?'

The light faded from her eyes and she stood up. 'We'll have to see.' She stubbed out her half-smoked cigarette in the tin ashtray. 'Now, I'd better get on.'

On receipt of my first cash wage sub, I celebrated with a lunch of beans on toast at the cafe, then sauntered down the old river path. There I found the car park, which served the Tesco store. Adjoining it was an open yard, surrounded by spiked railings, which held half-a-dozen commercial recycling skips.

This was the place that Rashid had chosen for the hand-over of the money Ginger had owed. Now the area was busy with shoppers trying to find a rare parking space, or else stopping to unload bottles, plastics and old clothes. By nine o'clock at night, I guessed it would be deserted.

My mind was in an angry sort of spin. I just couldn't get a picture of Ginger out of my head, his body slumped, head to one side with those dirty copper ringlets fallen over his eyes and his jaw hanging slackly open. Whatever else, he was a one-time brave young soldier who had fallen on hard times. Even when he was in the gutter, with not even a father to love him, there was still someone willing to suck the last lifeblood out of him. No one deserved that.

An idea began to crystallise in my mind.

The drug dealers wanted their money. Was it their pride at stake, or the defence of their power base in the lowlife community? It didn't seem to matter that someone had died. Or that it was just a few measly pounds owed by a down-and-out addict who'd once laid his life on the line for his country.

While Ginger and others had fought and died, or were hideously maimed, people like these were allowed to thrive back home, a seemingly ever-expanding and festering underclass. And no one seemed willing or able to do anything about it.

I turned away abruptly and entered the automatic doors of the busy Tesco outlet. In a few moments I'd located the aisle I wanted. I picked up two pairs of the heaviest denier tights I could find and casually slipped them into my pocket.

I was pleased Lexi had ordered me to tidy up and given me the clean clothes, otherwise I think the counter cashier at the bank may have taken a less helpful attitude to my unusual request. I placed two five-pound notes in front of her. 'Could you possibly change these for two-pence coins?'

She raised an eyebrow and smiled. 'That's an unusual request. Usually the other way round.'

'Fruit machines,' I replied amiably, as if that explained everything.

'Give me a few minutes.'

A short while later she returned with two stout linen bags and handed them over. I felt the weight in my hand and smiled to myself before thanking her and returning to the cafe. Gem and Lexi were busy serving a handful of customers and didn't appear to notice me as I slipped in. There was no one at the back of the kitchen where I was due to begin my end-of-day washing-up duties. Quickly I took the two packets of tights from my pocket and opened the first one.

With a pair of chef's scissors I cut the two nylon legs off at the knees and put one foot-section inside the other for strength. I then dropped the first two hundred and fifty coins inside and knotted the open top to form a weighty sausage. I left ample material outside the knot to form a handle. Then I repeated the process with the second bag of coins.

I had just finished when I heard Lexi enter the kitchen. 'Ah, there you are, Dave! I didn't see you come back. Think maybe you give up your job.'

'No way,' I replied, shoving the two coin sausages out of sight. 'It's the only thing that's keeping me from going mad.'

And even as I spoke the words, I knew it didn't sound true. That somehow the madness in my head was just about to start.

# Thirteen

I was sitting on a bench with Mahoney in the town square and the time was moving towards nine o'clock. We were just finishing a supper of leftover ham and salad scraps from the cafe. 'Never eaten so well since you pitched up, Dave,' he said, wiping his mouth on the cuff of his greatcoat. He looked up as I got to my feet. 'Where you off to, then?'

'Got to see a man about a dog,' I replied lightly.

His eyes narrowed a fraction. 'Don't do anything stupid about that Muslim gang. I saw that look in your eyes earlier today. I saw it in the eyes of someone else once, a long time ago.' He hesitated, then added, 'I'm not afraid of them, Dave, and I don't want anyone paying off Ginger's bill on my behalf. Let them sing for it.'

I gave a sort of crooked smile. 'Now there's a thought.'

He nodded. 'Catch up with you later.'

I moved swiftly across the square. The nights were beginning to feel distinctly chillier as autumn made its first tentative approach, and there were few pedestrians about. My apprehension grew as I approached the Tesco store, and I was conscious of the two bags of coins weighing heavily in the large cargo pockets of my combat jacket.

After the comparative dimness of the street, the harsh strip lights of the supermarket hurt my eyes, as I made my way towards its rear exit. But I was only vaguely aware of the late-night shoppers, a bawling kid seated in a trolley. The customers I could see in my head were wearing turbans and pancake hats, the women covered in robes and veils.

Suddenly I was back in Baghdad, moving in, adrenalin pumping and heart thudding. Knowing the others were closing in, too, the trap about to snap shut. I was unaware of the supermarket's air conditioning. Sweat gathered on my palms and in the small of my back. As I pushed my way through the exit door to the rear car park, I could have sworn that I could smell that familiar dusty, desert air.

I halted, took a deep breath and tried to focus my mind. Slowly the images of Baghdad and its people faded away, melting under the harsh floodlights reflecting off the parked vehicles. The temperature dropped rapidly and suddenly I felt almost chill.

Then I heard the voices, drifting from behind the spiked railings in the yard where the big recycling bins were held. I could identify three Asian men as I approached, all dressed in the usual designer trainers, baseball caps and baggy sports-wear. One had a dog.

The first gang member guarded the entrance, laconically propped against a concrete fence post as he sucked heavily on a spliff. His free hand was stuffed inside the zip front of his hooded top. My best guess was that he had some sort of weapon in there, probably a knife.

Over his shoulder, I could see two other young men. The shorter of them I was able to identify as the leader Rashid's number two, the slightly gormless-looking Amir with his sallow face and immature beard. He was holding court, with a small tote bag open at his feet.

Amir's protector was an older lad with a bodybuilder's physique and a shaven head that glistened in the lamplight. Beneath the flat, broad forehead his eyebrows knotted in fierce concentration as he struggled to restrain a monstrous dog on its short leather leash.

I'm no expert, but if the stout and muscular snub-faced dog wasn't actually a pit bull, it was something pretty damn close. There was no doubt in my mind that it was some type of fighting dog and I remembered reading somewhere that, with a snapping jaw pressure of over three hundred pounds, it could take your face off with a single bite. And if it got you in its teeth, its inbred tenacity meant it wouldn't unlock you until it was dead. Or you were.

It was certainly doing its best to terrify the two skinny young hookers who were proffering money to Amir.

He thought it was very amusing. 'Don't worry, girls, Saddam is a pussycat.'

Both girls, dressed in gaudy miniskirts and sparkly tops, had instinctively pulled back, so that the dealer's outstretched hand couldn't grasp their money. 'Even I can see it's a dog,' one of the girls snapped sarcastically.

Amir shuffled a bit to his right, out of reach of the dog's mouth, so that he could take the girl's cash. He dipped into the tote bag at his feet and handed over four small packets. 'Don't you go scoring off those Chip Shop dudes now, girls. Got me? You stick with us.'

One of the young women glared sullenly as she put two packets in her shoulder bag. 'It's a free country.'

Amir tried to give a cocksure sort of grin that didn't quite come off. 'Course it is. Except I'll give you a loyalty discount next time – and I *won't* set Saddam on you! How about that?'

The girl tugged at her friend's arm. 'C'mon, Hazel, let's go.'

Together they edged past the dog and arm-in-arm scurried away, their high heels clacking loudly on the tarmac. The three Asian men exchanged glances and giggled at each other as they watched them go.

I was disappointed that Rashid was not among them. But, anyway, I intended that he was going to receive a very clear message.

Amir suddenly saw me as I stepped out of the shadows. 'Ah, it's Jock's friend . . .'

'Dave,' I reminded, as I stepped past the man guarding the yard entrance.

'I wondered if you'd show,' Amir smirked, 'or if we'd have to come looking for you.'

The pit bull took a distinct dislike to me and began a low growl. It edged forward and the studded leather lead snapped taut. I hadn't anticipated the presence of a fighting dog. It would have to be dealt with first.

I said, 'I always keep my word, Amir.'

'Sure, sure,' the youth said impatiently. 'So where is our money?'

'Here,' I said, wrapping the loose end of one stocking from the cargo pocket of my jacket round my hand. 'I hope you don't mind loose change.'

Amir frowned as he realised he was staring at the foot of a stocking filled with coins. 'What the . . . ?'

The dog had to go, there was no other option. I raised the cosh and brought it down with every ounce of strength I could muster. Its owner stepped back in surprise, but the animal stood fast. I was aware of its wide blinking eyes the second before the blow struck its skull directly between its ears. I thought I heard the sound of cracking bone. There was a stifled whelp and the dog's front legs collapsed untidily before it rolled over completely and lay still.

Its owner took another step back, his mouth dropping open in surprise.

Behind me, I was aware of the man who'd been guarding the yard. As I turned I could see him pulling a long-bladed knife from inside his hooded jogging top. Light from the overhead lamp glinted on its edge. I drew out the second cosh with my left hand. The knifeman lunged at me, just as I swung the weighty nylon cosh directly into the side of his face. His eyes widened momentarily as he tried desperately to hold on to consciousness, and then lost it. His knees collapsed under him and he went straight down in a heap.

The dog's owner recovered and dived towards me with his hands outstretched. But he was too muscle-bound to move quickly. I was able to sidestep out of the way, leaving my foot behind to trip him up. As he stumbled I brought the right-hand money-cosh down into the back of his neck. I heard what sounded like teeth cracking as his face pounded into the paving stone. He started curling up into a foetal ball and whimpering softly.

I turned swiftly back to face Amir. Not surprisingly the blood had drained from his face. With eyes wide in horror, he took a step back and raised his hands.

'No, no, please!' he gabbled, indicating the open tote bag by his feet. 'Take the money, take the smack!'

'I don't want your dirty money,' I snarled. 'I don't want your drugs. I want you and scum like you dead. Off this planet. Men like Jock, men like Ginger . . . they fought for the freedom of scum like you, and they paid a heavy price!'

'Please, mister, I don't want to die!'

I swung the two coshes, one in each hand, and then let them fall to the ground with a resounding crash. I'd sort of half-planned to smash Amir's head in, to make *him* pay the price for Ginger's death. But I was starting to feel my blind raw anger ebb away now. I couldn't do that to an unarmed man who was surrendering.

I looked at him and said, 'You killed Ginger.'

He shook his head. 'I didn't mean to. The stuff must have been too pure for him. That's not my fault. If he'd been trying to come off it, it might have been just too much. Please!'

'Shut it,' I ordered. 'Take the belt off your jeans.'

'What?'

'You heard.'

Looking worried, Amir slipped the plaited leather belt from its loops and nervously handed it to me. 'Turn round and put your hands behind your back.'

Quickly I wound the belt around his wrists and locked it into a tight knot. Then, without warning him, I grabbed him by both shoulders and lifted his feet clear of the ground, hooking the back of his jacket over the seven-foot railing spikes.

I let him hang with his feet dangling, his two injured body-guards and the dead dog at his feet.

'Remember this,' I said. 'Don't ever threaten drug users or their friends again. It's *simple* . . . don't *give* credit!'

A sudden thought occurred to me, and I fished in the pockets of his top. Of course, there I found the ubiquitous mobile phone.

I flicked on its camera mode, stepped back and took a couple of snaps.

Amir, just hanging there, stared at me, not a word passing his lips.

As I moved away, I punched 999 into the phone keypad. When the duty receptionist of the emergency services answered, I said: 'I'm calling from Swinthorpe high street. There's been a fight in the rear car park of Tesco. Two men need urgent medical attention.'

# Fourteen

'There's a storm brewing,' Jock Mahoney said.

We were seated on a bench opposite the cafe when he stared up at the slow massing of angry cloud.

'You can smell it in the air,' I agreed. I'd just finished the day's washing-up and was more than ready for my cigarette.

That morning the two of us had been to Ginger's cremation. Gem and Lady Penelope had been the only other mourners. It had been a bleak affair and had left us feeling quite depressed.

'We'll need good shelter tonight. The multistorey car park's OK. You going to join me?'

I shook my head. 'I prefer the open air to the smell of damp concrete.'

Mahoney shrugged.

It was then that I noticed Gem standing at the cafe door. She saw us, waved and came over.

'Want me to go?' Mahoney asked darkly.

Gem smiled. 'Oh, Jock, I'm sure Andreas doesn't *really* mind you sitting here,' she said. 'He just has grumpy moods sometimes.'

'Aye, and he made himself clear enough *in* one of his grumpy moods.'

I noticed she was carrying the local weekly newspaper. 'Is that today's?' I asked.

'Yes, have you seen it?' she asked eagerly.

I shook my head as she spread the front page out on the bench between Mahoney and me. 'Good God,' I said suddenly. 'They've actually used my picture. Blacked their faces out, of course. That'll be for legal reasons.'

Mahoney peered at the headline, reading out loud, "Vigilante tames drug gang".'

When I'd told Gem what I'd done the day after the scrap in the Tesco car park she'd been angry with me at first, but then reluctantly agreed to download the picture I'd taken onto her computer and email it to the *Journal* for me.

I'd then thrown the phone in the river. I wanted nothing that belonged to those scrotes and certainly nothing that might link me to the 'scene of the crime'.

'The gang won't like that,' Mahoney said. 'Public humiliation.' He looked at me and held my gaze. I could see the anger in his eyes. 'I didn't ask you to do this, Dave. You be careful. There's no need to go stirring up a hornets' nest. And never mind them, *you* could end up doing time.'

Gem picked up the paper. 'Well, no one seems to know who beat them up and hung one of them up on the railings. Someone is reported to have said it looked like some old tramp did it.' She glanced at me and grinned widely. 'Anyway, it says the police arrested the gang members. Got them with all the evidence, drugs and money. And a knife. Says they've been charged . . . but two are still in hospital.'

'Shame,' Mahoney murmured.

'The RSPCA says a dog was also killed,' Gem added, frowning. 'In a very cruel manner. They think this man is very dangerous.'

Just then Mahoney said earnestly, 'This could be trouble.'

Walking swiftly along the riverside path was Rashid, followed by half a dozen of his Muslim gang members. He turned over the bridge and drew to a halt in front of us.

He glared down at the newspaper before looking directly at Mahoney. 'You have made one big mistake, Scotsman.'

Mahoney said, 'What's your problem, Rashid? You got paid, didn't you?'

Although Amir must have told his gang boss it was me who had actually taken out the two other members, I noticed that Rashid was studiously avoiding looking at me. Perhaps he was just embarrassed that I'd been able to flatten two of his so-called hard men. Instead he focused on Mahoney.

'A big mistake,' he repeated, then turned and strode swiftly away, his followers struggling to keep up with him.

Gem's eyes followed them as they crossed the second bridge that led to the town square. 'He's a nasty piece of work. I've heard all sorts of stories. One kid actually had his tongue cut out after talking to the police. No one would give evidence against any gang member after that. They can do what they want. There's even a rumour some of them have been to those training camps in Pakistan.'

Mahoney shook his head. 'Ach, Gemma, I would na' lose any sleep over him. He's nothin' more than a wee prick with the single brain cell of a cockroach.'

*        *        *

And that night I certainly didn't lose any sleep over Rashid or any of his squalid little gang. In fact, I had a deep, dreamless sleep – until, that is, I was rudely awoken by a loud crack of thunder. It seemed to be immediately overhead and I awoke with a jolt. It suddenly began to rain. Heavy drops for a couple of moments and then it began to come down in torrents as though someone was turning on a tap. The sound of it beating on my camouflaged canopy sheet, tied as a simple lean-to shelter, was almost deafening.

I curled up in my waterproof bivvy bag and tried to force myself back to sleep.

But now the demons were awake, and once that happens you just know that sleep is going to elude you until the dawn.

What had I done with my life and why had I done it?

I tossed and turned, remembering the horrors of Iraq and Afghanistan. Not only the horrors, but the sheer, insane exhilaration of combat. It was an almost primeval experience of heart-stopping fear, killing before you are killed . . . and the profound relationship that forms with your fellow soldiers. Bonds so intense that mean you would unthinkingly die for a mate, even if you didn't particularly *like* him as an individual. Nothing could replace that, and no civilian can understand it.

And why had I done it? Because it was simply the only life I'd known, and the only thing I knew how to do. Then I continued to do it because of the comradeship and those moments of combat madness you rarely get outside special forces. I certainly hadn't done it for the greater good or – God knows – even for my wife and family.

Then, after the mine and my injury in Helmand, came the terrible truth. It was all over for me. It may have started because of the bad dreams, but also because, I realised, I'd never know such good times again.

And, when I stopped and looked around in the cold light of day, it seemed that all the wrong people were in power and control everywhere. Those people had sent me and my colleagues, many now dead and many more hideously injured, to the wrong places for the wrong reasons. To Iraq in a hunt for weapons of mass destruction that didn't exist, and to destroy links with al-Qaeda that it didn't have. That was, of course, until *after* we arrived. Then bin Laden's men lined up in droves to help drive Western forces out of the country.

After that we were sent to take on a smoke-and-mirrors war of attrition in the tribal wasteland of Afghanistan – once a hideaway for the al-Qaeda leadership, which could now find sanctuary in any rogue state in the world. And there were plenty of them to choose from.

Those same politicians seemed to have failed their people in every way. I knew first-hand that the armed forces were in meltdown, and I was just starting to realise that the entire fabric of my country's society had been allowed to rot away over the years. Nobody ever did anything, and no one seemed to care. Why else would even Swinthorpe, the happy and drowsy market town of my youth, have vicious rival drug gangs roaming the streets undeterred?

Finally sleep must have crept over me. I awoke with a start at around six-thirty in the morning. The rain was still falling, straight down, heavy and persistent. I cursed. My bivvy bag was waterproof, but my temporary shelter wasn't, the earth already turning to mud. By the time I'd scrambled out of the bag and started packing up, my clothes were sodden.

I reached the cafe like a proverbial drowned rat. Yet when Gem opened the door to let me in, I was slightly surprised she made no comment.

'I'll put the kettle on,' was all she said in a flat voice.

I dumped my bergen in the corner and shrugged off my wet combat jacket. 'You sound a bit in the dumps,' I observed.

She sniffed, clearly trying not to cry. 'Do I?'

'What's wrong?' I asked, but the answer was at least partly staring back at me when I looked at her. One eye and cheek was bruised, and there were more marks on her arms. 'Who did that?'

She stared at the ceiling, her mouth in a tight thin line. Then she looked at the floor, not wanting to have to say what she knew she had to. 'Steve. Y'know, my BF.'

I suddenly remembered. 'You were going last night . . . to the doctor's.'

Gem nodded. 'He confirmed it. I was so thrilled. I couldn't wait to tell Steve.'

'And he wasn't so thrilled?' I guessed.

'You can say that again. He was like a madman. Accused me of trying to trap him. He said all sorts of crazy and horrible things. Said it wasn't his, I must have been sleeping around.' She took a deep sigh. 'Then he lost it. He was shouting. Grabbed me, shook me, then slapped me round the face. Made such a racket my neighbours called the police. They're always complaining about him playing loud music . . .'

I said, 'I'm so sorry, Gem.'

The kettle began to steam. She shrugged. 'No matter,' she said, busying herself mixing a couple of coffees. 'I'm probably better off without him.'

From what I'd heard of him, she would almost *certainly* be better off without Steve in her life. Gem had told me some things herself, and Lexi had muttered a few telling words under her breath whenever his name was mentioned. He'd once worked at the cafe as a kitchen hand, which was how he'd met Gem. But he also had a strong drug habit, which he paid for by small-time dealing. Unfortunately, when funds were low, he'd thought nothing of stealing from Andreas's till. Apparently he had a skin-deep charm and cheeky jack-the-lad attitude that people warmed to – but those people did not extend to the cafe owner, who sacked him on the spot.

Gem and I took our coffees out to the backyard. There were a couple of chairs and an old wrought-iron table under a lean-to with a roof of clear corrugated plastic. We sat down and I began rolling us a couple of cigarettes. A curtain of rainwater dripped all around us.

'Steve might have turned out different,' Gem said thoughtfully, 'if he'd joined the army. Or any of the forces, really. Might have turned out a bit like you.'

I smiled at that. 'Not sure I'm any role model to follow.'

'When did you join?'

I thought back. 'I was a young teenager when I joined the Army Cadets. My home life was pretty rough. We lived in a small house on the Evinmore estate. My old man was a violent drunk, quite happy to thrash me, or my mum, at the drop of a hat. It was when the Falklands War started – 1982 – before your time . . .'

'Only just,' Gem replied. 'My dad fought there.'

'Really?' That surprised me for some reason. 'Anyway, I was enthralled by that weird and controlled TV news coverage. Then I read all the books and magazine articles afterwards,' I continued, remembering. 'At the time, life felt lonely as hell for me at home. I just remember envying the obvious camaraderie of the British troops.'

'You wanted a new family to escape to?' she suggested.

Gem wasn't far wrong there. I said, 'Pretty much. I enjoyed the Army Cadets and I couldn't wait for my seventeenth birthday to sign up to the real thing. That was in 1985.'

'And it was the right decision?'

'It was for me. Best decision I've ever made. I loved every minute of it.'

As always, I left it there. I didn't go on to mention that I so loved the life and so craved excitement that, in 1991, at the age of twenty-three, I passed selection for 22 SAS Regiment.

I'd been just in time to see behind-the-lines action in the First Gulf War following Saddam Hussein's invasion of Kuwait. Years of variety followed with fascinatingly different types of mission and combat in Northern Ireland, the Balkans and Sierra Leone. By the time the Second Gulf War kicked off in 2003, I'd worked my way up through the ranks of the Regiment to become a Warrant Officer First Class.

'You *see*,' Gem said emphatically, 'Steve *could* have made something of himself. He used to talk about it, but I think the drugs gradually got to him, pulled him down. I begged him to get a proper job, but he got by on his benefits and petty drug dealing.'

I'd finished rolling the cigarettes and handed one to her. 'So what now?' I asked.

She accepted the flame from my old Bic lighter – I'd used it ever since I found Zippos weren't so reliable in the Afghan desert.

Inhaling deeply, Gem blew a long, slow stream of smoke into the yard. At last she said, 'It's got to be over. Not just for my sake, for the baby's. After this . . .' Tentatively she lifted a finger to her cheek and flinched when it touched her skin. 'I don't have a choice.'

I nodded. 'I think that would probably be the right decision.'

She looked at me and smiled for the first time that morning. Placing her hand on my forearm, she said, 'Thanks, Dave. Thanks for talking.'

'It's nothing. I'm glad if it's helped.'

She frowned. 'And what about you? What are you going to do?'

Her interest rather took me by surprise. 'Me? Oh, I don't know. I haven't thought. I'm still trying to sort my head out, if that makes sense?'

She looked at me thoughtfully. 'You went through some bad times in Iraq and Afghanistan?'

I shrugged. It was a difficult question to answer. In one breath I was inclined to say yes, there was a lot of bad shit. But in the next breath I'd be saying I miss it. Miss the excitement of living life on the edge, missing my comrades who had become as close as brothers. Blood brothers, at that.

When I didn't answer, she said, 'I noticed you've got a slight limp, I hope you don't mind me saying. Was that the result of an injury?'

I smiled grimly. 'Is it that obvious? My lucky leg. Mostly only hurts in damp weather, although the muscles are pretty weak too. More titanium than bone now.'

Gem looked aghast. 'And you call it your *lucky* leg?'

'It was a touch and go amputation,' I explained.

'Oh, I see.'

I held out my cigarette and watched its glowing tip. '*S-o-o* lucky,' I said quietly. 'I should have lost the leg or even my life in that explosion. Instead young Andy died trying to save me.'

'Andy? Another soldier?'

'Andy Smith. He was a newbie. Only twenty-four. Lovely lad.' I smiled as I recalled his early days with my team. 'He took a lot of stick from us old-timers. Given rotten jobs. But he took it all in good heart. He had a baby son and was due to get married after the tour . . . It's *me* who should have died. It's not fair.'

Gem placed her hand on my wrist. 'Don't say that, Dave, please.'

I stubbed out my cigarette end. 'I'm sorry. I know that sounds odd. But I've had my best years, Andy had his in front of him.'

Suddenly she frowned and when she spoke she sounded almost angry, 'Then you should *live* your life *for him*! I can't believe he wouldn't have wanted you to do that.'

That threw me for a moment. 'Easier said than done . . .' I began.

'And you can start by *not* living like a tramp!' Her stern expression suddenly melted away and her smile broke through like sunshine after rain. 'You looked like a drowned rat this morning. You'll die of pneumonia if you carry on like that . . .' A thought occurred to her. 'Dave, it's a thought, why don't you come and stay at my place for a bit. It's small but it's got two bedrooms. There's just a bit of clutter in the other one.'

'Oh, I couldn't,' I began.

'Yes, yes, you could,' she came back, warming to the idea. 'You could be my lodger for a while.'

I'd grown fond of Gem. She was likeable, kindly and down-to-earth. I had a feeling it could work out. Tentatively, I said, 'I suppose we could give it a try.'

She grinned with enthusiasm. 'Come over tonight with me after work. Do you like fish? I make a mean fish pie. Me nan taught me, she was a smashing cook.'

'Sounds good,' I said, and meant it.

'Then that's a deal.'

And a good deal it turned out to be. Gem's pad was a rented two-bedroom terrace house on the run-down side of town near the railway sidings. It was in a fairly dilapidated state but at least it was warm and dry, apart from a damp patch in the spare room that was allocated to me. I also had the opportunity to have a bath and to throw my clothes into the washing machine.

For the next few days it was to rain almost without let up. At least I could look forward to nicely cooked, simple meals and a comfortable night's sleep in a proper bed. Gem knew I couldn't afford the going price for room rentals, but she even turned down my much lower offer of a contribution. So in return, in the evenings, I got to work with a brush and roller and the paint pots I found under the stairs. Apparently this was a task boyfriend Steve had promised to do for her a year ago, but had never quite got round to it.

It was nearly ten o'clock one night when I'd just finished painting the staircase banisters a fetching shade of blue.

'Very nice,' Gem said. 'Are you stopping now? The news is on and I've made a brew.'

I nodded. 'Cheers, Gem. I'll just put the brush into soak.' I reached for the bottle of white spirit. 'You know, you really should get your landlord to tart this place up properly.'

'You're joking. I never see him – and nor do his letting agents. He just takes a like it or lump it attitude.' She shrugged. 'And at least I can afford the rent here.'

Leaving the brush in a jam jar of white spirit, I followed Gem into the living room where the irritating anthem of *News at Ten* was just beginning on television, drowning out the rattle of rain against the window. I sat in the spare armchair as the newscaster began. Another soldier had died in Afghanistan. I groaned. I really didn't need this.

Gem glanced in my direction. Guessing my reaction, she grimaced in an expression of sympathy.

At that moment the front doorbell chimed. Gem stood from the settee and went towards the door. 'I've a nasty feeling I know who this is,' she said.

'Steve?' I guessed. 'But you've told him it's over.'

Gem said, 'I'm not sure it's sunk in yet.'

As she went into the hall, I took the opportunity to switch off the television. By the time it went back on, hopefully that particular news story would be finished.

I heard the door open, and the sudden noise of gusting wind and splashing rainwater. Then it was Gem's voice. 'Just *what* are you doing here?'

'What d'ya think, Gem? To see you, speak to you.' The man's voice was a bit high-pitched and reedy, the enunciation a little slurred.

'Have you been drinking, Steve?'

'No.'

'I can smell it, Steve.'

'Just a couple of Stellas, that's all. There's no harm in it.'

'I'm not talking to you when you're drunk, I've told you.'

'I'm not drunk. I just want to talk to you, to say sorry.'

'Sorry?'

'For the other night. I was out of order. Let me in, Gem,' he pleaded. 'It's pissing down out 'ere.'

I sensed her wavering and mentally willed her to stand firm. But of course she didn't.

I heard Gem's voice again. 'OK, then, but just for a couple of minutes. I've got an early start in the morning.'

Something told me it wouldn't be a wise idea for him to find me in the armchair with a mug of tea. So I rose to my feet and positioned myself in front of the electric bar-fire in the 1960s grey-tiled hearth.

'Yeah, Gem, it came as a bit of a shock, see,' he was explaining as he pushed open the door to the living room. 'Kids aren't really my scene, yeah—' He stopped in mid-sentence as he saw me. 'Who's this?'

Steve Cranford was tall and thin with spidery legs that were encased in tight denims. The hood of his dripping Nike waterproof top was down. A long, pointed nose protruded from a pinched face, which had the spotty and pitted complexion of someone who regularly feasted on burgers and fizzy drinks. It was the face of a wayward adolescent and hardly belonged with the thinning sandy hair of a man approaching his thirties.

'I'm Dave,' I said. I smiled broadly and offered my hand. Unsure, he accepted it in a weak handshake. His hands, I noticed, were long and bony with engorged veins.

'I told you about Dave,' Gem put in hastily. 'I told you about him, he's working at the cafe with me.'

I knew Cranford was supposed to have some barrow-boy charm, but I didn't sense he was displaying any tonight. He took a backward step. 'So what's he doing *here*?'

'Staying for a few days, that's all.'

'Very cosy. Since when you been taking in hobos?'

'It's just till he can find a place of his own,' Gem replied defensively.

Cranford glanced at me with disdain, then looked around the room. 'As soon as I turn my back for a couple of days . . .'

'You said you wanted to talk,' Gem reminded.

'Not in front of *him*!' he snarled.

'I'll make myself scarce,' I offered.

'No!' Gem said, probably more sharply than she intended.

She placed a hand on my arm. 'Anything you've got to say, Steve, you can say in front of Dave.'

Cranford glared at me, and I could see he was swaying slightly. 'Say in front of him? *Him?*' His voice was starting to rise several more octaves. 'Who's *him?* Lover boy? He's old enough to be your father. You, sleeping with a bloody tramp!'

'That's enough!' I interrupted sharply. 'Wind your neck in, Steve. If you can't keep a civil tongue in your head and keep your voice down, you'll have to go.'

'VOICE DOWN!' he bellowed suddenly, arching forward so that his face was only inches from mine. 'WHO THE FUCK ARE YOU TO TELL ME TO KEEP MY VOICE DOWN IN MY OWN GIRLFRIEND'S PAD!'

I felt flecks of his angry spittle land on my cheeks.

Suddenly there was a loud knock on the adjoining wall.

'Please, Steve,' Gem pleaded. 'I don't want any more trouble with the neighbours.'

Cranford yelled at the wall. 'FUCK THE BLOODY NEIGHBOURS! NEED TO MIND THEIR OWN BLOODY BUSINESS, NOSY SODS!'

With that he reached down, picked up the wooden coffee table and hurled it against the wall. On impact, the cheap timber shattered into half-a-dozen pieces. The banging on the wall began again.

I stepped forward. 'That's enough, Steve. You're leaving,' I ordered, grabbing his arm.

It was my own fault. I hadn't really been expecting much resistance from this spindly lout. His vicious backward elbow jab caught me in the ribs. A cracked rib creates excruciating pain, way beyond the minor damage of the injury. Winded for a moment, I fell back, stumbling over the armchair and landing in an ungainly heap on the carpet.

I think Cranford had even surprised himself, as he leaped forward to cash in on his unexpected success. He aimed his right foot at my head and kicked with all his might. But I was more alert now, and managed to block the blow with both hands, grabbing one of his flashy trainers. As my fingers purchased a grip around both heel and toe, I twisted viciously and rolled my whole body to the left, taking his foot with me.

He came down like a felled tree, his back thudding heavily on the floor.

I rolled back, trying to climb to my feet, the pain stabbing in my ribs.

Then a loud banging on the front door began. I looked up and saw Gem staring at me, perplexed. The violent knocking continued. It took a second for me to realise the doorbell wasn't being used.

'Open up! Police!'

# Fifteen

The pain in my ribs was excruciating as I lay there, winded.

Steve Cranford crawled awkwardly into a sitting position and looked up as Gem showed PC Tiddy into the room.

'Shit, you was quick,' Cranford muttered, shaking his head.

The young constable looked down his nose at the two of us sprawled on the floor. 'Not that quick. Just happened to be driving past the end of your street when we got the call. Complaint from your neighbour.'

'*Again,*' a new voice said. It was female.

Only then I noticed a second figure, half-hidden behind Tiddy.

For a moment I was confused, thinking it was a man. That was until she pulled off the tweed-weave trilby hat and a confusion of auburn curls fell around her shoulders. Although she was dwarfed by the tall beat copper standing next to her, I could see she was at least five-seven. She wore short-heeled pumps with dark trousers that were mostly hidden by a stylish navy trenchcoat. Her face was open with high cheekbones. She wore no make-up apart from a trace of mascara on the lashes of her rather cat-like, deep violet eyes. She addressed Cranford, her voice light but firm. 'Remind me, Steve – it is Steve, isn't it?'

Gem's boyfriend had now managed to move into a full sitting position. 'Yeah, Steve Cranford.'

'Well, Mr Steve Cranford,' the plain-clothes officer continued, 'when was it we last met? Was it three *or* four nights ago that I was last called here by your neighbours?'

'Er, five, I think.'

She stooped over so that her face was only inches from his. 'When you decided you'd beat the crap out of your gorgeous girlfriend here! *Just* because she told you she was going to present you with a lovely bouncing baby!' She straightened her back. 'Get up off the floor, Mr Cranford. You're making the place look untidy.'

Then she turned and looked down at me. 'And are *you* going to lie there all night? Or are you going to stand up and introduce yourself to me properly.'

I obeyed her instructions and climbed painfully to my feet. 'I'm Dave.'

'Dave who?'

I decided there would be little point in lying about my name to CID. My time was up and I'd just have to be man enough to face it. 'Dave Aston,' I said.

'Are you now?' There was a hard glint in the violet eyes as she appraised me and glanced down at my offered hand. After a second's hesitation she accepted it with a brief, firm shake. She said, 'Detective Constable Christy. Jane Christy. That's spelled like Jesus Christ with a Y.'

'Pleased to meet you,' I said, 'just sorry about the circumstances.'

Christy nodded and turned to Cranford. 'And what are we

going to do about you? Do you really think my colleagues and I have nothing better to do than to keep coming round here to sort out your domestic squabbles? Look at you, Mr Cranford, you're a grown man. For once, why don't you just act like one?'

'He just turned up here,' Gem explained. 'When he saw Dave here, he just started throwing a strop. Dave asked him to go and it kicked off.'

DC Christy thought for a moment, then said to Gem, 'I suppose there's no chance of a cuppa?'

'That would be nice,' PC Tiddy agreed quickly.

'Oh, yes,' Gem said, 'I'll make a fresh pot.'

As she scurried off to the kitchen, DC Christy looked around the room, taking in the shattered remnants of the coffee table. 'And would either of you two gentlemen like to give me your version of events? Looks like we interrupted a real dogfight.'

Cranford said, 'I come round here to talk to Gem and found *him* here.'

'You mean Mr Aston?' Christy checked. 'Bit late to call round, isn't it?'

'No law against it,' Cranford snapped back. 'I needed a couple of bevvies . . . a bit of Dutch courage. Know what I mean?'

'Dutch courage to say sorry to the pregnant girlfriend you hit?' Christy asked.

But the irony appeared to fly way over Cranford's head. 'Gem can get a bit mouthy when she's angry, yeah!'

'I'm not surprised,' Christy replied. She pointed to the settee and armchair. 'Now why don't you two gentlemen take a seat while we sort this out.'

I took the settee and left the armchair for Cranford.

'Now, when I was here the other night,' Christy continued, 'Miss Wilkins said she didn't want to press charges against you. And in return you gave me your solemn word that you would not raise a hand to her again – and refrain from any antisocial behaviour likely to disturb your neighbours during any future visits.'

'I didn't hit her!' Cranford protested. 'I hit *him* – when he started trying to throw me out.'

I pointed to the wreck of a coffee table. 'After you smashed that against the wall.'

'Boys boys!' Christy pleaded, just as Gem returned with a tray of tea for the police officers.

The female detective took her mug in both hands and sipped at it appreciatively before turning her attention to me. 'So, Mr Aston. What's your role in all this?'

'I'm just staying here for a few days,' I replied.

Cranford sneered. 'He should be on the streets. Gem told me about him. Got him a job at her caff. He's a tramp.'

'You mean itinerant?'

'Whatever.'

'I've met Mr Aston before,' PC Tiddy intervened. 'A couple of times, in fact.'

'He's *not* a tramp!' Gem protested. 'He's been down on his luck and sleeping rough. He's got a part-time job where I work. I've invited him to stay here for a while.'

'For protection?' Christy asked.

Gem shifted awkwardly, and glanced sideways at Cranford. 'Partly.'

Sniffing at the lingering odour of paint, Tiddy added, 'And for a bit of DIY help, it seems.'

Christy ignored that. 'Well, the protection thing seems to have backfired a bit, doesn't it? Looks like the two of you have been going at each other like a couple of prizefighters.' She held me in her gaze. 'I'm not sure that's what Miss Wilkins had in mind about her protection.'

'It wasn't *over* when you arrived,' I replied darkly.

She raised an eyebrow. 'Just begun, eh? Then I'm glad we arrived when we did. Maybe someone could have been badly hurt.'

'Possibly,' I said under my breath.

Tiddy said, 'I believe Mr Aston was in the army.'

'I wondered,' Christy said. 'And so this town is your new choice of residence?'

'I was born here. Grew up on the Evinmore.'

'And where were you living before you came back here?'

'Hereford.'

'I see.' She glanced round at PC Tiddy. 'Ray, why don't we run a check on Mr Aston. It's nice to know about newcomers to our happy little town.'

The constable started to operate the radio on his lapel. 'Not here, Ray. Why don't you use the car radio?'

Tiddy nodded and headed for the door. He and the female detective constable were of equal rank, but it was obvious who was in command of the situation.

When he'd gone, DC Jane Christy regarded me closely. 'I see you're wearing jeans and a T-shirt,' she observed.

I frowned. She was certainly a red-hot detective, I thought sarcastically. 'So?'

'Do you still possess some of your old army clothes? Jacket, camo trousers, that sort of thing?'

'I do.'

'And are they with you now?'

'Yes.'

'And you've been wearing them while you've been living rough?'

I had a nasty feeling I knew where this was going. But, there again, it would be pointless to deny it. 'It's the best kit when living rough.'

She nodded thoughtfully and placed her empty mug on the sideboard. 'It's just that we've had reports lately of someone who's been involved in two rather violent incidents in the town. His description might well be said to fit yours, Mr Aston. And he was wearing army DPM trousers.'

I feigned an air of innocence. 'Really? Do you have a name for your suspect?'

A slight smile played at her lips. Somehow I could tell that she knew, that we both knew. It was a game of cat and mouse. 'Unfortunately not,' she replied. 'The victims are not talking. Perhaps they are afraid.'

I said, 'Perhaps they should be.'

Her eyes narrowed a fraction. 'Perhaps it's the man in the army trousers who should be worried. His victims were from two rival drug gangs. Nasty, ruthless people.'

I felt my anger rise. 'Two rival drug gangs in a nice little town like Swinthorpe,' I replied. 'Then it's a shame they've been allowed to flourish.'

Christy nodded slowly. 'It is indeed, Mr Aston, and we in the police are doing all we can to contain them. But we will also not put up with vigilantes taking the law into their own hands.'

I nodded my understanding. 'Two blacks don't make a white,' I suggested. I couldn't be sure if she'd picked up the edge of sarcasm in my voice.

'Quite.'

At that moment PC Tiddy returned to the room. His little black piggy eyes were glistening with anticipation as he could barely wait to announce, 'Well, looks like our friend here's got one conviction for grievous bodily harm. An attack on his former civilian employer. And his details are wanted in relation to another more recent incident, by another force. In Hereford.'

DC Christy looked back at me and thought for a moment. 'We'll need an address and phone number for you,' she said. 'In case of any further requests from Hereford.'

I gave her the number of the replacement mobile I'd bought.

'You can use this address,' Gem offered quickly.

The detective nodded. 'Very well.' Then she paused for a moment before saying, 'Seems like you have some anger issues, Mr Aston. Or perhaps it's *management* of that anger?' When I didn't answer, she added, 'Had you been serving in Afghanistan?'

I inclined my head. 'And Iraq.'

Those deep violet eyes softened a fraction. 'I understand if things are difficult for you, Mr Aston, I really do, but I've got to put people's safety first. Especially vulnerable people like Gem here.'

'Of course,' I agreed.

She looked at Gem. 'It's up to Miss Wilkins here. Now, I gather that you believe Mr Cranford is the father of your baby?'

Gem nodded emphatically. 'He is.'

Cranford nodded in grudging agreement.

DC Christy smiled with a little hint of triumph in her expression. 'And, is it your intention to keep Mr Cranford in your life . . . in *some* way?'

'Yes,' Gem said without enthusiasm. 'He's the father of my child. It's only right. He knows he could have moved in with me any time he wanted. He still can.'

I groaned inwardly but said nothing. How could she be both so forgiving and so naive?

'Then,' Christy suggested, 'perhaps it's not such a good idea for Mr Aston to lodge here too – when the two of them clearly don't get on. We wouldn't want any more breaches of the peace, would we?'

I could see that the detective constable had a point. I said, 'This arrangement is only temporary. I'll move out tomorrow.'

Gem looked confused. 'Dave, you really don't have to.'

'Good idea,' Cranford snarled.

Briefly Gem's expression lightened, as if for a moment her dreams were all going to come true at once. 'So you'll come and live with me, proper like?'

Cranford suddenly shrugged, looking like he was being

trapped. 'Well . . . not sure about that . . . but it's not right that old bastard living with you!'

'Language,' Christy warned.

'Maybe you could take in a female lodger,' I suggested. 'It would help with your expenses.'

'It's possible, I suppose,' Gem said, taken aback at the suggestion, her dreams vanishing as soon as they had arrived. 'So you are definitely going to leave?'

'I think it best.' I turned to Christy. 'I'm working at the Athena Cafe. Could I make that my address?'

The detective's expression softened. 'If that's where we can find you, that'll be fine.'

She clearly considered she was on a winning streak. 'And you, young man,' she said, addressing Cranford, 'will you promise Gem not to turn up here unannounced again? And not late at night like this, disturbing the neighbourhood.'

Cranford looked uncertain.

Christy added, 'Then we can forget about this, and Ray and I can get back to the station.'

'All right,' Cranford muttered grudgingly.

I offered him my hand and, after a moment's hesitation, he shook it with a limp grip.

Christy moved towards the door, placing a hand on Cranford's arm. 'Would you like me to take your friend out with us?' she asked Gem.

When the girl nodded, Christy turned to me. 'Remember what I said, Mr Aston.' Her voice was low and slightly husky. 'We'll have no vigilantes in Swinthorpe.'

And then she and Tiddy, and Cranford, were gone.

Gem puffed out her cheeks. 'Wow, some police lady.'

I smiled. 'I wouldn't want to meet her on a dark night.'

'Thanks for everything, Dave. I'm so sorry about what happened.'

I felt my ribs and winced. 'I'm just sorry for the mess. I should have done better.'

'You really don't have to go, you know.'

I said, 'I think it's best. The weather's supposed to improve tomorrow. Anyway, I've promised our local sheriff now. Better not to cross her, I think.'

The next evening I met up with Jock Mahoney and Edwina in the market square where they were sharing a bottle of wine on one of the benches. The rights were drawing in and there was a real chill in the air. Both, I noticed, were now wearing old and frayed woollen scarves.

'Hello, stranger,' Mahoney greeted on my approach. 'Been going soft, I heard.'

I nodded. 'Stayed with Gem for a few nights. It was a kind offer.'

'I'll say,' Edwina acknowledged. 'Better than anything I've ever had.'

Mahoney looked serious. 'And did that include beating up that waster of a boyfriend of hers?'

I was amazed. 'You know about that?'

'No secrets in Swinthorpe, Dave.'

'Well, I didn't beat him up,' I replied. My ribs were still tender – if I needed a reminder. 'In fact, Steve got the better of me – *before* the police turned up.'

Mahoney held me in a hard gaze. 'You need to watch yourself, Dave. You're making yourself enemies. You're not in the army any more and the law won't protect you.'

Edwina giggled. 'Oh, don't be so hard on him, Jock. It's nice to have someone who will stand up to those ghastly druggie thugs. The police don't seem to do anything.' She reached over and hugged my arm. 'I like to think of you as my cowboy in the white hat. You know, the good guy.'

I'd been starting to feel a bit guilty, what with DC Christy's scolding and now a warning from Mahoney. So Edwina's words cheered me a little. 'Thanks for that,' I replied as she handed me the wine bottle.

'It's not just you,' Mahoney said. 'I'm the one who got the threat from that little shit Rashid, remember? I was the one who'd promised him the money Ginger owed.'

I was concerned. That had been quite a few days ago. 'Have you had trouble from them?'

Mahoney shook his head irritably. 'No, Dave, it was probably all talk. I'm just saying that you need to keep calm. Lady Pen here and I – and our other friends on the street – have got enough shit to contend with.'

It was only then that I realised that Mahoney seemed genuinely unsettled. 'I'm sorry,' I said.

He noticed the concern in my eyes. 'Nah, Dave, don't worry about it! Just keep things cool, eh?'

I smiled awkwardly. 'No more rocking the boat, I promise.'

'Good lad.' He reached out his hand and I grasped it. 'So you're back on the street now?'

'Looks like it.'

'Back to Coronation Gardens?'

I nodded. 'And you're still on your personal park bench?'

'Until the weather gets real cold,' he replied. 'Thinking about it, only another few weeks and the town's soup kitchen will open.'

On that cheerful note, Mahoney and I left Edwina and strolled back across the square, past the ancient stone poultry-cross market enclosure and across the bridge by Andreas's closed cafe.

On the way, outside the bus shelter by the Debenhams department store, a gaggle of unkempt Asian youths shouted abuse at us.

We ignored them and trudged on. 'Were any of them from Rashid's lot?' I asked.

Mahoney shrugged. 'Could be, but I didn't recognise anyone in particular.'

When we reached Mahoney's bench, we parted company and I made my way into the nearby bed of trees and shrubs. It was actually quite nice to be back and I set to work stringing up my camouflaged basha shelter and laying out my kip-mat and sleeping bag.

Once settled, I made some coffee on my mini-stove and took a mug out to Mahoney. But when I arrived I found him fast asleep, snuggled up in a blanket that he'd sworn to me was in the pattern of his own family tartan. It was a story I hadn't believed for a minute. His face was a lineless picture of peace and innocence.

Smiling to myself, I tossed out the contents of the mug, and returned to my little camp. Within minutes of bedding down I, too, was far away in a weird world where British bobbies, in Victorian uniforms and waving truncheons, were chasing Taliban fighters down a maze of alleys and mud compounds in Helmand, just like a bizarre variant of a Keystone Cops movie.

I'm not sure what disturbed me first. I think it may have been the smell of burning. It was followed a split second later by an almighty scream that will haunt me until the day I die.

# Sixteen

That smell. It was somehow familiar, sweetish.

I began to stir, suddenly waking, thinking I'd overslept and that the pork roast was already on the table, getting cold. I'd be in for a tongue-lashing from Sally.

My eyes opened to find myself staring not at the bedroom ceiling, but the roof of my basha.

I sniffed the air again, shifted onto one elbow. The meat had burnt.

I shook my head. What bloody meat, for God's sake? I'd been asleep. There was no damned meat.

Then I heard the noise, the fierce crackling sound. That sound that you hear when you throw a tinder-dry birch log onto the red-hot embers of a fire. I turned my head towards the noise and was dazzled by the bright white and yellow light pulsing across the lawn from the raging pyre.

I knew that smell now. A blazing military vehicle in Iraq and the stench of live human flesh on fire.

'AAAAGH!!'

It was that sound again, astonishingly loud. But this time shorter, cut off with the abruptness of a guillotine blade falling.

Where the hell was I? This wasn't Iraq, or Afghanistan . . .

the smell was all wrong . . . God I'd been having that nightmare again.

As realisation struck, I threw aside the top of my sleeping bag and sprang to my feet. Ignoring the stones and thorns on my bare feet, I raced between the shrubs and out onto the grass. The sheer force of the heat from Jock Mahoney's body, burning on the wooden bench, hit me like a wall.

In the dark-grey wash of early morning I could just discern a group of figures melting into the distance. I saw one of them raise his fist and punch the air. It was the bright-red jogging top that reminded me I'd seen him before – one of the Muslim gang members.

He was shouting triumphantly. I'm sure the words were *Allahu Akbar!* but I could have been mistaken. Nearby a middle-aged woman with a small dog on a lead stood still, staring blankly in shock at the burning body.

'Call for an ambulance!' I shouted at her.

Seeing me appear from beyond the fire, she took a backward step. She shook her head and muttered, 'I don't have a phone.'

*For God's sake!* I thought savagely, and rushed back to my basha. I grabbed my mobile from beside the sleeping bag. Shit! No power, dead flat. Sod! I had no time to mess around. I ripped the DPM camouflage sheet from its mountings, turned and raced back towards Mahoney.

A male cyclist in a Lycra suit and plastic bone-dome had stopped beside the woman with the dog. He had his smartphone out and was hastily tapping in a number.

As I approached the body I realised that the flames were

dying down, the worst of their job done. The stench of methylated spirit stung my nostrils along with the acrid mix of charred flesh and material. It was all too late, I realised.

Then the crumpled dark figure lying in the centre of the ebbing fire suddenly sat bolt upright, as if trying to stand.

I took an involuntary backward step. After a brief second, the man fell slowly, almost reluctantly, back into the bed of licking flames.

I stepped forward again with the basha sheet spread between my outstretched hands and dropped it over him to douse the flames. It was a disgusting feeling as I rubbed my hands over the material, feeling the heat and the strange consistency of cooked flesh beneath it. At last the flames were gone, and just a putrid-smelling smoke issued from the outer edges of the sheet.

With reluctance I peeled it back, away from what had once been his face. It was now a blackened mix of charred flesh and scorched beard. Dark eyes stared blindly back at me from the yellowed whites.

'God, Jock,' I breathed. 'I'm so sorry.'

I reached out and grabbed his wrist. There may have been a faint pulse, but I couldn't be certain. I looked around anxiously for help. There was the huge and ancient plastic B&Q bag in which he kept his few worldly possessions. Only feet from the bench lay an empty bottle of methylated spirit and an open box of matches, its contents spilled out on the asphalt path.

It seemed like an age that I just sat there. I felt the cool morning air on my face, only dimly aware of the grey murk lightening the dawn sky. Half-a-dozen passers-by gathered near the woman and her dog and the cyclist, but no one ventured any closer to me.

In fact, I imagine only minutes had passed before I was aware of the urgent sing-song siren of the police panda car. It worked its way around the garden's barriers to the scene of carnage. Close behind it followed the huge red bulk of a fire-tender, edging up onto the pavement and into the ornamental grounds.

I heard car doors slam, but didn't look up.

'My God,' said a young male voice. 'Is this what I think it is?'

I recognised the voice of PC Tiddy. I turned around. The young constable, his face drained of blood, stood beside WPC Sharon Sharman. Behind them the firefighters gathered, nothing for them to do now.

'It's Jock Mahoney,' I said.

'Yeah.' Tiddy gulped as he recognised me. 'What, oh, Dave, isn't it? Er, Dave . . . ?'

'Aston,' I helped.

'Is he still alive?'

'I'm not sure.'

Tiddy kicked at the empty meths bottle. 'Set fire to himself, I suppose?'

'A smoking accident?' Sharman suggested.

'No,' I replied darkly, squeezing Mahoney's wrist, trying to give him comfort. 'Someone tried to murder him.'

Again Tiddy tapped the meths bottle with the tip of his toe. 'Not what the evidence is suggesting to me.'

'Jock didn't drink meths,' I replied wearily. 'Some bastards

set him alight. Youths, I think. I saw them in the distance –
over there.'

His gaze followed the direction in which I jabbed my
finger. 'No one there now.'

'Of course not,' I said. 'They weren't going to hang around.
Ask that woman with the dog.'

While WPC Sharman remained with me, Tiddy reluctantly
left us to ask the witness what she'd seen. He returned after a
few moments. 'The lady's a bit confused, Mr Aston. Came out
wearing her reading-glasses by mistake, apparently. Didn't
notice anyone until she saw the – er – fire – er, Mr Mahoney's
predicament. The first *person* she saw was you . . .'

At that moment the newly arrived ambulance crew rushed
over and we stood back. As the paramedics went to work,
manoeuvring him onto a stretcher, I thought I saw a movement in Mahoney's arms.

'Is he still alive?' I asked.

The ambulance woman glanced up. 'Just . . . who are you?'

'His friend. Can I come with you?'

The two paramedics lifted Mahoney between them. 'Sure,
but I have to warn you, he might not make it to A & E.'

I nodded and started to follow. Suddenly I found PC
Tiddy at my side. 'I'm joining you,' he asserted. It didn't
sound as though he meant he was coming to keep me
company. 'WPC Sharman will stay at the scene.'

I said, 'At first I thought Jock was dead.'

'There must still be some hope for him,' Tiddy replied as
we reached the open rear doors of the vehicle. 'Ambulance
crews don't take corpses. Brings bad luck.'

That, at least, offered a sliver of hope, but it still didn't look good to me.

With Mahoney rapidly masked up for oxygen and given a drip by the medics, the vehicle was quickly on its way to the district hospital. It was a surprisingly uncomfortable ride for a state-of-the-art ambulance, the suspension struggling with numerous speed bumps. The female paramedic had just managed to take down the few details I could tell her about her charge when we arrived at the casualty department. Someone had called ahead and we had an emergency welcome party waiting for us.

The NHS takes a lot of flak, but sometimes its performance can be exemplary. My hopes for Mahoney's survival rose slightly as he was spirited away by the team of doctors and nurses. PC Tiddy shuffled off to find a drinks-vending machine and returned to the waiting area with two plastic mugs of dishwater tea. He handed one to me.

I took a sip. 'Shouldn't you be looking for those yobs?'

'All in good time, Mr Aston. We only have your word that they were there. The old woman didn't see them.'

'Doesn't my word count for anything?'

'Of course,' he replied diffidently. 'But then you were also the first person at the scene of crime.'

'Jock had upset that Asian drug gang,' I said. 'Their leader is a bloke called Rashid.' Of course I didn't mention that it was actually me who had caused the *problem*. In truth I wasn't ready to dwell on that too much. 'I heard someone yell out Islamic slogans as they ran away. "Allahu Akbar" or something like that.'

'What does that mean?'

'God is most great. Or Praise be to God.'

Outside I noticed a local taxi pull up and a stocky, middle-aged man in a crumpled beige raincoat climbed out. He paid off the driver, then turned to let the yawning automatic doors allow him in. He was rough-shaven with a few strands of curly grey hair combed over the top of his balding head. Jabbing a thumb at the bridge of his spectacles in order to focus his vision, he surveyed the waiting area. The smile on his thick lips was instantaneous when he spotted PC Tiddy.

He headed straight for us. 'Hello, Raymond!' he greeted, his hand extended.

Tiddy took it without enthusiasm. 'What d'you want, Bernie?'

I was mesmerised by the bright canary-yellow cardigan peeping through the gap in his raincoat. 'Think you can guess, Raymond. Some poor devil set alight in Coronation Gardens.'

'How d'you know that? It's only just happened.'

The man tapped the side of his nose. 'I have my sources. Victim was one of the local down-and-outs, I gather?'

I didn't care for his description. 'Jock Mahoney,' I said. 'He's ex-Royal Navy. Served in the Falklands.'

He appeared to notice me for the first time. 'Sorry, mate. Do I gather you're a friend of his?'

I nodded.

He reached his arm across in front of Tiddy, much to the policeman's irritation, to shake my hand. 'Bramshaw. Call me Bernie. I work on the *Journal*.' His grip was firm. 'And your name is?'

'Dave. I was the first on the scene.'

'Dave who, exactly?'

For a second I thought of saying Jones, as I was still known by Andreas at the cafe, but that seemed pointless in front of PC Tiddy. 'I'm Dave Aston.'

Bramshaw hesitated, seeming to search for the right words. 'Someone said it was attempted suicide.'

I shook my head. 'It was attempted *murder*, Bernie. That Muslim drugs gang.'

Bramshaw's thick eyebrows raised like a pair of draw-bridges. 'Really? The ones from Rosebury Street on the Evinmore estate?'

'I think so. Headed by a guy called Rashid.'

Bramshaw pulled a battered notepad and a biro from his coat pocket, and began scribbling. 'Call themselves Swords of Allah.'

'Look, Bernie,' Tiddy intervened. 'This is all speculation. Nothing's proven.' He glanced at me. 'We have several suspects . . . And, anyway, how d'you know that Muslim gang calls itself that name? What was it? God's Swords or something . . . ?'

'Swords of Allah, Raymond,' Bramshaw repeated. 'And I only know because I have taken the trouble to find out.'

Tiddy said stiffly, 'I'll pass that information on to my superiors.'

'Please do,' Bramshaw replied. 'I look forward to reporting on the dawn raid and big drugs bust in the *Journal*.'

Tiddy smiled uncertainly, but I'm sure the irony of the journalist's reply flew right over his head.

At that moment a doctor wearing green scrubs and cap emerged from one of the emergency treatment cubicles. 'PC Tiddy, isn't it?'

The constable rose to his feet.

'I think you'd better come in.'

Tiddy glanced at me, unsure.

I said, 'Don't worry, Ray. I'm not going anywhere.'

'If he tries to do a runner,' Bramshaw added helpfully, 'I'll hang on to his shirt tails.'

Tiddy grunted, turned and, clutching his cap in nervous hands, followed the doctor.

Bramshaw looked at me. 'The lad's a bit out of his depth. We don't get many attempted homicides in Swinthorpe.' His fixed smile faded. 'I'm afraid it isn't looking too good for your friend, Dave. I knew those Muslim boys would overstep the mark sometime. The cops have done bugger all about them, or the other drug gang. That lot are mostly white. Rival gangs, you see.'

I was curious. 'I saw there was a photograph and story in the *Journal* this week. Some vigilante taking on a couple of drug dealers . . . Is that the same gang?'

Bramshaw nodded. 'Sure is! It was the best story we've had in years, but I got it in the neck for running it.'

'Really, who from?'

'The editor,' Bramshaw explained. He removed his spectacles and began cleaning the thick lenses with a grubby handkerchief. 'I'm just the humble assistant editor and chief reporter, you see. The story broke late while the editor was schmoozing at some drinks party with the city fathers and local councillors. I couldn't reach him and made an executive decision. Big mistake.'

'Why?'

'Everyone wants to think of Swinthorpe as a sleepy market town. The editor and the paper's owners are paranoid about anything that might stop advertising. So they never attack stupid or wrong decisions by the local or county council, the NHS, the police . . . That's why we have the most boring local paper in Britain. The editor wouldn't know a story if it came and bit him on the arse.'

I smiled at that. 'But you do?'

Bramshaw replaced his glasses on the bridge of his large, red-veined nose. 'I'm Fleet Street – or I suppose we have to call it Wapping nowadays – an old hand. I got kicked out over some phone-hacking accusations. You know, the junior royals and celebs. I was a scapegoat.'

'Innocent?' I asked.

'Driven snow, me.'

'So you ended up here?'

Bramshaw sighed. 'I've still got a mortgage to pay off. The *Journal* was the only paper willing to take me on at the time.'

'And how did you know about the attack on Jock so quickly?'

He looked just a little proud of himself. 'I was scanning the local police radio frequency over breakfast. Nearly choked on my cornflakes. Most exciting thing that's happened in this one-horse town for years.'

Icily I said, 'If you don't count the bubonic plague, I suppose.'

Bernie Bramshaw shrugged and gave a tight smile. 'Sorry, that was a bit insensitive, I suppose.'

'Just a shade.'

'So, Dave – don't mind if I call you Dave? – what happened this morning exactly.'

My first instinct from long experience in the SAS was to keep my mouth firmly zipped. But then I thought, if no one was doing anything about these drug gangs, then the public needed to know. That meant someone had to tell them. This might be a start.

So I gave Bernie Bramshaw a potted version of events, not mentioning anything about my own involvement, and certainly nothing about being the 'vigilante' behind his recent scoop.

'So you'd been sleeping rough nearby?'

I nodded. 'I was the first on the scene.'

He chuckled. 'I see, that's why our friend Raymond is scared you'll do a runner.'

Just as the journalist finished laughing, the screen of the cubicle opened again and PC Tiddy emerged. He looked white and visibly shaken. Taking a deep breath, he announced, 'I'm afraid Mr Mahoney is dead. They were unable to save him. His injuries were just too severe.'

I shouldn't have been surprised, but because he was still breathing when we got him to the hospital, I think I'd convinced myself he'd survive. The truth came to me like a sledgehammer blow and I fell back in my chair, feeling physically winded.

# Seventeen

Bernie Bramshaw was equally shocked. 'Good Lord,' he muttered. 'What a disgusting thing to have happened. In Swinthorpe of all places.' I saw his eyes blinking in disbelief behind the lenses of his spectacles.

PC Tiddy drew himself to his full height, and tilted his chin a fraction as he looked down at me. Why was it, I wondered, that he looked like he was thinking what the hell should he do next?

'What's going on?' a female voice demanded suddenly. 'Ray?'

I hadn't noticed the entrance of DC Christy before she appeared in front of me with WPC Sharman at her side.

Jane Christy was wearing the same tweed-weave trilby hat and blue trenchcoat as she had been the other night. Her complexion was a little pasty and I wondered if she might have been called straight from her bed.

'Ah, Jane.' Tiddy sounded surprised and not altogether pleased. 'Didn't know you were on shift. Er, it looks like we have a murder on our hands.'

'We have indeed, Ray.' The detective constable looked tired, her sharp cat's eyes a little duller than I remembered. 'I've just come from the crime scene. SOCO are there.' She turned to me. 'A horrible business. I am sorry, Mr Aston. I understand Jock was a friend of yours?'

I was surprised she recognised me, let alone remembered my name. 'It was pretty grim,' I admitted.

Tiddy looked at me accusingly. I don't think he could get it out of his head that I might have had a hand in Jock's murder. 'Mr Aston was at the scene of the crime.'

Christy puffed out her cheeks and blew gently in an expression of exasperation. 'Putting out the flames, from what I've heard – after someone had set fire to his *friend*.'

'Islamists,' Bramshaw chimed in helpfully. 'That lot from Rosebury Street.'

'Thank you, Bernie,' Christy said tartly, turning to him. 'And why are you here so early in the morning? Unshaven and . . . are they pyjamas under that hideous jumper? Been earwigging on the police net again, have we?'

'Certainly not!' Bramshaw protested.

PC Tiddy wasn't listening. He shifted awkwardly, then looked at me with a strangely fierce expression. I just knew he didn't like me and he certainly wasn't going to let go of me yet. 'Mr Aston, I should like you to come with us to the police station to answer a few questions.'

Christy muttered something under her breath.

I forced a smile in Tiddy's direction. 'I'll be happy to help in any way I can.'

I was to spend the rest of the morning being quizzed at Swinthorpe Police Station.

Actually it was Jane Christy who led the gentle interrogation, plying me with endless cups of lukewarm tea as she went over and over what had happened that morning.

Later we were joined by a detective inspector. His name was Tony Ryan.

A big-boned man in his forties, it struck me that everything about him was grey: a tired grey suit, grey hair and a grey pallor to his skin. Even his eyes were on the grey side of blue. He appeared listless and impatient, as though he'd rather be anywhere else than sitting with us in the interview suite.

Christy was trying her hardest to pin me down on the motive that anyone might have for murdering Jock Mahoney. I told her about Ginger's debt to the Swords of Allah gang and how Mahoney had agreed to pay it off.

'And was it?' she asked me keenly.

'As far as I know, yes,' I replied.

'How much was owed?'

I shrugged. 'About ten pounds, I think.'

'Ten pounds?' she echoed.

I nodded.

'So this murder wasn't about money, was it? It was about hurt pride – and revenge.'

I said nothing.

Christy sat back in her chair and regarded me across the desk. 'That incident that made the front page of the *Journal*. A couple of those Muslim gang boys humiliated, with a photo of one of them hung up on a fence and their dog killed . . . Did you read about it?'

I shook my head. 'We don't have money for newspapers. Only ever read the *Big Issue* really.'

A tic of a smile, or maybe irritation, flickered on her lips. 'Two coshes were found at the crime scene. Coins in bags made from women's tights. Five pounds in each . . .' Her eyes narrowed. 'Do you get it?'

I played dumb. 'Ten pounds?'

'Exactly.' She paused. 'Was that the money that Jock owed? Was that the payback? Was that the reason why Jock was killed?'

I was starting to feel uncomfortable.

'There were a lot of coins in those coshes,' Christy said. 'So we checked with all the banks and large stores in town. One of the HSBC tellers remembered someone coming in for coins on the afternoon of that assault. She didn't recognise him.'

Inspector Ryan spoke for the first time. His voice was gruff with the hint of a southern Irish accent. 'Was that you, Mr Aston?'

I played the usual politician's get-out-of-jail card, 'I'm afraid I don't remember.'

Ryan said, 'You work part-time at a cafe, don't you?'

'Yes. The Athena.'

'Are you ever asked to get change for the till?'

I suddenly realised I'd been handed a lifeline. 'Sometimes,' I lied. 'I guess banks are being asked for change every day – by a lot of people.'

Christy glanced sideways at her boss, but he was more interested in his watch. He clearly didn't think he had a case, and I could see why.

I took a chance. 'Didn't this bank branch have a CCTV camera?' I asked.

There was a pause before Christy answered with a small sigh, 'Yes, Mr Aston. But I'm afraid it had developed a fault that morning. The pictures were not very clear.'

'That's a shame,' I said.

'Or very lucky for someone,' she replied. 'I contacted Hereford police about their interest in you. Apparently there was a case of very serious assault on a serving member of the army. But there were no witnesses to the actual attack and the victim himself declined to press charges. You seem to be on a lucky streak just now, Mr Aston.'

That rankled. 'Forgive me. I don't feel too lucky just now.'

Inspector Ryan appeared to have had enough. He rose to his feet. 'You're free to go, Mr Aston. Thank you for your help. I'm very sorry about your friend. But, I'm afraid, Mr Mahoney lived on the wrong side of the street, so to speak. And a pretty mean street at that. Having anything to do with drugs brings its own rewards, I'm afraid, and its own dangers. Your friend unfortunately paid the price.'

That annoyed me. I remembered what Bernie Bramshaw had told me. 'Then shouldn't Swinthorpe's police be doing something about it? Like stopping that drug gang?'

Ryan spared me a withering glance. 'We do all we can, Mr Aston, but the whole country's turned to drugs and violence. Our resources are limited. All society's paying the price for it. Your friend just happened to pay the highest price of all.' He turned towards the door. 'Now, if you'll forgive me, I've got a meeting with my super.' He smiled stiffly. 'Believe it or not, it's about tackling our local drug problems. Goodbye, Mr Aston.'

As he left, I saw Jane Christy's eyes follow him until the door swung closed.

I could tell that she felt let down by him.

After a moment, I said, 'I suppose there'll be a post mortem?'

She seemed momentarily distracted. 'What? Oh, yes, of course.'

'Any idea when Jock's funeral might be?'

Her expression hardened. 'No, Mr Aston, I'm afraid not.'

In fact, the funeral was three weeks later.

Meanwhile I kept my head down, avoiding the city centre and places where I knew members of either drug gang hung out. Gem told me that Jock's murder had made a small slot on the national TV news and the inside pages of the tabloids. I wasn't sure if that was down to the horrific manner of his death, or if I detected the hand of Bernie Bramshaw behind the scenes, trying to rebuild his journalistic reputation.

The morning of the funeral broke bright and crisp in mid-October. Dying leaves on the trees, which lined the driveway of Swinthorpe crematorium, shone like burnished copper against a cloudless sky.

Edwina and I travelled first class to the tired-looking 1960s red-brick building in the back seat of an unmarked police car, courtesy of DC Jane Christy.

After Mahoney's murder I had vacated my leafy copse in Coronation Gardens. The Asian gang probably had a good idea that's where I camped, and I had no desire to end up the same way as my Scots friend. I moved between several different sites, none of which could be easily viewed by passing pedestrians. Each night I would change location.

A few days earlier, a car had pulled up by the benches in the market square where I was sitting with Edwina. We'd been sharing a supper of leftovers from the cafe.

To my surprise, it had been Jane Christy who emerged from the car and walked over.

She removed her trilby hat and smiled down at us. 'Evening, Dave. Hoped I'd find you here.' She nodded at Edwina. 'Lady Penelope – hi – we have met before.'

'Yes, young lady,' came the stiff reply. 'I remember all *too* well.'

Christy shrugged and dimples showed each side of her smile. 'Sorry . . . I was young and green behind the ears back then . . . Am I forgiven?'

Edwina grunted. 'Let me think about it . . .'

The detective sat down. 'May I join you?' She smiled apologetically. 'You know, when you're young you tend not to think about other people's circumstances. Why they're like they are, why they're *who* they are? When I took you into the nick for being drunk and disorderly—'

'You mean for being merry,' Edwina interjected.

'In a public place,' Christy countered.

'On Christmas Eve.'

Christy let that drop. 'The custody sergeant taught me a lesson. When I took you into the custody suite, he told me to never be judgemental. People are who they are through nature or nurture, he said – all stirred up by life's experiences. There, but by the grace of God, go any one of us. He told me you Lady P came from one of the most respected and influential families around here. He said he didn't know what it was, but there'd be a reason why you were singing carols in the shopping mall.'

Edwina grunted. 'Because it was Christmas?' she replied tartly.

'Why?' Christy asked. 'I really would like to know.'

The elderly eyes narrowed. 'Would you now? Well, I'll tell you, DC Christy, I was unhappy and alone at Christmas and the bottle of cider had made me happy. Helped me forget I had been kicked out of my home years before and that my family had disowned me.'

'Why had they done this?'

'Because my mother had died giving birth to me,' Edwina replied. 'And my father, a brigadier general in the army, never forgave me for that. He just couldn't handle it. I hardly ever saw him from one year to the next.' She paused for a moment, remembering. 'It was nursemaids and nannies for me – oh, and one rather odd uncle who took a bit of a shine to me. Then it was the very best boarding schools. Wasted on me, I wasn't academically bright. But I did like home sciences. God knows why. I think because the only adult friend I had as a kid was our home cook. I adored her right up until she died.'

'When was that?' I asked.

'In the swinging sixties,' she chuckled. 'I was there *and* I remember it. Talk about life in the fast lane! London, Berlin, Switzerland, the Riviera.'

Christy smiled. 'High society, eh?'

Edwina almost choked on hearing that. 'Good God no!

The aristos, the debs and my family circles would have nothing to do with me. I was in with the so-called jet set. I was kicking over the traces with the bad boys of rock, film industry moguls, actors and actresses. Smoking, drinking, doing drugs. That was when my father had enough. Cut me off from the family completely.'

'How dreadful,' Christy said. I could see it now, and so could she. 'All because you were looking for love.'

Edwina sniffed heavily. 'Well, something like that. Being *really* wanted by anyone – apart from my teddy – would have been nice. I couldn't keep scrounging off friends, sleeping on their sofas. So eventually I enrolled at culinary school and got a job as a cook. Private houses, ski chalets, directors' dining rooms, yachts. Still the good life. But a few inappropriate affairs with the wrong men and the wrong time . . . and it was back to the bottle, I'm afraid. In those times Jack was still the only friend I could truly rely on, who never asked questions.'

'Jack?' Christy asked softly.

'Daniel's.'

The detective constable realised her mistake. 'Ah, I see.'

Edwina concluded, 'Nowadays I've mostly given him up for a cheaper model.' She looked at Christy, then reached across and touched her arm. 'Yes, my dear, you *are* forgiven. Thank you for asking. You know, I'm not sure anyone else ever has . . . But then you didn't come here to just listen to me prattling on about my silly life story. What is the real reason for your visit? Not to arrest me again for being merry, I hope?'

Christy shook her head. 'I just wanted you both to know that Jock Mahoney's funeral will be next Tuesday. Eleven a.m.'

I'd given evidence at the inquest, along with the dog walker and the cyclist. The coroner found that Jock had been unlawfully killed by person or persons unknown.

Christy added, 'So obviously it is now officially a murder inquiry and we are on the case.'

I remembered the words of Bernie Bramshaw. 'But *are* you really?' I asked.

'Really what?'

'On the case. For instance, do you have the names of any suspects?'

Her eyes narrowed. 'No, not yet. We are short on witnesses. Even you didn't actually see it happen. And, if our suspicions are right, we're talking about a very tight-lipped community.'

Edwina grunted. 'So, again, nothing gets done! We'll *all* be murdered in our sleep before any action is taken by the police in this town.'

'Trust me,' Christy insisted. 'This really is a priority investigation.'

'So I really can afford to hold my breath, can I?' Edwina muttered.

Christy ignored that. 'As friends of Jock, I wanted you both to know that I managed to track down his family. His wife and one of his adult children will be coming – although, not surprisingly, her new partner has decided not to attend. She will be paying for his funeral. I suggested that it might be appropriate for the service to be held jointly for him and for his friend Ginger.'

'Jock would have liked that,' Edwina agreed emphatically. 'Ginger had a poor send-off.'

The detective smiled thinly. 'Mrs Mahoney wasn't so keen at first, but relented. I am afraid that Mr Adcock, Ginger's father, still did not want to know, nor any other relatives I spoke to. At least it will appear now more as the joint service for two good ex-military friends. I also spoke to SSAFA and gave them the details. Not sure what good that'll do.'

'SSAFA?' Edwina queried.

'The forces' charity – er, Soldiers, Sailors, Airmen and their families, I think.'

Christy had obviously gone to a lot of trouble, probably much more than she needed to.

'Thanks,' I said. 'We appreciate what you've done.'

She said, 'It's what *they've* done. They both did their bit for their country. A soldier, a sailor . . .' She pulled a tight smile. 'Anyway, maybe one of you would like to think of saying a few words. I'm sure Jock's wife wouldn't mind.'

Well, I certainly wasn't one for speech-making. But a few days later, as Jane Christy parked the car in the area outside the crematorium gates, Edwina was rehearsing her 'few words' and jotting down adjustments in her notebook.

I was aware of a number of cars pulled up on the grass along the gravel drive, suggesting that all the official parking spaces inside were taken. Of course, given the conveyor-belt turnover of funeral ceremonies, it was difficult to ascertain who was enjoying such a popular 'send-off'.

However, as Edwina and I approached the ugly, modern vestibule with Jane Christy, the answer became clear. The place was packed, overwhelmingly with males in early or older middle age. There were several army and navy berets in evidence, and blazers adorned with a variety of British Legion and other regimental lapel badges.

'I can't believe this,' I murmured.

'Nor can I,' Christy replied. 'Look, I think this is Mrs Mahoney.'

The widow was a tall and slender creature dressed in a black silk suit and wide-brimmed hat. The flawless skin defied her fifty-something years.

'Detective Sergeant Christy?'

'Detective Constable,' the policewoman corrected. 'You must be Mrs Mahoney?'

'Call me Greta. Such a wonderful turnout, I can hardly believe it.' Jock's wife scanned the sea of unfamiliar faces. 'I think someone's been on Twitter or Facebook, or something. Most of these are navy people who knew or served with Jock. Come to pay their respects.'

The man at her side, who appeared to be Jock's son, added, 'I think the others must be friends of Ginger Adcock.'

I said, 'Ginger was with the Cheshires.' I glanced around, noting the berets and lapel badges. 'It looks like some of his former comrades are here.'

Greta appeared to notice me for the first time. I was wearing my best kit, smart DPMs freshly ironed for me by Gem. 'Are you Jock's friend? The one Sergeant Christy told me about?'

'I'm Dave. Dave Aston.'

'You're in the army? You knew that *other* chap then, in Bosnia?'

I shook my head. 'I'm ex-army. I only got to know Jock and Ginger recently.'

I looked around for Christy, but she had gone. She'd disappeared into the crowd.

Then I noticed a cluster of journalists and cameramen and a van from the region's ITV news. No one had given a stuff about him when he was alive. Now that he'd died in horrific circumstances, he'd become a people's hero.

Inside the chapel the organ began to clear its steel lungs. It filled the air with a deep and stirring background requiem by John Taverner that I recognised, but could not name. Cigarettes were discreetly extinguished underfoot and people started to drift towards the entrance.

I turned back to Greta. 'By the way, this is Edwina. She has known your husband and Ginger for a long time. She was a good friend of both of them.'

I'm not sure what Greta made of Swinthorpe's 'Lady Penelope'. I had given Edwina a few pounds to spend on an outfit from the Oxfam shop and she really looked quite splendid in a black pepper and salt tweed skirt, fitted dark jacket and a jaunty hat complete with a colourful partridge feather.

The two women shook hands. 'I've heard a lot about you. I can't say you're what I expected.'

Edwina smiled. 'This is my bag lady's Sunday best,' she said in a voice that would nowadays have been much too smart for the BBC. 'Not what I usually wear on a Tuesday. This is special in respect for dear Jock.'

'I'm sorry,' Greta said, taking a backward step. 'I really didn't mean to offend.'

'You haven't, dear,' Edwina assured. 'Jock and Ginger were both great friends of mine. They always looked out for me, as

I did for them. Would it be acceptable to you if I said a few words?'

There was a beat of hesitation before Greta said, 'Yes, yes, of course. I'll ask the vicar to call on you – when he thinks it's a good moment.'

It was time for Jock's wife to join her family and the slow tide of mourners moving into the chapel. The pews filled up quickly and there were clearly too many to squeeze between its ugly bare brick walls.

I hung back in the open vestibule with those who could not fit inside, many of them seemingly Ginger's ex-army colleagues. Several were smoking. At least out here we were onlookers, rather than participants. I took the tobacco tin from the cargo pocket of my smock and opened it. I'd prepared half-a-dozen roll-ups and lit one of them now. I felt I needed one.

'Filthy habit,' a voice said.

I turned to find myself looking into Bernie Bramshaw's crumpled face. He was wheezing slightly from the exertion of having tried to run from his car. 'Thought I wasn't going to make it!' he gasped.

I smiled. 'I'm not sure you *are* going to.'

'What? Oh, no. Must get fitter. Promised the missus last New Year. At least I gave up the fags.'

'So I can't offer you one?'

'Jesus, no. I couldn't go through that hell again!' He fumbled in his raincoat pocket and produced a small leather-bound flask. 'Discovered a nice new friend instead. I hate *funereals.*' That was how he pronounced it. 'This'll get me through.'

I suddenly realised there was a pasty-faced teenager with him, a gormless-looking lad with an unworldly spiky haircut.

'Who's this?' I asked.

'Oh, oh – I call him *Jedwood.*' Bramshaw chuckled at his own joke. 'He's what passes for a photographer on the *Journal.*'

I nodded towards the congregated ex-servicemen. 'Former comrades of Jock and Ginger,' I said. 'Might make a good picture.'

To my surprise Bramshaw turned to the lad. 'Hear that, Jed? Go and do your stuff. Might use it on the front page this week – *if* you get a good 'un.' He turned to me. 'He's fresh from uni. A degree in *media studies,* or some such bollocks. Still, he's willing, and makes a good cup of tea.'

The burble of voices around us fell silent as the pallbearers approached with Jock's coffin.

I threw away my cigarette stub and stood on tiptoe to try to hear the preacher. All I caught were the words at the end of his very brief introduction. '. . . *He who believes in me will live, even though he dies* . . . That is from John 14. Verses 1 to 2.'

Jock's son spoke briefly to the congregation, saying how the family had lost their beloved father for so many years, but now happily – if belatedly – found him again. There was a thank-you to his 'shipmates' for attending, and to the mates of Jock's friend, Ginger.

The preacher led us into a tuneless rendition of 'He who would valiant be . . .', which was followed by a reading of Psalm 46.

With slightly more confidence, the hotchpotch of family and former servicemen made a better job of the more familiar 'The Lord's my shepherd . . .'

A brief reading from Corinthians by Greta Mahoney was followed, as was only to be expected, by the sailors' anthem, 'For those in peril on the sea'. The voices in the congregation, especially those at the back around me, rose in heartfelt unison.

It was then that the preacher waved and Edwina climbed to her feet with all the elegance and confidence of a winning MP at a by-election.

She perched a pair of gold-rimmed glasses on the bridge of her nose, glanced down at her notes, and looked up sharply. 'Dear Mrs Mahoney, family and friends of both Jock and Ginger Adcock.' Each word was beautifully enunciated, crisp and clear. Pure county. 'It has been my privilege to know both these gentlemen for several years, when I have shared the time of their fall from grace.

'Both fell through the net that society puts out to help its troubled warriors. They were missed by the good charities, which try so hard to help. But the fierce and maybe misplaced pride, independence and determination of these men – taught by the military – sometimes works against them.

'Many of our former heroes – or servicemen – fill our prisons or lie uncared for on our streets. Hidden under cardboard boxes. I know, because that is where I met them. I am the prodigal daughter of an aristocratic family. My father was a brigadier general. Sometimes I think I was given everything, maybe too much. Too much of everything except what really mattered. Love and affection. When I fell from grace there was no sympathy for me.

'Then, eventually disowned by my family, I met Jock and Ginger in this town. I was very scared, very lonely. There was no sympathy from them either . . . Just unqualified friendship. Unjudgemental. A love between comrades. In our different ways we had been fighting the war of life, and failing. We were all injured, all wounded. Some, of course, can cope with those injuries better than others.

'Together we created a life between us that was bearable, just about worth living . . . until those two dreadful times . . . Within days of each other . . . when both men died. And with their lives gone, I fear that, without their support, others among us will feel more vulnerable.'

Edwina hesitated then and looked up over the congregation. I knew her eyesight wasn't that good, and her glasses were bought from a charity shop. She could just as well have been staring at Jane Christy, yet somehow I felt she was looking straight at me.

'Out there, *someone* knows who was responsible for the callous murder of our friends. Yes, Ginger, too, was effectively killed – albeit without a weapon. Someone must bring the perpetrators to justice, or else there *is* no justice in this modern world. Justice not just for me, for them, but for the country for which they once fought and never really stopped.'

Edwina finished abruptly and stepped down from the podium. In the chapel and all around me, the congregation suddenly erupted into heartfelt applause. Jane Christy caught my eye and smiled.

It was then that I saw the sudden flash of red. The teenager in the bright jogging top was half-hidden behind one of the brick columns of the vestibule. He'd obviously been lurking in the crowd and was now creeping down the steps to the car park.

I was shocked and furious at the same time. There was no mistaking the sallow face with its acne-riddled skin and the lifeless black eyes. I'd seen him standing alongside the Muslim gang leader, Rashid. And I swear it was also him who had shouted at me when I emerged from my sleeping bag to see Jock in flames.

The boy slipped away across the car park, moving swiftly without a backward glance.

As the sound of Rod Stewart's 'Sailing' drifted hauntingly from the chapel, I followed down the steps in pursuit. Edwina would have her justice.

# Eighteen

I cut across the cemetery at right angles, taking a short cut between the tombstones. It allowed me to reach the main road before the teenager.

Crossing the road to the other side, I entered a public telephone box. I lifted the receiver and pretended to make a call.

Moments later, my quarry appeared at the crematorium gates. He glanced over his shoulder to make sure he hadn't been followed.

Satisfied that he was safe, he lit a cigarette. Then he sauntered over the main road.

As he walked past the box, I was undecided whether or not to grab him there and then. In that second the opportunity was lost.

Thinking quickly, I slipped off my army smock top, rolled it up and tucked it under my arm. The teenager would have recognised me all too easily in that. At least I was wearing a dark-blue polo shirt underneath. I pushed open the door, crossed back over the main road and followed at a discreet distance.

It was nearing lunchtime and he'd be wanting food. Maybe he would join the gang in town for a burger or KFC, I thought?

But no, he headed towards the ring-road underpass that would eventually take him to the Evinmore estate. It seemed our brave Muslim warrior was going home for his meal.

Rosebury Street was the main shopping broadway in that part of town. It brimmed with retailers serving each and every need of its ethnic community. It was known as 'Little Calcutta' to the residents of Swinthorpe, although the community was essentially Pakistani, not Indian. There were takeaways, grocers, herb and spice merchants, haberdashers and foam-cutters, halal butchers, Internet cafes and money-dealers.

The teenager took one of the narrow side streets that ran off both sides of Rosebury Street. I turned the corner and watched him walk down the hill beside narrow Victorian two-up, two-down terraced houses. They fronted the pavement without any kind of garden.

My quarry disappeared into one of them. When I reached it, I walked straight past. Number 21. Neatly painted door and windows, I noted, and a clean and well-scrubbed front step. Fresh white net curtains suggested a house-proud family.

There was going to be no easy way to do this. I used the black-painted knocker and rapped twice, loudly. No voices came from within. I rapped again.

The door swung open abruptly. The youth looked up at me, a sandwich in his free hand.

I smiled. 'And you are . . . ?' I asked.

'I am Ali.'

His mouth dropped as the loop in his brain completed the circuit. Recognition and connection. But it was a nanosecond too late. His hand moved to close the door, his sandwich taking flight. I pushed forward with the weight of an angry bull. The door crashed back, knocking chips of plaster from the wall. I followed in, my right hand around his skinny throat as I thrust him hard against the door to the front room. I heard the wood splinter under the force.

'No!' he gasped. 'Leave me, you bastard! Fuck off!'

'Where are your parents?' I demanded.

'Out – shopping!' he replied, using both hands to try to prise my forearm from his throat.

In response I pushed it in even harder. 'You've just been to the cremation of Jock Mahoney, right?'

'No!' he gasped. 'I don't know what you fuckin' mean! I have been nowhere!'

That riled me. 'You soddin' little liar. I saw you there. I've just followed you!' Spittle showered his face, but I just didn't care.

'No, I've been nowhere!'

'And you are with Rashid's gang. You were there when Jock was set on fire!'

'No, mistah! You have it all wrong. I know nothing!' Moisture was starting to brim in his eyes. No longer lacklustre, they were bright with terror.

'*YOU* SET FIRE TO HIM!' I accused, my voice rising to a scream.

Ali was in tears, starting to blub. 'No, mistah, believe me, I know *nothing*!'

My inner anger overwhelmed me. I was back in Baghdad, after the bombers. Another lying, murdering bastard. Another home raid in the early hours. Operation Knight hadn't finished yet.

I released his throat, but grabbed the collar of his shirt. I opened the front room door using his head. Inside the room was clean and immaculate. Two young girls, maybe eleven or twelve years old, sat on the floor, a selection of toys between them. They stared up at me, their mouths open in speechless horror.

I ignored them and pushed on, dragging Ali with me. We went to the staircase where I half-hauled and half-pushed him up the steps. Grabbing his hair, I threw him into the bathroom. As he stumbled, an expensive smartphone fell from his pocket. I kicked it into the corner.

Ali stood and stared back at me, his mouth gaping.

I pointed to the bath. 'Put the plug in!' I ordered. 'Turn the fucking cold tap on!'

Ali was starting to tremble now, really tremble like a naked man in a blizzard. He couldn't stop.

'Remember killing Jock *now*, do you?'

The water began to gush. 'I remember nothing . . .' Ali began to gush like the water, blubbing with fear. 'I don't know what you are talking about! Please let me go!'

'I'll let you go,' I snapped back, 'as soon as you tell me the truth. It's that simple.'

A weird silence followed for several long minutes. I stared straight at him, never losing focus for a second. Ali glanced at me, glanced down at the fast-filling bath, and back at me again. I knew he wondered what was going to happen next. His trembling increased. A damp patch suddenly began spreading across his trousers from the groin.

'Sit on the bath!' I ordered.

Shocked at the words breaking the brief silence, he obeyed instantly. I reached forward and pushed him over and into the water. It splashed up like a geyser. Water slopped heavily on the floor, the taps still running full on.

I grabbed a thick bath towel from the rail. In a couple of seconds I had it over Ali's face, pressing his head down under the water. I held it fast, counted to ten.

In Iraq I'd witnessed the Americans 'water-boarding' their captives a dozen or more times. I knew the form, this was my version.

I released him, pulling the towel free. 'Why were you there, Ali? Why were you there?'

'I don't know what . . .'

I didn't even let him finish his sentence. Towel down again, hard over his face, counting again. This time longer. Twelve. It seemed like for ever to me.

Ali came out of the water like a surfacing whale. He was gasping, spewing water everywhere.

'Try again, Ali! Why were you there?'

He heaved in air, barely able to breathe.

I started to push him down again. 'No!' he spluttered. 'Please stop! I go because I am ordered.'

I pulled his head free of the water. 'Ordered by who?'

'By Rashid.' He spat out more water, and opened his eyes. 'And for myself. To ask for forgiveness.'

'Forgiveness?' I asked. 'From who? Jock was dead.'

Ali was recovering, regaining his senses. 'I don't know. From Allah, from God . . . maybe from myself.'

A red cloud was forming in front of my eyes. 'You did kill him, Ali, didn't you? It was *you* who set fire to Jock!'

'No, no!' I saw the fear in his eyes.

But it was too late. The towel was over his face and down he went, under the water, his legs flailing. Water slopped over the bath sides. By now, I thought, it must be seeping down through the ceiling below.

I dragged him clear of the surface again. This time I'd forgotten to count. I think I nearly drowned him.

He coughed up water, violently, and some vomit. He gasped and gasped, his eyes closed.

'So you set fire to Jock?' I demanded again.

Ali was defeated, a wreck. He nodded slowly. 'Rashid ordered me to do it.'

'You had no choice?' I asked, very quietly.

'No,' he answered.

I stepped back, an idea forming in my mind. 'Get out! Get out of the bath now.'

Still coughing and spluttering, he struggled to get a grip on the smooth enamel surface. I left him to it while I looked around, searching for his smartphone.

I found it and switched the camera mode to 'video'. Ali at last climbed out, his clothes sodden and dripping onto the bathroom floor. He was sobbing quietly.

I indicated the toilet seat. 'Put the lid down,' I snapped, 'and sit on it.'

As he obeyed, his trembling became more severe. Being cold was adding to his fear, so much so that his teeth began to chatter.

'Stop that, Ali!' I ordered, perching on the edge of the bath. 'Get a grip on yourself.'

I looked down at the screen on the phone and pressed record. 'What is your name?'

It took a moment for Ali to realise what was happening. 'What? Er, Ali. Kamran Ali.'

'And what is your address?'

'You know, we are here . . .'

'Just answer my questions, Ali, and you won't get hurt.'

He squirmed awkwardly on the seat as he told me his address.

'How old are you?'

'Nineteen, nearly twenty.'

'Are you a student or at work?'

'I'm not a student. I don't have a job.'

'Why?'

He shrugged. 'How should I know? No one wants me.'

'So how do you get money to live?'

'I gets me benefits . . .' His voice faded into a croak. He coughed up some bathwater. 'Fuckin' Jobseekers an' that.'

'That's not much to live on,' I suggested.

Another shrug. 'I get by. Doin' this an' that.'

I said, 'You mean working for Rashid?'

He looked distinctly uncomfortable. 'What you mean?'

'Doing drugs with Rashid. You're part of his gang, aren't you? I've seen you.'

'No, I ain't no part of that.'

So now he was back to lying again. I said, 'Ali, we can do this the easy way or the hard way. Your choice.'

He glanced over at the bath. After a moment, he said, 'Yeah, right, I sometimes works with Rashid.'

'He's the boss, right? He runs the gang that calls itself Swords of Allah.'

Ali looked down at his hands, clutched together on his lap, and nodded.

'And if he says jump, you ask how high, right?'

He gave a half-hearted laugh at that. 'Yeah, somethin' like that.'

'And *he* told the gang to set fire to Jock Mahoney?'

'Might have done . . .' This time it was me who glanced back at the bath, just to remind him. 'Yeah, OK, he did. While the tramp was sleepin'. That man had dishonoured the gang, made fools of us.'

'Was it *you* who actually used the matches and methylated spirit?'

There was a pleading expression in his eyes. 'I didn't want to, mistah, honest! I was in Rashid's bad books. He said I hadn't yet proved myself in the eyes of Allah. He said doing this would prove I was a worthy Muslim, an Islamic warrior. Otherwise I wouldn't get to go for trainin' an' that.'

'Training where? With who?'

'I don't know. In Pakistan. Or this place called Yemen, or somethin'. Is that in Pakistan?'

I decided it was a waste of time to give him a geography

lesson. 'So why did you go to Jock's funeral this morning? Did Rashid really order you to go?'

Kamran Ali sighed and nodded. 'He wanted to know what was happening, who was there. But I volunteered to go.'

'Why?'

'To make my peace with him.'

'With Jock.'

Another nod of the head.

'Because what you did was wrong?'

He glanced across at the bath. 'Yes.'

I'd heard enough. I had what I wanted. I turned the camera off, snapped the phone shut and dropped it into my pocket.

Grabbing his arm, I pulled him towards the door. The two young girls were crouching at the top of the stairs, staring towards me in terror.

I forced a smile. 'Nothing to worry about, girls. Nothing to fear.' I looked at Ali. 'Which is your room?'

'This one here.' He pushed the door open. It was a scene of adolescent chaos. An unmade bed, football posters on the wall, and DVDs scattered amongst the dirty clothing left all over the floor.

'Get those wet things off,' I ordered. 'Put some dry stuff on. You've got four minutes . . . I'm counting.'

He went to close the door. 'Leave that!' I snapped. 'And don't go near your laptop or any telephones.' And I certainly wasn't going to let him get out of the window or shimmy down a drainpipe.

Ali's terror-driven quick change must have taken all of a

record three minutes. When he re-emerged, I propelled him to the top of the stairs. The two girls stood aside as we went past and started our descent.

We'd nearly reached the bottom step when the front door opened.

The couple stared at me and their son and I stared back at them. They were both short and in their fifties. He had a greying beard, wore glasses and a laced prayer cap. A collarless white shirt showed beneath a modest dark jacket. His wife was plump, her figure disguised with a long-flowing and colourful dress and a headscarf.

The man quickly found his voice. He blinked rapidly and tried to hide his fear. 'And *who* are you?'

I smiled with reassurance. 'I'm making a citizen's arrest of your son. He's been a bad boy. Don't worry, I'm not going to hurt anyone.'

Mr Kamran frowned. 'But I *am* worried. My daughter phones me to say that a stranger has burst into our house and has dragged my son upstairs. They were terrified! So *what* is your name, who *are* you?'

'My name is Dave Aston and I'm the friend of a man who was murdered here in Swinthorpe a few weeks ago. Someone set fire to him on a park bench.'

'The tramp?' Mrs Kamran piped up. 'I was reading about it. And it was on the television.'

'What has this to do with us?' her husband demanded.

'Allow me to explain,' I said in the most reassuring voice I could find.

In an uneasy silence, the couple sat down on the settee and

we stood in front of them. I pressed the play button and handed them the smartphone.

Ali's parents watched the replay in deathly silence, the cold light of the screen highlighting their features.

When it was finished I took the phone from them. Mrs Kamran looked up at her son. 'Is this true, Ali?'

The teenager said nothing, just nodded and hung his head.

His father shook his head sadly. After a pause he looked at his son and said, 'I am going to call the police.'

'Good,' I said. 'It'll save me the trouble.'

It didn't exactly go as I had planned.

A male detective sergeant called Butler and his uniformed custody sergeant took barely five minutes before deciding to arrest me. I was charged with a litany of offences. It didn't all register, but it included breaking and entering, aggravated burglary and grievous bodily harm. I think attempted kidnap for ransom might also have been in there somewhere.

I was put alone in a police cell, given a plastic mug of cold tea and left to cool my heels.

It was about two thirty when the door opened. DC Jane Christy entered with the custody sergeant who had actually arrested me. She sat down on the bench and removed her hat.

She placed it on the cushion between us. 'You missed a good wake, Mr Aston. The prawn vol-au-vents were delicious. It was all really very moving.'

I said, 'I'm pleased. Glad you enjoyed yourself.'

Christy's face was expressionless. She reached into the

pocket of her trenchcoat and extracted a smartphone. 'Is this yours, Mr Aston?'

The detective seemed so cold and distant now, so different from when we'd been listening to Edwina's life story a few days earlier. I said, 'Call me, Dave.'

She didn't blink. 'Is this yours, Dave?'

'Yes.' I hesitated. 'Well, no, actually it belongs to the lad. Kamran Ali.'

'So do we add *theft* to the list?'

I smiled. 'It's not stolen. You've got it . . . More important, have you examined it? Have you seen that little scrote's confession?'

It was Christy's turn to smile, although there didn't seem to be much humour in those narrowed cat's eyes of hers. 'Yes, I saw what passed for a confession. My boss, DI Ryan, has seen it, too.'

'Good,' I said, happy that things were starting to move. 'And what did *he* think?'

'Dave, can you explain to me why, on the little film clip, young Ali is so *wet*? Not just wet, but dripping. His clothes, his hair and face. He looked petrified.'

With a sudden sense of dread, I realised where she might be coming from. 'We were in the bathroom.'

'You tried to drown him?'

'No, certainly not. I just wanted him to tell the truth.'

'That's not what Ali says. He says he only told you what you wanted to hear. That was because you attempted to drown him. What did you call it in Iraq, "water-boarding"?'

I shifted uncomfortably. 'It wasn't *exactly* like that.'

'I would hope not. I'd hate to think of Swinthorpe being twinned with Guantánamo Bay.' She took a deep breath and looked directly at me. 'Have you got a cigarette, Dave?'

I pulled the tin from my pocket, then glanced up at the forbidding sign on the wall.

She waved a hand. 'Sod that, Dave. I've managed without for three weeks now.' Our eyes met again. 'You've broken me.'

The custody sergeant shook his head in a show of slow despair as he watched Christy take my roll-up. Nevertheless he offered her a light as my Bic had been taken off me when I'd been charged.

She exhaled, long and slow. At last, she said, 'I know you meant well, Dave. But you *haven't* got a confession. Even the words don't add up. You're an amateur, for goodness' sake. Now Ali denies everything he said, claiming he was tortured, tricked and bullied. He may be a bit of a dunce, but he's not stupid.' She took a deep breath and studied the tip of her cigarette. 'You however . . .'

'Ali killed Jock,' I insisted. '*He* was the one, acting on Rashid's orders. He admitted it.'

She smiled and placed her hand on my wrist. 'Dave, I realise that. But you've now blown any chance of a conviction out of the water. You tortured the confession out of him – at least, that's how the CPS or any court will view it. Even my boss, Ryan, who can be a bit right of Genghis Khan, waved it away.'

I fell back against the wall. 'So Bernie Bramshaw is right. You're not doing anything to stop these people. Your hearts just aren't in it.'

Jane Christy ignored that. 'Look, Dave, if you ever want to bring these people to justice, you have to do so using *legal* methods, and collect *real* evidence. Anything else, and *you* are more likely to end up in prison than them.'

'Legal methods,' I echoed, 'real evidence.'

She sucked again on her cigarette, inhaling deeply. 'The good news for you is that young Kamran Ali has spoken to his solicitors. He will not press charges or give evidence. Nor will his parents. Inspector Ryan has decided you can go.'

It took a moment for the words to sink in. I climbed slowly to my feet. 'I caught Jock's killer. I got a confession.'

Christy smiled tightly. 'I'm sorry, Dave. It's just not enough.'

'*Legal* methods,' I repeated. '*Real* evidence?'

She just smiled and nodded sympathetically.

Anger was building inside my head like a thunderstorm, until it felt that my skull would split. Under my breath, I murmured, 'If that's what you need, then that's what you'll get.'

I was aware of her eyes on my back as I left the police station.

# Nineteen

'So you were the one who was arrested?' Gem was incredulous.

The next day, I had finished making the day's sandwiches when she joined me at one of the outside tables for a cigarette.

'And Ali didn't want to press charges?' she asked.

I shook my head. 'No – on his solicitor's advice. You know why?'

'Because you could bring up his confession in court? Say about him having killed Jock?'

I grunted. 'Well, I might try, but I don't expect I'd get that far. You know what judges and lawyers are like.'

'Not really.' She stubbed out her cigarette in the tin ashtray. 'But it all seems very unfair.'

I stared out at the river where a flotilla of swans was competing with the ducks for scraps thrown by tourists. 'I can't see that anyone's likely to be convicted. Both Jock and Ginger were just considered down-and-outs. I don't think anyone really cares.'

'But we do, Dave, don't we?' She put her hand on my forearm. 'What are we going to do about it?'

'We?' I echoed.

'Yes, well . . . you, anyway.'

Yesterday, in the heat of the moment, I'd pledged to avenge the deaths of my two friends. I had decided I'd employ the sort of tactics we might have used in the SAS. Full-on surveillance. Now it didn't seem such a clever idea. I had virtually no money, no equipment, no team, no backup and no transport.

Thinking aloud, I said, 'A bicycle would be useful.'

'A what?'

'A bicycle.'

'For what?'

'For surveillance, following people.' I could just visualise it. In Swinthorpe centre it would be ideal. 'Maybe I could nick one.'

'That's *not* a good idea, Dave.' She smiled and shook her head. 'But I could lend you one.'

'*You?*'

'Well, it's not actually mine. Steve bought it last Christmas. A sort of macho mountain bike. Part of his keep fit campaign that never happened. He never even took it out of my house.'

The idea appealed. And with a mountain bike, at least I wouldn't be peddling around like some district nurse out of an Agatha Christie whodunnit. 'Gem, that sounds like a great idea.'

That afternoon I visited a discount clothes shop and, with my meagre accrued earnings, bought a selection of three jogging bottoms and 'hoody' tops in grey, black and dark blue, all of which could be interchangeable. I then purchased some cheap trainers, sunglasses, and a mobile phone on pay-as-you-go for thirty pounds.

That evening I collected the sturdy mountain bike from Gem's place and began the wobbly process of relearning what they say you never forget! After another night in a new and obscure location, way off the beaten track, I could barely wait for my morning's work in the cafe to finish.

With demand for the sandwiches increasing rapidly, along with my earnings, it was now at least ten in the morning before I finished production. Leaving my bergen in a kitchen cupboard, I donned my shades and hooded top, before setting off on the mountain bike for Ali's family house.

Of course, I was at a distinct disadvantage. I didn't know if the youngster was at home or out with his gang. I dragged the bike off the road at the top of the street and sat astride it, parked in the shade.

Nothing. Minutes passed, then hours. His parents came back, loaded down with bags of shopping. Twilight came, and then nightfall. Cold, aching and hungry I continued to wait. I wasn't as tough as I used to be. I'd had enough. At ten, I decided to get a cheeseburger and chips, then head for my latest home, this time in a multistorey car park.

As I headed off down the high street I saw Ali returning home, coming from the town centre and hunched against the north-easterly wind. I couldn't help wondering just what the hell he might have been up to.

There was one good thing. He didn't see me, let alone recognise me. He didn't even look up when I cycled past on the damp and deserted high street. He was about as sharp as a chocolate knife.

*       *       *

The next day I arrived at the cafe an hour early, worked like a demon, and had finished by eight thirty. I was aware of Lexi Simitis watching me, a slightly concerned expression on her face. I was working much, much faster. Hopefully the quality of the sandwich-making was as good as always, but as a result I would be losing money.

From my point of view, the important thing was that I arrived at Rosebury Street just before nine o'clock. Druggies like Ali normally tended to work late and sleep late. This morning he was up relatively early. He was unshaven and yawning as he started his journey into town. It struck me that his stride was unusually purposeful.

He appeared totally unaware of his phantom shadow, a cyclist in indistinct hoody and shades, cruising silently in his wake.

When he reached Coronation Gardens, the reason for his sense of urgency became clear. The Swords of Allah had taken over the children's play area, its members seated on the swings and roundabout, smoking and talking among themselves. I counted seventeen of them, with more arriving every few moments. Their ages varied from around sixteen to late twenties. Virtually all wore hoods or woollen hats.

A group of mothers with prams and toddlers stood near the entrance gate, looking on with clear irritation. None of them had the inclination to confront the gang, which had hijacked the playground.

I cycled past to the public toilet block nearby. Wheeling my bike into one of the cubicles, I bolted the door. It was a squeeze, but I wasn't at all sure how safe my only mode of transport would be if I left it outside, even for a few minutes. Hopping onto the seat, I had a clear view of the play area through the slatted glass of the window.

Moments later, Rashid strode into view. Beside him walked the gormless Amir, who I'd last seen in a picture on the front page of the *Journal*, hooked up on a railing outside Tesco. Two new heavies had replaced the ones I'd hospitalised. They walked a few steps behind, alert and swaggering in the wake of their boss.

One of the mothers seemed to realise he was the leader and approached Rashid, blocking his path.

'I've seen you here before!' she challenged. 'Is this your gang of hooligans?'

The lofty Rashid looked down at her with an air of disdain. 'What are you talking about, woman?'

For a moment she glared back up at those anthracite eyes and glossy black hair. She seemed to pale and her voice wavered. 'This is a children's playground.'

His lips twisted into a smirk. 'These are children . . . just a bit older.'

'It's intimidating. Your – er – friends are frightening them.'

Amir giggled. 'I think they are frightening *you*.'

The woman stood her ground. 'Unless you go away,' she threatened, 'I'll call the police.'

'And just what do you think they'll do?' Rashid replied in a smooth, quiet voice.

One of his new bodyguards stepped forward. 'Piss off, lady. Or I'll break your little girl's fuckin' legs for her.'

Rashid raised a hand. 'That's enough.'

A small girl clutched at her mother's coat and stared up at the worried-looking grown-ups.

'I'll call the police,' the woman repeated defiantly.

Rashid smiled sweetly. 'You do that, madam, if you think it will make any difference.'

Amir leaned forward. 'And, remember, we'll soon find out where you live.'

The mother sneered. 'Oh, yeah . . .'

'And your daughter looks like she's at . . . maybe her first year at school? Not many junior schools around here.' Amir raised his mobile telephone and, using the camera function, took a snap of the little girl. 'One for my album.'

The bodyguard leaned forward again, until his face was mere inches from the woman's. 'Like I said, missus, piss off!'

It was game, set and match to Rashid's thugs.

The brave mother scurried away and rejoined the other women and their children, who were already pulling back.

Rashid strode into the play area and scrambled up onto the roundabout. He was a naturally commanding figure and all his followers immediately stopped talking and looked in his direction.

'I've called you today because those white tossers, Jak Twomey's gang, have sent word they want a powwow with us. Looks like he wants to discuss the turf round Swinthorpe. Like he don't like the competition from us.' There was a murmur from the audience who watched on in rapt admiration. Rashid was getting into his stride: 'My guess is they want to agree with us to carve up the turf. And who do you think will want the lion's share – just 'cos they claim they was here first!'

A low growl of disapproval came from the gang members.

Amir, who stood on the ground in front of him, punched the air with his first. 'We will tell them what we think of that! Just because we are Muslim they think they can taunt us and degrade us! We have an answer to that! *Allahu Akbar!*'

'*ALLAHU AKBAR!*' the audience dutifully responded.

Rashid continued, 'We will meet Twomey here at nine o'clock tonight. Here, on *our* own turf. We will show them the reality of who is in control. You will all be here by nine o'clock this evening. Your crew leaders will text you with your individual orders . . . Now you can all dismiss except for our three crew leaders. I want you to remain behind to discuss our strategy and tactics for tonight. *Inshallah!*'

Dutifully the group dispersed, chatting excitedly in small groups while three older members hung back, waiting to join Rashid and his senior cohorts. They gathered together on the roundabout, their voices lowered as they debated their plans in earnest.

I was able to hear nothing more from then on.

I struggled to get my mountain bike out of the cubicle and then began my wobbly ride across the park towards Swinthorpe Police Station.

It was just my luck to find WPC Sharon Sharman on the front desk. 'Mr Aston, isn't it? I didn't recognise you with the hood and sunglasses.'

I couldn't resist it. 'That's the general idea,' I replied.

But my words flew over her head. 'So how can I help you?'

'Is it possible to speak to DC Christy?'

'She's not in.'

'At lunch?'

'No, the dentist. She won't be in until tomorrow.' Her rose-bud mouth puckered into a reluctant smile. 'Can I help you – or PC Tiddy?'

Of all the cops in all the world . . . The station seemed to teem with officers, the numbers having swollen over the years to match the town's growth. So it was my turn for the reluctant smile. 'Er, I don't think so. What about Inspector Ryan?'

'Is it important?'

'I think so – otherwise I wouldn't be here.'

'Would you like to tell me about it?'

'Not really. I'd like to speak to Tony Ryan.'

'The inspector's in a meeting. He may be a while.'

'I'll wait.'

'I'll tell him as soon as he comes out.'

I sat down in the empty lobby reception and began my long wait. One hour passed, and then another. One by one the seats in the waiting area filled up. Another couple of hours ticked by.

Suddenly the large figure of Inspector Ryan burst into reception without warning. His grey eyes narrowed as I stood up and offered my hand. 'Mr Aston,' he said, but there was no enthusiasm in his greeting. 'What can I do for you?' He made it sound as though doing something for me was the last thing he wanted to do.

I said, 'Hopefully, it's what I can do for you.'

'Oh yes, and what's that?'

I glanced around at the semicircle of faces. 'Perhaps we could talk somewhere a little more private.'

'What? Oh, yes, I suppose so.' He didn't bother hiding his irritation. 'Follow me.'

He led the way out, past the desk, to the interview rooms. He ushered me into one of them.

'Right, Mr Aston,' he said as he took a seat on one side of the only desk in the room. 'Let's make this snappy. It's been a busy day.'

I took the opposite chair. 'In Swinthorpe?'

'Things do *happen* sometimes, Mr Aston,' he grunted, barely able to bring himself to look at me, 'believe it or not.'

I said, 'Well, something is happening tonight. There's going to be a meeting between the two major drug gangs. The Chip Shop Boys—'

'Jak Twomey and his shower?'

I nodded. 'With the Swords of Allah.'

'Who?'

'The Muslim gang who killed Jock and supplied Ginger.'

'Yeah, yeah . . .' He dismissed my words with an irritable wave of his hand. 'The Rosebury Street louts. Don't dignify them with fancy names, Mr Aston. They're all just pond life, maggots.'

I said, 'The maggots are meeting tonight. Nine o'clock in Coronation Gardens. I think a turf war is starting. I've a feeling it could get nasty.'

Ryan stroked his chin as he contemplated me for a few long moments. 'Do you now, Mr Aston? And do you think I'm worried if these two sets of lowlifes beat the hell out of each other? Mutual assured destruction would be the perfect answer.'

'But it's never clean like that,' I replied testily. 'Swinthorpe could end up like a mini-Manchester.'

There was a slight pause before Ryan asked, 'How did you find out about this?'

'Surveillance.'

'So you had a camera and microphone?' He smirked. 'Like when you were in the SAS?'

'I had eyes and ears,' I replied testily. 'And a mouth that's quite capable of giving evidence.'

Without warning, he rose to his feet. 'Well, Mr Aston, I've seen quite enough of your evidence gaining techniques. I appreciate your information about tonight and I'll brief our street patrols accordingly. I'm sure they'll keep a lookout for any trouble.' He paused. 'But just a word of advice. I know it's difficult – Afghanistan and all that – but try and let go of your obsession with these Muslim boys.'

I replied sharply, 'It's nothing to do with Afghanistan. This is about my hometown.'

Ryan clearly felt he'd spent enough of his valuable time on me. Impatiently, he called on WPC Sharman to show me out. His final words were, 'Remember what I said, Mr Aston.'

Minutes later, as I cycled hurriedly back across town, I found myself seething at how I had just wasted so much of the day.

I was in a bad and un-talkative mood as I washed up back at the cafe. I was even grumpy with Gem when she tried to make conversation. Of course, I could see Inspector Ryan's point. I wasn't doing myself any favours in getting obsessed by Rashid and his gang. But now I knew there was likely to be some kind of showdown that evening, I couldn't resist the temptation to observe whatever was going to happen.

There are no gates to Coronation Gardens and I was able to enter them by cycling straight across the lawns from the nearby pavement. I avoided the criss-crossed web of tarmac footpaths and kept to the shadows cast by the many stands of trees and beds of ornamental shrubs.

I approached the kiddies' playground from behind the toilet block. To my irritation it had been firmly locked and bolted for the night. But then I found two large municipal wheelie bins parked at the back of the building. Hiding my bicycle and bergen behind them, I used the saddle as a foot-hold to climb up onto one of the bins. That gave me access to a metal downpipe, which allowed me to scramble onto the flat roof.

I had a perfect view of the playground and a ventilation pod to use for cover.

My timing turned out to be perfect. I'd barely settled down when the first of Rashid's gang members started to arrive. The face of my watch told me it was just turned eight-thirty.

It occurred to me that if the Chip Chop Boys had been a bit sharper they, too, might have arrived earlier to recce the scene of the rendezvous with their archrivals. As it was, Rashid had it all his own way. Every couple of minutes, more of his followers turned up. As I'd learned earlier that day, the gang's hierarchy comprised three crew leaders who acted as gangmasters to three sub-groups. Within minutes they had dispersed into the surrounding darkness. I heard some of them below me in the shadow of the toilet block, talking in whispers. I caught the distinct smell of cannabis smoke.

Rashid, Ali and his two bodyguards sprawled nonchalantly on the kiddies' merry-go-round, idly pushing it back and forth.

A woman wandered in off the edge of the road and sat on a bench. She was in view of the playground, but also any passers-by. The skin-tight red skirt and black patterned tights said more than any advertising billboard. She lit a cigarette and waited for the night's business to begin.

It was exactly nine o'clock when I became aware of the approach of the rival gang. Their excited, high-pitched conversation was interspersed with nervous laughter. It sounded like there were quite a number. I counted fifteen as they emerged into the arena of light cast from the nearest street lamp.

Jak Twomey strode along the footpath at the head of his gang, which was spread out behind him. Clearly the leader, he was tall like Rashid, maybe even taller by an inch or so. But, in contrast, he was very thin and looked decidedly undernourished. I imagined he was probably hyperactive and lived on a diet of narcotics, burgers and KFC – without the salad.

His shoulders were also badly hunched in the hooded top he wore, hands thrust deep inside the pockets of his jogging bottoms. A large, spiky nose and dark little raisin eyes peered out from under the peak of a baseball cap.

Despite his slightly goofy look, there was something about him that demanded attention. He was a leader of sorts, and I got the feeling that violence and cruelty would mean little to him.

His younger brother, Aaron, suddenly skateboarded into my peripheral vision, and glided up to him. He skidded to a dramatic halt.

'What gives, bruv?' I just made out from Twomey.

'Careful, Jak,' the youngster warned ominously. 'I think it might be a—'

A teenager's car, with blasting hi-fi and souped up exhaust, rattled past on the nearby road. I missed the exact words.

Twomey shrugged and smiled, confident.

I was certain Aaron's older brother had been warned that he could be walking into an ambush or some type of trap. But he was cool, laid back. Almost horizontal. He muttered something and the four older youths behind him moved away, fanning out to offer three-sixty degrees of cover as they reached the kiddies' playground.

Rashid shifted from the roundabout, his inner group of followers turning to face the arrival of the Chip Shop Boys in the dim ambient light.

The Asian gang leader raised his hand. 'Jak,' he acknowledged. 'It's been a time.'

Jak Twomey took a tobacco tin from the pocket of his jogging top and plucked out a roll-up. 'Smoke?'

Rashid shook his head.

'So this is business, not pleasure.' It was a statement, not a question.

'This is not your hometown, right?' Twomey began.

Quietly, Rashid answered. 'It is now.'

Twomey sneered. 'Yeah, now . . . but not always. We is the born and bred in Swinthorpe. Generations, yeah? My dad, his dad . . . Our dads' dads. Get me? You understand that?'

Rashid nodded. 'Of course.' His voice was quiet and calm.

Twomey looked satisfied, and lit his roll-up with a plastic lighter. 'So you come lately, yeah?'

Rashid did not blink. 'So what?'

'Then that's settled. We understand you must earn a living. We're not unreasonable. And we don't want no trouble, 'cos that's just plain stupid and no one wins. 'Cept the filth.'

Rashid nodded without a word.

Twomey continued, 'So we will offer you some quarter of the trade in this parish, yeah?'

'How do you propose to do that?' Rashid asked.

'Simple, bro'. We know this parish inside out, where the trade is. You have Rosebury Street, and the riverbank. We have the rest of Evinmore estate and the town centre. We'll draw up lines, make it easy.'

Rashid shook his head slowly. 'You ever heard of free enterprise, Jak?'

'Sure.'

'Like competition, like in the United States. Well, that's what you *got* here now – like it or not! End of story.'

Twomey looked as though he'd been slapped around the face.

The Asian gang leader raised his hand. I had to admit that the effect was good. On the unspoken command, figures slowly began emerging from the darkness. A few came from the bushes behind Rashid, some from the left of the playground and some from the right. Those who had been hiding behind the toilet block also advanced.

I saw Twomey swallow hard. They were encircled by probably more than twice their number. I squinted to see knives or machetes or even baseball bats. There were none, but the gang still looked mean and ready for action.

The circle closed in. Twomey tilted up the peak of his baseball cap with his thumb. Clearly it was a signal.

His four minders, covering three-sixty degrees of the gang's position, produced their hardware. Street light glinted on black gunmetal.

I couldn't be certain at that distance, but they looked like old Czech Skorpions with the folding stocks removed. Not the newest, but still deadly.

There was a low but distinctly audible gasp. Suddenly, the threatening circle stopped closing. As the weapons pointed there was a tense silence. If those Skorpions went off, there would be carnage.

Then I started to hear the faint backward shuffle of trainers on the grass as the members of the Swords of Allah slowly backed away.

# Twenty

'You had your offer, Rashid,' Jak Twomey said. 'You had your chance. Now it's withdrawn. You don't operate here no more. Get me?'

The Asian stood calmly in the playground as his followers melted away into the shadows. 'Don't threaten me, Jak. You and your people will be sorry, I promise you that.'

In my peripheral vision I saw that the hooker was standing up, moving away as she spoke on her mobile phone. I wondered vaguely if she'd got herself a punter.

Meanwhile Twomey ignored Rashid's warning. He continued, 'As from now we reclaim Coronation Gardens. Any of your scum found doing business here – or anywhere else in town – will be shot. And don't think we are afraid to pull the trigger. If you wanna trade, sure – but some place else. Not Swinthorpe, get me?'

Carefully and deliberately, Rashid gathered saliva in his mouth and spat at Twomey's feet. Behind him his young brother Aaron and his two new minders shifted awkwardly. I guessed they were worried they might have to pay the sacrifice for their leader's brave words.

One of the Skorpions swung in Rashid's direction.

Just then, the high-pitched *eye-ore* scream of a police car siren tore through the quiet night air. I caught sight of the pulsing blue lights.

The brave protagonists on both sides broke away from each other like a starburst, all running in different directions.

Two police cars pulled up at the edge of the gardens, doors flying open. As the uniformed officers ran forward the prostitute left the park bench. She was on her feet, wearing impossibly high heels. She still had the mobile phone in her hand as she pointed her finger. 'That way, boys!' she yelled.

I dropped down off the toilet-block roof onto the lid of a wheelie bin, then onto the mountain bike. I threw back my hood before pedalling across to the prostitute.

I had wondered if she was some sort of police informer. It took a long moment before the penny dropped and I recognised DC Jane Christy.

'Good Lord,' I said. 'I thought . . .'

She smiled tightly. 'I'm a woman of many parts. And no, this isn't my day job. I've heard all those jokes before.'

'Just undercover then?'

Her eyes followed the police officers disappearing into the darkness. 'I don't think they'll have much luck.'

I said, 'At least you seem to have broken up a possible major scrap between the two gangs.'

Another plain-clothes cop had joined her. 'Hardly *West Side Story*,' the man said.

Christy glanced sideways at him. 'You've already met DS Sam Butler.'

'Didn't know your name,' I said as I shook hands with the police sergeant.

'Likes his musicals,' Christy added.

Butler was short and stocky with a flat face that was the colour of pale gammon. He wore an old-fashioned duffel coat and had no hat on his shaven head. 'Now, what were the gangs in that called?' he asked.

'Sharks and Jets,' I helped out.

'That's right! How times have changed,' Butler muttered. 'What's it now? – Swords of Allah . . . and the Chip Shop Boys. Wasn't that a pop group?'

I said to Christy, 'I didn't think Inspector Ryan was going to do anything about this meeting.'

'He wasn't.' She turned to Butler. 'You got a spare ciggie, Sam?'

He frowned at her. 'I've given up. Six weeks now. So should you.'

'Piss off, Sam. I have. I'm just having a relapse.'

'Another one?' Butler asked.

I jerked the tobacco tin out of my jacket pocket. 'Will a roll-up do?'

She peered down at them. 'Very neat.' Plucking one from the tin, she accepted the flame from my lighter. 'Ryan left a message that you'd called and had given the information about tonight. He thinks the drugs scene here is a lost cause, so he's now delegated it to me.'

'Good thing, too,' Butler said. 'Otherwise nothing would have got done. You said they had guns?'

'The IC1s did,' Christy replied. 'About three or four. Bigger than handguns. But I don't know what type.'

'Skorpions,' I offered. 'Czech-made. Technically, they're a

machine-pistol. 7.65mm. Like a small SMG.' She looked puzzled, so I added, 'They're like small sub-machine guns. And the Muslims didn't appear to have firearms.'

She nodded her agreement. 'But I'm sure the IC4s had knives and stuff. I thought you might have called up CO19.'

Sam Butler smiled to himself. 'Pre-disposed at the time required. Their night for target practice, or some such.' He glanced at his watch. 'Better call off my dogs before one of them decides to win a gallantry medal and gets himself shot.'

The detective sergeant wandered back towards the police cars as he talked on his radio.

Christy exhaled a long stream of smoke and said, 'Without Sam nothing would have got done. He's very supportive. Loves this town, like I do.'

'We all do,' I added.

'And where were you when all this was going on? I didn't see you.'

I inclined my head. 'On top of the lavatory block.'

'Don't let Sam hear you say that. He'll do you for importuning. He's a total homophobe and hates drugs.' Her lips parted in a kink of a smile. 'Apart from that, he's pretty well balanced for a copper.'

I returned her smile. 'Whatever – I'm glad he gave his support. The situation could have got nasty.'

Out-of-breath uniformed officers were starting to emerge from the shadows, moving towards us.

She said, 'We couldn't have done it without you, Dave. Just promise me you'll take care.'

'I will.'

'I've heard rumours that Rashid is still looking for you. He's put a price on your head. Two thousand pounds.'

Somehow I hadn't been expecting that, and her words sent an involuntary shiver down my spine. I laughed it off. 'Is that all?'

She gave me a disapproving look. 'Have you got a place yet?'

I shook my head. 'I'm not earning enough. I'll need at least seventy a week for a small room.'

She said, 'I've heard a new hostel's opening next month. On Monmouth Street. Bed and breakfast only. I could put a word in for you.'

I didn't want to seem ungrateful. 'Thanks,' I said, but we both knew there was no enthusiasm in my voice.

We parted company and I cycled back across Coronation Gardens towards the city centre. While my natural inclination was to find a pitch alone to sleep, Christy's warning that Rashid had actually put a price on my head was still a bit unsettling. I decided, for once, to go to an area where Lady Penelope liked to sleep. It was popular with other down-and-outs and I reasoned that there should be safety in numbers. But I'm not sure I had really convinced myself.

The covered rear entrance of the carpet warehouse was on the other side of town. It provided shelter from both wind and rain. As it backed onto a railway embankment, it was also unobservable from any road. That allowed the occupants to have a brazier burning on winter nights without any complaints from nearby residents.

The fitful flames cast long dancing shadows around the concrete cavern as I drew up on my cycle and dismounted.

'Who the *fuck*'s this?' came an angry voice from the inner gloom.

I slipped the bergen off my shoulders and dumped it on the floor. 'Hi,' I said, peering at the row of pale, indistinct faces. 'Is it OK, if I stay here?'

A huge figure emerged from the darkness. He was a good seven feet tall with a halo of wild black hair and a long beard. He was clad in a long, dark greatcoat that just served to emphasise his height. Dark, crazed eyes glowered down at me from below bushy brows. It was as though he'd been called to play Samson straight out of Central Casting.

'You are army man!!' he bellowed accusingly, as he glared at my DPM trousers. 'I kill you! I do war crimes, so you do not scare me! I kill you!'

Involuntarily I took a backward step.

At that moment, Edwina's voice rose imperiously to my defence. 'Do shut up, Manni. This is a friend of mine.'

Manni bent down and squinted at me. 'You? Friend of hers?'

I nodded. 'I'm Dave.'

The giant now had an expression of incomprehension.

Edwina appeared beside him. 'Out the way, Manni. Thank you for protecting us, but you can take it too far sometimes.' She turned towards me. 'What are you doing here, Dave?'

'A change of scenery.'

'Good thing, too. You'll be much safer here. You saw what happened . . .' She suddenly realised that she hardly had to remind me about Jock. 'Come with me.'

I shouldered my bergen and followed her with my bike to a far corner of the concrete cave. 'Who's Manni?' I asked. 'Jewish? He sounds Slavic.'

She gave a snort of laughter. 'I don't know if he's Jewish. He's from Manchester. Says he lived in Serbia. Don't know how he got here or why he's allowed to stay.'

I glanced back. 'He's a bit . . . mmm . . . volatile.'

'You'll find the word you're looking for is *volcanic*.' She giggled. 'We get no trouble from *anyone* when he's around. He'll go off on one, then a few minutes later he'll be fast asleep like a babe. Suffers from some weird disorder.'

We came to her supermarket trolley with her bedding laid out beside it. 'There's a space here. It doesn't catch the rain and it doesn't smell of dog's pee.'

'Thanks,' I said, leaning my bicycle against the wall.

'I've already eaten, I'm afraid,' she said apologetically. 'But I do have a little gin.'

I dumped my bergen. 'I do have a flask of hot tea.'

She looked taken aback. 'Dear boy, I do believe you've turned the corner.'

I smiled. 'Maybe. But which one?'

At that moment my recently purchased mobile rang. No one ever called me, so the sudden noise made me jump. I glanced down at the screen. It was Sally.

'Hi, Sal.'

'Dave? You OK?'

'I'm fine. You and Daisy?'

'Yes.'

I hated this sort of conversation.

'That's all right then,' she continued. 'I wouldn't have troubled you, but Duffy's here. You know, Brian Duffy. Your sergeant.'

My smile was involuntary. 'Yes, I know who you mean.'

'He's here. He called to see if I had a number for you. I hope that's all right?'

'Sure,' I said. 'I'll speak to the old bastard.'

'I'll put him on . . . Brian, it's Dave . . .'

'Hello, boss. How you doin'?'

'I'm OK. And you?'

'All this truck drivin' is drivin' me bonkers, but apart from that . . . I've got someone with me. He just turned up at me door.'

I don't know why, but immediately a picture of Charles Houseman, with his smarmy charm and crinkly blond hair, flashed in my mind. 'Who?'

'The little Injun fella, Ravi, remember? With us on your last mission.'

I clearly recalled the smart operator and linguist from the Special Reconnaissance Regiment. He'd been a regular and welcome visitor when I'd been hospitalised for months at Selly Oak. At the beginning in Afghanistan, I'd thought of him as just another sharp spook working alongside House-man. Although Ravi and I had got on well, I still wasn't entirely sure how far I'd really trust any of the intelligence mob.

'Ravi's Sri Lankan,' I corrected flatly.

A new voice came on the phone. 'I'm *British*, Dave. My *parents* are from Sri Lanka.'

I heard Duffy push him away. 'Well, boss, wherever he's from, he turned up here and forced me to go out for a drink with him. Says he'd like to meet up. You know, a few jars for old times.'

The thought of 'old times' was the last thing I needed. I was trying to start a new life. I had enough on my plate just now with my latest friends – and enemies. It suddenly seemed as though my past was trying to catch up with me, surrounding me, smothering me.

I began to sweat. 'Look, Brian, I'm sorry. Some other time.' I switched off.

'Everything all right?' Edwina asked.

'Sure.'

'Fancy a tipple of that gin. I've got some orange juice.'

I raised an eyebrow. 'Do they go together?'

Edwina giggled and produced two plastic beakers from one of her shopping bags. 'Dear boy, when times are hard, *anything* goes together.'

The next morning, I worked furiously and had finished preparing all the sandwiches by eight thirty. I was painfully aware that I was working myself out of a decent living wage.

Before I left, Gem phoned to say she wouldn't be in because of morning sickness again. Andreas was none too pleased, especially when I said I wouldn't be able to help out and fill in for her.

At least it meant that I was away on my bicycle and had reached the top of Ali's road at nine o'clock. I pulled up my hood, lit a cigarette and waited.

It was just as well, because he was up a little earlier than usual. A white Ford Escort with a fancy spoiler and go-faster livery pulled up outside his family home. An air horn blasted out a brief anthem that would have woken anyone trying to have a lie-in that morning. Ali emerged, shoulders hunched, and slid into the rear passenger seat. It was over-filled with other gang members, its suspension dangerously low. Mesmerising hip-hop music blasted from the car's speakers and the engorged chromium exhaust outlet burbled as the car pulled away.

I let fly after it, speeding down the hill towards the city centre. I cursed as I pedalled like fury, losing my quarry several times on the journey into town. At least I did eventually manage to catch up each time. For once I was grateful for the 'job lot' of traffic lights the council had recently purchased – clearly designed to bring total gridlock to the town centre.

The Escort eventually pulled up outside Swinthorpe College on the far side of town, where three of its passengers spilled out. One of them was Ali.

They crossed the busy arterial road to a car park that mostly served staff and pupils at the college. Because it was surrounded on all sides by earth embankments and high shrubs, it was also popular with drug dealers.

To my surprise, Ali and his two mates split up and moved surreptitiously into position behind some trees. They appeared to be waiting for someone.

The first person to emerge from the car park was Jak Twomey. Those hunched shoulders and the slightly comical swagger to his gait were unmistakable. His two minders, who had been armed the previous night, were walking close behind him. All the time, his younger brother Aaron circled the group on his skateboard like a frigate protecting three heavy man-o'-wars.

When they sauntered along the pavement towards town, I was expecting Ali and his two Muslim friends to follow. I don't know why, it just seemed logical. In fact the next person to emerge from the car park was Gem's boyfriend, Steve Cranford. Tall and spidery-limbed with faded spray-on denim jeans, he looked every bit as unhealthy as I remembered him.

It didn't take a genius to work out that he'd probably just scored off Jak and the Chip Shop Boys. Although he wasn't exactly running, there was an urgency in his stride. I realised he would be anxious to get back to his home and shoot up.

It was then that Ali and his two Muslim mates broke cover and started to follow Cranford. I found it amusing to watch their amateur efforts to set up a 'surveillance box', as we call it in the business. It was amusing, yet nevertheless effective, because their quarry was so intent to get home for a fix that he noticed absolutely nothing.

I let them get ahead, then settled down at a comfortable distance on my bicycle, following them following Cranford.

Because he took a shortcut with which I was unfamiliar, it came as a surprise to suddenly realise where we were heading. A pedestrian alleyway that ran between garden fences opened up onto a street of neat two-up, two-downs that had been built in the 1930s. We were in Leyton Grove, the street where Gem lived.

Turning left onto the pavement I could see Cranford waiting at the front door of her house. He was unaware of the three youths standing behind him at the gate of the tiny garden. The lawn was guarded by a line of new bush roses that I'd planted for her.

I ditched my mountain bike at the end of the alley and went forward on foot. The front door of Gem's house had opened and Cranford was stepping inside. Already the three pursuers were through the garden gate. Cranford turned, suddenly alerted to the commotion behind him. They pounced on him, pushing him in through the open door. I broke into a sprint. I'm not really sure I'd thought things through; my only concern was for the safety of Gem and her unborn child.

I leapt the low fence, in the heat of the moment completely forgetting I was disabled. However, my bad leg hadn't. The pain shot through it like a lightning bolt as I landed. I yelped in pain and collapsed onto the grass.

As I regained my senses and looked up, Ali's two minders were staring back at me from the doorway of the house. They didn't know me, and didn't know that it was me who had hospitalised their two predecessors. But Ali, of course, would never forget me after I'd water-boarded him in his own bathroom.

He pushed his way out from behind the two burly minders. He blinked in surprise. 'You bastard!' He looked at one of the minders. 'He tried to kill me! He works for the cops! He's dangerous! Smash his head in!'

The two minders exchanged glances and shrugged. Lying there, sprawled on the grass, I didn't look like much of a threat to anyone.

In truth I didn't feel like one either. But I was on the ground and vulnerable to two thugs who looked like they knew how to handle themselves. As they closed in on me, I glimpsed Cranford and Gem in the doorway behind them.

The first heavily booted foot came flying straight towards my face.

Grabbing the foot with both hands, I twisted it inwards sharply.

I heard the ligaments rip in the minder's knee and the sudden grunt of pain as he went down.

The second thug took a backward step, now wary. Ali was at his side, a knife in his hand. 'I told you he was dangerous!' he warned

The second thug smiled, showing two gold teeth. He was a big and shaven-headed brute of a man. He wore a long linen jacket over a T-shirt that had hidden most of the machete which he now drew. Its razor edge glinted dully in the grey morning light.

'Don't you worry, Ali. He's no danger to you now.'

# Twenty-One

Trying to ignore the searing pain in my leg, I struggled to my feet.

The thug was hunched low, weighing the machete in his right hand. There was a grin on his face. He was a slightly slimmer build than his downed comrade and more muscle than fat. And he looked more menacing. His eyes were dark and cold and without emotion.

Behind him I could see Gem holding on to Cranford for protection.

'Steve,' she implored, 'for God's sake *do* something!'

Cranford's face was sheet white and he was shaking. I guessed he was scared as well as still desperate for his fix.

I hunched forward, matching the thug's posture, and we began edging around his stricken comrade like two Sumo wrestlers without the nappies. Thank God for that extra few feet that kept the two of us apart. It gave me a few seconds' thinking time. If *only* I had an idea of how to disarm this brute of his machete. My leg throbbed and my mind was a blank.

Suddenly the thug spoke. I think it was because he knew he had me. I had no get-out clause and it showed in my eyes. 'My name is Saif,' he said quietly. 'You should know this, because today you are going to die. And it is only right you should know who has killed you.'

I think I murmured, 'Thanks for that, Saif,' but it may have been something less polite. We had now shuffled some three-sixty degrees around his injured comrade on the lawn.

Discretion seemed a desperately better option than a failed attempt at valour. 'Why don't you and Ali just take your friend here to hospital,' I said. I tried to make my voice sound authoritative, as though it was me holding the machete and not the other way round.

Saif smiled slightly and spat on the ground. He edged to his left, and so I edged to mine.

There was a sudden movement behind him, but his bulk hid the front door from my view. Then Cranford was there, his tall and uncoordinated frame like a demented spider as he launched an attack on Saif with one of Gem's metal kitchen chairs.

Cranford really went for it, throwing the whole strength of his weedy frame behind the effort. The chair legs struck Saif's head and broad shoulders and bounced off. But the blow had caught the man by surprise and pushed him forward. He toppled onto his mate.

I seized the opportunity and dived for the wrist of the hand that held the machete. I grabbed it with both hands and twisted, but the machete remained firmly in his grasp.

Above, just in my peripheral vision, I saw Ali slash his knife at Cranford. The blade sliced a line of dripping scarlet across his knuckles. He yelled in pain. The kitchen chair fell onto Saif's shoulders and bounced off again. His grip on the machete tightened even more.

Sweat was stinging my eyes as I wrestled with Saif on the ground. His free hand pounded at my head and my ribs. He packed a powerful punch.

Through my tear-streamed eyes I saw a vision and for a second I could have sworn I was dreaming.

He stood tall, towering above me. Magnificent against the blue sky and cloud, sun streaking through the wild grey-white hair and beard from behind him, so that he looked like a god. Maybe he was God. I heard Saif's sharp intake of breath beside me, the smell of almond lozenges nauseous to my senses.

Then the god-like giant lunged to his left. Great ham-like fists grabbed one of the inch-square stakes that supported Gem's newly planted roses. He wrenched it free of the ground. Black moist soil dripped from its shaven tip as he held it aloft. Then he struck, with huge force and a perfect aim. It went straight into Saif's bicep like a lance. The man's yell was ear splitting, the machete dropped onto the grass.

I saw someone else, dark and swarthy, jump the garden fence and snatch up the discarded weapon. My eyes narrowed, finding difficulty in distinguishing the man's darkly handsome features. For a second I thought it was another of Rashid's mob. It took a second longer for me to recognise him.

He grinned, showing perfect white teeth straight out of a Hollywood dentist's catalogue. 'Hello, Dave. So very good to see you again.' It was Ravi.

Before I could answer, Saif made a huge effort to push me off him. Ali helped the injured man to his feet. There was blood everywhere, the rose stake thrown aside. Between them, Ali and Saif collected up the fallen thug and dragged him away with them towards the gate.

The god was not a god. It was big Brian Duffy. 'Want me to call the cops, boss? Or just give 'ems a kick up their arses on their way?'

I struggled to my feet. 'No, no point. Let them go . . . God, am I glad to see you.'

Duffy grunted. 'Wouldn't think so. You's hung up on us yesterday. You's missus says she thought something was wrong. You didn't sound right.'

I asked, 'So how the hell did you find me?'

'Wasn't rocket science,' Ravi replied. 'Your wife said you were working at the Athena Cafe in town. The owner said if anyone knew where you were the lady who lives here would.' He looked over towards the door. 'And this lovely young person must be she, I assume?'

Cranford scowled.

Gem took a backward step, confused. I guessed that for a moment she thought Ravi might have been a member of Rashid's gang.

'Ravi's one of ours,' I assured. 'Used to be Special Recon Regiment.'

'Army?' Cranford asked.

Ravi noticed the man's hand. 'My God, we must stop that before you bleed to death.' He snapped a pristine white handkerchief from his pocket and applied a makeshift bandage to Cranford's hand. 'You need to see a doctor.'

'Let's get inside,' Gem said, anxiously looking up and down the street, 'before they come back. I'll make some tea.'

'Now you're talkin', lass,' Duffy said, and replaced the stake in the ground beside the rosebush. 'I could murder a cuppa.'

'I'll be mum,' Duffy offered and splashed tea into an array of unmatched tea mugs.

Ravi had been helping Cranford to get cleaned up in the upstairs bathroom. I assumed that Cranford had then managed to shoot-up his latest purchase because he seemed a lot calmer when he came back downstairs several minutes after Ravi.

As Gem joined us, I asked, 'So why did you come here, Steve? You promised DC Christy to keep away.'

He looked indignant. 'It was just to pay Gem what I owed her? Nothin' more.'

I looked at her. 'You been lending him money again?'

Her cheeks coloured. 'He's been desperate. It wasn't much. And he has been paying me back.'

I frowned. 'How'd you get the money, Steve?'

He shrugged. 'A bit of this and that, you know.'

'You mean thieving?'

'No!' he said affronted.

'Then what?'

He snarled at me. 'It's nothing to do with you. Why don't you piss off?'

Gem said, 'Steve has been paying me back, but I think he owed that Muslim gang a lot of money. That's why they followed him here.'

'I've been trying to use them white guys,' Cranford chimed in, now that Gem had stood up for him. 'Known as the Chip

Shop Boys round here. They're a bit more easy to do business with, like.'

'How much do you owe them?' I asked.

He shrugged. 'I dunno. Two, two-fifty.'

'That's a lot,' Ravi commented.

Cranford's anger flared. 'What's it to you, you Paki know-all? Never even seen you before.'

Duffy intervened. 'Then you should be damn pleased you's seen him today, young sir. Ravi an' me just saved your useless hide, I think.'

Cranford blinked, but before he could retort, Ravi said, 'You've got to get that hand seen to.'

'What's it to you?'

'I know about these things. It's bad.'

'How'd you know?'

'Afghanistan, Iraq . . . Gangrene . . . you could lose your hand, even your arm.' Ravi smiled. 'Let me call you a taxi.'

'I can't afford no taxi.'

'I'll pay.' He turned to Gem. 'Do you have a number? By the way, this tea is lovely.'

She blushed. 'Thanks so much. It's only PG.'

His teeth shone. 'And an excellent PG at that.'

Ten minutes later and we'd got rid of Cranford. Gem had insisted on going with him and invited us to call the place our own and help ourselves to lunch.

I collected my bike from where I'd dumped it in the alley, then put my new cafe-training to good use. After raiding the fridge and larder, I created a pile of sandwiches. Unfortunately Duffy insisted on helping, so his rough-hewn doorstep wedges, stuffed with filling, hardly matched my neat buffet-table efforts. Gallingly, Ravi clearly preferred Duffy's pile and, to be honest, so did I.

As we began to empty our second pot of tea, I said, 'It's great to see you, Ravi, but what prompted this sudden idea for an old boys' reunion?'

Ravi had trouble in swallowing a chunk of Duffy's generous filling, then cleared his throat. 'Remember Chas Houseman? To be honest it was him that gave me the thought. He called round unexpected.'

'Me, too,' Duffy added. 'Just turned up.'

I nodded. 'Sally said he'd been asking where I was.'

Ravi said, 'I don't think Chas is the touchy-feely reunion type. It was really *you* he wanted to find. Of course, none of us knew where to find you. Well, Brian knew which town as he dropped you here. But he didn't think you'd appreciate Houseman turning up out of the blue.'

I nodded at Duffy. 'You were damn right there,' I said.

'Chas is OK,' Ravi added, noticing my unenthusiastic tone. 'Just a bit difficult to get to know.'

I said, 'I don't think I'll bother.'

'I had got to know him well,' Ravi continued. 'We got on OK. But this time he was worried about something. Real worried.'

'What about?' I asked.

'Some computer memory stick that's gone missing.'

I shrugged. 'What would I know about that?'

'Says he gave *you* a copy for safe-keeping.'

I shook my head. 'I don't remember.'

Ravi sighed. 'Well, I get the distinct feeling Chas might be in some sort of deep trouble over losing it.'

Duffy seemed perplexed. He didn't always appear quick-witted but, in fact, his jocular and robust demeanour hid an exceedingly sharp and thoughtful mind. 'So what was it about that meeting with Zam-Zama that was so secret?'

Ravi flashed his perfect top set. 'Chas might have been drunk, Brian, but not that drunk. When I pushed him, he just closed up.'

At that moment the front door opened and all heads turned. Gem entered the room alone.

'No Steve?' I asked.

She shook her head. 'I left him when they took him into the cubicle. If I was there when he came out, it might have made things difficult. He'd probably insist on coming back.'

'Don't *let* him,' I advised. 'He'll *never* change.'

'So those people were from a drugs gang?' Ravi asked. 'A Muslim gang. And Steve owed them money?'

Gem nodded. 'He's a fool.'

Ravi's smile was charming. 'But still your boyfriend?'

She patted her belly that showed the earliest signs of swelling. '*Ex*-boyfriend . . . but he is still the father of my child.'

Duffy appeared not to be listening; this sort of thing was not his scene.

Ravi continued, 'But Steve has a habit and you've been helping him out – because you're still in love with him?'

Gem smiled awkwardly. 'No, I don't love him any more. But he *is* part of my life. I can't change that.'

'I don't think you want this Muslim gang being part of your life, too,' Ravi said. 'They were carrying knives and machetes. Looked a ferocious lot.'

Gem nodded. 'They murdered one of Dave's friends just recently. Set him alight.'

Ravi looked at me, aghast. 'Is this true?'

I said, 'I've been living rough. I got to know Jock. He was ex-navy. There'd been a sort of run-in with the Muslim gang. One morning they set him alight on a park bench. I tried to save him, but . . .'

Duffy frowned. I think he found it hard to accept that his former 'boss' was now reduced to sleeping on the streets. 'Did the cops get the killers?'

'No,' I said. 'It was pretty obvious, but there wasn't an eyewitness. I was there, but the gang was already running away. The cops are following it up, but they haven't got very far yet.'

'Because this Jock character was an itinerant?' Ravi guessed.

I nodded. 'And because it's difficult to get evidence against drug gangs. Wall of silence. Closed community and all that stuff. People feel threatened, scared of reprisals if anyone talks. And I think there's a lack of police effort.'

'That's not right,' Ravi said. 'Perhaps we should give them a kick up the arse – or give them a hand.'

Duffy looked at him curiously. 'Are you bored or somethin', Ravi?'

Ravi grinned. 'Just maybe.'

I said, 'I think the cops are scared of the situation getting out of hand. There are two rival gangs. One is British white locals and the other second generation Asians – they're more the incomers. They're fighting over the turf. The Muslims were the toughest, but suddenly now the white gang has got hold of some firearms. It could get nasty.'

'Bloody hell,' Duffy murmured. 'In my day it wus cata-pults an' air pistols.'

'You should do something,' Ravi said to me. 'Give the cops some real evidence.'

He was trivialising this, and it hit a raw spot. 'Drop it, Ravi. This isn't one of your intel wargames.'

He smiled and I could almost hear that brain of his buzz-ing. 'Maybe it should be, Dave. The police need evidence, so get it for them. Kosher evidence. You say that in this turf war, suddenly the white guys . . . ?'

'The Chip Shop Boys,' Gem helped.

Ravi laughed. 'Really? Well, the Chip Shop Boys suddenly have guns. That must put the Muslims at a disadvantage.'

I said, 'I reckon.'

'Then it's a perfect opportunity.' Ravi sounded triumphant.

I didn't understand. 'For what?'

'To get in with them. To infiltrate.' He grinned widely. 'Who knows more about guns than you? You can offer to teach them, show them. Even be a bodyguard for them. With your background—'

'You're nuts,' I said. 'Anyway, I'd be out of my depth, outnumbered. Anything could go wrong . . .'

'Who Dares Wins,' Ravi said.

I don't know how he had the gall or bad taste to say that then. The motto of the SAS. I glowered at him. 'Piss off, Ravi!'

But the Sri Lankan-born spook wasn't in the mood to be deterred. 'I could see this working, honestly?'

'I couldn't,' I said. That was it.

'You wouldn't be alone,' Ravi said. 'I'll back you up.'

'Not getting bored by civvy life by any chance?'

Ravi smiled slyly. 'Since you've both mentioned it . . . *very!* I admit it. My dad died earlier this year and left me a lot of money. Trouble is I don't know what to do with it – or myself.'

'Lucky old you,' I said unkindly.

'Give the money to charity,' Duffy scoffed. 'And rejoin the army. They're desperate enough.'

'I'd not go back to Afghanistan.' Ravi shook his head. 'I've had enough of that place. Bloody mission impossible.'

'Then just go home,' I said.

'Good point,' Duffy said, looking at his watch. 'Needs to get back to my HGV. Places to go, people to see. You comin', Rav?'

Ravi fixed his gaze on mine. 'I'm staying, thanks, Brian.'

I said, 'I sleep rough.'

Ravi replied, 'Not tonight, you don't. My treat.'

'You's serious?' Duffy asked.

'Yes,' Ravi replied. 'Thanks for the lift, Brian. But I'm staying.'

The big man rose from his chair. 'Well, forgive me, I'm off.' He looked at Gem and offered his giant paw of a hand. 'Thank you, young lady, for your kindness and hospitality.'

He turned and glanced at Ravi, then me. 'You two, you's both insane.'

Then he was gone.

# Twenty-Two

Steve Cranford did not return to Gem's house again that day.

In the afternoon, becoming concerned at having not heard from him, she rang his mobile. It was switched off. She then tried the local A & E where she had left him earlier. Apparently he had been treated and discharged. Once again she tried his mobile; it was still off.

'Gone to ground,' Ravi guessed. 'I don't blame him. Scared stiff, I shouldn't wonder.'

Later I cycled off to the cafe to complete my washing-up stint for the day, before heading into the city centre to meet up with Ravi again.

It was a large riverside pub that had been stripped of its charm by a popular chain, which sold cheap beer and plastic food. They may have destroyed the decor, but even they couldn't destroy the view. Swans and ducks patrolled back and forth on the dark-green water that flowed swiftly beneath overhanging willows.

I settled down to enjoy a pint of local bitter.

Ravi indicated the bergen that I had dumped on the seat beside me. 'I've booked you into a room,' he said pointedly.

That annoyed me. 'Thanks,' I said, 'but no thanks. I don't

have the money and I don't want to survive on charity. Yours or anyone else's.'

Ravi shrugged. 'Then treat it as a loan. But *I'm* certainly not working out of a cardboard box under a railway arch. And nor are you, if you seriously want to sort out this gang of murderers.'

After a long and thoughtful swallow of beer, I said, 'I'm not really sure that I do.'

Ravi raised a cynical eyebrow. 'No? You don't want to bring the killers of your friend to justice? I don't believe you. Maybe I don't know you *that* well, Dave, but from what Brian Duffy's told me . . .'

I raised a hand. 'OK, yes, of course, I'd like to get justice for Jock, and for his friend Ginger . . . I'm just not sure I'm ready yet.'

'On the contrary,' Ravi said slowly, 'I think you've never been more ready. Look at you, you've let your life slide down the pan and you're living like a dosser . . . or should that be tosser? A complete tosser. It's about time you started fighting back.'

I allowed the words to sink in. They should have hurt, but they didn't. I should have been outraged, but I wasn't. And I realised why. Because I knew that they were true.

Grudgingly I asked, 'What d'you suggest?'

'You book into your room. We'll get a decent steak and chips, and have a few beers. And you bring me up to speed about what's been going on around here.'

'That sounds like a good idea,' a voice said.

I turned. Because Bernie Bramshaw had been standing at end of the bar with his back to me, I hadn't recognised him.

Now the chubby face, bald head and thick spectacles were unmistakable. 'Sorry, gents.' He looked straight at me. 'It *is* Dave, isn't it? Dave Aston? Didn't mean to earwig. I always have a pint here after work. Thought it might be you talking.'

Damn well *knew* it was me, I thought. Not many people go round town with eighty-litre bergens on their backs.

He added quickly, 'Had been hoping to speak to you at Jock's funeral, but I couldn't find you after.'

'Shame,' I said flatly. I wasn't too sure what to make of Bramshaw.

I took the opportunity to break up the party. Shouldering my bergen, I looked down at Ravi. 'I'll go to my room then. See you later.'

He nodded. 'Reception will know which one.'

Reception did. It was probably the cheapest that Ravi could get, a little attic space that must have been home to a scullery maid in an earlier age. But I couldn't blame Ravi for that. If someone held on to your ankles while you leaned out of the window, there was possibly a nice view of the river.

I waited a few minutes before returning downstairs. To my annoyance, Bramshaw was still there, now having joined Ravi at our table and chatting to him like a long-lost mate.

'Got you a pint of Ringwood, Dave,' Bramshaw said extravagantly. 'Hope that was all right?'

I grunted churlishly. 'Thanks.'

'Room OK?' Ravi asked.

As I nodded my appreciation, Bramshaw said, 'Gather you two served together in Afghanistan. Dark horse you, Dave.

One of our Hereford heroes, I gather. We'd better behave ourselves in Swinthorpe from now on, eh?'

I glowered at Ravi, who appeared blithely unaware of my irritation.

He said, 'Bernie's been telling me a bit about Swinthorpe. Its problems with rival drug gangs and what have you. Getting a bit serious, I gather.'

Bramshaw intervened, 'Only in the past three years or so. There's been a growing element of Asians here since the sixties and seventies apparently. Always polite and hard-working, but never integrated particularly well. In those days you got a bit of "Paki-bashing", as the tabloids liked to call it – young white racist thugs, but no serious problems between communities.'

'But now?' Ravi pressed. He saw the sudden change of expression on Bramshaw's face. Ravi laughed lightly and affected an Indian accent, 'I'm one hundred per cent copper-bottomed British – born, bred and educated. My parents were from Sri Lanka, or Ceylon as they used to call it.'

'Ah, right!' Bramshaw said. 'Well, anyway, things changed with new generations. We've seen it on a larger scale elsewhere – like the Midlands and Yorkshire – work drying up in the industries where they traditionally worked, especially textiles. Youngsters, often not well educated, end up being jobless and on benefits. They get fed up being the underdogs. They feel victimised and start clutching at their ethnic identities for protection.'

'And militant Islam takes hold?' Ravi suggested.

Bramshaw shrugged. 'For some of them, our wars in Iraq and Afghanistan just fuelled the divide. Some Muslim clerics love to pour oil on the fire. Often I think it's done to boost their own sense of power than with any real malice. We've got one in Swinthorpe. Mullah Chadhar, preaches at the local mosque.'

I was surprised. 'I've never heard of him.'

Bramshaw gulped down the last of his beer. 'Well, you wouldn't unless you were a young Muslim. His activities certainly never get reported in *my* newspaper. I tried to write a piece once, but my editor spiked it. Might upset our rose-tinted image as an English tourist spot. Mind you, I think Chadhar got a small mention once on a *Panorama* TV programme. But that was on so late at night that no one saw it.'

'When did the drugs start?' Ravi asked.

I could answer that one. 'Since the beginning of time, when I was a teenager here. Small-scale weed and heroin.'

'And coke in the nineties,' Bramshaw added. 'But there's been a big acceleration in the last couple of years. That's when the Muslims began appearing on the radar. Even the last six months . . . it's become noticeable here on the streets, the police mentioning it a lot. And violent crime.'

'Like Jock's murder?' Ravi asked.

Bramshaw nodded. 'Sure, like Jock's murder.'

There was a brief silence and I stared at the frothing head of my new beer. 'And *now* their rivals have got guns.'

Bramshaw blinked. 'What?'

Suddenly I wished I'd kept my mouth shut. 'Oh, nothing.'

'You mean the white guys?'

Reluctantly I nodded. 'Jak Twomey's lot.'

'The Chip Shop Boys,' Bramshaw murmured thought-fully. 'Guns?'

I said, 'I think Rashid and the Asians had been getting too big for them to handle. Throwing their weight around.'

Ravi drew in a deep breath. 'As I said earlier, this may be a window of opportunity. It strikes me Rashid hasn't been having too much luck lately with his security. Bernie tells me his hard men were ridiculed by some local vigilante and pictured in his newspaper. Today, you, me and Brian sorted them out when they came after Steve Cranford. *Now*, we know their opposition have got firearms! Strikes me the Muslim gang might feel the need for some very serious assistance.'

I frowned. 'Like us?'

Ravi grinned. 'Some ex-military hardmen.'

Bernie Bramshaw almost choked on his beer. 'Am I really hearing this?' he asked.

I think Ravi suddenly realised his mistake. As Bramshaw turned towards my colleague, I shook my head vigorously. Ravi caught my eye and added quickly, 'I'm just fantasising. It's down to the police to deal with that sort of thing.'

I wasn't sure Bramshaw was convinced. 'Well, if you guys decide to go after them, you know you can always bank on me for support. Anything I can do.'

Ravi smiled. 'But with one condition, I suppose?'

Bramshaw understood. 'As always, Ravi. My only rule – any story must be *my* exclusive.'

'And, I wonder,' Ravi asked absently, 'what would be the easiest way to meet up with this gang leader called Rashid?'

'How about Friday prayers?' Bramshaw suggested. 'Anyone who's anyone amongst the local Muslims will be there. The mosque is a converted school on Rosebury Street.'

There had been complaints about it from nearby residents, but still the muezzin call to *Jumu'ah*, or congregational Friday prayers, continued to be played some twenty minutes beforehand each time. It was relayed on a worn-out tape deck over a loudspeaker that had seen better days. Somehow the mellifluous charm of the sound was lost without the accompanying desert warmth and spice-scented air that I remembered in Iraq or Afghanistan.

Today, Swinthorpe's streets were cold and damp. Its mosque had formerly been Rosebury Infants, a sprawling Victorian school that had been sold off ten years earlier.

We pulled up outside in Ravi's beloved Lexus saloon. It had been the first purchase he'd made with his inheritance. He'd returned by train to his home to collect it and driven back to Swinthorpe. 'She's the child I never had,' he laughed.

'More like the mistress you could never afford,' I countered.

Ravi ignored that. 'The religious service shouldn't take more than an hour,' he assured. 'Friday's not a weekend holiday in the UK, so they tend to keep the sermons short so that they can fit prayers into a working lunch hour . . . I've been to prayers undercover so many times in my life, I think Allah must think I'm one of his.'

There was a distinct waft of cologne in the air as we reached the school gates on which the locals were converging. It was very noticeable that the dress code appeared to be 'smart casual', but no ties.

I thought I recognised the tall young man who stood at the entrance, distributing prayer sheets. He may have been a member of Rashid's gang, but I couldn't be certain. As I approached, he frowned at the sight of my 'smartly casual' DPM trousers.

Ravi intervened. 'This is a friend of mine. He's interested in our faith. Is it all right for him to attend and observe?'

The man looked dubious, but smiled thinly and said, 'Of course, he is welcome. Please, he must remove his shoes.'

'Of course.' Ravi returned the smile and accepted a couple of the prayer sheets. He turned back to me. 'Come this way. Hope you haven't got holes in your socks.'

Leaving our shoes by the door, we followed the stream of men towards the main assembly hall, while the females in the congregation separated into a large former classroom.

Ravi and I joined the back row to kneel in prayer. 'Who's taking the service today?' Ravi asked the man next to him.

'Probably Mullah Chadhar,' came the reply. 'He is very good. A nice man. It is your first time here?'

'Yes, I am visiting a friend. He is here with me, a non-Muslim.'

I nodded my acknowledgement and exchanged smiles.

Ravi then bowed his head and murmured some words I didn't understand. He'd told me earlier these were two cycles of voluntary prayer called *tahyatul masjid salah* that are offered in greeting to the mosque.

A member of the congregation stood to give the call to prayer just before the imam, Mullah Siraj Chadhar, entered from the door of a side office. Chadhar was stooped and slight. He had a frizz of long white hair and flowing beard that created the impression of an aurora of light around his head. At the centre of his face were tiny pale-blue eyes, enlarged by highly magnifying pince-nez and a thin mouth disfigured with ageing gold fillings.

He greeted the congregation in warm but reedy-sounding Arabic. With my basic understanding of the language, it was easy enough to follow. Then he slipped into English for his sermon.

If I was expecting a tirade of abuse against Westerners or infidels or unbelievers, I would have been disappointed. In fact, in friendly tones, he preached how much his Muslim congregation should make allowances for those in whose country they lived. They should offer friendship and love, treating everyone as individuals and respecting individual views. I felt almost disappointed.

As he finished his *khutbah*, Ravi glanced sideways at me. 'Prayers next,' he said. 'Go and sit over there.'

Visiting was one thing; joining in prayers would have been a step too far. I climbed to my feet and made my way to an empty bench set against the rear wall of the hall. As I sat down, the rest of the congregation rose, standing shoulder to shoulder in the direction of Mecca. Then, the sea of bodies dropped to its collective knees and foreheads touched the ground in supplication.

As Ravi had advised me, the imam began to lead his flock in two cycles of ritual prayer.

Suddenly I found a man sitting next to me. It was the man who had welcomed us at the mosque gates.

He said, 'I hope you have found this interesting?' His breath smelled faintly of almonds.

I nodded politely. 'Very, thank you.'

Someone else passed in front of me and sat on my other side. His backside landed heavily on the bench. It was Amir, the gormless-looking number two of Rashid's gang, who I'd last seen hanging from a railing behind Tesco.

No, not quite true. I'd seen him hanging from the railing in a picture on the front page of the *Journal*.

'Hello, Amir,' I said. 'Glad to see you managed to get down. Nice photo in the paper.'

'Mistah Aston,' he hissed. 'You gotta cheek coming here!'

The man with the almond-smelling breath said, 'Quiet, Amir. Imam's saying *salat*.'

I said, 'I want to talk to Rashid.'

'And I think *he* will want to talk to you,' Amir retorted.

'Then I think we should take him into Mullah Chadhar's office,' the other man said. 'I'll get his friend.'

Amir nodded his agreement and indicated for me to follow him. Meanwhile the other man walked across to Ravi, rudely interrupting his prayer.

I suspected that Mullah Siraj Chadhar's large office had formerly belonged to the school's head. There was an impressive wooden desk with a green leather top and four beautiful and matching captain's swivel chairs in deep, buttoned upholstery. The mahogany bookcases, that no doubt had once been laden with school textbooks and administrative folders, now boasted a vast range of Islamic holy books and scriptures.

I'd just taken a seat in front of the desk when Ravi came in with Amir.

'Take a seat,' Amir ordered.

Ravi was dressed in cool casual, a pale-grey mohair suit and an expensive yellow silk shirt with no collar. Pure urbane, Muslim chic. His presence was both classic and naturally commanding, there was no denying that. I noticed that both Amir and his colleague were regarding him with unmistakable respect and caution.

While everyone was eyeing up everyone else, but before any more words were exchanged, the panelled door opened again.

This time it was Rashid who entered.

He looked worried, harassed. His first scowling glance was at me, his second at Ravi.

It was obvious that he decided Ravi was the more important of the two of us. He held him in his gaze as he asked Amir, 'What in the name of Allah is going on here?'

Ravi showed his irritatingly immaculate teeth in one of those dazzling smiles of his. He rose to his feet and offered his hand. 'I am called Ravi Khan. I am a friend of Mr Aston.'

Ravi Khan, I mused. Might as well have been John Smith.

Scowling, Rashid ignored the offered hand. 'Are you trying to be funny, Ravi – or whatever your name *really* is? Mr Aston is no friend of mine – or my colleagues – as I am sure you are aware.'

Ravi's Warner Brothers smile didn't falter for an instance. 'Perhaps not. But circumstances change. He believes that you are very possibly in need of his help. In fact, let us say, *our* help.'

Rashid clearly found it hard to contain his anger. 'I don't think that is very likely. Explain yourself.'

'Mr Aston and I are former soldiers,' he stated baldly. 'Mr Aston and I were in the British Army until quite recently. We were in different elements of what is known as special forces. You understand?'

This time Rashid's shoulders relaxed a fraction and his dark eyes narrowed with interest. 'Go on . . .' he demanded.

'You and your colleagues have already fallen foul of Mr Aston's tender mercies, I believe?'

Rashid grimaced, ignoring the sarcasm, and nodded his head.

'He says there is no reason for you to continue to be enemies,' Ravi continued. 'You have had your differences, but now they are settled. You are equal. It is time to survive and thrive together in the same town. So why be enemies when you can be friends?'

I had to hand it to Ravi, he had an unbelievably silken-tongued charm. Rashid watched cautiously, but said nothing.

'You and your organisation are in trouble here,' Ravi said plainly. 'That is *why* you need our help. You can deny it, but it doesn't change the truth. You've seen what Mr Aston can do with his bare hands, let alone with weapons. Firearms that your rivals now have, but that you do not.'

Rashid sneered. 'That is what you think?' He turned to Amir. 'Fetch one of them for me, now.'

Amir grinned and proceeded to open the door of a large in-built cupboard behind the desk. He brought out something wrapped in bubble wrap and opened its contents onto the desk. A gleaming .45 Colt automatic clattered onto the polished wooden surface.

Gleefully Amir reached out and grabbed the grip in his right hand. He held it in the air above his head.

Getting carried away, he yelled 'Allahu Akbar!' triumphantly.

It was at that moment that it happened.

# Twenty-Three

The bullet went straight through the ceiling, the sound of its discharge vibrating around the confines of the office.

I snatched the weapon from Amir's grasp as he stood in open-mouthed shock at what he'd just done. Petals of plaster floated down from around the neat hole in the ceiling.

'Is there anyone upstairs?' I demanded as I removed the magazine and checked that the breech was clear.

Rashid shook his head. 'Just an attic for storage.'

'You are lucky you didn't bring the whole ceiling down,' Ravi said. 'I think my point has just been made. *Always* check the magazine and clear the breech when handed a weapon. You most *definitely* need our assistance.'

The door burst open. Mullah Siraj Chadhar stood there, a vision in white: wild hair, flowing beard and pristine robes. The blue eyes seemed to gleam like tiny, hard diamonds. What he lacked in stature he certainly made up for in sheer presence.

He appeared to be very angry. 'What is going on here?' he asked Rashid. His voice was reedy and rasping. 'Was that a gunshot I heard?'

'I am afraid so,' Rashid replied. 'It was an accident.'

White brows raised above the azure eyes. 'I am most relieved to hear that, at least,' Mullah Chadhar said snappily.

He turned to the man who had earlier greeted Ravi and me at the gate of the mosque. 'Wait outside this door. Make sure we are not disturbed.'

The man nodded and slipped past the clergyman, who in turn looked at me.

'You fired that weapon?' he asked.

I placed the automatic and the magazine carefully on the table. 'No, it was Amir here. Got a bit overexcited.'

Mullah Chadhar's eyes went from me to Ravi. 'And who are you two gentlemen? You are from the police, from the authorities?' He didn't wait before adding quickly, 'I had absolutely no idea that anyone in my flock had firearms, or that they had them on the premises. Such a thing would be utterly prohibited.'

'Same with drugs, I suppose?' I muttered under my breath.

'Shut up,' Ravi hissed at me from the corner of his mouth. Then he turned to Mullah Chadhar and smiled broadly. 'Sir, with the deepest respect, we have come here to offer assistance. Shall I say assistance in your—' Ravi slowed and put heavy emphasis on the word '—pastoral work? The work that is done in the community by Rashid and his followers.'

I could hardly believe it. Ravi was making the Swords of Allah sound like a bunch of social workers.

'My friend,' Ravi continued, nodding in my direction, 'has had his disagreements with Rashid. They are now resolved. The point is, we are aware of the activities of Rashid's group. We know they need to have better security than they currently enjoy . . .'

Mullah Chadhar smiled demurely. 'I know nothing of Rashid's group, as you call it, or its activities.' He made his way around the desk to the huge upholstered chair and sat down. 'I am sure you understand.'

'Of course,' Ravi replied. 'But Mr Aston and I do. We are both former soldiers and we are both seeking employment where our specialist skills can be put to good use.'

'Ah!' Mullah Chadhar said, suddenly understanding. Resting his elbows on the chair arms, he interlaced his fingers. 'And where did you serve?'

'Most recently in Afghanistan.' Ravi didn't hesitate or blink an eye. 'We were both discharged. Mr Aston's was on medical grounds. Unfortunately, mine was a dishonourable discharge. A complete misunderstanding.'

Chadhar's blue eyes glittered. 'I am sure.'

'But sometimes in life,' Ravi added pointedly, 'you have to break the rules in order to survive.'

Chadhar glanced up at Rashid who was now standing beside him. 'Rashid, I think you might listen to these gentlemen. Of course, it is nothing to do with me. That is just my advice. But please get that dreadful gun, and any other weapons that anyone else may have stored here, taken away. This is a house of God.'

Rashid indicated for Amir to pick up the gun and magazine, which he quickly pocketed.

'Now if you will forgive me, gentlemen,' Chadhar said dismissively, 'I have another sermon to prepare.'

Rashid inclined his head, indicating for the rest of us to follow him. The assembly hall had mostly emptied, but a quite a few members of the congregation remained, chatting in small groups.

'We'll talk outside,' Rashid said. 'Not in here. We don't want to be overheard.'

The sun was making a shy appearance and the pavements were beginning to dry. Rashid led us through the gates to a spot by the railings where an evergreen bush sheltered us from the chill northerly breeze.

As I walked alongside Rashid, behind me I could hear Ravi talking to Amir: 'We can begin by offering to show you how to handle a gun safely.'

Rashid stopped and turned. 'I will make the decisions here.'

'Don't want to shoot yourselves in the foot, do you?' I pointed out, not bothering to hide my sarcasm. 'That won't impress your opposition too much.'

He ignored that. 'First, Aston, I want to know I can trust you . . .' He glanced at Ravi. 'And Mr Khan here, of course.'

Ravi's smile was dazzling everyone again. 'Of course, anything.'

'Two days ago,' Rashid said, 'I understand you and Mr Aston were in a fight that hospitalised one of my members. They were seeking a certain Steven Cranford. He is a cheap junkie who owes us money. We have to re-establish our position in this town. It must be known that we can't be messed with.' Rashid looked directly at me. 'He is the boyfriend of the girl who works with you at the cafe. I want an address for him, a place where he can be found. That should not be too difficult for you. Get me Cranford and then maybe we can talk.'

Before I could utter a word, Ravi said brightly, 'I don't see that being a problem. And I perfectly understand you want to be certain of our ability and loyalty to you.'

'Ravi . . .' I began, but he waved my protest aside.

He said, 'Rashid, just let me have an email address and a phone number where I can reach you. Nice and secure, of course. Nothing that could compromise you.'

The man stared at Ravi for a moment, then fished in his pocket for a scrap of paper. He found an old parking ticket and scribbled a couple of lines on the back with a biro.

'Twenty-four hours,' Rashid said, handing it to Ravi.

Ravi inclined his head politely, 'Even sooner, if I can manage it, boss.'

'Steve Cranford is a bad man,' Ravi said lightly, as we walked back from the mosque. 'We both know that. Gem knows that. Hell's bells, Dave, even Steve himself knows that.'

I said, 'I'm still not comfortable handing him over to Rashid.'

Ravi shrugged. 'So what's Rashid going to do? Just put the frighteners on him, and mark his card. It's about time Steve Cranford learned to respect other people and paid his dues. Whether that be drug dealers or pregnant mums.'

We separated at the edge of town, Ravi heading back to the hotel and me to the cafe, ready to do the afternoon washing-up stint.

Gem was sitting outside, smoking a cigarette at one of the tables.

'This really is my last one,' she said guiltily. 'I promised the doctor.'

'Good,' I said, opening my tin of rollies. Everyone I knew seemed to be giving up the habit or trying. 'You don't want to deliver a pint-sized baby now, do you?'

She giggled. 'Actually, Dave, I rather think I do.'

I laughed. 'But not one with a fag in its mouth, eh?'

'Ah, not really that, no,' she replied with a smile.

I took the plunge. 'Has Steve been around again?'

She shook her head. 'Not since I took him to hospital the other day.'

'Is he still staying at his usual digs?'

'Actually, I don't think he is.' She drew deeply on her cigarette. 'To be honest I think he's got behind on his rent there. Said he was thinking of moving on. Could well be at his sister's place as he knows he can't stop at my house no more.'

I didn't fully trust her on that. 'You're sure?'

'Absolutely. If he loses his temper again, he could hurt the baby.'

'Where does his sister live?'

'She's got a flat on the Evinmore estate, one of the tower blocks. She's got a couple of kids, so there's not really room for Steve. She won't be too pleased having him there.'

'Have you got his number?'

'His mobile, yes. Why?'

Thinking off the top of my head, I said, 'A job he might be interested in.'

She giggled. 'Really? Does it involve getting up in the morning?'

'Ravi came across it, some sort of self-help charity that works with drug addicts. Only a few hours a week, but at least it pays.'

Gem shrugged. 'I guess you never know,' she said without conviction, and jotted down the number for me.

She returned inside to work and I tried Steven Cranford's number. I just got his voicemail and decided against leaving a message. After I'd finished my washing-up stint, I tried again.

'Yeah?' he sounded like he'd just got out of bed, which probably meant that he had.

'It's Dave Aston here.'

'Oh, yeah, and what do you want?'

'Something you might be interested in.'

'Like what?'

'A charity is looking for a street support worker, stuff with addicts. Just a half-day a week, but it pays in the region of fifty quid. Not at all bad. Thought you might be interested.'

'Why don't you do it?'

'They want a reliable addict or ex-addict.'

'Where did you hear about it?'

'I didn't. It was my mate, Ravi.'

'The Paki.'

'Yes. Interested?'

'Maybe.'

'You at Gem's sister's?' He confirmed that he was. 'Give me the address. Ravi and I will pick you up tomorrow morning. Go see them. Nice people. What's a good time?'

'Er, eleven. No, say half-past.'

I wrote down the address and hung up before he could change his mind.

In fact I was with Ravi in his Lexus car by nine the next morning. It was Saturday and I wasn't doing a weekend shift at the cafe that week. We were parked opposite the block of flats where Steve Cranford's sister lived, in case he changed his mind and decided to give us the slip.

As it approached eleven-thirty, Ravi climbed the stairs while I took the shaky, urine-tainted lift to the fourth floor, so that we didn't miss him by chance. It was his sister Grace who answered the door. She had her brother's sandy hair, roughly pinned up off her face. She was dressed in a T-shirt and grubby joggers and was bare-footed. In one hand she held a lighted cigarette and in the other she cradled a mixed-race baby girl. Another child, an open-mouthed boy of about four, clung to her left leg.

'Is Steve in?' I asked.

She looked from me to Ravi, as dapper as always, today wearing a slick grey suit. 'You from the Social?'

'No, we're mates. I'm Dave and this is Ravi.'

Cranford, carrying a can of cola, suddenly appeared behind his sister. He was wearing jeans, and a grubby singlet hung on his scrawny body.

He squinted over her shoulder, suddenly recognising me. 'Oh, shit, is that the time?' he asked groggily.

'Eleven thirty,' I confirmed helpfully.

'Give me five,' he muttered, noisily clearing the phlegm from his throat and disappearing back inside the flat.

In fact we had to give him fifteen. Time to visit the bathroom, splash cold water on his face and have his first heroin fix of the day.

Wearing a black jogging top and a Nike baseball cap, he emerged with hands thrust deep in his trouser pockets. His first words were, 'I'm not sure about this.'

'Nonsense,' Ravi replied brightly, setting a swift pace for him and me to keep up with. 'You're just the sort of person they're looking for. An ex-junkie going straight.'

Cranford grunted. 'And fifty quid for what . . . ?'

'Just talking and giving advice,' I said quickly, 'as easy as that.'

'Why think of me?' he asked suspiciously. 'You don't even like me.'

'Yes, I do,' I lied. 'Well, I care about Gem. It helps her if her baby's father could at least earn a living wage.'

We reached Ravi's silver Lexus saloon. 'Bit posh,' he observed.

'Give up the drugs, Steve,' I said. 'And you might have one some day.'

He climbed into the back. 'Bit rich coming from you,' he countered. As someone who was living on the streets, I can't say he didn't have a bloody good point.

'Let's go for a pint,' Ravi said, 'while I contact the client. What's a good place?'

We settled on the Monk's Mill, a huge barn-like pub in the middle of town that had been converted from its original purpose. We sat outside in the uncomfortable autumn chill, so that we could smoke while Ravi set up his laptop on one of the tables beside the foaming mill race.

I fetched three beers and returned to find that Ravi had telephoned Rashid's mobile phone and left a voicemail message.

We waited in awkward silence with little to say to each other until Ravi's cellphone played its weird and irritating tune. 'Hello, yes it's me, Ravi. We have Mr Cranford with us, as promised. When and where would you like us to meet for the interview? As soon as possible I would imagine.'

Ravi listened intently for a moment and scribbled down an address in his pocket notebook. He requested confirmation. 'Fairoak estate?'

'I know it,' I said. 'About twelve miles south of here.'

'We'll be with you in about thirty minutes,' he concluded, looking at me for agreement.

As he hung up, I said, 'It's a small industrial park.'

We finished our drinks and made our way to the car. The drive was on the two-lane fast road to the coast, through a wide and flat river valley with farmland on both sides. The industrial park was on the outskirts of the sprawling village of Fairoak. Historically, the village had once vied with Swinthorpe for political prominence in the region. But Swinthorpe, with the weighty religious authority of the abbey on its side, had won.

At least Fairoak now boasted a modern business estate of prefabricated buildings. Mostly the companies appeared to be in light engineering, food packaging and general distribution.

It was outside the gates of one of the latter that Ravi pulled up. NIGHTHUB-UK read the large weathered sign outside the closed wired gates. The place looked tired and neglected. The red paintwork on the bargeboards, windows and doors of the two-storey building was neglected, blistered and peeling. The edges of the concrete parking bays were overgrown with weeds and scattered with rubbish. Bindweed had grown and died still clinging to the twelve-foot high security fence that was topped with rusting barbed wire. If I'd been told that

NIGHTHUB-UK had gone out of business a year ago, I'd have believed it.

'You sure this is the right place, man?' Cranford sounded concerned.

'Of course,' I replied and sprang out from the front passenger seat.

I sauntered over to the gates and looked left and right along the empty concrete apron that ran in front of the building. There was a rickety-looking intercom box hanging from the gatepost.

I pressed the tit and a voice squawked: '*Yes?*'

'Dave here. I've got Steve Cranford with me.'

'*Wait. We'll be out.*'

I returned to the Lexus and indicated to the other two to join me. Ravi looked nonchalant but I noticed that his eyes never ceased scanning the deserted depot frontage. Cranford made no such attempt to hide his increasing nervousness. 'This don't feel right,' he muttered.

'Here we are!' I said as a side door opened next to the depot's big steel up-and-over doors. Two men emerged, both Asians.

Steve Cranford made a backward move. He stepped straight into Ravi's and my vice-like grips, twisting his forearms around and up into the small of his back.

'Hey, what the *fuck* is this?'

'Shut up, Steve,' Ravi hissed, 'and you *won't* get hurt!'

One of the two Asians opened the gates and indicated for us to go in. I thought I recognised both men as players from Rashid's gang.

Cranford jerked his head around and shouted at me, 'You fucking bastard!!'

In retaliation, he had both his wrists forced simultaneously up into his spine. He gave an involuntary yelp of pain. Ravi had even less sympathy for him than I did.

There were a number of vehicles in the gloomy interior: three or four white Transit-type vans and a couple of nondescript saloons. Straight ahead of us, lights were on in a partitioned office area. There was a large desk and Rashid sat behind it, his acolytes on either side of him.

Among them I recognised Amir, who I'd hung from the railings. Ali, who I had water-boarded in his bath and Saif, who had been speared in Gem's garden by Brian, were also in the group. You could almost feel the hot hatred glaring in our direction.

Ravi spoke immediately. 'Gentlemen, I know we haven't always seen eye to eye, but let this be a new beginning. I promised you Steve Cranford, and here he is.'

Cranford was beginning to tremble uncontrollably and his skin was slippery with sweat under my fingers.

I said, 'You can put the frighteners on him and agree arrangements for him to repay you. We'll see to it that he does.'

Rashid looked to Amir. 'Take him out the back.'

I added, 'When we leave, we'll take him with us. No heavy stuff, right?'

Rashid raised an eyebrow. 'You can't work for us, Aston, *and* be his fuckin' social worker.'

Ravi cut in to prevent the situation deteriorating. 'Let's

talk guns, Rashid, let's talk security. If those idiots in the –
what is it? – Chip Shop Boys have started toting, then your
people are going to need to know how to handle themselves
without blowing holes in ceilings or in each other.'

Amir glowered at Ravi as he and a colleague took Cranford from us and began to haul him to some place in the back
of the warehouse.

Rashid said, 'We already have someone who looks after
security.'

The man who stepped forward was of middle height, his
thick waist emphasised by a long, embroidered waistcoat that
he wore over Western clothes. His moustache and beard were
crinkly, and heavy like the tortoiseshell spectacles he wore.

I sensed resentment, and trouble.

'Mr Aston,' he stated. His handshake was firm and warm.
'And Mr Khan . . . I am Jooma Khan. Snap! – as we say in
England. As you might imagine, I have heard about you, Mr
Aston. You are clearly not someone to be messed with. I had
put a price on your head. I had been making plans for you . . .'

He let the words hang in the air and I felt a cold shiver
between my shoulder blades. I felt an involuntary tremor.
Then he smiled suddenly. 'And now you appear in front of
us, offering your services.'

Rashid was impatient. 'OK, Jooma. So what do you think?'

Jooma raised a hand. 'Be patient.' The authoritative tone
he used to Rashid surprised me a little. Their security man
turned to one of his colleagues and took hold of a Colt automatic, probably the same one I'd seen earlier at the mosque.

'You know what this is?'

I glanced down. 'The classic US .45 Browning. M1911 automatic. Replaced by American forces in the mid-80s by the Beretta 92F.'

I picked it up. Everyone around the table took an instinctive backward step. 'Lovely piece,' I added. I weighed the weapon in my hand and replaced it on the table.

Jooma smiled. 'You seem to know your guns, Mr Aston. You were special forces, I am told?'

I always found it hard admitting this. 'Yep. My experience and expertise covers everything you and Rashid's – er – team needs. Weapons training, close protection, surveillance, assault, interrogation . . .'

'And where would you start?'

Ravi was straight in there with the diplomatic bit in case I buggered it up. 'With you, Mr Khan. Working *with* you and your existing plans. But, of course, we have our terms to agree.'

Jooma's eyes narrowed. 'What sort of terms?'

'Our advice is essential for the very existence of your business,' Ravi replied coolly. 'I expect our terms to reflect that. Perhaps a percentage slice off the top of proceeds. Say, twenty per cent.'

'It is not my decision,' Jooma replied. 'But even eight or ten is unlikely. More realistic is a not insubstantial fee for services rendered.'

'Like?'

Jooma shrugged. 'Five hundred pounds a day.'

'One thousand.'

'Perhaps.'

'Each.'

A hesitation. 'That is possible.'

'While under contract,' Ravi smiled gently. 'Minimum three months, including weekends.'

I tried to do the sums in my head, and failed. It was a lot of money.

There was another hesitation from Jooma, so Ravi added, 'Remember our service includes vital issues for your organisation's survival. Like mastering the use of firearms within your team . . . that would be our very top priority.'

Jooma opened his mouth to reply, but his words were drowned out by a tremendous metallic crashing noise from outside.

The two Asian men who had let us in earlier came rushing back in, panic-stricken. One of them yelled, 'Rashid, we're under attack! Those white bastards have crashed the gates! And they've got guns!'

# Twenty-Four

Thinking faster than I did, Ravi snatched the Colt and magazine from the table.

'They've rammed the gates,' the Asian added. 'Must be a dozen of them.'

The remaining gang members rushed out of the partitioned office to see what the commotion was all about.

Ravi followed them towards the front door of the warehouse, palming the magazine into the automatic as he went.

There was a sudden report of gunfire. Members of the Chip Shop Boys were either firing at us, or letting off rounds in a stupid display of exuberance.

I turned to Jooma. 'You've got more guns here?'

He was looking bewildered. 'Yes, of course.'

'Can you let me have one?' I snapped.

'Er, of course.' He turned to Rashid. 'Get them quickly.'

As the man turned to go out the back door of the office, I called after him, 'For God's sake, don't arm everyone – or there'll be carnage. Just one for me!'

Jooma gave me a strange look, hesitated a second, then called out, 'And *for me*, please, Rashid!'

The weapons must have been stashed just outside the office as Rashid returned almost immediately with three packages. He passed two of them over to Jooma and me. While Rashid fumbled sorting out spare rounds to put into the empty magazines, I was surprised to note that Jooma was quite practised. The guns were all second-hand Colts in reasonably good condition.

I had a magazine filled and loaded in moments and left the two of them still loading while I joined Ravi and the others at the front of the warehouse. There was a large and locked up-and-over vehicle gate, and an adjoining personnel door through which we had entered earlier. Next to it was a long and narrow horizontal window. The dirty glass was rein-forced with thin steel mesh as well as iron security bars on the outside.

A few members of Rashid's gang were peering apprehen-sively out at Jak Twomey's white yobs. They had driven a blue Land Rover Discovery – no doubt stolen for the purpose – through the compound gates. In the process they had managed to get the beast entwined with broken metal poles, mesh and barbed wire, so that it resembled a vicious hornet caught in a spider's web. Although they'd brought down the gates, they'd actually pulled them down on top of themselves.

Two youths were trying to find a way through, while a couple more were shooting wildly in the air or at the ware-house in an attempt to intimidate everyone inside. Finally another two used the roof and bonnet of the Discovery as a bridge over into the compound.

'They're through,' Ravi observed.

One of the yobs raised his hand. He was armed. 'Watch it!' I shouted.

More rounds were heard and bullet holes appeared in the wooden personnel door. Other shots noisily blew ragged holes through the metal up-and-over doors.

If our attackers had known what they were doing, they'd have shot the lock and hinges off the personnel door, crashed in and killed everyone they'd wanted to in seconds. Or taken us all prisoners . . . whatever their crazy plan might have been.

I said calmly, 'Let's give them something to think about.'

Ravi looked at me. 'But no corpses eh? This isn't Iraq.'

I didn't need reminding. I lowered the wrist of my gun hand onto my left forearm for support. Aiming the pip of the barrel, I put a solitary round through the front windscreen of the Discovery. The effect was amazing.

Their own noisy barrage having momentarily subsided into silence, it was broken a split second later by the sudden violent explosion of glass. It was like surprising a stalking cat from behind – the men almost literally jumped at the shock of it. They hadn't been expecting a return of fire. Suddenly the odds were dramatically changed.

Ravi added a few rounds around their feet, seeing the telltale kicking dust on the tarmac. Now the men began to dance.

Rashid and Jooma Khan appeared at our side. 'What is happening now?' their security chief asked.

I said, 'They're having second thoughts, I think.'

Moving closer to the window, Rashid raised his gun.

I brushed the barrel aside. 'You won't be needing that.'

Sure enough, the Chip Shop Boys' advance party was scrambling on the slippery bonnet of the Discovery. They were desperately trying to get back over the wire. Meanwhile the driver revved furiously in an attempt to extract the vehicle from the tangled web of steel and mesh.

'You two are cool under fire,' Jooma observed and I noticed the irritated expression on Rashid's face as he heard the words.

The Discovery finally pulled free and the remaining members of Jak Twomey's gang scrambled aboard. Tyres screeched in a final display of idiotic machismo as the vehicle reversed, then shot forward and away out of the estate.

We waited, expectantly, for them to regroup and return. Minutes ticked by. It didn't happen. The weekend hush returned, settling uncannily over the industrial estate. Only the mangled fence was testimony to the few minutes of noise, madness and mayhem.

At last, Jooma said, 'We'll keep watch, but I do not think they will return now. We'll have our own private contractors repair the fence right away.'

'But it's a Saturday,' Ravi pointed out.

'These people are from our community,' Jooma replied evenly. 'When we say jump, they know it is best to ask "how high?". Or in this case, how soon?'

An hour or so later, a firm of local Asian contractors was reinstating the fencing.

When we eventually sat down, it was alone with Jooma Khan. That had displeased Rashid, but Jooma was clearly higher in the pecking order under Mullah Siraj Chadhar.

'Firstly,' Jooma said, 'you must understand that currently I am the one responsible for *security* in all the undertakings of

Mullah Chadhar. That this is necessary is in itself sad, because he is a very good and holy man. It is just his – and indeed my own – misfortune that we are both originally Afghanistani or Pakistani nationals. Therefore, we have become automatically – and most unfairly – mistrusted by some elements of the British establishment of late.

'It is not helped that some of his congregation have, sadly, become involved in low-level drug dealing. Mullah Chadhar does not condone this – indeed he positively condemns it. He is actively trying to teach his pupils to leave that evil world alone. Nevertheless, that activity can attract revenging types – anti-Islamists, Zionists and racist groups – to attack him and his congregation members. It is a very real threat and a worry.'

I could almost believe he believed this bullshit himself. He was so convincing, he almost had me feeling sorry for them. The truth I'd learned was that Mullah Chadhar was in fact a secretive fundamentalist who hid his provocative jihadist agenda well, pretending to be a moderate. He'd been rumbled by some in the media and, no doubt, others in intelligence circles. Mostly, however, it seemed to me he was doing a good job in preserving his facade of respectability.

Ravi was listening intently and wearing an expression of deep concern. 'You know, Mr Khan, I really *do* understand. Life is not easy for us Muslims in this country any more.'

Jooma seemed to fall for Ravi's supposed sympathy. 'Some members of Mullah Chadhur's congregation are picked on by racist white youth gangs. Just lately they have been using firearms as you have just witnessed here. That is why we too must likewise protect ourselves. There is no other reason why you would see them here.'

Taking Ravi's lead, I nodded my understanding. 'Then you *must* also be sure your people are safe with firearms and do not harm themselves or others unintentionally.'

Jooma appeared to agree with this. 'I'd like them used as a *deterrent* – as indeed, I have just seen you use them – rather than a method of attack. We are not trying to attract police attention . . . just to survive in peace.'

'Bless,' I murmured under my breath.

Jooma looked at me curiously, blinked, then continued. 'Perhaps you could train one or two of Rashid's most trusted, mature and sensible colleagues in the safe use of firearms. And their minimal use for maximum effect.'

Ravi said, 'We can find a firing range. Somewhere very out of the way.'

The security chief raised an eyebrow and nodded. 'Also I might appreciate your very *personal* assistance. We soon have an important visitor from overseas. What you may call a VIP. Very Important Personage. It would be terrible if he were accidentally targeted by some idiot racists.'

I said quickly, 'Close protection is one of our specialities.'

'Then let us meet again shortly,' Jooma said, 'and consolidate our plans. We can also confirm your remuneration then.' He consulted the calendar on his desk. 'It is Saturday and I am busy . . . I suggest Tuesday. Midday?'

Ravi and I looked at each other and nodded.

At that moment daylight began flooding into the partitioned office as the main steel up-and-over door was cranked open.

The air was suddenly filled with diesel fumes as a couple of white vans parked in the warehouse were started up.

I was alarmed. 'Where's Steve Cranford?' I demanded.

The first of the vans was already manoeuvring its way through the metallic chaos left by the Discovery.

'He's being taken somewhere for his own safety,' Jooma assured calmly. 'There is no need to fear.'

'I told you he was to return with me . . .' I began.

Jooma fixed me with his dark eyes. 'Those who are not with us, Mr Aston, are against us. Remember that.'

I felt Ravi's restraining hand on my shoulder. 'Cool it, Dave. Don't forget, we're being tested.'

'This is two-way traffic,' I replied angrily, shaking off Ravi's grip. I glared into Jooma's eyes. 'That was my half of the deal.'

The man appeared not to hear. He looked down at his desk, picked up a file and opened it. As he began to read, without looking up, he said, 'I shall see you two gentlemen at twelve noon on Tuesday.' His tone was utterly dismissive. 'We can discuss the issue then.'

We had a late sandwich lunch back at the hotel. I had tracked down an Ordnance Survey map of the area and we sat with it in a quiet alcove in the bar, away from prying eyes.

I brought over two beers from the bar. 'I've been trying to find some possible places for training,' Ravi said, the map spread out in front of him. 'But then you're the one who knows the area.'

I took a couple of gulps of beer and peered down at the map. I'd been considering it myself since our meeting with

Jooma Khan earlier that day. 'The old chalk pits,' I said. 'Near a place called Wykham Woods. About fifteen miles south of here.'

'Got it,' Ravi said, almost immediately. 'Not far from the Fairoak industrial estate, where we were this morning.'

'The woods were always private,' I said, 'and the chalk quarry had been long abandoned when I was a boy. Probably a housing estate now.'

'Not according to this,' Ravi rejoined. 'It's still marked. Although these maps can be a good ten years out of date by the time they're printed.'

I said, 'Let's check it out. No time like the present.'

Thirty minutes later, Ravi's Lexus was nosing into the cinder-surfaced car park of Wykham Woods. It was as quiet and magical as I remembered from boyhood, some four square miles of unspoilt mixed woodland surrounding a dilapidated old manor and collapsed greenhouses that were once home to a rare orchid collection. I think it had been left open to the public with the help of some sort of trust set up by the last owner before he died. It was a magnet to deer and wildlife and boasted carpets of bluebells in late spring.

We entered the wood and followed the track south, then crossed through some undergrowth to a collapsed wire fence that marked the edge of the chalk pits. The lunar landscape before us had a sad and abandoned air to it. Once-white cliffs of hewn chalk were now greying with age and weather, and scattered with the odd abandoned vehicle wreck and a variety of domestic detritus, from mattresses to disused washing machines.

'This will be good enough,' Ravi said, surveying the scene. 'So what now?' I asked.

He was looking very pleased with himself. 'I have a plan, Dave. Fancy a trip to London?'

In fact, a trip to London was the last thing I fancied. But Ravi was already on his smartphone. He waited impatiently for a few moments with it clamped to his ear.

'Hello, Egor!' Ravi raised his eyebrows expectantly. 'Yes, it's me . . . Yes, it's been a while . . . Ah, yes, well enough, thank you. Yes, you guessed. About that small favour you owe me. Like *your life*.' There was a pause and I could just make out the sound of deep laughter coming from the handset. 'It's urgent. Is tonight possible? Yes. Where? OK . . . I'll find it. Ciao.'

Ravi switched off and pocketed his phone. 'Right,' he said. 'Let's go and get our glad rags on.'

# Twenty-Five

My glad rags were a pair of clean jeans, a crumpled white shirt with fraying cuffs and a borrowed dark suit jacket from Ravi. It was a shade too tight to button up properly. According to him I looked quite cool, but I think he was just being kind.

On the journey up to London in Ravi's Lexus, the radio tuned to Classic FM, he explained he had arranged for us to meet a certain Egor Baran.

'Egor is a Russian,' Ravi explained, casually steering the big Lexus with one finger on the wheel. 'He was former FSB, electronic intelligence, the successor to the old KGB. Cut his teeth in the Cold War and during the Soviet invasion of Afghanistan. Then privatised himself with some ex-FSB computer specialists in the late nineties. They've got a web of companies all over the world in most of the major cities. That includes London. Egor is in the centre of the web, or near the centre. The UK branch is currently called DarkStar Ethernetics – but blink and it'll have a new name. Just about every Internet bug, virus or scam originates from Russia. Don't ask me how or why, it's just how it is. Egor appears to hire the cream of each year's university computer geeks from Moscow and St Petersburg.'

'How did you meet him?' I asked.

'We wanted some stuff done in Iraq,' Ravi replied lightly. 'To get inside Iraqi politics and both sides of the insurgency. Basically we wanted to place worms to hunt around inside their computer networks.'

'Don't we have our own people who can do that?' I asked.

Ravi chuckled as though I were an innocent. 'Yeah, well, yes, but not as good as the Russians. Anyway, we needed to do that in cahoots with the Yanks – sort of black electronics op in cyber space. So we needed a third party. Egor was our man.'

'Successful?' I asked.

'Stunningly so,' Ravi said. 'And cost a fortune. What we didn't know at the time was that he also used the information we fed him to infiltrate some eighty per cent of the MOD system. It cost the poor old British taxpayer a few million quid of *insurance* money to Egor to get it all resolved.'

'And his *life*?' I asked. 'On the phone you said he owed you.'

Ravi suddenly placed both hands on the wheel, as though to steady himself. 'His company tried a similar trick on his own country, on Russia. Their government's reaction was different to that of the Brits. Let's just say, I did him a favour to divert the flak heading his way. A not-so-innocent Chinese computer hacker based in Tiawan took the blame – and paid the price. Gunned down on his way to have his lunchtime pot noodles.'

Ravi peered forward through the rain-smeared windscreen. 'Ah, I think this is it!'

We were in Knightsbridge. Ravi eventually found an empty parking space, pulled in and fed the meter. There was a chill breeze and fine drizzle in the air as we walked the two blocks. It was a corner building, which used to be a bank. Two heavyweight bouncers in dicky bows stood outside the entrance to the 'Hammer&SickleKlub'. That was the spelling and style on the discreet brass plaque beside the closed doors.

'We're not members,' Ravi said to the larger of the two men. 'We're personal guests of Mr Baran.'

The bouncer eyed us suspiciously as he spoke into the microphone on his lapel for confirmation.

While we waited, Ravi whispered to me, 'Typical Egor. The hammer and sickle emblem is banned in most ex-Soviet nations – like the swastika in post-war Germany – but Egor flaunts the name proudly. Politically incorrect to a fault.'

I overheard the crackling voice emanating from the bouncer's flesh-coloured earpiece. He nodded at us to follow him up the half-dozen steps. The twin mahogany doors swung magically open to welcome us in.

A tsunami of body heat and deep, throbbing music came out to meet us. The lobby, with its reception and cloakroom, was all gilt and red carpet and red flock wallpaper. It resembled an open mouth surrounding the stairs, which plunged down a gaping black hole to the inner soul of the venue.

A skinny girl, with heavy make-up and dressed in the club uniform of black leather dress and thigh-length boots, was waiting for us. With a painted crimson smile, she led us into the noisy depths. It could have been a contemporary version of Dante's inferno. The crowded basement dance floor was illuminated only by spotlights and surrounded by under-lit neon tables and grey chamois sofas the size of beds. So-called music pumped out of giant speakers beside the black DJ's pulpit. Behind him, on the dark red wall, was a large hammer and sickle emblem in moulded gilt.

It immediately struck me that the male clientele was well heeled and mostly aged over forty. The women, all sleek and slender, were decidedly younger.

There was a momentary pause in the pulsing sound waves. I don't know if it was house, trance or garage, I just knew I was happy to give my eardrums a rest.

A voice from behind us said, 'Dear Ravi, old friend!' The man's words were deep and rich like those of a Shakespearean actor with an unhealthy fondness for cigars and cognac. 'If you are seeking a good honest Russian wife or girlfriend, you have come to the right place!'

Egor Baran emerged from the darkness of the dance floor. A tall and exquisitely beautiful woman followed a pace behind him.

'Egor, you old rascal!' Ravi was grinning widely as he shook the extended hand. 'I was thinking more of a mistress.'

'No problem. Even one who will bump off your wife for you, if you want.' The Russian guffawed at his own bleak humour. '*Anything* can be arranged – for a friend.'

'Ah,' Ravi rejoined, 'you mean anything can be arranged – *for a price!*'

Baran chuckled. 'That as well. Did I neglect to mention that bit? Yes, indeed, anything for a friend *and* a price.'

Baran was tall, broad-shouldered and in his forties. His hair was dark and severely receding, but that was hardly noticeable. Anyone's attention was naturally drawn to his strong facial features, the prominent nose and high cheekbones, and the penetrating eyes that were a deep, almost hypnotic blue. Like me he wore a shirt, jacket and jeans. Unlike me, I think they were likely to have been Tommy Hilfiger, hand-stitched Hugo Boss and Calvin Klein, but not necessarily in that order.

'This is Veronika,' Baran said, turning to the beautiful creature who was now standing next to him. She was sheathed in jade-coloured satin. 'Spelled with a K if the police ever ask you. Like the mantis, she is prone to killing her men after making love and taking their money.'

The divine Veronika, half her hair plaited into a tiara while the other half splashed onto the white skin of her shoulder, nudged her man playfully. 'Don't say such things, Egor! Some people may think you are not joking with them!'

'Ah, am I not!' Baran replied before introducing Ravi as an old business acquaintance.

'But, Egor, you still have your life *and* your money!' Veronika retorted a little sharply, just as her green eyes caught mine, seemingly for the first time. 'And this gentleman?'

I was thinking this gentleman wouldn't mind being killed after making love to this creature. At the moment my life was shit, and the money hardly mattered – I didn't have any.

'This is Dave,' Ravi said. 'A good friend of mine. We fought together in Afghanistan.'

Her flawless brow splintered into the finest of hairline fractures. 'I'm sorry. I see on the television that you have bad times there. Just as our Russian soldiers had. Just as Egor had.'

'They weren't exactly good times,' I agreed.

Baran said, 'It is perhaps sad but amusing to see you Westerners make all the same mistakes in Afghanistan that we Soviets made. Does no one ever read history, or learn from it?'

'Apparently not,' Ravi replied.

The big black DJ, dressed in a flowing multi-coloured kaftan, was making his way back to his control podium with a bottle of cola.

Baran indicated the nearby spiral staircase leading to the upstairs balcony floor that had once been the ground floor of the original bank building. 'He'll start again in a minute. It's quieter up there.' He looked at Veronika. 'A bottle of Clicquot. And three glasses.'

She nodded and turned, all three of us men admiring the sway of her hips as she faded into the nightclub's gloom.

'Your mistress?' Ravi ventured.

'My office manager,' Baran replied flatly.

The music was awakening again, and the punters were drifting onto the floor. Each woman that I saw seemed to have no expression on her brightly painted face. The mood was quieter now, sexier with Nina Simone and some jazz number, the title of which I couldn't quite recall.

Upstairs, the balcony overlooked the dance floor. Like the lower level, there were leather sofas and neon-lit tables all around, some with hookah water bowls. One fairly large area was partitioned off with darkly tinted glass. It was empty.

'Our VIP lounge,' Baran explained.

He ran a plastic zip card through the electronic lock and pushed it open. As we passed through into the lounge I had the distinct impression from the thickness of the glass that it might have been bulletproof. The area had its own quietly throbbing musak and welcome air conditioning, a sort of microclimate of its own.

We sat around one of the tables. 'So how can I help?' Baran asked. As he spoke he took a cigar from his pocket and began unwrapping the cellophane.

'There is a criminal gang involved in drugs,' Ravi said. 'In a big town in the south of England. They are getting too big and dangerous. The police are doing nothing . . .'

Baran lit his cigar, inhaled the heavy smoke without a cough or a splutter, and let the stuff exhale slowly out between his teeth.

Ravi paused. 'Er, don't smoking rules apply here?'

The Russian smiled and shrugged. 'Do I give a fuck? Everyone is told after they join. Anyone reports, they know what to expect. We know where they live. No one has yet said a word, but many are happy to join me.' He tipped the ash into a smart, charcoal glass ashtray. 'And why should this gang be of interest to you?'

I interrupted. 'They murdered a friend of mine.'

'We want to gather evidence that will convict them,' Ravi said. 'Stuff the police and Criminal Prosecution Service won't be able to ignore. I've got a telephone number and email address.'

A faint smile crossed Baran's face. 'That is all I need.'

'You'll do it?'

'I don't see why not.' The glistening eyes hardened. 'But that will be it. We will then be fully squared up, I think you say?'

'Nothing owed,' Ravi agreed. 'All square.'

Veronika then returned with a silver tray, on it a bottle of Veuve Clicquot champagne and three cut-crystal flutes. I noticed the bill of one hundred pounds, which Baran deftly signed off with a flourish of his gold pen.

Only three glasses was the signal for the delectable Veronika to leave us alone to discuss man things.

When she'd gone, Baran got straight to the point. 'You want to know all you can about these people, yes? Perhaps get inside their computer networks?'

Ravi nodded. 'If we can do that?'

'Of course. Do these people know you have their email address?'

'Yes, and I have something legitimate to send them.'

'Excellent!'

'A map.'

'Even better.'

Ravi took the Ordnance Survey map from his pocket and put it on the table. 'This area here. Wykham Wood and the adjoining chalk quarry. I've marked it with some notes for them.'

Baran placed a pair of designer spectacles on his nose and tilted the map so he could see it by the neon light of the table. 'That will be ideal,' he murmured. 'This can be corrupted by a simple instruction to download one of our Trojans.'

I'd heard that IT expression before, but I wasn't sure exactly what it meant. 'Like the famous Trojan Horse of

Greek mythology,' Baran explained affably. 'It is welcomed into the target's computer, but once in there, we can open it without them knowing and it will wreak havoc – or in this case, allow us access to all the files on their computer. The cost? Between nine hundred and one and a half grand, depending on the complexity.'

I was puzzled. 'What about firewalls and security systems? Won't they stop it?' I asked.

Baran smiled. 'That's what you are paying for. Any security system can only detect and protect against a *known* virus, of course. We are creating a *new* one – just for you. Our laboratories are upstairs. Come, let me show you.'

We finished our drinks and Baran led the way to a door marked Fire Exit. It opened onto a stairwell and landing. Steps led down to the front reception and up to the next floor. We followed Baran upwards where we were confronted by a plain grey door with a heavy-duty electronic lock.

Baran punched a code into the touchpad and opened the door into a stark office. Its bright fluorescent lights shone down on bare polished wood flooring and plain white walls. There were no decorations of any sort, no pictures, no ornaments, nothing that might hide a bugging device or miniature camera. Aluminium blinds covered the windows and the banks of glossy black computers and their associated paraphernalia sat on see-through smoked-glass tables.

Another electronic lock protected a smaller, solid-partitioned inner office. This was the keep of Egor Baran's castle. Again the desk was glass and clear of any clutter. He sat on an uncomfortable-looking ergonomic chair made of bright-red plastic and opened the Ordnance Survey map in front of him.

'I will scan the section of the map you want,' he announced. 'As you know, images – like pictures or maps – are made up of thousands and thousands of tiny spots called pixels. To the computer each will instruct in binary language – "Draw red, draw red, draw red" . . . or "Draw green, draw green, draw green . . ." But just one pixel will carry the secret instruction "Download TJN blah, blah, whatever." While he is online, unknown to the user, the computer will go to an unnamed Dark-Star webserver. Once there, it goes to the file storage account where the Trojan virus is waiting. It will download immediately into his computer. Within seconds it will have infected his hard drive and I will have total access to all its contents. That includes passwords, bank accounts, telephone numbers, email or postal address details. As long as it is switched on or even just a Wi-Fi connection, I will have full access to his computer.'

'Amazing,' I breathed.

'How long will it take you to set up?' Ravi asked.

Baran shrugged. 'Usually three or four working days.'

Ravi frowned. 'I need it for Monday.'

'Do you now?' There was a sarcastic edge to Baran's voice. 'Let's see . . . It's Saturday night. Sunday is not too busy. For an old friend, Monday morning I will email you a copy of the map. Give me your number. And remember . . .'

'Don't open it?' Ravi guessed.

Baran steepled his fingers together. 'Unless you want me to have access to your dirty porn and other secrets, too, just save it and pass it on to your target.'

Ravi rose to his feet. 'Egor, I am most grateful.'

'My pleasure,' Baran replied. 'You and your friend can come down to the club and enjoy the rest of your evening.'

'Sorry, we must get back.'

Baran looked suitably disappointed as he showed us down the stairs, said goodbye, and then waited with the two bruisers on the door. He kept watching us until we disappeared into the wet and misty Knightsbridge street.

'Do you trust him?' I asked as we approached the Lexus.

There was a thoughtful pause. Ravi said, 'Not as far as I could throw him.'

We drove straight back to Swinthorpe.

I treated myself to a couple of shots of whisky from the hotel minibar before having a shower and crashing out naked on the crisp white sheets.

At around four in the morning I woke up in a cold sweat. I'd been dreaming. I was back in Baghdad again.

We were raiding a bomb-maker's compound in the dead of night, but instead of being in darkness it was lit up like a fairground. It was crazy, all wrong.

I wanted to abort. But Chas Houseman was there, countermanding me. The mission must go on, he insisted. Big Brian Duffy was there, Ravi, Andy Smith, the whole team shouting and yelling as we attacked and entered the compound. There were explosions all around us, bullets firing as I entered the house.

It was dark inside, just a little girl's face looking up at me.

Big wide eyes. But it wasn't the face of an Afghan child. It was my daughter Daisy.

'*Daddy, what are you doing here?*'

Her words were still sounding in my head. So clear, so real.

The hotel room was claustrophobic, airless. I crawled off the bed, made my way to the window and threw it open. Welcome cool air wafted in and I breathed deeply. I shook my head, but the vision of Daisy wouldn't go.

I realised at that moment just how much I missed her.

What the hell must she think of me? How could she cope with having such a spineless idiot as a father? This really had gone on long enough. Somehow I must regain control of my life. To go on like this was to surrender to my demons, to let them win without a fight.

I poured some water from the cooler and downed a couple of tumblerfuls. Then I threw myself on the bed, feeling fresher and calmer. Confused thoughts scrambled through my head, fighting for attention as I tried to plan how I might get my life back together again.

I was still struggling with it all when I must have drifted off.

The next thing I knew was Ravi knocking on my door, ready to go down for breakfast. I joined him fifteen minutes later and told him I'd had enough of hotel life. He said he understood, but I wasn't sure he did.

After topping up with a full English, I headed for the streets of Swinthorpe and the market square. There, as anticipated, I found Edwina sitting on one of the benches, an old blanket wrapped around her legs. She was talking earnestly to the Serbian wild man known as Manni.

She broke off her conversation as soon as I approached. 'Dave, dear boy, I've been so worried about you! Where have you been?'

I sat down beside her. Manni glared at me; I wasn't sure he remembered me. But then he said, 'Hello, army man. Remember me? I am war crimes killer. I look after this lady.'

I said, 'Yes, I remember you. Once met, never forgotten.' I turned to Edwina. 'I've been slumming it in a hotel. An old friend turned up and treated me.'

Edwina gave a snort of feigned envy. 'Lucky you to have friends like that. Did you nick any sachets of shampoo? Or soap would be nice?'

I shook my head. 'No, and I couldn't stand the central heating.'

'Fussy bugger.'

Manni said, 'Policewoman comes looking for you. The one who dresses as man with tits.'

Edwina glanced at him. 'Language, Manni,' she admonished. 'Oh, yes. DC Jane Christy, wearing that trilby of hers. Looking for you. Had a man with her.'

Why was it I felt a sudden sensation like a trickle of ice water down my back? 'What was his name?'

'She didn't say, but I gathered *he* was the one who wanted to talk to you.'

'What did he look like?'

'Handsome bugger, I suppose. Forties, I'd say, with a bit of a tan and gold fair hair going to grey. Bit smarmy.'

'Houseman,' I breathed. 'What did you tell them?'

'What could I tell them? I had no idea where you were.'

She reached out her arm and touched mine. 'Dear Dave, you aren't in any trouble, are you?'

I forced a grin. 'Not that I'm aware of.'

'Good, because DC Christy asked that you contact her as soon as you can. I said I'd pass the message on when I next saw you.'

I said, 'Then I'm the invisible man, understand? You haven't seen me.'

Edwina sighed. 'Yes, Dave. I've seen nothing and nobody.'

'Have you heard from Steve?' Gem demanded.

I'd been trying to avoid being alone with her since the cafe opened on the Monday morning, but it was impossible. Ravi had turned up for one of our Daybreak Specials, sitting outside with his fancy Wi-Fi laptop and a cup of steaming cappuccino. She had caught me as I sat beside him to have a cigarette.

'No, Gem. I was hoping you might have.'

She shook her head, as she placed a plate with a bacon and egg roll on the table. 'And nor has his sister. I just called.'

'Don't worry,' I said with more reassurance than I felt. 'We should be seeing those people tomorrow. We'll have news then. Probably bring him back with us.'

At that moment, Ravi's laptop gave an energetic little bleep. 'Ah!' he said, 'an email from Egor. There it is. "Dear Ravi, a gift from your old friend. Good to see you. Map attached as requested. Veronika sends her love. Egor."'

'Don't open the attachment,' I reminded.

'Certainly not,' Ravi replied absently, starting to tap on his keyboard. 'Just filing it safely away, and writing a short note to that bastard Rashid. Giving him the location of the quarry for shooting practice and the map attachment.'

I said, 'We're seeing him and Jooma Khan at midday tomorrow. Maybe suggest we all visit there in the afternoon.'

'Good idea,' Ravi answered, tapping away like a demon. 'There, all done. No problems.'

Well, no problems for Ravi perhaps, but I had just one with my boss, Andreas Simitis.

I managed to catch him alone in the afternoon. I thanked him for having given me a break, the opportunity to earn a few pounds. 'But, Andreas, I have to move on. Some things have come up. I have to deal with them. And I have to get my life in order.'

The Greek stared at me hard. 'What are you saying, Mr David?'

'I'm sorry. I won't be back tomorrow.'

He scowled. 'You leave me? I will be ruined. Since you are here, my business goes up. They like your sandwiches.'

I smiled and shook his hand. 'Then break the habit of a lifetime, Andreas. Put more filling in the sandwiches.'

I awoke early the next morning in the loading yard of the carpet factory. Overnight it had become a refugee camp. It was November now and there was a glistening coat of frost on the blankets and cardboard sheets covering the dozen sleeping bodies.

While I lit my gas stove to boil up some water, people began to stir. The owners of the store were very tolerant, but everyone knew they had to clear the area by the time the store opened at nine o'clock.

Edwina and Manni joined me, clutching their empty mugs, ready to be filled.

My mobile rang. It was Ravi. 'I just got an email from Rashid. He's swallowed it – hook, line and sinker. He's obviously opened the map attachment – our Trojan should be right in his computer now.'

'Great,' I said.

'But there's been a change of plan.' For the first time I became aware of the slightly higher, nervous note in Ravi's voice. 'Rashid wants to meet us earlier than planned. Can I come over and pick you up now?'

'Of course.' I gave him directions to the carpet store, then asked, 'What's going on, Ravi?'

'I'm not sure. Something's odd. Tell you when we meet.'

I just had time to get my kit together before Ravi's Lexus pulled up outside the rear gates. I said goodbye to Edwina and Manni and lugged my bergen over to the car, dumping it in the boot.

As we pulled away, Ravi said, 'After receiving his email, I phoned Rashid. He sounded a bit strange. Hard to put my finger on it. He said there'd been a change of RV. The gang have pulled out of that warehouse on the Fairoak estate. After all that shooting on Saturday, worried neighbours called the police. They must have arrived just after we left. Our friend Jooma Khan did some quick thinking on his feet. Explained away the wrecked gates and fence as an attempted robbery. He thought it had gone wrong when the robbers realised the warehouse was occupied over the weekend.'

'Didn't the cops find anything?' I asked. 'Surely the place was full of drugs – not to mention firearms.'

'According to Rashid, they lost interest when Jooma said nothing had been stolen from the warehouse because it was empty. The white gang must have been acting on wrong information. A bunch of wallies.'

'But the gunfire?' I asked.

Ravi shrugged. 'I expect Jooma just denied there was any use of guns. Doesn't sound like any member of the public actually *saw* anything. So it was just a non-event at the weekend on a deserted industrial estate. Not much to get the police too excited over.'

'Suppose not,' I said. 'So where are we having the meeting now?'

'Apparently some farm not too far away. I've got the directions,' Ravi said, pointing to the scrap of notepaper on the dashboard. 'And another development. A bit weird.'

'What's that?'

'That VIP of theirs who's coming over . . .'

'The one we've offered to protect?'

'That's him. He's arrived a few days early. He's here now. Seems to have got everyone in the gang a bit jumpy.'

'What's so weird about that?'

'Not that. His name. It rang a bell with me straight away.'

I was getting irritated with Ravi's games. 'What name, for God's sake?'

Ravi said, 'Masood Babur.'

It took me a moment, a long moment. My mind was flying like a time machine, back across the streets of Hereford, aching hours of physiotherapy in Headley Court, the seemingly endless operations on my leg in Birmingham Selly Oak, the painfully long flight back from Afghanistan, the dust of the giant Chinook helicopter as it tried to land, and the house like a Pakistani wedding cake.

The house of Dr Zam-Zama, Taliban warlord and drug baron.

I could barely remember the sullen-looking man who had taken us into the meeting with Chas Houseman at Zam-Zama's house.

But I remembered his name. The man who'd described himself as Zam-Zama's number two.

'Masood Babur,' I echoed. And as I whispered the name I felt the caterpillar's crawl on hairs down the back of my neck.

# Twenty-Six

The mere mention of that name seemed to change every-thing.

The sun passed behind a cloud as a new front rolled in from the south-west. A chill wind began rustling the trees.

Tall wooden gates guarded the entrance to the yard and farm buildings. Unusually, there were scrolls of razor wire running along the top of them. On our approach, two members of the Swords of Allah gang appeared from a small shed beside the entrance. It looked as though the men might be concealing weapons beneath their jackets. They also seemed edgy.

Ravi's electric side window glided open. 'Ravi Khan and Dave Aston,' he announced with a smile. 'We are expected.'

One of the guards glanced down at the clipboard in his hand. 'I know.' He turned his head away and called to some-one on the far side of the gate. 'They're here. Open up.'

The car edged into the muddy yard. One of the two men who had opened the door indicated the smaller of two enclosed barns in front of us. There were half a dozen vehi-cles parked in front of it. As we drove over and stopped beside them, a small door to the barn opened sharply.

It was Jooma Khan himself, the gang's head of security, who was there to meet us. He wore his long signature waistcoat with its intricate Arabic embroidery. I don't know if it had been the result of the shootout at the warehouse on Saturday, but his reaction to us seemed distinctly warmer. The lips within the distinguished thick beard were smiling, as were the eyes behind the tortoiseshell spectacles.

However his friendly manner did not extend to shaking hands with us. 'Mr Khan and Mr Aston, it is good to see you both again.'

As he stepped aside to let us in, I saw that Rashid had been standing behind him. The leader of the Swords of Allah made no attempt to conceal the Colt automatic in the waistband of his trousers.

Rashid beckoned us. 'You two, come on in.'

Ravi and I exchanged glances, uncertain. Ravi shrugged and clearly made a decision to continue. My guess was he reasoned that a number of these gang members were armed and we could be in big trouble if we changed our minds now.

It was dark inside the barn. There was only ambient light from a small, lighted area at the far end of the building. We were ushered forward in silence.

To me it felt that we were entering some sort of filmset. Industrial plastic sheeting had been spread out on the ground beneath a couple of arc lamps, forming a stark pool of light. All around this small arena stood members of the gang. I recognised a number of them. That included Rashid's number two, Amir, with his gormless expression and sprouting beard, and young Ali, who I had water-boarded.

Directly opposite Ravi and me stood a man I had not seen for a long time. In fact I had not seen him since our meeting at the house of Dr Zam-Zama. I would never have recognised him in a million years, and I doubt if Ravi would have either.

With a sudden thrill of excitement, I realised it was exceedingly unlikely that Masood Babur would recognise Ravi and me either.

Babur was taller than I remembered. His hair was neatly trimmed, and he wore a small moustache. He stood there in a plain white shirt and black trousers. His eyes were still sullen as I vaguely remembered. But they also seemed distinctly harder than my memory of them. I recalled he'd told us he'd lost family to an American air strike. What else had happened to him since, I wondered? How deep did his hatred of all things Western run now?

'We are all here,' Masood Babur stated suddenly. His English was much better than I recalled. Now he talked with more confidence, and definitely with more authority.

The silence in the circle of gang members was absolute. Everyone listened, the atmosphere tense.

After a moment, he added, 'First I must thank you all for your welcome to me – especially the warmth of Rashid, on behalf of Mullah Siraj Chadhur. It is only my second visit to these shores. So I appreciate the friendship you have shown me. I also bring greetings from those of your number who have in the past made their way from here to wage jihad in my own homeland.'

There was a ripple of murmured comment and nodding of heads amongst the youthful chain of onlookers. I wondered how many recruits had been offered up from my own hometown to be slaughtered amongst the ranks of the Taliban in the badlands of Afghanistan.

Masood Babur paused for a moment, clearly seeking out someone amongst the rows of unfamiliar faces. 'Ah, dear Jooma Khan. Our hard-working security expert, who has taken such care to get me into this country with a new name and identity. Helping me to escape the attentions of the UK Border Agency. There you are. Do step forward.'

I glanced sideways at Khan. He looked uneasy and was sweating profusely. Perhaps it was the effect of the heavy waistcoat he wore, and that thick black beard can't have helped. He waved his hand. 'It is nothing,' he muttered.

Babur's voice dropped an octave. 'I *said* step forward,' he repeated. 'Come and accept the honour.'

Khan shrugged and shuffled into the centre of the brightly lit circle until he was face to face with Dr Zam-Zama's man from Afghanistan. 'There now, Mr Khan, that is not so difficult. Why the reluctance to accept praise, I wonder? After all, as I said, you have been working so hard, have you not?'

I noticed Khan was avoiding the other man's eyes. 'Thank you,' he mumbled under his breath.

Masood Babur appeared suddenly to lose interest in Khan. Instead he turned his head and looked at Ravi and me.

'Now, you two gentlemen,' he said. 'Jooma and Rashid tells me about you. That you have served in the British Army, yet have offered your services to them? I have this correct?'

Ravi took a deep breath. 'We are out of the British Army now, sir. My friend Dave here and I both personally believe that we should never have been in your country. But we were soldiers and had to follow orders. We have both now left. Dave was injured and I – er . . .' Ravi's acting abilities could have won him a bit-part in *EastEnders* '. . . fell foul of military law, shall we say.'

'You are a criminal?'

Ravi's smile held steady. 'In that I traded with your people. Supplied luxuries that they wanted.'

'In return for what?'

'A little hashish. It was a tough time.'

I could swear a ghost of a smile illuminated Babur's face for a split second. 'But now?'

'Times are still hard for my friend Dave and for me. You will be aware of his relationship with your friends here. The trouble he has caused them single-handedly to protect his defenceless friends. That fierce courage and loyalty, and his skills are offered to you now, along with my own. We both need money and we both offer skills and total loyalty in return.' The smile fell from Ravi's face. 'As an Afghan you will understand the concept of the mercenary soldier?'

That seemed to strike home. After a pause, Rashid spoke for the first time, looking directly at Ravi. 'I received your email with your map. This Wykham Woods, it looks like a good place to use weapons. For firearms training, you said?'

'You clearly need it,' I added firmly. 'And we'll offer close protection to Mr Babur, or whoever you wish to keep safe.'

Babur nodded his understanding. 'Indeed, I understand the concept of the mercenary. You say you offer skills, but as for total loyalty . . . ? Of that I am not so sure.'

Rashid had now moved to stand beside Babur, his right-hand man. He said, 'Oh, but I think we can establish that.'

There was a brief, chill silence. I noticed that Babur's eyes appeared very dark, cold and without emotion. His lips moved almost imperceptibly. 'Proceed.'

Jooma Khan stood to one side, observing the proceedings with obvious apprehension.

There was a sudden commotion to the left of the circle as Rashid called out an instruction. Gang members stepped aside as two burly minders entered. A skinny, hapless individual was half-shuffling and half-carried between the two of them. He was doubled-over and barely able to place one foot in front of the other.

I knew instantly who it was, despite the fact that the hood of his Nike waterproof had fallen over his bowed head. There was no mistaking the spidery legs in the faded jeans.

'Steve . . .' I breathed.

'What?' Ravi demanded irritably.

'It's Steve Cranford.'

Recognition dawned. 'Oh, my God.'

In unison, the two heavyweights pushed the man forward. Whether or not he was tripped, I don't know, but he dropped to his knees in the middle of the circle facing Ravi and me. He tilted his head up and the hood fell back off the head shorn of sandy hair. His white, pitted face turned up as if to try to see me. Trails of congealed blood ran over his cheeks from sightless eyes. Two more trickled from his ears, one still wet and creeping down his neck like a grotesque invisible snail.

Even the members of the circle took a united gasp of surprise.

'See no evil, hear no evil,' Babur said softly. 'Now he will speak no evil. It is the price of defiance. *Allahu Akbar!*'

Suddenly the camera on a mobile phone clicked and flashed. Then another, and another.

More of the audience decided to copy their comrades. The repeated clicks sounded strangely like a swarm of insects. I took a step forward but I felt Ravi's restraining hand on my arm.

Cranford's thin fingers scrabbled in the air, trying to identify something, someone to help him. The word *'Please ...'* escaped his parched lips.

Babur ignored the plea. 'So, Mr Aston, you will be first to prove your loyalty and allegiance to your new masters. Rashid ... give him the gun. Just one round.'

I'd barely had time to register the words when I felt the cold gunmetal in my hands. I stared down at the .45 Colt.

'One shot,' Babur reminded.

My mind was in a blur, a total spin. This was the oldest trick in the book. Kill your own to prove your loyalty to your former enemy. It was part of many terrorist organisations' rites of passage. The Provisional IRA had been fond of it, as well as the corrupt regimes of Saddam and Gaddafi.

One shot. I had just one shot. Did I use it to take out Babur or Rashid? Who else had guns in the surrounding crowd? I was sure that at least one of the minders who had brought Cranford in was armed; I could see the bulge of the shoulder holster quite clearly.

'Do it now!' Babur commanded, his voice rising in its pitch.

Another pistol had appeared in Rashid's hand and now he was toying with it impatiently.

My heart was thudding so hard I believed it would burst out of my chest at any moment. Sweat was breaking out across my shoulders and on my forehead. It was trickling into my eyes, making them sting. I couldn't do this. I couldn't kill Cranford. He didn't deserve this. He'd already been blinded and his ears tent-pegged – a favourite but nasty little Taliban trick to punish those who dissented from their views or orders.

'For God's sake!' the voice beside me said.

Ravi snatched the Colt from my grasp.

He pointed and fired. Mobile phone cameras flashed. The single shot to the head blew Cranford backwards at an awkward angle, so that he toppled sideways onto the plastic-sheeted flooring.

Ravi looked pale. He swallowed hard. 'I am sorry. My friend has more soul than I do. I lost mine some time ago.'

Babur ignored that and looked hard at me. 'Not good enough. Mr Aston, you must shoot too.'

Rashid took the Colt from Ravi, removed the magazine and added another single round.

The gun was back in my hand. Rashid raised his own gun and pointed it directly at Ravi. I had no way out now. I checked the Colt, aimed quickly at Cranford's inert body and pulled the trigger. It twitched with the force of the impact.

Blood was thudding in my temples as I stared down in blind rage at the body and at what Ravi and I had been forced to do.

I was barely aware of the bizarre and grotesque ritual that
followed. The smoking Colt was passed to each member of
the circle in turn, together with a single round. One by one
they stepped forward, shot a single bullet into Cranford's
corpse, muttered 'God is Great', turned and handed it to the
next man in the line.

The process, clearly Masood Babur's new initiation ceremony, seemed to go on for ever. I felt sick.

'For God's sake, Dave!' Ravi hissed. 'Get a grip.'

We were back in Ravi's Lexus, leading a small convoy of
vehicles towards Wykham Wood.

'Do you realise what's just happened?' I said. 'We just
murdered Steve Cranford.'

Ravi looked uncomfortable, the light gone from his eyes.
'Actually, Dave, *I* did. But under duress, in self-defence –
with a gun pointed at both of us. I don't know what the law
would make of that, but I'm sure it's not murder.'

I glared sideways at him. 'This isn't Iraq, or Afghanistan.
We should go straight to the police now.'

This time Ravi smiled thinly. 'That lot. You've already told
me what a useless shower they are. A murder charge will be a
self-fulfilling wish for both of us – and nine months in custody
before the case gets to court. No, Dave, we stick to the plan.
Get some decent evidence against them. You heard what
Rashid said. He's got the emailed map attachment. With any
luck our little Trojan is jogging around his computer hard
drive, even as we speak. Get the evidence and *then* we go to
the police.'

I shook my head in despair at his gung-ho attitude. 'And when Steve Cranford's body is discovered? We might not have the luxury of that much time.'

Ravi swung the wheel to take us into the small car park that marked the entrance to Wykham Wood.

There was no more time to talk. As we climbed out of the car, a green Range Rover and a minibus pulled in beside us. Rashid had brought with him his most trusted half-dozen gang members, including Amir and young Ali.

I led us through the gate into the woodland. Further on we went between tall hedges of glossy rhododendron and along a track of recently fallen dead leaves. After a quarter of a mile I left the track, weaving through a scattering of holly trees to a perimeter fence.

Beyond the boundary, open grassland fell away to the first of the chalk pits. A faded sign read: 'Strictly No Entry'. I pushed it aside and stepped over the collapsed strands of barbed wire. As I'd thought, it was an ideal location, totally private and not overlooked by any road or any housing. I remembered from my childhood that there was always shooting going on in this area, the usual targets being rabbits, crows, pigeon or game birds.

Ravi and I spent a couple of hours putting everyone through their paces. It was safety first, of course. Getting everyone routinely checking that the chamber was clear and the catch on when receiving a weapon. And to remove the magazine completely if it wasn't being used.

Some of them had difficulty getting their heads around these golden rules. They'd obviously seen far too many movies and video games. I don't think they quite believed that in civilian life more people died through accidents with firearms than by deliberate action.

Likewise they tended to forget to take off the safety catch before trying to fire. Ravi would dance in front of one of them, goading, 'Go on, shoot me, shoot me!'

Young Ali cautiously pointed the Colt near the man's feet and pulled the trigger. Everyone stopped and stared, wondering what would happen. Of course, nothing happened.

'You've left the safety on,' Amir pointed out smugly. Everyone laughed and Ali kicked at the ground in his frustration at being shown up in front of the others.

I had a brainwave after we'd put out three posts and mounted them with circular cardboard rifle targets that Ravi had bought from a sports shop in Swinthorpe.

'We'll need to keep scores,' I said, turning to Ravi. 'You got pen and paper?'

He produced a notebook and a biro.

I turned to the youngster I believed had killed Jock Mahoney. 'Name?'

'Ali.'

I shot back quickly. 'Ali what?'

'Kamran Ali,' he shot back.

Before anyone realised it wasn't actually necessary for keeping a score, I'd gone around the whole group, each member offering up his full name.

Ravi caught my eye and winked. The contest began.

The time sped by and it was soon time to leave. The gang members had clearly enjoyed the practice and lessons, and at least Rashid seemed pleased. After all, I ensured his was the winning score.

His face was flushed with pride as he packed away his weapon. 'Tomorrow there is an important event,' he told me as we started walking back towards the vehicles. 'A big delivery of product. You understand what I mean, yeah?'

'Product?' I repeated. 'I think I know what you mean.'

'I want you and Ravi to organise security.'

I nodded. 'Where is this to take place?'

'You get told tomorrow. After you know the details, you don't go no place, understand? Until it's over.'

I shrugged. We didn't have much option. 'What about Jooma Khan?' I asked. 'He's our head of security, after all. Does he agree with this?'

Rashid glared at me. 'Don't you worry about him. You just be awake at seven tomorrow morning. We will finalise your pay deal with Mr Babur.'

I said, 'We told Jooma Khan our terms.'

Rashid didn't blink. 'I know. They will be met.'

'So we'll see you then,' Ravi confirmed as we reached the car park.

I didn't need Ravi to persuade me it was time to give up my life as a nomad – or at least sleeping under the stars and travelling around the city on a bicycle. He was not short of a few quid, and I finally relented at his insistence to pay for my room at the hotel for a while.

Something about him had changed. At first he seemed to have been treating this whole thing like a game. I realised he was missing army intelligence a lot more than he let on, and recent events had been filling that vacuum for him. But now there'd suddenly been a seismic shift in his attitude and his demeanour. To save us both he'd just been trapped into killing an innocent man. The fact that the man was a wastrel and had alternatively faced life being both blind and deaf hardly made it any easier.

In life, the hardest person to forgive is often yourself.

I think Ravi was beginning to realise that now, and he wasn't happy. I sensed he'd like to be on his own with his thoughts for a while. So when we got to the hotel, I dumped my bergen in my room and left immediately on foot for Gem's house, promising Ravi I'd be back later.

I knew Gem would have been worried about Steve Cranford. For good or ill she obviously still felt something for him. And I had been the idiot who had recklessly placed him into the hands of his killers, never dreaming that just a few days later I'd be witnessing his death and taking part in the macabre murder ceremony. I felt incredibly guilty.

To be honest I had no idea what I was going to say to her. Obviously, I couldn't tell her I knew he was dead. I just felt I ought to offer her some sort of comfort.

But, as I rounded the corner into her street and saw the two white police cars parked outside Gem's house, I realised it was too late for that.

# Twenty-Seven

Detective Constable Jane Christy opened the door of Gem's house.

A rapid blink was the only sign of her surprise at seeing me there. 'Ah, Mr Aston.' There was hardly any hesitation before she added, 'I was about to come looking for you.'

I smiled awkwardly. 'About the disappearance of Steve Cranford?'

Christy remained poker-faced. She was not wearing her hat and a profusion of auburn curls cascaded onto the shoulders of her trenchcoat. 'About the believed *murder* of Steve Cranford,' she corrected with a level voice.

I tried to feign surprise, but my acting abilities were rubbish. '*Murdered?* . . . Are you sure?'

The violet eyes narrowed. 'Well, *someone*'s been murdered. We believe it is Steven Cranford, but the body hasn't been formally identified yet. Murdered by person or persons unknown. A gunshot to the head and multiple gunshots to the body. A bit of a mess. The corpse was found wrapped in industrial plastic sheeting and dumped in a country lane lay-by south of the town. A dead end only used by tractors at a nearby farm. No witnesses yet and certainly no CCTV.'

'Grim,' I said, and meant it.

'I understand you collected Steve Cranford from his sister's flat on the Evinmore estate on Saturday. You and your ex-army buddy called Ravi Azoor?'

I nodded.

Christy stood back to let me pass. 'You'd better come in. I'll warn you, Miss Wilkins is not very happy.'

I stepped into the hall and through the lounge door. Gem was sitting on the sofa, her hands clasped together with those of WPC Sharman. PC Tiddy stood behind them, in an earnest whispered conversation on his radio.

Gem looked up as I entered the room. Her tears were glistening like snail tracks down her cheeks. She went to stand up. 'You bastard . . . !' she began.

'Now, now, Miss Wilkins,' Sharon Sharman urged, restraining her. 'Please stay calm.'

'Please, Gemma,' Christy said, 'I know you're upset. We're all upset about it. But let's hear what Dave's got to say.'

But Gem was hardly listening. 'You bastard!' she repeated. 'You told us some charity wanted a druggie to warn kids about stuff. You told me and Grace and Steve he'd get paid – like some sort of outreach worker. Then you went and handed him over to those Muslim tossers! I don't believe you!' She glared pure vitriol at me. 'And I *trusted* you!'

Christy gestured for me to go back into the hall and asked quietly, 'Is this true?'

I nodded. I was hardly in a position to deny it. 'Steve wouldn't have come with us otherwise. Obviously Ravi and I had no idea they were going to kill him. Steve only owed them peanuts.'

'So it was a gang pride thing?' Christy pushed. 'Street cred?'

'Terror tactics,' I replied tersely. 'Rule by fear.'

She stared into my eyes. 'Why the hell did you do it, Dave? I don't understand.'

Suddenly I snapped. 'They murdered Jock Mahoney, for God's sake! And Ginger with crap drugs. And your Inspector Ryan did nothing. You may have wanted to, but he did *nothing*! I just wanted to get in with the gang, find out about them. Get this precious bloody *evidence* you cops seem unable or unwilling to find.'

Christy swallowed hard. I knew my words had hurt, but she wasn't about to give up that easily. 'Well, maybe now you know a bit more about them than you wanted to.'

'That they're killers?' I gave a snort of derision. 'I do believe I told you that. I still didn't *dream* that they would actually kill Steve.'

The expression in Christy's eyes said 'More fool you', and I couldn't deny she was right. But all she asked, quietly, was, 'And your friend, Ravi Azoor? Ex-army intelligence, I gather. We're checking him out. Facts aren't very forthcoming from the MOD, I'm afraid.'

I said, 'He was with the Special Reconnaissance Regiment. Close-up intelligence gathering. Their forerunners were 14 Int in Northern Ireland.'

'Do you know where he is now?'

I nodded. 'We've got rooms at the Riverside Lodge Hotel in town. I'm due to meet him later.'

Christy paused thoughtfully for a moment, before asking,

'And where did the two of you take Steve Cranford on Saturday?'

'To a warehouse on the Fairoak industrial park,' I replied. 'A firm called – er – Night . . . something . . .' It took a moment to recall the name. 'That's it . . . NightHub UK. Looked like some sort of distribution outfit . . . run by the Swords of Allah gang.'

'For their drugs distribution?' she asked. She was putting two and two together fast and making five.

'I would guess so.'

'There was some trouble reported there on Saturday,' Christy murmured. 'We're still investigating. An attempted break-in that went wrong.'

'It was,' I replied. 'By the rival Chip Shop Boys gang. Ravi and I were there at the time, delivering Steve Cranford.'

'To his death?'

'We didn't know that,' I replied wearily. 'We thought they'd just give him a severe talking to. We wanted to discover more about them.'

'And did you?'

'We found out that Mullah Siraj Chadhar is the real head of the operation in Swinthorpe,' I replied. 'I'm guessing it covers more than just this town.'

Christy raised an eyebrow in surprise. 'You have been busy. I understand your impatience, but I'm afraid you've been going about things all the wrong way.'

'Offering our services to the gang was the *only* way,' I returned icily. 'It's led us to meet one of the major suppliers from Afghanistan. The Border Agency might be interested in the name. Masood Babur. He's in the country already. Ravi and I are supposed to be providing close protection for him.'

PC Tiddy had been pacing up and down in the lounge, beyond the sofa where Gem sat with WPC Sharman. He had been chatting away on his radio in a low voice. Now he stopped and waved at us standing near the door. 'Jane,' he called over. 'We're just getting reports in. Looks like mobile phone footage of Steve Cranford's execution. Posted on some radical Muslim website. A warning from the Swords of Allah.'

Gem clasped her hands to her face. 'Oh, my God . . . !'

Christy said angrily: 'Not in front of Miss Wilkins, Ray, for goodness' sake. She's been through quite enough.'

Tiddy swallowed hard and looked apologetic. 'Sorry, Jane.'

The detective constable turned back to me. 'My God, you've got a lot more explaining to do, Mr Aston.'

I swallowed hard, but said nothing.

She said, 'First I want to talk with your spooky mate.'

'Ravi will be at the hotel.' As an afterthought, I added, 'But can we do this quietly – maybe without marked police cars? I don't want word getting back to the gang.'

She looked at me curiously. 'Do you *really* believe you'll be working with them again after this?'

I shrugged. God only knew the answer to that one.

Before we left, I attempted to speak to Gem, to say how sorry I was about Steve Cranford. But she was too full of tears and anger to want to listen.

Christy arranged for an unmarked car to pick us up from Gem's house and drop us around the corner from the Riverside Lodge.

As we entered the door I noticed Ravi seated at the bar in earnest conversation with the *Journal* reporter Bernie Bramshaw. The man looked to be in good form, laughing as he gulped from his beer glass.

'Oh, dammit,' Christy muttered under her breath.

Bramshaw still had his wits about him, spotting our approach immediately. 'Hello, Dave, how you doin'?' he greeted. 'And you've got my favourite cop with you, Swinthorpe's gorgeous answer to Miss Marple.'

'Hello, Bernie,' the detective replied with a forced smile, then regarded Ravi. 'Mr Azoor, nice to meet you again. Just a shame catching you talking to the Anti-Christ.'

Bramshaw's smile crumpled. 'That's a bit harsh, m'dear. Let me get you both a drink.'

Christy said, 'This isn't a social visit.'

I added quickly, 'Steve's body has been found. Multiple gunshot wounds. There's even some phone-cam footage on the Internet.'

'Oh, no,' I heard Ravi murmur.

I caught his eye and shook my head gently. 'There's no faces shown, apparently . . .'

Meanwhile, Bramshaw pounced. 'The missing junkie, Steve Cranford? Shot? Where was the body found?'

'No, no!' Christy protested. 'It's not even confirmed it's him yet. I'll keep you posted, as soon as I know anything.' She turned to Ravi. 'I must talk with you urgently.'

He smiled his charming toothy smile. 'Sure, my room?'

Saying our goodbyes to Bramshaw, we left him in the bar and traipsed up to the rather musty-smelling bedroom that was mostly only rented out on a Saturday night when one of the local lads got unexpectedly lucky.

Christy declined an offered drink and seated herself in the only armchair.

I think Ravi wanted to steal a lead before the detective constable had a chance to ask too many awkward questions. As he poured himself and me a tot of whisky, he said, 'I've heard from our Russian friend, Dave. He's starting to find out a lot of interesting stuff.'

I explained, 'We've got someone to hack the computer of one of the Muslim gang leaders. The one called Rashid.'

Christy blinked in surprise. 'Oh, gentlemen, I really think enough is enough!'

But Ravi pressed on, 'It looks like they're part of a much wider operation. Maybe UK-wide, according to Egor. He's found connections with London, Glasgow, Manchester and Bristol – that's for starters. Quantities are huge. Many of the statistics are encrypted, but a lot of it is pretty obvious in open-code – once you know what you're looking for.'

Her expression softened. 'You boys have been busy,' she murmured. I don't think she knew what to make of all this.

Ravi studied the whisky tumbler in his hand. 'There's something else that Bernie Bramshaw was just telling me. He's been cultivating one of the brighter youngsters in the English gang.'

Christy nodded. 'The Chip Shop Boys.'

'A lad called Aaron.'

I added, 'He's the leader's younger brother.'

'Aaron reckons there's a very big heroin delivery due for the Swords of Allah gang.'

That was interesting. 'Jak's gang know about that?' I murmured. 'I'm sure that shipment is why Masood Babur is over here. To supervise its safe delivery and distribution.'

'Would make sense,' Ravi agreed. 'Thing is, though, Jak's gang plans to seize it off the Muslims for themselves.'

'How the hell did Jak's gang find out about the shipment?' I asked. 'Who leaked the information?'

Ravi took another sip of his whisky before replying. 'Young Aaron reckons there's an informer in the Muslim camp. God knows what his *motive* could be? Aaron didn't know *who* he was, but he says he was an older man. Beard and thick glasses. Dressed more traditionally and wore an embroidered waistcoat.'

I frowned. 'That sounds remarkably like Jooma Khan.'

'Who's he?' Christy asked.

'Jooma is the Swords' head of security,' I answered. 'Sort of right-hand man to Mullah Chadhar, alongside Rashid who runs the drug gang.'

'So what sort of game would he be playing?' Ravi asked himself.

Christy shook her head in disbelief. 'God, you two and Bernie Bramshaw really seem to be putting us to shame.'

I was curious. 'So why aren't the Swinthorpe Police more active against narcotics?'

Christy shrugged. 'Don't ask me. Inspector Ryan came over from Northern Ireland when the RUC changed its name. He's very old school, but also wanted the quiet life, I think. He'd had a tough time over there. And the super . . . well, he's due to retire. He's a freemason and well-in with the city fathers.'

Ravi added, 'Bramshaw reckons your detective super-intendent is in denial. Like his editor on the *Journal*. Thinks Swinthorpe is like it says in the tourist leaflets. Some leafy, crime-free idyll.'

Christy stood up from the armchair. 'Well, gentlemen, I've got a dilemma. I really need you both down at the station for questioning over the disappearance and subsequent murder of Steven Cranford.'

'We've told you all we know,' I replied. 'Tomorrow could be our big opportunity to break open at least one of two drug gangs. Get vital information – and *evidence* about their operation.'

'I realise that,' Christy came back irritably. 'But, after all, I am a mere DC. It's way above my swimming depth. My sergeant is on holiday in Tuscany with his missus and my superintendent is on a special course in Hendon.'

'And Inspector Ryan?' I asked.

She glanced at her watch. 'Drinking down the Eight Cats – I'll have to call him in.'

Ravi and I exchanged glances. DC Jane Christy didn't sound like she was relishing the idea.

'Well now,' Inspector Ryan said. 'What do I do with you two?'

Ravi and I were sitting in the interview room at Swin-thorpe Police Station when the man joined us. His session with other police officers at the nearby Eight Cats pub had been interrupted.

DC Jane Christy had organised tea for us, and a takeaway pizza. She had made no attempt to interview us, separately, which I knew she would have done under normal circumstances. But then PC Tiddy and his probationer Sharon were always with us when Christy was not present, so there was no chance for us to collude prior to any eventual interviews under caution.

We gathered that Inspector Ryan had been back from the pub for some considerable time, perhaps the best part of an hour, before he finally appeared with Christy by his side. His hair was dishevelled and his tie loose at his open shirt collar. He wasn't obviously drunk and his Northern Irish accent was still sharp, but he did look tired.

He pushed the wing of lank greying hair back off his brow. For a long moment he stared at us both, as if marshalling his thoughts into words. 'From what I understand from DC Christy,' he said finally, 'you two would normally have been arrested and charged in connection with the abduction and murder of the druggie and serial pain-in-the-arse Steve Cranford. However, young Christy here has been giving me some long cock-and-bull story about some amateur sleuth thing you've been up to regarding Swinthorpe's increasing gang violence.'

He hesitated to allow himself a smile. It sat unhappily on his face and I had the distinct feeling it didn't happen often. But perhaps it was just the alcohol that had mellowed him.

'Always get away with it, don't they?' he said suddenly. He said it to no one in particular, so perhaps it was directed at himself.

'Who do?' I ventured.

Ryan belched lightly. 'The scrotes, the scumbags. Happened in Northern Ireland. And it happens on the streets over here today. They do bad things, we catch them, and the soft politicians with their secret social agendas and eye to the next election let them go. Some criminal justice system, this! Don't do it again for the sixty-ninth time – here's a community service order. Clear up dog shit in your local park, though they never do and no one makes them. Hug a fucking hoody. Won't be saying that when they've burned down our so-called civilisation.'

Ravi cleared his throat. 'That's some speech, Inspector.'

Ryan viewed him from under hooded eyes as he perched on the edge of the table. 'You suggested to DC Christy to not contact the MOD direct, but to enquire about you via Special Branch.'

'Helps to tug the right strings,' Ravi acknowledged. 'In the right order.'

'They talked highly of you, Mr Azoor.'

'Ravi, please.'

'In the sneaky-beakies,' Ryan said. 'Now the Special Reconnaissance Regiment, I understand. Once 14 Int. Tell me, did you ever serve in Northern Ireland?'

Ravi nodded. 'Some time ago.'

'Not many Paki shopkeepers in Armagh.'

The other man allowed himself a faint smile. 'Not many.'

Ryan continued, concentrating on his words. 'The people at the MOD say if you're onto something, have some information to offer, we should listen. Take heed. If you have infiltrated some criminal organisation, it would likely be in our interests – police interests – to let you run with it.'

'That's good,' I said.

The Irishman turned his gaze on me. 'Sorry, chum, you didn't get quite the same glowing testimonial.'

Ravi intervened sharply. 'Dave's top rate, he's had some tough times, some injuries . . .'

Ryan waved him to silence. 'Burnt-out case. Know how he feels . . .' He stopped abruptly. 'Oh shit, I need a cigarette!'

As he fumbled in his pocket, PC Tiddy gave a polite cough and pointed to the smoke detector on the ceiling. 'Sir . . .'

'Oh, for Christ's sake, Constable, use your initiative and take the bloody battery out.'

While Tidy pulled over a chair to step on, I used the opportunity to light a roll-up of my own. Christy produced an old chipped glass ashtray from the table drawer.

Now shrouded in a smoke cloud of his own making, Ryan looked happier and more relaxed. 'Jane here tells me you think this local Muslim drugs gang could be part of a nation-wide operation?'

'Appears to be,' Ravi confirmed.

'And there's a big delivery due tomorrow?'

Ravi said non-committally, 'That's the word. And Dave and I are supposed to be providing the security. It's an ideal opportunity to learn more about the whole Muslim network . . .'

During the pause, Ryan contemplated for a moment before saying, 'Which you can't do if you're being held here for questioning . . . Is that it?'

Ravi smiled thinly. 'I'm afraid so, Inspector.'

Another pause followed. Then Ryan appeared to reach a decision as he stubbed his cigarette butt out in the ashtray. 'Right, I tell you what. In view of the advice from the MOD, I'll let you two run with the foxes. But for a limited time. Then I will want you both in here for an official interview under caution – about your part in the disappearance of Steve Cranford. Understood?'

'Thank you,' Ravi said. 'I'm sure that's best.'

Ryan grunted and looked at the policewoman. 'And I'll hold you personally responsible, DC Christy, to make sure that happens. Right?'

She didn't seem too pleased. 'Yes, boss.'

He looked back at Ravi and me. 'Right, you two. Get out of my sight. And let me get back to the Eight Cats before closing.'

# Twenty-Eight

The call from Rashid came through to Ravi's bedroom in the Riverside Lodge at seven in the morning. Ravi then immediately got on the intercom to me. Fifteen minutes later we met in the saloon bar where breakfast was being served.

What I really wanted was a cigarette, but I made do with a black coffee and a croissant.

'It's a freezer container truck,' Ravi said. 'It's coming from Cherbourg and landing off the Poole ferry at midday. Then it's heading to a food-packing plant.'

'What's the official cargo?' I asked.

Ravi shook his head. 'That's all I got from him. He sounded very nervous. Wants us to meet him in a pub car park at eight thirty to go over the plan for its protection.'

'Have you called Jane?'

He smiled thinly. 'Yes. She wanted us to go into the station and get ourselves wired for sound. I told her to forget it. She has to trust us or it's no deal.'

'And?'

'She didn't like it, but I think she understood it would be too dangerous. If we were searched, we'd end up like Steve Cranford – or worse. She finally accepted she'll just have to hear from us as soon as we can get in touch.'

By eight o'clock we were pulling out of the car park and heading north in Ravi's Lexus.

'The Ratting Stug,' I observed wittily as it appeared around a bend in the narrow B road.

Ravi grinned. 'Or the Stag Inn and stagger out.'

It was obvious why Rashid had chosen this place as a rendezvous. The run-down building was by the river in the middle of nowhere, situated between two villages. The car park was on the opposite side of the road to the Rutting Stag pub itself. An inconspicuous white Mondeo and elderly red Toyota estate were parked together in the far corner, half-hidden in the wreaths of autumnal mist that drifted in off the slow-moving water.

Unlike the nose-first positioning of the other two vehicles, Ravi reversed his car in and left the engine running, ready for a fast getaway. I doubt he even thought twice about it, it was instinctive. Always anticipating the unanticipated.

We climbed out and waited by our car, letting Rashid come to us. As we waited, I noted that the Mondeo and the Toyota estate were filled with gang members, the windows starting to fug.

After a few moments, Rashid climbed out of the Mondeo passenger door. His hands were thrust deep inside the pockets of his leather bomber jacket and his shoulders were hunched against the chill air.

Ravi moved straight in to take control. 'Morning, Rashid. What is our strength?'

The gang leader looked puzzled. 'What?'

'Manpower,' Ravi snapped impatiently. 'Who've you got in the cars? How many?'

'Er, oh, ten including me.'

'And just the two cars?'

'Yes.'

'How many of your men are armed?'

'All of them, of course.'

Ravi raised his eyes, imagining the carnage that could happen. He said firmly, 'Arm only those who passed our training yesterday with top marks.'

'That will make only seven.' The man looked crestfallen.

'Excellent,' I replied. 'Get the others disarmed *now* and stow weapons and ammunition in the boot of your car.'

'Then I want to see our destination,' Ravi added. 'The food-packing plant.'

'That is secret . . .' he began.

'Not if we're going to protect you, it isn't,' Ravi snapped back. 'Clear it with your bosses, if necessary. But I'm telling you, it's all or nothing.'

Rashid thought for a moment. 'OK, it's near to here. I'll take you.'

Ravi continued, 'Then Dave and I want to drive to Poole using the route the truck will use. OK?'

Rashid nodded.

When he'd disarmed half his men and placed the guns in the boot of his car, he joined Ravi and me in the Lexus.

Following his directions, we left the pub car park, crossed an ancient stone bridge and drove east for a couple of miles.

'So what's in the truck?' I asked.

'Halal meat,' Rashid replied absently, as he studied the passing countryside. Then he added, 'Frozen.'

'Increasingly popular,' Ravi murmured.

Rashid nodded. 'Especially as everyone is cashing in. Even supermarkets sell it and who can trust them? Real Muslims want the real thing.'

'From where?' I asked.

'Ours was from Tajikistan, north of Afghanistan. Now it is from Iran.'

Ravi said, 'Because Tajikistan's getting extremely tough on heroin trafficking.'

Rashid ignored that. He lit a cigarette and puffed on it nervously. 'The meat is sourced and labelled from Turkey. Slaughtered and frozen there. Then across Europe by road.'

'Frozen meat has always been a good one,' Ravi observed. 'Customs have to have precise target intelligence. Otherwise the load is ruined and compensation will cost a fortune.'

'And it comes to this processing plant?' I asked.

Rashid indicated the road ahead. The high wire fence, topped with razor wire, was just appearing at the side of the tight two-lane road. There was a weatherworn sign reading *A&O Meats* beside the wire gates. Apparently it stood for Arabian and Oriental.

'Where do you distribute to from here?' Ravi asked.

Rashid shrugged. 'All over UK. Mostly big conurbations with high Muslim populations. The product is good quality, finely processed and popular in specialist delis.'

I grunted. 'Which of the two products are you talking about?'

Rashid sneered back at my sarcasm. 'Don't take the fucking piss.'

Aware of the growing antagonism, Ravi said, 'Right, let's take a look around.'

Beyond the fence, a modern but tired-looking prefabricated shed had an abandoned look about it. I could see only three old saloon cars on the weed-infested concrete apron and no sign of life except for two rather mangy mastiff dogs that started barking at us when we stood outside the gates.

'Is there any regular staff here?' I asked.

Rashid nodded. 'Just half a dozen. Local people. That's all it needs to keep things ticking over. When there's a delivery, we bring in our own boys.'

'Can we go inside please?'

'Why?'

'To check security,' I replied. 'We don't want to find your friendly Chip Shop Boys waiting to sing you a song when you turn up with your goodies, do we?'

Rashid scowled at me, but could hardly miss the sense of what I said.

Inside, the warehouse was in good order. It was clean enough, but somehow looked jaded and unloved. Only a couple of the workers were in evidence, Asian in appearance and wearing protective whites and mop caps. They viewed all of us boredly as we made our way up a set of steel steps to an upper deck of offices. The phones were connected but the computers appeared to be switched off. There was virtually no sign of any paperwork. Under the circumstances that was hardly surprising.

Back on the ground floor, a couple of forklifts guarded rows and rows of pallets containing boxes and shrink-wrapped cans of food. The produce was mostly Asian and oriental delicacies. Another sector housed walk-in refrigeration units where rows of carcasses hung, awaiting their appointment with various dull aluminium vats, mincers and a small canning machine. Although modern, the entire plant didn't appear overly automated.

A long steel table ran down the central open space of the painted concrete floor. My guess was this was where the gang would gather to unpack and repackage the heroin in readiness for its final distribution.

Before we left, I arranged for two of Rashid's semi armstrained goons to remain at the plant with all the doors and windows to be locked until the actual arrival of the shipment.

That sorted, Ravi said, 'Let's get started on the route back down to the ferry terminal.'

I already had my notebook out and was making observations.

The route down to Poole from the plant started with a few miles of narrow country lane. After that it reached some dual carriageway, but was mostly fast A road. The journey would normally have taken around one hour and forty minutes.

While Ravi drove steadily, I made notes and took a few photographs on my mobile phone camera. We finally parked outside a dockside cafe at just gone eleven.

The other passengers from the Mondeo and the Toyota estate grabbed a snack at one end of the cafe, while Ravi and I took our teas with Rashid to a quiet corner.

I poured three spoons of sugar into my mug. 'Rashid, you say we have WT radio connection between our three cars?'

He nodded. 'In fact we have five sets in total. One is already with the delivery driver.'

'So that's one for each of our three cars?' I checked.

'And one for Jooma Khan, so he will know immediately if anything goes wrong.'

That made good sense, I thought. After all, Jooma was supposed to be in charge of security.

'Does the driver have any special instructions?'

Rashid shook his head. 'Just not to stop anywhere for fuel or to eat. Anywhere that could make him the victim of a criminal hijack.'

'Does he normally have an escort?'

'No. We are always afraid that may draw unwanted attention to him – and put members of our organisation too close to the product.'

I understood that it was often drug gang routine to keep well away from its own product in transit – so they couldn't be easily associated with it by law enforcement authorities.

'But this time it will,' I said decisively. 'We'll have the Mondeo directly in front and the Toyota estate immediately behind. Split your gunmen between the two. But they must be under *very strict* orders. They are not to shoot under any circumstances unless directed by you. And to avoid killing any attackers *if at all possible*. The last thing your people need is police investigating any more homicides.'

'It is wise to escort?' Rashid seemed very unsure.

I could hardly tell him we'd had a tip-off from Bernie Bramshaw via the Chip Shop Boys. 'Yes, this time it is. We don't want any slip-ups, especially when Babur is over here.'

'And our car?'

'We'll follow a few vehicles back. Give ourselves time and space to react if anything goes pear-shaped.'

Our drinks finished, Rashid went off to brief his gang members. Ravi and I glanced at each other with tight smiles. So far, so good. Unfortunately Bramshaw only knew about the attack plan, not the when and where.

At twelve twenty, under a cloudy sky that was shedding spits and spots of drizzle, the cab tractor unit and refrigerated container from Turkey rolled off the ferry.

As soon as it left the terminal gates, the white Mondeo slipped in front of it. A mile up the road the red Toyota estate fell in behind the truck. Two vehicles back, Ravi positioned himself in our Lexus with consummate ease.

Mostly the journey was uneventful, although there were a couple of moments of heightened tension. There had been a road accident on the dual carriageway, the lanes narrowed with cones and police cars with flashing lights. Later some roadworks appeared that hadn't been there on the way down.

After an hour, just a few minutes behind schedule, we reached the Swinthorpe ring road. I looked down from the raised carriageway at the spires of the abbey and wondered transiently about Lady Penelope and her friend. Suddenly they seemed a lifetime away, like another kind of nightmare to the one I now found myself in.

We circled a roundabout and broke off north, along the winding main road that headed in the general direction of Swindon and the north-west. The traffic was sparse and I was seriously beginning to think that our intelligence from Bernie Bramshaw was wrong. After all, just how much information would gang leader Jak Twomey have entrusted to his kid brother Aaron?

Then our leading Mondeo, now behind a random blue Transit van, took a right-hand fork off the main road and down a lane that ran through a swathe of silver birch. The container truck followed with the rest of us.

I noticed that a jade-green Escort had settled in behind our Lexus.

Golden leaves swirled all around under the archway of bare branches as our little convoy motored on. There were now no vehicles between our Lexus and the red Toyota estate in front.

Ravi eased up on the gas and as the gap between us and the Toyota widened, I could see further up ahead, beyond the truck to the blue Transit that was leading.

Suddenly the Transit began to slow, brake lights winking. I saw it signal and turn right. In front of it was a yellow sign with black lettering – DIVERSION ROADWORKS. That hadn't been there on the way down.

We all turned, one vehicle after another, into an even narrower country lane. I glanced down at the map I had been following. The lane led past a farm and then returned a half-mile further on to the main lane we had just left.

Ravi took his eyes off the road for a second to look at me. We didn't have to speak. I flicked on the hand-held radio: 'Sword Leader to all taxis. Be on alert. Make no sudden moves.' The response was vague and garbled.

Then a voice was shouting in my ear, 'Police ahead! Police ahead!'

'Sword Leader here!' I snapped. 'Who's calling?'

'Sorry . . . White taxi calling. Police . . .'

I peered forward to see a uniformed policeman at the side of the road. He was waving on the innocent blue Transit, which in turn was followed by our white Mondeo.

Then the officer stepped into the middle of the road and pointed to the driver of the container truck, indicating for him to pull over into a lay-by under the trees. I heard the protesting squeal of air brakes as the driver obeyed. Another officer waved the following red Toyota estate on. It dutifully obeyed. It was when both officers produced weapons that I knew for sure they were impostors.

When that happened Ravi had reacted with lightning speed and edged over onto the grass verge. I glanced in the rear-view mirror. There was no sign of the jade-green Escort that had been behind us.

I was on the radio, 'Sword Leader to White and Red taxis. This is a heist, this is a heist! They are not traffic police, but they are armed!' I took a deep breath. 'Listen carefully. Drive on until you are out of view and pull over. Send your trained armed personnel back only. Be cautious and do not fire unless your life is under direct threat. Understood? Over.'

The response was a series of garbled grunts and words. Radio discipline was totally non-existent.

'Do you read me?' I snapped.

Finally someone thought to say, 'Roger, Leader.'

Ravi looked at me and shook his head in an expression of despair. 'Let's get on before they get away with it.'

As the three of us scrambled out of the car I said to Rashid. 'Let Ravi and me do the talking. And keep your gun out of sight unless you're directly threatened, right?'

He clearly didn't like being given orders, but I didn't give him a chance to backchat. Ravi and I kept close to the side of the lane as we scurried forward to where the big container truck had been pulled over under the trees. Cars were still passing us, following the diversion, and waved on by the man in the police uniform.

We tucked in under the tail of the truck. Through its wheels we had a better view of the roadside clearing. There were two plain white saloon cars parked, probably stolen because they could resemble patrol vehicles. I counted six individuals, three more of whom were in what looked like police uniform. I recognised a couple of the others as members of the Chip Shop Boys gang. Two of them had our driver face down in a bed of leaves beside the cab. They were tying his hands behind his back.

I turned to Ravi. 'Let's keep this simple. Surprise, and let them go.'

'Shock and awe?'

I nodded. 'Armed police, OK?'

He understood.

Leaving Rashid gawping, Ravi and I moved forward, out into the open where we could see all half-dozen of the rival gang. I fired two shots into the air.

The effect was stunning. All sound stopped in an instant.

The gang members froze and their urgent chatter ceased. Birdsong fell momentarily silent.

I yelled at the top of my voice. 'DON'T MOVE! ARMED POLICE! ARMED POLICE!'

Ravi decided to join in. 'THROW DOWN YOUR WEAPONS! MOVE AND WE FIRE!'

'DO IT NOW!' I yelled.

I don't know what the members of the white gang thought. All I could witness was that they were totally disorientated by the sudden turn of events. I was wearing a baseball cap with a long peak, so I'm not sure anyone recognised me. They probably did think it was a genuine police ambush.

The Muslim gang members from the two other cars began appearing through the trees at the other side of the clearing.

Noticing them, the six members of the Chip Shop Boys looked at each other, unsure what to do.

I suddenly realised that one of the men standing over our driver was their leader, Jak Twomey. There was a look of horror on his face as he saw the Muslims emerge from the trees. Whether he recognised them in his panic, or genuinely thought they were police, I don't know. But he clearly decided this was not the time for an unequal shoot-out.

He threw down his weapon and hurriedly thrust his arms into the air. 'Don't shoot, don't shoot!'

I waved my gun in the direction of their two white cars. 'Leave that driver and just go,' I told Twomey. 'GO NOW!'

He hesitated, not believing what he was hearing, not understanding this unexpected offer of escape.

'GO!!' I screamed at him again.

There was a sudden flurry of activity as the six gang members followed Twomey's example and began running to their cars, falling over themselves in their desperation to get in and start the engine. All the people in our party gathered in the clearing.

The two white cars slewed out into the lane, back wheels fishtailing on the tarmac in their haste.

I turned to Rashid. 'They won't be back. Get our lorry driver on his way. He'll be shaken up. I suggest you go with him. I'll speak to you tomorrow.'

Rashid opened his mouth and shut it again. His eyes remained sullen and hostile, even when his lips moved. 'Thank you. *Allahu Akbar.*'

I headed back towards the Lexus with Ravi, pausing only to pick up a police officer's cap that had fallen in the leaves. There was a label inside: *Swinthorpe Playhouse: Fancy Dress Dept.*

The big container truck coughed back into life and Ravi and I watched as it lumbered out onto the leaf-strewn tarmac with its secret high-profit load. The Muslim gang's red Toyota estate escorted it, leaving the clearing deserted. The meat processing plant was just a mile or two away. Our job was done. A wood pigeon called forlornly for its mate.

I felt suddenly exhausted, and took my tobacco tin from my pocket. Ravi declined a rollie as I lit up and exhaled.

Then he nudged me. I'd forgotten about the jade-coloured Escort that had been behind us when we'd followed the diversion. I hadn't registered that it had never overtaken us. The reason was now apparent. It had pulled over into the bushes someway behind our own vehicle. Its two occupants crossed the road towards us.

DC Jane Christy had been in the driving seat. She removed her trilby and shook out her hair. 'Well done, lads,' she congratulated. 'And no one hurt.'

Ravi was even more annoyed than I was. 'You bugged my car?'

I knew why he was furious. Early on in surveillance training you are warned by your veteran tutors never to forget that just because you are following someone, it doesn't mean that someone else couldn't be following you. But, of course, no one ever had been. Until now.

Inspector Ryan looked happier than I'd ever seen him, which wasn't saying a lot. 'And we've been tracking you all by helicopter. I take it the final destination is that meat-processing plant you visited earlier today?'

I nodded. 'From there, it looks like processed halal meat gets distributed around the country, pretty much alongside the heroin.'

Ravi said, 'I'm having copies of their distribution network emailed to me later. Apparently it's virtually a national operation.'

'You'll get us copies?' Christy asked.

'Of course,' I assured.

Ryan added, 'Then this operation will go national. I'm planning a video conference this afternoon with the Home Office, the Met and the other major constabularies.'

I grinned. I was sure Jock would have been proud of us.

Then the smile froze on my face. Over Christy's shoulder

I could see the scruffy figure of Bernie Bramshaw scurrying along the road. I could just make out the outline of another car beyond the green police Escort.

'Hope I haven't missed the party!' he declared breathlessly.

Christy scowled at him. 'You've been tuning into our wavelengths again!' It was a statement, not a question. 'That *is* a criminal offence.'

Bramshaw beamed, his face radiant with happiness and perspiration. 'As if! Can't say I didn't follow you, though.'

It was Ryan's turn to look a little embarrassed that it had never occurred to him that they too, in turn, may have been tailed. 'You're pushing your luck, Bernie.'

The reporter ignored that. 'Don't forget . . . the tip-off about this attempted hijack came from me . . .' He saw the look on Ryan's face. 'Oh, don't worry, your big story is safe with me. I'll sit on it until the time is right. I just want the promise that when it does break you'll give me a twenty-four-hour head start. It could be my route back to the nationals.'

Christy's frosty glare melted a fraction. 'I promise you, Bernie. When the time is right, you'll be the first to know.'

'Meanwhile,' Ryan said, looking at me, 'I want you and Ravi back at the station with me now. I want us to be filled in on everything you know before my video conference this afternoon.'

'Fine,' I replied. 'Just remember we are due to meet Rashid and Masood Babur this evening.'

'There'll be no problem there,' Ryan confirmed.

'Oh, by the way,' Christy said. 'There's someone waiting to

see you at the station. A *charming* gentleman. From the Foreign Office. Calls himself Houseman.'

'Houseman?' I echoed.

She nodded. 'A bit of a lady's man, I think.'

# Twenty-Nine

'Hello, Dave. Long time, no see.'

Chas Houseman was seated casually on the edge of the table in the police station canteen. The array of drained plastic coffee mugs surrounding him suggested that it had been a long wait. He wore the off-duty army officer's uniform of cavalry twills and a tobacco linen jacket over a blue check Charles Tyrwhitt shirt.

'Hello, Chas,' I replied evenly.

'You're certainly not an easy man to find.' His white smile was a little fixed and his blue eyes glittered with more ice than warmth as he regarded Ravi standing at my side. 'I'm surprised our mutual friend didn't tell you I was trying to find you.'

Ravi's eyes avoided his. 'It was mentioned,' he said smoothly. Then, to me, 'Can I get you a coffee, Dave?'

I nodded. 'Cheers. Black and very sweet.'

Ravi turned to DC Jane Christy, who had shown us to the canteen where Houseman was waiting. She said, 'A tea please, milk and no sugar.'

Houseman pulled out a hard-backed chair and sat astride it like a horse. 'Well, Dave, you certainly know how to cover your tracks. Thank goodness Jane here gave me a call.'

Christy saw my look of displeasure. 'Sorry, Dave. I would have told you I was going to call him, but in all the excitement I'd forgotten all about Mr Houseman's earlier visit. I'd promised to call him next time you showed on our radar.'

I ignored that as I pulled up a chair for myself. 'So what did you want, Chas?'

'To talk about old times.'

'I'd rather forget them.'

'Of course.' The smile was back. 'Must have been a tough time for you.'

I didn't want to go down that road. I said, 'Have you heard about the drugs operation in Swinthorpe?'

He nodded. 'Inspector Ryan was telling me about it this morning.'

'And the arrival here of Masood Babur,' I added. 'The number two to Dr Zam-Zama.'

Houseman said, 'Isn't that extraordinary?'

Ravi arrived at my side with a tea and two coffees, handing one to me.

There was nothing that I could read in his eyes. I said, 'Ravi and I are trying to find out what we can, pass on the info so that Inspector Ryan can take some action.'

'That's nice,' Houseman replied.

Suddenly he smiled, dismounted his chair and stood up. 'Any chance of a chat in private with my old muckers?' he asked Christy. 'No offence. It's just a security thing.'

Christy was taken aback. 'Oh, of course. I think there's a room free.'

Ravi and I exchanged puzzled glances and shrugs as she showed us to a side room off the canteen. There was nothing much in it: a peeling plastic-topped table in the middle was surrounded by a motley collection of old armchairs. A dart-board adorned one wall and there was a pile of lads' mags in one corner. It didn't look like a haunt that catered much for females in the force.

It seemed to suit Houseman's purpose. As she left, he perched himself on the edge of the table.

He dispensed with any niceties. 'I gather you and Ravi might have got yourselves in a bit of bother with the law.' He squinted. 'Abduction of some junkie. Even part of some conspiracy to murder.'

Anger suddenly flashed inside my skull, like a pulse of red light. What the fuck was Houseman playing at? 'It's no concern of yours, Chas,' I said testily. 'I'm long out of the army now.'

'That's as maybe,' Houseman continued. 'But anyway I've advised the police to drop any further investigation or charges against the pair of you.'

Ravi looked pleased. 'Wow, thanks, Chas.'

Houseman added, 'I've given Ryan the word that it won't get past the CPS. Not once the Home Office knows you two are involved. You know, your history and so forth.'

'I guess we owe you a big thank-you,' I said ungraciously.

His smile widened a fraction. 'No – but maybe just a small favour.'

'Which is?'

'Your last mission. Supporting Ravi and me during an exceedingly dangerous meeting with Dr Zam-Zama.'

I said, 'I'm hardly likely to forget it.'

'After the meeting, I gave you a memory-stick to look after.'

'It's against Standing Orders to bring a memory-stick into theatre,' I reminded.

'I don't do Standing Orders,' he replied, then repeated, 'I gave it to you to look after.'

I frowned. 'Just before I was blown up?'

He seemed to miss the sarcasm in my voice. 'Yes.'

'I don't remember.'

'You *must* do.'

'Well, anything like that – small and important – I'd have put in the inner secure pocket in my combat trousers.'

'It was important. A video copy of my meeting with Zam-Zama. Not the most sophisticated of arrangements, I know. But I didn't want to go in and get caught with a secret camera, or anything. So I got him to agree for us to video our meeting. I recorded it on a simple wide-angle webcam on my laptop.'

Houseman could see the look of disbelief on my face. 'Without a copy of it for himself, Zam-Zama would *never* have agreed. It was a two-way insurance policy for both sides,' he insisted. 'Each of us had a record of the meeting, each a copy of the video. So neither side could *deny* the deal that had been done.'

I frowned. 'Sounds like that deal was pretty important. What was it?'

'You know I can't tell you that, Dave,' he replied. I wondered for a moment if I could detect moisture gathering in his eyes. 'But I can tell you that I made a copy of the video on my laptop and gave the memory-stick to you . . . in case anything happened to me on the way back. Belt and braces.'

'Wrong decision then,' Ravi observed, 'as it turned out.'

I shrugged. 'Anyway, Chas, I haven't seen it. Sorry. Our translator Abdullah was shot and then we were blown up by a mine. Young Andy Smith died. Brian Duffy saved me and I was taken away by helicopter. The medics took my trousers off – and almost my bloody leg with it!'

Houseman raised his hands defensively. 'Yeah, sorry, Dave, I didn't want to bring back painful memories. But something might have happened to that memory-stick, anything. It's important that it's tracked down.'

I said, 'Most probably in the ashes of that fire where they used to burn clothes outside the hospital in Camp Bastion.'

'Someone would have gone through your pockets,' Houseman pressed on earnestly.

I was losing patience. 'Then it would have found its way back to camp HQ at the time. Or else army intelligence, or even Hereford. Presumably you've tried all of those?'

'Of course.'

I'd had enough of this. I couldn't help but wonder why he wanted the bloody thing so badly. 'Sorry, Chas,' I said, 'that's the best I can offer.'

I made my move towards the door and left Houseman and Ravi to follow me out into the canteen.

Christy looked up from the table. 'You forgot to take your drinks. They'll be cold.'

At that moment her mobile phone began to trill. She cursed and picked it up, putting it to her ear. As she listened her forehead fractured into a frown. 'When was this?' she asked as Houseman and Ravi joined us.

Getting her answer, she echoed, 'Shot in the head? . . . I'll be right over.'

She snapped her phone shut. 'There's been an attempted murder in the Rosebury Street area, not far from the mosque. Looks like a drive-by shooting. Someone on the back of a motorcycle with a gun.'

'Is this to do with the Muslim gang?' I asked.

Christy bit her lower lip. 'Not sure. That attempted intercept of the drugs shipment this morning – who told you about it? Bernie Bramshaw, right?'

'That is correct,' Ravi affirmed.

'And who told him?'

'Aaron of the Chip Shop Boys gang.'

'And who told Aaron?'

I said, 'Aaron said it was a member of the Muslim gang who had tipped them off. His description sounded remarkably like that of Jooma Khan.'

Suddenly Chas Houseman seemed interested. 'Did you say Jooma Khan?'

That surprised Christy. 'Yes. Why, do you know him?'

Houseman looked awkward. 'Not sure. Name sounds familiar. Might have cropped up on my radar.'

Christy was irritated at the interruption to her thought processes. 'Why on earth would Jooma Khan want to tip off a rival gang? He was the Swords' head of security.'

'*Was?*' Houseman asked.

'The man just shot by the motorcycle pillion,' Christy said, 'was wearing a long embroidered waistcoat of the type Jooma Khan always wore. The indications are that it could be him. But there hasn't been a positive identification yet . . . I need to get down to the hospital pronto.'

Bernie Bramshaw was already in the waiting area at A & E when Ravi and I arrived with Christy and Chas Houseman.

The journalist approached us. 'It's Jooma Khan,' Bramshaw confirmed. 'I know him. A leading light at the local mosque.'

Christy looked harassed. 'How is he?'

'Didn't look too good to me.'

Just then a doctor appeared from one of the cubicles. He recognised Christy immediately and approached. The expression on his face said it all. 'DC Christy, isn't it? I'm afraid the guy didn't make it.'

'Did you get a name from him?'

'He didn't have a mouth to speak with. A bit of a mess, I'm afraid.'

She paled. 'We'll need an official identification.'

The doctor stepped back to let her through. Houseman went with her and the rest of us followed in.

Houseman bent over the cot, then nodded. 'It *is* him. Jooma Khan.'

Christy looked at him oddly. 'So you *did* know him?'

'Our paths had crossed,' the other muttered and, straightening his back, he plucked a mobile phone from his pocket.

'But how . . . ?' Christy began.

Houseman waved her to silence, turned his back on her and returned to the waiting area, talking earnestly to someone on the other end of the line.

Some ten minutes later we left the cubicle and rejoined Houseman, who had finally finished his call. He looked directly at Christy. 'Sorry about that, Jane, I had to make some urgent arrangements. A private ambulance will be coming to remove Mr Khan's body. The Home Office will take care of everything.'

Christy was taken aback. 'The Home Office? This is a murder inquiry . . .'

I noticed that Bramshaw was listening intently, his notepad out and pencil poised.

Houseman shook his head. 'No, Jane, it was a very unfortunate road traffic accident. Horrible head injuries. Trust me. So there's no need for a visit to Mr Khan's home or for an investigation into any alleged offence – *apart* from this road traffic accident, of course.'

He suddenly realised that Bramshaw was scribbling furiously and turned on him. 'Will you put that away – and piss off out of it! Try to publish anything and you'll get a D notice slapped on it. Get it?'

Christy's mouth dropped. 'What exactly are you saying?'

'Everything will be taken care of. All you need to do is try and identify the owner of the motorcycle and whoever was riding it at the time.' He repeated. 'Everything else will be taken care of.'

Ravi shook his head in disbelief, suddenly realising what the man had just said. 'You mean MI5's "bin men"?'

The doctor had been discussing the case with a couple of his staff members and had only now worked out what Houseman was saying.

'Excuse me, sir,' he intervened, 'but you can't interfere with our procedures here.'

'This is now a matter of national security,' Houseman replied smoothly. 'It'll all be squared with your chief executive – if you'd be kind enough to arrange for me to speak to him. With your good self, of course. I'll explain the form and what happens in these matters.'

Christy had been looking on in astonishment, hardly believing what was happening. She tried to radio the station to speak to Inspector Ryan, but he wasn't available. 'Dammit, Wednesday, isn't it?' she remembered. 'He'll be playing golf with the super.'

Houseman left the doctor and crossed the waiting area to where the rest of us stood. 'As for you, Ravi. And Dave – I don't know what it is you think you're playing at? Are you trying to be private detectives, or what? Let the cops do their business, eh? Your help in this drugs business is not help, it's interference.' He turned sharply on Christy. 'Isn't that right, Jane?' he demanded.

Christy was starting to look indignant. 'Actually, Mr Houseman, I think you're a little out of order. Dave and Ravi have proved very helpful to our inquiries.'

I don't think he'd been expecting contradiction from a mere country detective constable. 'Well, I'm telling you, young lady. Theirs is dangerous interference in national security. You'll be getting official notification, but any investigation of yours into the Swords gang, Jooma Khan, or anything that's related to them, is going nowhere – until you are instructed otherwise. Do I make myself plain?'

I was incensed. 'What the hell's going on, Chas? What's got into you?'

The Hollywood smile was long gone. 'Nothing's got into me, Dave. I'm just doing my job. You and Ravi might have meant well, but you've been rocking the boat. So just wind your necks in – both of you!'

The doctor returned with a message that the hospital's chief executive was ready to speak to both himself and Houseman together. Apparently the chief executive had already received high-level calls from the Home Office and the Ministry of Health.

As Houseman disappeared down the corridor in animated conversation with the doctor, Bernie Bramshaw stared after them with such anger I was surprised his spectacles didn't steam up.

'The bastard,' he fumed. 'This whole thing is a bloody cover-up. That was my chance of a big story.'

Christy touched my arm. 'I don't like it at all. I'm sorry, boys, you've done so much. Taken risks. I feel we've let you down.'

'Maybe Inspector Ryan will run with it,' Ravi suggested. 'Fight back and not take it lying down.'

The detective shook her head. 'Not if I know Ian. He'll only push the boundaries so far. That's pretty much it.'

Bramshaw said, 'Well, it's still a story. *My* story.'

Christy frowned. 'Are you sure that's a good idea?'

Bramshaw grinned broadly. 'Why not? Don't we still believe in a free press?'

Ravi added, 'And we still have a contract with the Muslim gang. They owe us for services rendered. We'll break them yet.'

'You two be careful,' Christy warned. 'Don't get yourselves into any more trouble.'

'I never did like Houseman,' Ravi admitted.

Bramshaw laughed. 'I think that makes four of us. Plus the doctor. Anyone fancy a drink?'

'You've called me in for *this*, Bernie?'

The editor of the *Journal* was not a happy man. He wore a Harris tweed three-piece, a brown check shirt and a yellow knitted tie. The wild curly hair around his bald pate and his unruly beard seemed to be made out of the same material as his suit before it had been weaved.

There was no anger and no passion in his voice, as he added quietly, 'We've already got our front page story. The donkey sanctuary won't be saved. It has lost its case in the high court. There won't be a dry eye in the town. I think we'll add another five hundred copies.'

We were sitting among the rows of empty desks and computers in what was described as the newsroom, although Bramshaw had told me that the majority of the workstations were manned by the advertisement staff. Outside it was dark and raindrops glistened on the windows that gave a panoramic view of the market square.

Bramshaw tried to hide his exasperation. 'But, Donald, the

donkey sanctuary closing is hardly a scoop, is it? The sleepy country town suddenly finding itself at the centre of an international drug smuggling ring is just a *bit* more exciting!'

'I *suppose* so,' Donald Quigley said in a painfully reasoned tone.

Bramshaw pounced. 'From the war-torn badlands of Afghanistan, where our lads, our soldiers – some from Swinthorpe itself – have given their lives, comes in heroin from the poppy fields. The Taliban in our own backyard. Open gang warfare on the streets. Guns and lorry hijacks. Local-born SAS hero helps to expose the story!'

I winced at that, but Bramshaw was in full flow and ignored my expression of disapproval.

'And you have evidence of all this?' Quigley asked somewhat reluctantly.

'Yes, yes,' Bramshaw confirmed rapidly. 'And I got a photograph of the hijacked lorry. A bit woolly, long-distance – but it will do. And I can take a picture of Dave here.'

I wasn't expecting that. 'Oh no, you can't!' I protested.

Bramshaw steamrollered on. 'Anyway, Donald, there's plenty of material. At least seven-fifty or a thousand words.'

'We'll have to change page two and three as well.'

'*I* can do that, Donald. We've got until eleven tomorrow morning – that's why I called you in now. I'll write it through the night and redo the layouts. It'll all be ready for you crack of dawn tomorrow.'

Donald Quigley scratched at his beard. 'The city council might not like it. They're starting a new tourist drive next summer.'

I could tell Bramshaw was biting his tongue. 'The city council don't edit the *Journal*. We do, and we're journalists. Remember Watergate – publish and be damned. We can make a difference. The people of Swinthorpe deserve the truth!'

The editor smiled sheepishly. 'Yes, Bernie, of course you are right. I look forward to reading your stunning revelations tomorrow morning.'

'Wizard,' Bramshaw declared in triumph. 'I'll leave it all on your desk.'

Quigley seemed to be warming to the idea. 'I suppose *this* is what it feels like on the national red tops.'

'It's for you,' Ravi said. 'A gift.'

I'd just got back to the hotel when he joined me in my room for a whisky nightcap. I was about to tell him how Bernie Bramshaw had secured the front page of the Saturday *Journal* with our story.

I looked down at the smart Antler suitcase lying on the bed cover. 'What's that?'

'What does it look like?'

'A suitcase,' I replied irritably.

'Then that's what it is.' Ravi stared at me. 'We've got you off the streets, Dave. Step one. Now get rid of that bloody bergen of yours. Playing at tramps isn't cute. You're no Charlie Chaplin. You've got to get your life back. If for no one else, you owe it to that daughter of yours.'

That brought me up sharp. I'd barely allowed myself to think about Daisy since Jock had died. Not since I'd become fixated on avenging his murder.

I didn't say anything. I couldn't continue to push away anyone and anything that was there to help me.

Ravi poured some whisky into a tumbler and handed it to me. 'Empty the bergen. We'll chuck it out. Like throwing out your old life, all the baggage.'

I took a swig of the whisky. 'You sound like a bloody agony aunt,' I said acidly, but in truth I knew he was right.

I hauled the bergen onto the bed, undid the straps and began emptying the contents of the main section onto the top sheet.

'I've had an email from Egor Baran,' Ravi said. 'He's attached tons of stuff from Rashid's hard drive. Apart from email contacts all over the world – and I'm sure some of those will have al-Qaeda connections – there are details of what looks like the whole UK distribution network for the proc-essed meats and heroin. London, Manchester, Leeds, Glasgow, Birmingham . . . the lot.'

'That's incredible,' I said.

'You'll be a popular boy with Jane when she gets sight of this lot. You'll be in there, no problem.'

I'd separated my clean clothes from the dirty, and laid all the aluminium camping equipment in another pile. 'In?' I asked absently.

He shook his head. 'In with Jane,' he said. 'Hadn't you noticed? The way she looks at you. Like you're some cross between Batman and Superman. Lassie, even.'

'I don't think so,' I said, trying to remember any admiring glances and not recalling any. The opposite, in fact.

'Something else to interest her,' Ravi went on. 'Rashid has

a list headed "Traitors". They're mostly Arab or Pakistani names, but some English. About fourteen of them overall. There's a date against each. The last entry is Jooma Khan.'

I frowned. 'He was shot yesterday. So he *was* suspected as a traitor.'

'And Rashid put the date beside *his* name – *yesterday*.'

It raised that question again. 'Why did Jooma tip off Aaron about the shipment?' I asked aloud. 'And, if he was a traitor, just who was Jooma working for? . . . Oh, my God! Houseman knew him.'

'He was working for Houseman!' Ravi decided. 'For MI6! Or was it MI5? Either way, Jooma was one of ours.'

I'd emptied the bergen now. I turned it upside down and gave it a final, hard shake. An item dislodged from the inner seam of the rucksack bounced off the sheet and onto the floor with a metallic clatter. Before I could see what it was, it had disappeared under the bed.

I went down on hands and knees and scrabbled about blindly for a couple of moments before locating it amidst the dust.

I held it up. It was a computer memory-stick.

# Thirty

Ravi and I stared at each other across the bed.

'Is that it?' he asked.

I shrugged. 'How should I know? I don't remember ever putting a memory-stick in there.'

'It's obvious what happened,' Ravi said. 'When you were wounded, you were casevaced back to the hospital at Bastion. At some point, a hospital orderly went through all your pockets and stuffed all valuables, paperwork, ID and whatever into your bergen.'

I nodded. 'All done in a hurry. The memory-stick got stuck. Literally, probably at the bottom of the sack. And has stayed in my wardrobe back home ever since.'

Ravi reached across and picked it up, examining it closely. 'I suppose it's the one. It's not marked.'

'I don't think Houseman had time to mark anything. He just gave it to me to look after.'

Ravi finished his drink and held up the memory-stick. 'OK if I go through this on the laptop tomorrow? See what all the fuss is about.'

'Be my guest.'

'One other thing, when does the *Journal* come out?'

'Saturday.'

'Then I think we need to see Rashid about our wages of sin before then.'

I was stunned. 'Are you serious?'

'Yes, I am. We saved that gang thousands. Maybe tens or hundreds of thousands! I can see I've got to get you back into the habit.'

'Habit of what?'

'Earning a living.' With that he was gone.

My sleep that night was silky deep and dreamless. While Steve Cranford's death still hung over me like a dark cloud, other things were looking up.

Bernie Bramshaw had secured a front-page story for my dozy hometown that would shake up the nation and force the police to act. It looked like Ravi and I would get some money. I'd discovered the elusive memory-stick. And, apparently, Detective Constable Jane Christy had the hots for me.

It seemed like there was all to play for.

The next morning Ravi announced that we had an appointment with Rashid and Mullah Siraj Chadhar at the mosque on Rosebury Street after Friday prayers.

What I hadn't realised was that meant there was time for me to be dragged around on a clothes shopping spree at the local T.K.Maxx like a hen-pecked husband. Ravi had a sharp eye for both fashion and a bargain. I ended up with a stylish designer casual jacket and trousers that were only two seasons out of date, all for fifty quid from the final clearance rail.

The white collarless shirt was the perfect finishing touch for our visit to see Mullah Chadhar. Despite my greying fair hair and blue eyes, I felt a bit more in character amongst the

Muslim community, most of whom it seemed were coming out of the mosque as we were going in.

Amir, Rashid's gormless-looking number two, was waiting for us at the gates of the former Victorian-built infants' school. However, unlike his former sullen welcome, this time he was all smiles and flashing teeth, greeting us like long-lost relatives.

'Ah, Mistah Khan and Mistah Aston, it is so good to see you again! Come, follow me!'

As we walked, I noted the telltale bulge under the left armpit of his cheap charcoal jacket. Maybe it had been a mistake giving him five-stars for his weapons training. The old building was almost empty of devotees and we were led quickly to the office of the former head that was now occupied by Mullah Chadhar. The old man was seated behind his green-topped desk, slouched in his chair amid a cloud of glowing white hair and long beard. Behind him, standing upright with his back arched, was Rashid. I couldn't believe it. For once he was smiling.

Chadhar's tiny, bullet-hole blue eyes pierced through the lenses of his gold-rimmed glasses. 'Ah, gentlemen! I can scarcely believe that I am hearing such good stories about you since we last met. Of course, I do not know of the details of Rashid's work in the community – just that, at times, it can be difficult.'

Rashid said coyly, 'I am most pleased with the work you did for our commercial enterprise.'

I said, 'I trust it reached its destination safely?'

'Thanks to you, gentlemen. You said we needed your help and you were right.'

'We were discussing a contract with your colleague,' Ravi said. 'Jooma Khan. He is not here?'

The smile fell from Rashid's face. 'Unfortunately Mr Khan met with a traffic accident and is no longer with us.'

Ravi let it pass. 'We had agreed a fee.'

'You were *discussing* a fee,' Rashid corrected.

'We were *discussing* a fee of two thousand a day,' Ravi countered. 'And a three month contract.'

'That is unlikely to be acceptable,' Rashid said quickly. 'But for the work you have done so far, I have an envelope here with the cash. One thousand pounds sterling. Used twenty-pound notes.'

'Repelling an attack on your warehouse,' Ravi replied, 'a training session and safe passage for your delivery. I think that has to be worth two thousand.' He glanced at me. 'And there are *two* of us. I'd say five K minimum.'

Rashid glanced down as the old man looked up without expression.

It was Rashid's call. 'I understand.'

'And one thousand retainer for any future work,' Ravi added quickly. He paused. 'I assume there *might* be further work?'

Mullah Chadhar gently slid open the drawer of the desk in front of him. He extracted four more large brown envelopes.

Rashid said, 'We are in agreement. As you know we have an honoured visitor here from Afghanistan, whom you have met.'

'Masood Babur,' I acknowledged.

'He would like you to continue to train our people in close-protection. For his safety while he is here. You understand?'

'Of course,' I said.

'Our organisation expects other VIP visitors, too, Mr Aston,' Rashid continued. 'So this will be very important work for us.'

'It will be our pleasure, gentlemen,' Ravi said, as he gently picked up the brown envelopes. 'Oh, by the way, my infidel friend here, Mr Aston, is planning to convert to Islam.'

'I'm just so, so sorry,' I concluded.

The cafe was closed, the lights off, and Ravi and I were sitting at the last remaining table outside. I'd just gone over with Gem the nature of our involvement in what had happened to Steve Cranford. It was a short and highly selective account of events. And, of course, I made no mention of our presence at and participation in his actual killing.

She forced a smile. 'Thank you for having the courage to come and tell me. I was so angry when Steve died, I wanted to tear your eyes out.'

I put my hand on her arm. 'Understandable. Ravi and I thought maybe the gang would rough him up a bit, but had no idea he'd come to serious harm. We'd planned to take him back with us.'

She picked up her cigarette pack and lit one of its contents with a plastic lighter. 'I've nearly given up – honest!'

'I'm sure. Losing Steve can't have helped.'

Gem inhaled deeply and thoughtfully. 'No, it didn't. But I know I'm fooling myself if I ever thought he was going to be a part of my life in the long term. Certainly not a good part.

Can you believe, I still miss him? What do they call it? Women
who love too much?'

I said, 'We're all human.'

'That female detective, Jane something . . . ? She was good
to me. Very sweet and understanding.' Gem took another
deep inhalation of smoke. 'I couldn't believe that you were
actually trying to *do work* for the gang – that you took Steve
to them to prove yourselves.'

Ravi said, 'That's sometimes how it works with those sorts
of people. Ruthless types, criminals, terrorists and the like
can want insurance in blood. And no better insurance than
shared guilt.'

She exhaled and stubbed out her cigarette butt. 'And it
worked, you say.'

'It's still working,' I added.

'But the police aren't going to take action? I don't understand that.'

'Not yet,' I said. 'But they will. At the moment they're
being hampered by political interference.'

Gem looked baffled. 'I don't understand.'

'Neither do I,' I said, and meant it. 'Basically, it seems
the powers that be think police investigations could
compromise some sort of intelligence shenanigans. But
we've got Bernie Bramshaw on the case. He's persuaded
the editor of the *Journal* to run a front-page scoop in
tomorrow's edition.'

'Gosh, really?' That seemed to genuinely impress her.
'Last time that paper did anything was a campaign to restore
the town's minimum one-hour parking fee.'

'Well it's national, ground-breaking stuff tomorrow,' Ravi added.

At that moment my mobile rang. That happened so rarely that it took me by surprise. So did the name of the caller as I glanced at the tiny window. 'DC Christy?' I said. 'Hi.'

'Hello, Dave . . . Oh, and you don't have to be so formal. You can call me Jane.'

I grinned to myself. 'What can I do for you, Jane?'

'Are you still at the hotel?'

'Yes, we're staying there, but Ravi and I are visiting Gem just now. Gemma Wilkins – Steve's girlfriend.'

I heard the gasp of relief. 'Thank goodness for that.'

Suddenly I was concerned. 'What's the matter, Jane?'

'I can't believe it,' she said, lowering her voice. 'That man Chas Houseman has just turned up again. He's got a couple of plain-clothes officers from Special Branch with him. And a warrant for your arrest.'

'Arrest?' I asked. 'For what?'

'The assault on your former Family Officer. Luke Hartley?'

'You told me those charges had been dropped.'

'Well, they seem to have a life of their own, because they're back. If you were found guilty it would almost certainly be a custodial sentence.'

'What's going on?' I murmured, not expecting a reply.

'And they want to talk to Ravi under caution. I didn't get the details. Just something about the Official Secrets Act. It didn't sound good.'

'So what's happening now?'

'I tried to stall, but Ryan told them where you were staying. They're on their way to the Riverside Lodge as we speak. They'll be there any second . . . If you're at Gem's, can you stay there tonight?'

'I can ask.'

'Well, just don't go back to the hotel,' she advised earnestly. 'I'll try and keep you posted on developments. I've deleted your mobile phone number from our files. Only answer a call if it's from me. Not any calls from Inspector Ryan or anyone else.'

'Roger that.' I suddenly thought of something and turned to Ravi. 'Is your laptop back at the hotel?'

He shook his head. 'No way. It's in the car-safe in the boot, along with your blessed memory-stick.'

'Thank God for that,' I said, then thanked Jane and hung up.

I explained to Ravi and Gem what had happened. As I might have expected of Ravi, typically he showed little concern. However, Gem looked very worried.

'If you can't go back to your hotel, you can stay in my spare room,' she offered. 'There's only one bed though.'

Ravi smiled. 'That'll be great. I always keep a sleeping bag and kipmat in the car. For a dreadful moment, I thought you meant I had to share a bed with *him*.'

But Gem wasn't in the mood for jokes. 'What if the police do find you?'

'We'll cross that bridge as and when,' Ravi replied. 'What we've got to remember is that this is some kind of cover-up. Someone's clearly got something they want to hide. We just need to find out what it is.'

'About time we took a look at that memory-stick,' I said.

Gem took a deep breath. 'This is all too much for me. I'll get some supper on. I was thinking of Irish stew.'

While Ravi set up his laptop, I rang our hotel on my mobile and advised them that we had been called away on very urgent business unexpectedly, but wished to keep our rooms on. We'd return as soon as we could – probably in a few days' time. They had Ravi's credit card details, so there was no technical problem. When the receptionist started to sound hesitant – as though someone may have been talking to her – I hung up.

On the assumption that no one could just hang around on the off chance that we would turn up, our plan was to return unannounced, grab our things and leave before staff had a chance to call either Houseman or the local police. That was the plan, such as it was.

We'd kept in touch with Bernie Bramshaw and a little later he arrived at Gem's house. He was full of excitement having spent most of the day asleep after leaving the whole new front-page story on his editor's desk. I'd even allowed him to take a mugshot of me, artistically lit with heavy shadow so that I was unrecognisable.

He was surprised to learn that Houseman was after arresting us, but he didn't seem too concerned. I think for him the story was just growing and growing. Once he knew the background, he was as eager as Ravi and me to see the memory-stick film.

'*There! I think that's it! It's filming now . . .*' I jumped as Chas Houseman's clipped words suddenly entered the living room.

'Sorry,' Ravi said, 'too loud!'

Houseman's distorted face was peering out of the laptop screen at me.

Ravi hit the pause button, and Houseman's face froze.

'This must be Dr Zam-Zama's villa,' Ravi decided. 'Look, behind him you can see the red walls and gilt edging. Like a tart's boudoir.'

'So what has Houseman done?' I asked.

Ravi said, 'If you remember, we arrived at the villa and waited outside in the anteroom. We'd just met Masood Babur for the first time and he provided refreshments while House-man talked in private with Dr Zam-Zama. Houseman told us how he set up a webcam to record everything on his computer.'

'It still doesn't make sense to me,' I thought again, this time aloud. 'Those were supposed to be *top secret* talks.'

'They were,' Ravi explained. 'That's the point. It's what we call MAD in the intelligence trade. Like MAD in the Cold War. Mutual Assured Destruction. Both sides, East and West held enough nuclear weapons to ensure both sides would totally annihilate the other side in the event that one side fired first.'

'Sort of insurance,' I murmured.

'Exactly that. If you're a married man having an affair, the safest person to have an affair with is a married woman. You've both got too much to lose.'

Gem overheard that. 'That's not very nice.'

'But it works,' Ravi rejoined. 'So this was a secret meeting, but both sides have a record of exactly what was said. So it's not in anybody's interests to break the silence.'

I said nothing. The world of the intelligence spooks and para-politics was way above my head.

'So let's see,' Ravi said.

He pressed the play button and the slightly fuzzy frozen image of Houseman's face came back to life in the laptop screen. The man retreated back into the room at Dr Zam-Zama's villa. As he diminished in size, it was revealed that he and the Taliban warlord and drug baron were seated next to each other on two armchairs. In front of them was an ornate, marble-topped coffee table, which supported a tray of glasses and colourful bottles of cordial.

I'd forgotten just how big and impressive a character Zam-Zama was. Even when seated, it was clear he was well over six feet in height and even the folds of the white dishdasha couldn't hide the breadth of his chest and shoulders. Curls of greasy hair exploded from under the traditional pancake hat to merge with an equally long and wild black beard.

The voice was deep and resonant. It struck me he would have sounded good on the stage at the Globe in London. 'So, despite trying to bug my home, you ask me to trust you?'

'Indeed, doctor,' Houseman was saying, 'and I apologise for the attempt to spy. This is good Western bureaucracy at work, the left hand not knowing what the right is doing. It is *me* that you have to trust. Because what *I* want to offer you will be totally *unorthodox* and *unauthorised* – but it may just bridge the gap between us. That is why I will film this conversation and why we will *both* have a copy.'

'You have my undivided attention.'

Houseman was smiling gently. 'As I have already said, if

only we can put our differences aside for long enough to discuss what the other wants. We British are currently fighting a war with your Taliban fighters that is more ferocious than at any time since the Second World War.'

'We are winning.'

'For the moment,' Houseman conceded. 'But you know that you will not. Because America – and thereby Britain, too – cannot allow you. It would be too much loss of face. Washington will not countenance another Vietnam, another Saigon. There will be a surge, you will be crushed without mercy.'

'You think.'

'You *know*. In your head and your heart, doctor, you know that I am right.' He hesitated. 'So that is what *I* want. Some respite. Maybe you cannot offer us a ceasefire, but perhaps a temporary *cessation* . . . Perhaps until next year. That is not at all the same thing.'

Zam-Zama reached forward towards the low table. 'A cordial?'

Houseman smiled. 'Lime juice would be nice.'

'And ice?'

As it chinked into the glass, the doctor said thoughtfully, 'And what do we want? Well, it is time to gather in the opium harvest. The poppies will not wait.'

'I will offer you more than that.'

That clearly took Zam-Zama by surprise. 'You mean, in return for a *prolonged* cessation of activity in the British sector here in Helmand?'

Houseman added, 'I offer you personally, doctor. Not

your fellow warlords, not your fellow jihadists in Pakistani intelligence, or in Iran. This is *personal* between you and me.'

Zam-Zama ran his hands sensually through his own beard. Just watching the act made made me feel queasy. 'A personal offer?'

'For your own action and persuasion of others with the Taliban leadership. To take the kettle off the heat.'

The doctor was no fool. 'So you can regroup, reinforce and attack again in greater strength?'

But Houseman ignored that. Instead, he said, 'Much of this land is your fiefdom, yes? Vast areas of poppy fields.'

Zam-Zama nodded, caressed his beard again.

'Your personal friends control many more acres of poppy fields?'

Again the man nodded.

'That crop is refined and finds its way to Europe,' Houseman said. 'Especially the UK and Russia, where there are big addiction problems. There are middlemen, in Iran and in Tajikistan. Gangsters and warlords and narco bosses. Italian and Ukrainian mafias in Europe, Irish and Turkish in the UK. All want their pound of flesh, their cut of *your* product.'

'That is true.'

'And your percentage of the street value?'

'Minimal.'

Houseman waved his hand, light glinting on his chunky gold signet ring. 'But if your *own* distribution network went all the way into the UK, what would be your share of the profit?'

Zam-Zama didn't bother to answer that. 'Why would you want to do that?'

The SIS man said bluntly, 'Because we are desperate for a military breathing-space. And we need it now. And, besides, your country's heroin will flood into our country regardless. It may as well be you who benefits, if in return we save British life and limb – not to mention public opinion.'

'You would sleep with your enemy, Mr Houseman?'

'I'd sleep with the devil if it would save the lives of our young men,' Houseman replied tersely.

'A protected supply network into the UK?'

'Virtually,' Houseman conceded.

'It will generate huge funds for the jihadi war chest,' Zam-Zama murmured.

And I knew at that moment exactly what Houseman's thinking was. The Taliban already had plenty of funding from the Arab world. The main beneficiary of this seemingly crazy plan would be Zam-Zama himself. The greedy bastard might spread *some* of his gains to fellow Taliban warlords, but it was ten to a penny the lion's share would go in his own back pocket. More likely to be spent on harems, luxury villas, private jets and political aspirations than guns and bombs.

'There must be tangible results,' Houseman said. 'You will have to bring your considerable influence to bear. We must see a lull in activities. Use whatever reasoning you like. Talk, regroup or consolidate until next summer. Even to talk to NATO forces would be exceptionally good.'

The picture on the screen was poor, but I noticed the way Zam-Zama's eyes blinked slowly at that. He said, 'I will consider your proposals, Mr Houseman. Obviously my colleagues within the Taliban leadership cannot know of any personal understanding we may have. So there are three things I need you to do and they are interconnected.'

Zam-Zama paused and stared directly at the webcam to make his point. 'So that I can trust you, you must be personally complicit in our agreement. So that no one in the movement of jihad will suspect and accuse me of dealings with the infidel, there will be an attack on your convoy when you leave here.'

I gulped at hearing that and Ravi gave me a sideways glance.

Houseman looked deeply worried.

The warlord waved his hand. 'No, no. Do not be concerned. You will *appear* to be in trouble, but they will have their special orders. I have a very special team I shall deploy, my personal commandos. They are trained sharpshooters.'

'I don't understand,' Houseman said.

'Your interpreter, Abdullah. He has defied me, defied the Taliban and works for you. He insults me and insults my authority. He will be your sacrifice to seal this deal. When you leave here, make sure he will be in the passenger seat of the lead vehicle.'

I could scarcely believe what I was hearing.

Ravi gulped. 'That was your Shogun, Dave.'

'Abdullah will be taken out by my sharpshooter. It will be *your* commitment to our deal, signed in *his* blood.'

Houseman shook his head. 'I can't do that.'

'It's what you have to do if you want a deal. And if you don't agree, I cannot guarantee safe passage of your convoy back to Bastion. You may all die.'

There was a long silence. 'Do I have a choice?'

Zam-Zama looked directly at the webcam again. 'We will both have much to lose if our secret becomes public. And the camera never lies.'

Suddenly Houseman rose to his feet and crossed rapidly towards the laptop, his body filling the screen. Abruptly it went blank.

'Blimey,' Bernie Bramshaw said. 'That was something else. What happened next?'

Ravi said, 'When we left, our convoy was attacked.'

'It explains one thing that always niggled,' I added.

'What's that?'

'Why the Taliban suddenly stopped shooting,' I replied. 'The Shogun had blown up. We were all sitting ducks. Yet they stopped. It was unlikely they'd run out of ammunition.'

'It was all a show,' Ravi murmured, putting the final piece of the jigsaw in its place. 'And our interpreter Abdullah was shot dead in the lead vehicle. In your Shogun.'

My heart was thumping as I reached for my tobacco tin. 'God,' I said. 'Sacrificed by Houseman to seal the deal.'

'What Zam-Zama didn't know,' Ravi said, 'was you'd then go and drive into an old Soviet minefield.'

I nodded. 'That's the reason Houseman is so desperate to get our copy of the recording. To destroy the evidence.'

# Thirty-One

'So you had no idea about the secret deal?' Bernie Bramshaw asked, as we sat around the breakfast table together.

It had got so late the night before – after we'd watched the tape, talked endlessly and demolished a bottle and a half of whisky – that Bramshaw had decided he was in no fit state to drive home. Gem had offered him the sofa in the front room and he'd collapsed onto it without a second's thought.

Ravi shook his head. 'I had no idea about any deal. I was Special Recon. That's reconnaissance up close and personal. Houseman was MI6. I was just his battlefield assistant, so to speak. I wouldn't be entrusted with such stuff.'

'Amazing,' Bramshaw muttered.

'Crazy and unorthodox all right,' Ravi agreed.

'Perhaps it worked for a while,' I said. 'I was back in the UK at Selly Oak, but from what I heard the pace of enemy action did slow for a while.'

'It's hotting up again now,' Bramshaw said, 'according to news on the telly.'

I said, 'You can see why Chas would be so nervous about it getting out. Allowing – even encouraging – a Taliban warlord to import heroin into the UK.'

Bramshaw wagged a finger. 'On the basis that if he didn't someone else would!'

To my surprise Gem seemed to be following the complexities of it all. 'That wouldn't wash in the tabloids, would it?'

'The government would be crucified,' Ravi agreed. 'Not to mention Houseman himself.'

'There'd be chaos in Parliament,' I added.

'I've just thought of something,' Ravi said. 'I don't see Houseman giving someone like Zam-Zama carte blanche. A pipeline, a network, yes. But he'd want to see it controlled . . . We wondered earlier why Jooma Khan was killed by the Swords?'

'They referred to him as a traitor,' I thought aloud.

Ravi nodded. 'Is Zam-Zama's network infiltrated with security service agents?'

I added, 'So it could be controlled by Houseman's people at all times . . . ?'

'Even closed down by MI6,' Ravi suggested, 'when they decided it had served its purpose.'

'Jeez,' Bramshaw said, buttering another slice of toast, 'this story just gets bigger by the minute.'

There was no contradicting that. The journalist's words said it all. In the silence that followed we all heard the noise of something being pushed through the letterbox.

'Think your post has come,' Bramshaw said with his mouth full.

'Too early,' Gem replied, standing up. 'That'll be the newspaper.'

As she disappeared into the hall, the three of us looked at each other apprehensively.

Ravi grinned. 'I don't think life is ever going to be the same again.'

'Wapping, here I come,' Bramshaw said.

Gem re-entered the room, holding the *Journal* with both hands. She stared at the front page and looked up. She read, in a quiet voice, ' "Donkey sanctuary to close." '

Mrs Quigley answered the telephone when Bramshaw called.

In her best county voice, she calmly advised the deputy editor and chief reporter of the *Journal* that her husband was unwell and had taken to his bed. Donald Quigley had warned her to expect a telephone call from Bramshaw. He had told her to tell him that he was sorry, but he had taken legal advice about the drug gang story.

He had been advised not to run it after the paper's solicitor had spoken to the local police who had, in turn, passed him on to Special Branch in London. Someone called Houseman had advised that there could be serious legal implications for the paper if the story was run.

Bramshaw snapped shut his mobile phone. I could almost see the hot rage steaming from the man's ears.

'What now?' Gem asked.

Bramshaw took a deep breath and smiled widely. 'God moves in mysterious ways.'

'Yes?' Ravi asked, bemused.

'Bugger Swinthorpe,' Bramshaw declared. 'I'm obviously meant to take this further.'

'What d'you have in mind?' I asked.

'My old paper. The *Sunday News*.'

'Is that still going?' Ravi asked.

Bramshaw looked hurt. 'Of course. Not the circulation it had, I admit. Become a bit of a niche market. But sometimes a real scoop emerges amidst the tits and bums.' He suddenly remembered Gem's presence. 'Oh, sorry, m'dear, must watch my language.'

She smiled. 'That's OK.'

'I'd better get home,' he said. 'Take a shower and change my clothes. Then give Russ a call.'

'Russ?' Ravi asked.

'Russ Carver, my old editor. I'll keep you posted.'

With that he pulled on his raincoat, headed for the door, and was gone.

Ravi pushed away his empty coffee mug. 'Well, if there's no story in the *Journal*, we're still in business with the Swords. Let's see what we can do. I'll give Rashid a call.'

In fact, Rashid was pleased to hear from us and it was quickly decided that we should run a master class on 'close protection' in one of the back rooms at the Rosebury Street mosque that afternoon.

But first we had something a little more pressing – collecting our possessions left in our rooms at the Riverside Lodge hotel.

A lock-picker's kit was a regular issue in the SAS and, like many others, I had managed to hold on to mine when I left the army. Unfortunately it was in my bergen – which I still couldn't persuade myself to abandon – and in my room under lock and key! However, after ferreting around in Gem's kitchen and the tiny garden shed she had out the back, I collected a few bits of wire, a broken hacksaw blade and other items that I thought might do the trick.

It was just as well, because when we drove to the hotel and approached the unmanned reception desk, the keys on the hooks for our two rooms were missing.

Slipping quickly up the stairs, we went to Ravi's room first. I'd always been good at lock-picking. God knows why. Happily this lock hadn't been updated and even with my makeshift tools I had the door open in five minutes. I left Ravi to gather his stuff and went on to my own room. My door was trickier for some reason and I had to wave to a fellow guest, who came out of his room to stare at me suspiciously.

'Faulty lock, guv,' I explained. 'Hope I didn't disturb you.'

I hadn't and he seemed happy with the explanation. I don't think I'd ever packed a bergen so fast in all my life, even when I'd been under fire. I left down the back staircase and out through a fire escape door. It was with a huge sense of relief that I joined Ravi in his Lexus.

We then bought some false numberplates at a unit on a local industrial estate to replace those on Ravi's car, before treating ourselves to lunch at a quiet out-of-town pub.

In the afternoon, we drove down to the Rosebury Street mosque where we found Rashid waiting for us with a classroom of eager pupils. The whole subject of 'close protection' was far more my subject than Ravi's, and covered a much wider area than basic 'bodyguarding', which is what the gang members seemed to think it meant. No doubt that was down to having watched too many trashy DVDs.

So I went through the whole gamut of stuff from assessing the enemy and its likely or known capability, any established modus operandi, then applying it to the mission in hand. Then choosing from available communications equipment, vehicle types, protective wear, firearms. Theory lessons and practice followed in anti-ambush driving skills and moving your charge to and from a vehicle with safety.

After a couple of hours, I decided they'd had enough, especially when one of them fell asleep at the table. After Rashid had angrily kicked him awake, I promised another class the following week. We left the exact date to be arranged. Rashid, I noticed, was becoming increasingly friendly in tone. I think this training, along with his earlier firearms course, had made him feel seriously empowered.

Ravi and I had just returned to Gem's place when I received a call from Bernie Bramshaw.

'I've done it, boys!' he declared joyously. 'Carver's agreed to see us.'

'When?' I asked.

'Tomorrow.'

That was enough for me. 'Do you want us both?'

His voice lowered. 'Just you, Dave, if that's all right. I'm a little uncertain about Ravi. Nice bloke, but I'm not sure about his connections.' As an afterthought he added, 'Oh, and bring that interview recording.'

'Of course,' I said. We'd already made several copies and posted some to different trusted friends for safekeeping.

\* \* \*

'Tea with the Taliban.'

Russ Carver already had his headline, as he watched the rerun of the secret meeting on Bramshaw's laptop.

He may have been draped casually in a typist's swivel chair, but Carver hardly looked relaxed. His was the thin body and racing mind of a fast-thinking adrenalin junkie.

'Actually,' Bramshaw said, 'I think it was lime juice.'

The rather cramped, deserted office of the *Sunday News* was the nerve centre of one of the few national newspapers still in Fleet Street. I thought it had ceased publication years ago, but apparently it still had a hardcore old readership that liked comely naked females as part of its diet of sport and as little real news as possible.

The fluorescent strip lighting was off and the only illumination in the open-plan room was provided from the computer monitors flickering on the two rows of empty workstations.

Abruptly the film of the meeting ended. Carver's pale, gaunt and unshaven face stared at the blank screen in silence for several seconds. Then he brushed his overlong hair from his eyes.

'So this bloke Houseman agreed?' Carver asked. 'You left the meeting and on the drive back to base this Abdullah – an Afghan good guy – was shot dead by a sniper. Sacrificed to seal the deal.'

'You got it,' Bramshaw said.

'Jesus,' Carver said, and looked at me. 'And then you got blown up?'

I smiled thinly. 'That wasn't part of the plan,' I said. 'When

Abdullah was shot, I took evasive action by swerving off the
road – right into an old Soviet minefield.'

'But the deal went ahead,' Carver said. You could almost
see the paper's circulation figures clocking up in his eyes.
'British intelligence helped this Dr Zam-Zama set up a heroin
pipeline into Britain in return for turning down the heat on
the battlefield.'

Bramshaw nodded.

'God, and I thought journalists were cynical. Did it work?'

'For a while,' I said. 'But certainly not any more. It appears
to be getting much worse again. Much more emphasis on
IEDs.'

'Improvised explosive devices, right?' Carver asked.

I nodded. 'Zam-Zama's militia were never much into that.
They were more sharpshooters and ambushes.'

Carver was quick to grasp things. 'So you could argue that
Houseman made the deal with the wrong warlord.'

I said, 'Maybe, as things turned out.'

'But this UK drug distribution network is here, up and
running?'

'Yes,' Bramshaw confirmed. 'We think there may have
been agents recruited and planted in that network by MI6 –
probably in collusion with MI5. To monitor it and close it
down when it was deemed appropriate.'

'You know this?' Carver demanded.

I said, 'No, but a colleague of mine thinks that's highly
probable.'

'But you say that sort of *safeguard* . . . could be breaking
down?'

'It's likely,' I confirmed.

Carver swivelled round in his chair and lit a cigarette in defiance of the big No Smoking signs plastered on the walls. He stared out of the window at the double-decker buses splashing through the forlorn puddles of a dark and wet Fleet Street.

He exhaled a stream of grey smoke. 'We miss you, Bernie.'

Bramshaw said, 'I love you too, Russ. You always were the perfect liar.'

'What do you want for all this?'

'Take me back.'

The editor smiled grimly. 'I don't think the new proprietor will agree to that. He's trying to put the paper's past behind us.'

'It's a big story,' Bramshaw said. 'It stands up and it's got legs. It's worth its proverbial weight in gold.'

'Still the master bullshitter, eh, Bernie?' Carver chuckled. 'But for once you're right.'

'Thirty.'

Carver looked pained. 'Times are hard, Bernie. The good days are over.'

'That's because I don't work for you any more.'

The editor could have been playing at a poker table. 'Five.'

'Twenty-five.'

'Ten – if you stand it up with solid concrete legs.'

'Fifteen,' Bramshaw countered. 'With pictures and quotes.'

God knows where he thought he was going to get his pictures and quotes from. I had a nasty feeling Ravi and I might be featured in there somewhere.

Carver dropped his cigarette butt into a dirty coffee mug. It sizzled momentarily and expended a tiny puff of smoke as it died. 'A deal, Bernie. And the only reason is I've heard on the grapevine that there's a major secret security inquiry about to start in Westminster. About various things that have been going on in Iraq and Afghanistan.'

'It'll be the usual whitewash,' Bramshaw said.

'Apparently not,' Carver replied. 'It's said this inquiry's got real teeth. Well, we'll give it something to bite on, eh?'

At least, I thought, when the story broke the police will have no option but to take proper action against the drug gang. Hopefully, the killers of Jock and Ginger would finally get their just desserts.

Carver reached over the table and shook Bramshaw's hand, then mine.

'Will you leave a copy of that recording with me?' he asked.

Bramshaw shook his head. 'You've seen it, you don't need it. It'll be in our safer keeping unless your lawyers need a view.'

The editor of the *Sunday News* seemed to know he was beaten as he showed us to the door. 'Good to do business with you again, Bernie.'

As the two of us clattered down the concrete steps of the stairwell, I said, 'Fifteen thousand pounds, Bernie, that's amazing.'

I was still allowing that to sink in when my mobile phone began its trilling jingle in my pocket. It was Ravi. 'Hi, Dave, Gem said you're in London.'

I said, 'Yes, I'm with Bernie. We've just visited an old mate of his.'

I heard a faint grunt at the other end and a thoughtful pause. 'That's useful – because I've just had a call from Egor Baran. It was very quick, very enigmatic. Wouldn't tell me anything, just gave me another number to ring immediately. He didn't sound happy. Some woman – I suspect it was that girlfriend of his, Veronika – answered. She gave me another number to ring for an urgent meet in London.'

'You want me to attend the meeting?'

'I'm here,' Ravi replied tersely. 'You're there. Just be careful.'

He gave me a mobile number. When I called it, a woman answered. Just the word 'Hello' with its seductive, soft Russian accent, was enough to get my pulses racing.

I said, 'I'm Dave, a friend of Ravi's. I think we met.'

'I remember.'

'Then you are Veronika.'

'Please, no names,' she said hoarsely. 'This is a clean phone, but you cannot be too careful. When can you get to central London?'

'I'm in Fleet Street.'

'Then come straight away to Oxford Street. There is a burger bar . . .' She gave me the name and hung up.

'What's happening?' Bramshaw asked.

'Blessed if I know, Bernie,' I replied, putting my phone away. We'd both come to London in his car. 'I've got to see someone. Grab yourself a bite to eat and I'll catch up with you as soon as I can. We can drive back to Swinthorpe later.'

He wasn't too happy about that, but it couldn't be helped. I flagged down a passing taxi and headed off for Oxford Street through the quiet, wet streets.

When I arrived at my destination, I found only a dozen or so customers in the brightly lit burger bar. It took me a couple of moments to recognise Veronika. She was dressed in a grey overcoat and wearing a headscarf. The fact that she'd positioned herself in a corner – looking out into the restaurant area and close to the only escape route, via the kitchen – told me a lot about her.

As I approached, she looked up. Without a touch of make-up, she appeared remarkably plain. She patted the seat beside her.

Obligingly I sat down. 'Kiss me,' she said.

I did and almost immediately she pulled away. She smiled. 'Let's go.'

She picked up her shoulder bag, took my hand and we walked briskly out onto the street together. An irritating, spitting drizzle had begun. When I went to speak, she just shook her head and hurried on. She turned sharply down a side street, then another. And another.

Then she stopped, stepped into a doorway and pulled me in after her.

'Kiss me,' she ordered again.

But this time I realised she wasn't falling in love with me. She was watching over my shoulder to see if anyone had followed us. This was classic fieldcraft.

No one had followed. In fact I don't think anyone was on the streets of London on that miserable evening; I think the entire population was at home watching *The X Factor* on television.

After a few moments, she drew away. 'I think we are safe.'

Again she took my hand and led the way along several streets until we found ourselves outside a grubby little coffee bar with fugged windows and a neon sign that flashed intermittently. As she pushed open the door, the cloying warmth hit us. The place was empty apart from the owner, a fat Italian-looking man at the counter, who was reading a copy of that day's *Sunday News*. Reluctantly he looked up. It struck me that this guy could take lessons in how to run a cafe from Andreas Simitis in Swinthorpe.

I think Veronika looked at me properly for the first time. 'Coffee?'

'Black and sweet.'

We carried our respective chipped mugs back to one of the tables. Veronika used a beautifully manicured hand to wipe away the condensation on the window and peered out.

I decided someone had to get the conversation going. 'Where's Egor?' I asked.

She looked at me and blinked, almost as if she thought I should know the answer to my own question. 'Paddington Green.'

I couldn't believe that. 'The police station?'

'Of course. He is being held for questioning. His company was raided this afternoon. By the police. MI5 or Special Branch . . . I do not know. Egor had a short warning – he has many friends in many places. He has just enough time to give me this file.'

She opened her shoulder bag and produced an anonymous-looking grey cardboard folder. 'Egor has a message for you,' she added. 'He can no longer work for you. Your debts are even and square.' She stared blankly at the steam rising from the coffee machine. 'In fact, I do not think he will be working for anyone for some time.'

'This raid . . .' I began. 'Was it to do with . . . ?'

'Your friend's request? Yes. GCHQ was investigating.' She took a sip of the coffee, pulled a face and put the mug back down on the table. 'Apparently Egor's Trojan and its intercepts were discovered and traced back to his company.'

I shook my head in disbelief. 'And this file?'

'It contains copies of recent email communications. They are sent by someone called Rashid. He works for a man called Masood Babur, who is currently visiting here from Afghanistan. In turn Babur is the number two to a warlord boss in Afghanistan called Dr Zam-Zama.'

I nodded. 'That's right.'

Veronika shifted in the uncomfortable plastic chair, clearly eager to be going. 'Egor has discovered what appears to be a plot. Babur is planning to take over the drugs operation from Zam-Zama.'

I didn't really care if Babur wanted to screw his boss. As far as I was concerned they were all as bad as each other. I shrugged. 'So what?' I asked.

Veronika's nostrils flared with impatience. 'You don't understand. Babur has been in email correspondence with a man called al-Kuwaiti. Al-Kuwaiti is based in Abbottabad in Pakistan. Babur is planning to hijack the network from Zam-Zama *for* his new boss, al-Kuwaiti.'

I turned the name over in my head, not understanding why Veronika was getting so worked up about it. The name meant nothing to me. I said bluntly, 'I don't know who al-Kuwaiti is.'

She stared at me. 'Abu Ahmed al-Kuwaiti,' she said. 'Egor tells me he is the top personal courier of Osama bin Laden.'

Suddenly the world's most wanted terrorist leader had wandered onto the landscape.

# Thirty-Two

'It's incredible,' Ravi said. 'Al-Kuwaiti. I still don't believe it.'

It was Monday evening. He was seated with Bernie Bramshaw and me in the settee and armchairs around the electric coal-effect fire in Gem's front room. As she poured us tea, he was carefully studying the file that Veronika had given me.

'Who is this guy al-Kuwaiti?' Bramshaw asked. The journalist seemed almost to have moved in with us, sharing the spare room in Gem's house to type away on his old laptop. He was now paranoid that there would be a raid by MI5 on the offices of the *Journal* or, indeed, his own home.

'As his name suggests,' Ravi said, 'Abu Ahmed al-Kuwaiti is of Pakistani Pashtun parentage. He was actually born and grew up in Kuwait. Later he moved to Pakistan where he made a living as a money-changer in the tribal areas. Somewhere along the line he got involved with Osama bin Laden and became a trusted senior member of al-Qaeda. He was reported to have given computer training to some of the September 11 team.'

'So one of the world's most wanted,' I observed, accepting a mug of tea from Gem.

'I'll say,' Ravi agreed. 'Word was he'd been wounded and died in the Tora Bora mountains back in 2001 – when he was on the run with bin Laden himself. Story went that he'd bled to death in his leader's arms. It was only much later, in around 2004, that the rumour spread that al-Kuwaiti was still very much alive. I think it came from one of the Guantánamo Bay prisoners. He's currently reckoned to be Osama bin Laden's most trusted courier.'

Ravi tapped the paper in front of him. 'This indicates that al-Kuwaiti is currently living in a place called Abbottabad. And obviously he's now in touch with our friend Masood Babur.'

'So how exactly is this playing out?' I asked.

Bramshaw had clearly been putting his journalist's analytical mind to work in order to write his story in simple terms for the readers of the *Sunday News*. As he sipped at his tea, he said, 'Seems to me that our MI6 friend Chas Houseman did this dodgy deal with Dr Zam-Zama to buy a bit of peace back in 2006. The Taliban eases up on the pressure in return for a heroin network into the UK. MI6 reckons there'll be heroin here anyway, so why not? Besides, they plant their own people in the network to keep an eye on things, so the network can be *controlled* or closed down by MI6. Or, on home turf, that's more likely MI5.'

Ravi agreed. 'Things quietened down on the battlefield for a while and the plan works.'

I said, 'I think maybe Dr Zam-Zama's influence in the Taliban has diminished since the deal was first done.'

Ravi nodded. 'That wouldn't surprise me. I think Zam-Zama's more interested in himself than the Taliban movement. I somehow doubt they saw much of the profits.'

It was Bramshaw's *eureka* moment. 'Of course, that's why Masood Babur is here. Probably Mullah Chadhar – he's a known fundamentalist – realised what was going on and spilled the beans to Babur. Babur might be working for Zam-Zama, but he's also an old school, hard-line jihadist and wedded to the Taliban. I can guess where his true loyalties lie. He's also in with al-Qaeda and bin Laden's best mate al-Kuwaiti.'

I said, 'That's why Chas Houseman wants the video of his meeting. He did an unauthorised deal with the Taliban through Zam-Zama – and it's blown up in his face. Judging by Jooma Khan's murder, they could be losing control of the network in the UK.'

'And according to Carver,' Bramshaw added, 'there's a major inquiry beginning in Whitehall. My guess is, Chas Houseman's career is about to become roadkill.'

'Succinctly put,' Ravi agreed.

Having provided us all with tea, Gem had sat down with her copy of the *Journal* and begun reading all about the unhappy closure of the local donkey sanctuary, totally oblivious to our debate about international high politics and corruption.

Suddenly she asked, 'You know that bag lady in town? I mean the one with the posh voice they call Lady Penelope. You know her, Dave? She comes into the cafe sometimes.'

I dragged my mind back. 'What about her?'

'Do you know her real name?'

'Edwina,' I said.

'That's what I thought. And her surname?'

I couldn't remember. 'Something high-falutin'. Double-barrelled.'

'Hinckley-Fawcett?'

'Could be,' I replied. 'Why?'

'There's a small ad in here from a firm of solicitors. Want to speak to anyone who knows the whereabouts of someone called Edwina Hinckley-Fawcett.'

I said, 'You'd better make a note of their number. I expect she'll drop into the cafe before long . . . By the way, how are sandwich sales going?'

'Sales are down. Andreas has put his prices up.'

Bramshaw said, 'I'm all in. I'll have to finish the story for the *News* tomorrow. OK if I crash on the sofa again, Gem?'

'Don't outstay your welcome,' I intervened. 'It's not fair on the poor girl.'

That didn't seem to have crossed his mind. 'More fun here than being stuck at home with my missus.' He patted Gem on the knee. 'Besides, you don't mind, sweetheart, do you?'

'That's fine,' Gem replied wearily. 'It's quite nice having all this company for a change.'

Ravi turned to me. 'Time we got some shut-eye, too, Dave. A busy day tomorrow.'

While I had been in London, Ravi had been talking to Rashid. The Swords gang had apparently procured a new HQ, a small building alongside the Itchen river. Its location, I realised, would give direct access to the Solent, making it ideal for importing narcotics. Rashid wanted advice on making the place secure and would have his own gang of Asian workmen standing by to act on our instructions. I was looking forward to it.

At that moment, Bramshaw's mobile phone rang. He took it from his pocket and glanced at the screen before answering. 'Hi, yes, it's me,' he said in a deliberately lowered voice. He headed for the hallway, shutting the door after him.

Ravi was suspicious. 'I wonder who that is?'

I said, 'Probably Rupert Murdoch, offering him a job.'

The door to the hall opened again. Bramshaw stood there, his face drained and white.

'Goodness, Bernie,' Ravi said. 'I thought Halloween had gone . . . Looks like you've seen a ghost.'

Bramshaw shook his head, not listening, not getting the joke. 'That was Russ Carver. He's in a right panic. Gabbled off something about a raid on the newspaper office by Special Branch. They also called at his home. They've just left. He's on his way here.'

'What?' I couldn't believe it. 'You haven't given him this address?'

'I had to.'

'How bloody stupid.'

Bramshaw glared at me. 'He's not an idiot, Dave. I told him to make sure he's not followed.'

Ravi looked at me. 'What should we do?'

I thought for a moment, cobbling together a vague Plan B at the back of my mind. I said, 'It might be OK, but best be prepared. Put all our kit into your car and get it moved round to the next street. Then we can hotfoot it if necessary.'

Bramshaw frowned. 'Go on the run? I'm too old for that sort of caper. Count me out.'

'I have,' I snapped back, more irritably than I'd intended. I turned back to Ravi. 'Have you got any decent outdoor kit? Maybe some of your old army stuff, like your boots?'

Ravi looked pained. 'Well, unlike you, Dave, I wasn't planning to live rough. But I've got a sweater and an anorak in the car. And a cheap sleeping bag for emergencies.'

Gem was watching us, looking slightly amused and I think not fully appreciating the seriousness of the situation. 'I've got some green wellies. They might fit.'

'I'm a man,' Ravi protested.

Gem giggled. 'Size is everything. You're quite slim. What size feet do you take?'

'Eight.'

'Bingo,' she replied. 'I'm seven, but the boots are too big for me. Give me blisters.'

I shook my head in despair.

Having dressed for the outdoors, Ravi and I got our kit sorted and put it all in my trusty bergen. I was pleased I had not got rid of it. After it was dumped in the boot of the Lexus, Ravi drove the car around to the next street before returning. If things went wrong, we had an escape route planned.

We settled down and turned off the lights, awaiting the eventual arrival of Russ Carver.

I was asleep, but only just. I was in a room in Afghanistan, or maybe Iraq. It was pitch-black, but there were crowds of totally silent insurgents outside pressing against the windows like zombies, trying to get in. It was also Gem's spare bedroom and Ravi was sleeping on the floor beside me.

I opened my eyes. The sound of knocking was barely

audible. I swung my legs off the bed and shook Ravi's shoulder roughly.

'Someone at the front door,' I said. 'Get your boots on, just in case.' I left him to it and stepped onto the darkened landing. Moving past Gem's bedroom, I trotted down the stairs to the front door. A deep, shuddering sound of snoring came from the living room where Bramshaw was camped on the sofa. Then I heard Ravi's footsteps coming down the stairs behind me.

There was another soft tap on the front door. Uneasily, I peered through the fisheye spyhole. My heart was starting to pound. If it were the police or men in plain clothes, I'd just turn and run for the rear exit.

Russ Carver's thin face was dramatically side-lit from the glow of the porch lantern. He sucked on his cigarette impatiently as he stared back out into the street.

Breathing more easily, I opened the door. I could see the relief in Carver's expression. 'Dave, isn't it?'

I nodded. 'You drove yourself here, in your own car?'

'Yes. I'm sure I wasn't followed.'

As I stepped aside to let Carver in, Ravi moved past us both and out into the porch. He looked up at the sky and cocked his head, listening intently. Above the distant murmur of a car on the town's ring road, I could hear it, too. A light aircraft.

Ravi came back in and shut the front door as I turned on the light in the living room. Bernie Bramshaw was now awake, dragging his feet off the sofa and reaching for his spectacles.

All the commotion had woken Gem and she came down wearing her dressing gown and pyjamas. She knew instinctively what was needed and went to the kitchen to put a brew on.

Meanwhile I offered Carver a seat. He looked unnerved and I could see the slight tremor in his hand as he accepted the tumbler of whisky I'd poured him. 'Christ,' he said hoarsely, 'you guys really have stirred up a hornets' nest, haven't you?'

Ravi said, 'Listen, Mr Carver, you'd better be quick. We may have to leave here in a hurry. Tell us what happened?'

Carver took a deep swig from the tumbler and wiped his mouth on the back of his hand. 'They came to my house late afternoon, totally unannounced. I was at home with my wife. Apparently they raided the office at the same time.'

'Who were *they*?' I asked.

The editor pulled a face. 'God, you know what, I'm not sure they said. There were four of them in plain clothes. Someone flashed some sort of pass, not a badge. I think someone mentioned the Security Service.'

I said, 'Did one of them have a tan and crinkly fair hair?'

'Yes,' Carver replied. 'Smarmy fucker. He was the worst and did most of the talking. He clearly wanted a copy of the video of the meeting you showed me. He really did not like it when I told him I'd seen it but I didn't have a copy. He got really nasty. He said if I didn't cooperate, or attempted to print the story, I could expect a personal inspection from the Inland Revenue. And problems with my bank overdraft and credit rating. He also seemed to know about an *affair* I had with my secretary last year. Mentioned that in front of my wife – a big mistake.'

Ravi frowned. 'Mistake?'

'Beth went ballistic. We've always had an open relationship, ever since we met at university. I hadn't actually *told* her about this one. It wasn't important. But Beth was absolutely incensed that he tried to use this to silence me. She kicked them out and insisted I get in touch with you . . . do all I can to run the story – *somehow!* In my paper or another one. She's a great believer in the fourth estate, anti-capitalism and free love.'

'Good on her!' Bramshaw enthused.

'What happened next?' I asked.

'When Beth let rip, they said sort of menacingly that their visit had never happened, there would be no record of it. Then they left. That's when I phoned Bernie. I need to get hold of tangible evidence.' He saw the look on our faces. 'I had to call, it was my only way to contact him. But I have left my mobile phone *at home*. I know they can track people by that.'

'Was your car at home during their visit?' Ravi asked.

'On the drive.' He saw Ravi exchange glances with me. 'But, as I said, I'm sure I wasn't followed.'

Ravi said, 'If MI5 was following you, you wouldn't know. They may even have left a tracking beacon in your car. There's a light aircraft up now – I just heard it. MI5 has a secret airforce for surveillance and eavesdropping. Twin-turbo Cessna F04s, I understand. That could be one of them.'

Carver looked more shaken than ever. 'God, that's scary.'

I said, 'Seems like just now we're public enemy number one.'

At that moment, Gem arrived with a tray of mugs filled with tea. Eager hands reached out to grab them.

Carver said, 'So we might not have long before the cops or MI5 get here? Can you let me have the Zam-Zama meeting video?'

'I can let you have a copy,' Ravi said. 'I've sent copies to several people. One is a trusted friend of mine. He has made copies of it and sent them on to several friends of his.'

Carver shook his head in disbelief. 'I'd better move fast. At this rate, some bastard will put it on YouTube and the story will be out.'

'Only you know all the details, Russ,' Bramshaw assured.

'My friend is Nigel Greene, a retired solicitor,' Ravi said. 'He lives in the south of France now. Give him the codeword "Pandora" and he'll know it's safe to give you a copy.'

Carver grinned. 'I promise you, I'll break this bloody story somewhere. If not in the *Sunday News*, it'll be somewhere else!'

I wasn't sure I shared his faith. Even as I was thinking about it, my mobile phone rang. I glanced down at the screen. It was Jane Christy. 'Hello,' I said.

She dispensed with the niceties. 'Dave, you're in trouble. That creep Chas Houseman is back on the scene here and stoking a big fire. The CPS has been involved and Inspector Ryan's under pressure to reopen the Steve Cranford case, arresting you for abduction or conspiracy to murder – or both! They've tracked some Fleet Street editor to an address in Swinthorpe. It could be Gemma Wilkins's address. You're not there now, are you?'

I hesitated. 'No comment.'

'Oh, God!' Christy breathed. 'Then you haven't got long. Make yourself scarce. I've gotta go—'

The phone cut out and I switched off. I turned to Ravi. 'They know we're here. It's time to leave.'

'Thanks for your help,' Carver said. 'I'll try not to let you down.'

I'd been thinking earlier as I tossed and turned in my bed unable to sleep. It had become clear that Ravi and I would need some outside help if we were going on the run. I handed Gem a scrap of paper. 'When you have a chance, call this number. That's Big Brian, my former sergeant.'

She nodded. 'I remember him.'

'Tell him we need help.' I lowered my voice. 'I plan for us to be at Wykham Wood. It's a run-down private estate, about fifteen miles south of here. You can find it on an Ordnance Survey map. Ask him to meet us there *as soon* as he can – and bring some fresh pay-as-you-go mobile phones. Just cheap ones will be fine.'

Gem looked troubled. 'What if he won't cooperate?'

'If he says no, then you'll be talking to the wrong Brian.'

Bramshaw said suddenly, 'I think I heard a car.'

In the sudden silence that fell over the living room, we all heard the slamming of vehicle doors. Gem peered through the gap in the curtains. 'I can see shapes, people. Dozens of them. Out on the pavement. Coming this way!'

I turned to Ravi. 'Let's go!'

Gem reached up and kissed my cheek. 'Good luck, Dave. I'll contact Brian as soon as I can.'

Ravi waved to the two journalists as he made his way to the kitchen door. 'Don't forget,' he said cheerily, 'publish and be damned!'

Carver smiled bitterly. 'You know, I've a nasty feeling we will be.'

I followed Ravi out, through the kitchen and into the back garden – just as I heard a loud knock on the front door.

Then we were running down the path, ducking under the arms of the rotary laundry dryer, racing for the rear fence. In one practised movement we were up and over into the adjoining garden. I snapped on my mini-torch to show us the way along the crazy-paving path to the house and its side gate. Swiftly unbolting it, I found myself in the next street. There, waiting for us under the glow of a street light, was Ravi's car. I've never seen a more welcome sight.

'Sod,' Ravi said, slapping his jacket pockets with his hands.

'What?'

'I've forgotten my keys.'

My jaw dropped.

He grinned. 'Only joking!'

Before I could swear at him, he was already in the driver's seat and starting the engine. I was barely in through the passenger door when he pulled away from the kerb.

Ravi had left his lights off. There was sufficient ambient light to see where we were going. Just before we turned the corner we passed two uniformed policemen, who looked as though they had been deployed to cut off any escape attempt from the raid. The timing had been mercifully misjudged by some thirty seconds in their rush to mount the operation.

The two cops turned, bemused, as we swept by quietly, and without lights.

It was clear we'd be followed on monitors at the police CCTV control room. But it was the small hours of the morning and it was unlikely Swinthorpe was geared up to react very quickly to this sort of operation.

I directed Ravi to take the route for out of town, which would get us quickly onto the open road where there were no cameras. With its lights now on, the Lexus responded instantly to Ravi's foot with a muscled, silent strength.

Eventually I said, 'Pull in just ahead. It's a garden centre. Go into the car park and turn hard right. The perimeter hedge will hide us from the road.'

Ravi swung in, parked and killed the engine. I snatched my bergen from the boot and slung it over my shoulders.

Seconds later, we were crossing back across the main road and into a marked footpath which ran into dense, dark forest. In the distance I saw the pulsing blue lights of a patrol car racing towards us from the direction of Swinthorpe. High above and far away in the night sky, I heard the menacing throb of an engine.

I was drenched in sweat. For a split second, I was back in Iraq.

# Thirty-Three

The arch of trees engulfed us like a tunnel, leaves crunching underfoot. Behind us the lights and siren of the police car flashed by, quickly receding into the darkness. Silence cocooned us like a woollen blanket. It was broken only by our own footsteps and the discordant screech of an owl. Later, when we paused, the quiet was absolute. There were few clouds in the sky and it was a waning moon, the still air was crisp and would almost certainly make a frost on the ground by morning.

I knew this area well from my childhood. Although barely a five-minute drive from Swinthorpe town, it offered some twenty-five square miles of unspoiled countryside, dissected by a solitary winding lane and not a single village. Wildlife was left to its own devices. There were rabbits, badgers and foxes in abundance and it was a sanctuary for at least two types of deer.

Memories began flooding back so vividly that I barely needed the Ordnance Survey map and compass. The narrow beam from the small military torch was all I needed to confirm half-recalled landmarks as we made our way for half a mile before turning off. It was a hard scramble up a steep embankment. My right leg was beginning to throb painfully with the unfamiliar exertion.

'Where are we?' Ravi asked.

'A disused railway line,' I said. 'Used to run from Swinthorpe to the coast.' I paused for breath at the top of the climb. That's when I heard it again. 'The plane's still up,' I said.

'Some way off,' Ravi observed.

'Let's hope it stays that way.'

The old railway gravel crunched as we followed the line of the track that had been ripped out over forty years before under the Beeching cuts. We made fast progress, covering four miles in an hour before leaving the embankment at an old bridge,which crossed over the only lane in the area.

Some confusion followed. A marked footpath had been blocked by a zealous landowner. It was overgrown with spiteful brambles and barbed wire, forcing us to make a lengthy detour. Eventually, however, we arrived at the edge of the chalk quarry where Ravi and I had previously conducted our weapons training with members of the Swords gang.

Beyond it lay the peace and welcoming deep cover of Wykham Wood.

I led the way, crossing the perimeter fence and followed the soft, leaf-mould track to the right. First downhill, then up, wondering if I could find the dell that had once been Robin Hood's camp in my childhood.

I thought I'd got it wrong. Something had changed. We were at the highest point of the wood now. In daylight it had a commanding view of the three tracks leading up from the lower reaches of the plot. Now, nothing.

I cursed.

Then I passed a beech tree, its trunk bigger than I remembered, the etching in its bark made with my penknife as a youth still visible. I moved to the left. There it was, a deep depression in the ground. Anyone down there would not be seen unless a passer-by almost fell into it.

I looked back at Ravi and grinned like a big kid. 'Perfect,' I said.

We made do with the most basic of shelters for the night. Laying out a groundsheet first, we then stretched out a camosheet on a slant to form a primitive roof. It would keep out all but the most persistent rain. Then it was a mere question of rolling out our sleeping bags and crashing out for what was left of the night.

I fell into a deep and dreamless sleep. The rich smell of damp earth all around me was comforting in a way that was almost primeval. High above me, the wind whispered and rustled in the branches as I drifted into oblivion.

I awoke with a start.

The dog barked again.

I opened my eyes, and found myself staring into Ravi's face a few inches from my own. He stared back at me.

We both rolled over, in different directions, drawing our legs out of our respective sleeping bags. I'd kept my boots on, and quickly moved to the edge of the depression, while Ravi pulled on his borrowed footwear.

I glanced at my watch. It was twelve o'clock.

Some distance below, I could see the woman on the footpath. In summer she would have been hidden from view by wild shrubs and bracken, but now in winter her blue anorak and jeans were clearly visible. At her feet, a muddy golden retriever barked impatiently for her to throw the stick again. She obliged and the dog waited until it had disappeared into the thick carpet of leaves before racing off to find it.

I turned and waved to Ravi, giving him the thumbs up. Our campsite was as safe as it could be on a crowded island like Britain. Most dog walkers and mountain bikers would keep to the tracks, because the woodland growth was fairly dense, and we were a good hundred metres from the nearest one. We'd be safe if we kept to the basic rules. Unfortunately they included no smoking and keeping our voices low.

I started our gas stove and began making a breakfast of coffee and boil-in-the-bag porridge with apple flakes.

'Where the hell do we go from here?' Ravi asked, pulling a face at my culinary efforts.

I said, 'Wait until Russ Carver manages to get our story in print, I suppose. Then play it by ear.'

Ravi smiled stiffly. 'That's a big *if*, Dave. Houseman will do all he can to squash it.'

'He doesn't own the media,' I retorted. 'Still I guess we'll just have to wait until Gem or maybe Brian comes looking for us.'

Ravi didn't look happy. 'Deep joy,' he said.

Then I heard it. A voice was calling. Someone had lost his or her dog.

'This place is like Piccadilly Circus,' Ravi muttered.

'Sssh,' I urged.

There it was again. Distant. Female. 'DAVE! DAVE!'

Ravi laughed quietly. 'Got a dog named after you.'

'DAVE! RAVI!'

Ravi was taken aback. 'Hell! No one would name a dog after me. Is it Gem?'

I placed a restraining hand on his arm. 'Didn't sound like her voice,' I said. 'We need to be careful.'

Keeping low, I ran across the edge of the depression and peered over the natural earth rampart and down towards the path. For a moment I was confused. The figure on the track looked like a man. Maybe a gamekeeper or woodsman, in green boots, jeans and a body warmer. Of course, I should have recognised the tweed trilby hat that hid her mass of wild auburn hair. I could hardly believe my eyes. DC Jane Christy was looking right and left, peering intently into the under-growth on either side of her.

'DAVE! IT'S ME – JANE!' she called out again. 'ARE YOU THERE! I'M ALONE! NO ONE KNOWS I'M HERE!'

As I turned back to Ravi, I found him staring at me. His face looked quite white with shock. 'How did she know we were here?'

I shook my head. 'I've no idea. Someone must have told her. Bramshaw, Carver . . . ?'

Ravi bit his lip. 'Do we trust her?'

Again the voice, echoing coldly between the leafless trees. 'I'M ON YOUR SIDE! I MUST SPEAK TO YOU!'

I said, 'I think we have to. Otherwise they'd already have these woods surrounded by police.'

He looked doubtful. 'It's your call, Dave.'

'I'll risk it,' I said. 'I'll go down and speak to her. If she's playing games, at least you'll stand a chance of making a run for it.'

Christy was still calling out and she didn't hear my foot-falls in the leaves as I came down the hill behind her.

She turned suddenly. 'God, Dave! You scared me!'

'Sorry. You weren't expected.'

'I know, forgive me.' It was odd to see the tough female detective almost pleading. 'Gemma told me where to find you. I'm afraid I really bullied her, left her in tears. She refused to say anything so I said her new baby would likely be taken into care if she didn't cooperate.'

I couldn't believe my ears. 'You said *what*?'

'I didn't want to, Dave, believe me. But I had to. I don't think you know what deep shit you are in.'

'And you'll be in it, too,' I observed. 'Just by coming here.'

She shook her head. 'Yes and no. I made a decision last night. I'm leaving the force.'

'You're what?'

Her serious face melted momentarily and she smiled impishly. 'You're sounding like a recording. I said, I'm hand-ing in my sheriff's badge.'

'Why?'

'This case is the final straw.' She looked at me closely as though trying to determine if I really understood. I think she decided that I didn't. Looking around at the audience of trees, she said slowly, 'The job and its attitudes have changed,' she said. 'Since I joined as a probationer – what, fifteen years ago? – it's become more remote, more pen-pushing, more politically correct, more cliquey . . . It's all about careers and pensions, not protecting the community from crime. You nick young villains one day and the next they've got a community order they don't obey and give you two fingers.' She paused. 'Then there's *this* business.'

'Ravi and me on the run?'

'The whole thing. It's not right.' She held my gaze. 'There is no way we should be having officers from secretive government departments coming down here and interfering with our work, overruling us and taking command – clearly breaking all the rules in the process. I was with Houseman and Inspector Ryan when Gem's place was raided last night. I saw what happened, how that newspaper editor was threatened. How they treated Bernie Bramshaw. It made me ashamed to be a police officer. I've had enough.'

I took a deep breath. 'That's a gutsy thing to say. Inspector Ryan's going to miss you.'

She gave a snort of derision. 'I don't think so. We've never seen eye to eye. I've never wanted to go to his pub piss-ups – you're not one of the lads if you don't do that, it's expected. Get rat-arsed and show 'em your tits, that's what you're supposed to do if you're a girl with the boys in blue. If not, you're a spoilsport. Don't think it's changed that much recently, it hasn't. At least not at Swinthorpe nick.

'No, Ryan will be pleased to see the back of me. I like people, like to understand them. I want to work with them, not against them. I'm a Dixon of Dock Green kinda guy.'

I smiled at that. 'You can't just walk out, can you?'

'I'm not going to,' she replied. 'I could throw a sicky, get medically discharged over stress or something.' She paused, puffed out her cheeks and stared thoughtfully up at the rustling branches way above our heads. 'But I'd like to make a point. Go out with a bang, so to speak.'

'What do you mean exactly?'

'I want to help you and Ravi.'

I stared at her. 'Are you mad?'

She looked at me and grinned again. 'Probably.' She corrected herself. 'No certainly.' The impish expression melted away. 'You'll get no more help from Ryan. Certainly not now the big boys from London are here, breathing down his neck.'

'What can *you* do?'

Her eyes narrowed, the warmth in them giving way to the hard glare of an alley cat. 'Nothing without you and Ravi.'

'So that's it,' she said. 'Now I'm starting to understand.'

Ravi switched off his laptop. 'The battery's running low.'

She stared at the blank screen. 'No wonder Houseman is so desperate to stop news of his deal getting out.'

We'd been sitting around our tiny camouflaged campsite in Wykham Wood and the daylight was beginning to fade.

I said, 'Of course we don't know how far up the chain of command the decision went. Was it local in Afghanistan? Was it confined to the military, or did it go further? After all, Houseman is SIS . . . an extension of the Foreign Office. If it went that far, we could even be knocking on the door of Number 10.'

'It's possible,' Ravi said, 'but I doubt it. They were

desperate times back then. Our troops were taking a real pounding. Someone wanted a quick fix and this was it.'

Christy thought for a moment. 'So Houseman and whoever else was behind this hare-brained scheme thought they could control it – putting in their own people, like the late Jooma Khan, under cover. But Dr Zam-Zama is gradually eliminating them and running his own show.'

'But Zam-Zama's number two, Masood Babur, is a Taliban and al-Qaeda purist,' Ravi explained. 'According to reports from our Russian hacking expert, Babur intends to usurp Zam-Zama and take over the drugs network from him.'

The detective constable shook her head. 'I can't believe the amount of work you guys have done. If we'd been doing our job properly, Inspector Ryan and our team might have begun to unearth some of this.'

'The question is,' I said, 'what do we do next?'

Christy frowned. 'The gang has no idea of what's going on with you and Houseman?'

I said, 'Of course not. They don't know MI5, Special Branch and the police are after us. Babur and Rashid just think we're a couple of ex-army bad boys on the make, willing to do their dirty work for them.'

Christy tipped up the peak of her trilby with her thumb. 'Then why don't we continue letting them think that? If you're willing, that is? Get back in touch. From what you said, they might be wanting some professional help. I'll do all I can to help you get all the evidence that's needed.'

'Sounds great to me,' Ravi said.

It was now getting dark.

DC Christy said, 'I'd better get back while I can still see. I'll go back to the station and borrow some bits of surveillance equipment that might help us. Tomorrow I'll call in sick. I'll come here, maybe around ten.'

'Fine,' I agreed.

She smiled at me. 'Tonight I'll have a large whisky in a deep bath and have a long think about how to handle this.'

I said, 'I'll hold that image.'

'Cheeky.'

I indicated the surrounding trees that were losing form, melting away into the deepening darkness. 'I'll come with you to the car park.'

'I think maybe you'd better, or I could be wandering around all night.'

Ravi said, 'Then I'll get some grub on the stove. Fancy a nice boil-in-the-bag curry?'

I led Christy out of the depression and back onto the track, my eyes quickly adjusting to the darkness. We walked in silence. There was no noise apart from crisp leaves crackling under our feet and the irritable sound of rooks settling down in the trees high above our heads.

It only took ten minutes to reach the gravel car park.

I was surprised to find two cars parked there, fairly close to each other.

The sidelights on the black Saab blinked twice as Christy pointed her key fob at it. 'That's mine,' she said. 'Whose is the other?'

It was a battered green van with no windows in the cargo body. 'Probably a dog walker.'

Christy peered at the number plate. 'A dealer's name in Gloucester.' Then she observed, 'Tax disc is valid.'

Once a cop always a cop, I thought, as she climbed into her car and started it up.

I turned away and back into the woods. There was still no sign of the van driver as I made my way back up the track.

I'd been walking for five minutes when I suddenly stopped. I'd heard a sound. I could have sworn it was human, maybe someone cursing. But the underfoot leaves had made so much noise I couldn't be certain.

I thought again of the van in the car park.

Against my better judgement I left the track, stepping tentatively in the direction of the sound I had heard. Nothing. I took another step, then another. Suddenly I was sure I could hear heavy breathing.

I could feel the hairs on the back of my neck standing up like iron filings.

# Thirty-Four

My torch blazed into life, framing the bearded face with its piercing blue eyes.

'God, Brian!'

'Bloody hell, boss!'

In that split second, I don't know which of us was the most terrified.

'You scared the life out of me,' Duffy gasped. 'What's the matter wi' you? You asked that Gem to get in touch with me – so what you expectin'?'

'I'm sorry,' I said. 'Thanks for coming.'

'You're lucky I wasn't away. I'd just buried Mum, so was tidying loose ends.'

I remembered Constance, a proud and elegant woman from another age. 'I'm sorry.'

'Not as sorry as I was,' Duffy said. 'Broke her hip. The op was all right but the aftercare was shit. Didn't manage to feed and water her. Don't know what's the matter with nurses today. Got fancy degrees but don't know how to handle a spoon or a bedpan. My fault, I suppose, I was away truckin'. By the time I realised what was going on, it was too late. Got that MRSA thing she did.'

'I'm sorry,' I repeated.

He shrugged. 'I think she just lost the will to live. Still . . . all done now.' He took a deep breath. 'So what the hell are you and Ravi up to? Spoke to that nice young lass, Gem, whatever . . . she gave me some garbled cock-and-bull story. Not sure I could follow it. If I did, I can't believe half of it's true.'

'It's true enough,' I replied. 'Have you got some new mobile phones?'

He held up a plastic Asda bag. 'She didn't know how many you wanted. So I thought of a number and doubled it. Special offer. I got ten of them and put twenty quid on pay-as-you-go for each.'

'Good thinking.'

'That's five hundred you owe me. My friendship only stretches to beer, not money.'

'I'll pay you.'

'Sorry, boss, no offence, but you're a tramp. Tramps don't have money.'

'Ravi's got money.'

That seemed to satisfy him, and I led the way back to our camp on the top of the hill.

The three of us had a quiet but cheerful reunion, sitting around the small fire and eating a fairly disgusting curry, washed down by a bottle of whisky that Duffy had thought to bring with him.

We decided we'd make contact with Rashid the next day with our new communications set-up. Each of us had three phones, plus one spare. We noted each other's numbers for future reference and gave each phone a separate alphabetic identity. Finally Duffy made his way back to his van to spend the night in a modicum of comfort.

Neither Ravi nor I slept well that night. My mind was certainly spinning round and round, yet unable to reach any decision or conclusion. After several hours I was sure I would never get to sleep – that's when it finally happened.

We woke with the first light at around seven fifteen in the morning. I got some beans and bacon on the stove, while Ravi went to the car park to find Duffy and invite him to join us for breakfast.

When we were done, we broke camp, leaving the place without any sign of our ever having been there. Once back in Duffy's van, we ran the engine and heater to warm up and chatted over our options.

I was anxious to contact Rashid to let him know we were still in business, but I felt it wiser to wait until Jane Christy returned. Moments before ten o'clock she arrived as promised, parked and approached us.

She looked quite different from before, wearing snug jeans tucked into green Dunlops and a dark-pine body warmer over a rather dull plain sweater. Her hair was hidden under a navy woollen beanie hat and she wore no make-up at all. You wouldn't have remembered her from a crowd, you wouldn't even have noticed her in one. It was then I recalled she'd told me she'd done a lot of undercover work in the CID. And with a smile I recalled the convincing hooker in Coronation Gardens. That suddenly seemed such a long time ago.

The rear doors of Duffy's van were open and I was seated on the back ledge. 'How was that bath?' I asked.

'What?' Momentarily she looked perplexed. 'Oh, that! Good, thanks, Radox works wonders on the body and the mind. But I kept the shower curtain closed to stop any naughty little imaginations creeping in.'

'Ah,' I replied to her banter. 'So that's what it was.'

She dumped a tote bag of equipment by my side. 'I borrowed some stuff from the station last night. I also asked a few discreet questions. Everyone is looking for you. Ravi's car has been located in a garden centre car park, but there were no clues as to where you might be. Inspector Ryan is making you two his top priority.'

'Is Houseman still around?' Ravi asked.

'Yes. He'd checked into a hotel in the town for the night.' She pulled a face. 'And when I phoned in from my deathbed with flu an hour ago, I asked after him. Apparently House-man was already back at the station and ruffling more than a few feathers.'

I said, 'I want to call the Swords' gang leader, Rashid.'

'Fine.'

'Do you have a tap on his mobile?'

Christy shook her head. 'No, we only have Mullah Chad-har's landline on file – just in case. You're the one with all the numbers. Of course, I don't know what taps Houseman might have.'

Somehow I didn't think he would have any. It seemed to me that he was only now getting closely involved with this part of the devil he had helped to spawn. I decided to use my new mobile phone, allocated as C. I then wouldn't use it again until I had to.

I hid the caller's identity, then punched up Rashid's number.

His voice was testy, irritable. 'Hello, who's that?'

'Me, Dave.'

'Why are you withholding your number?' he demanded.

'Security,' I snapped back. 'And I've changed my number.'

'Oh?' he seemed chastened, perhaps remembering the lecture Ravi had given him on telephone security in the modern age. 'Where the hell have you been? I've been trying to get hold of you. Masood Babur needs to talk to you urgently.'

I repeated. 'I changed my number. Security.'

'Yes, yes.' He sounded annoyed, assuming I thought he was a fool. 'Can you come to us?'

'Of course,' I replied smoothly. 'Tell me where and when.'

'Can you come now? To an address in Southampton.'

Apparently it was their new HQ on the River Itchen. I raised an eyebrow. 'We're on our way,' I said. 'Give us a couple of hours.'

'Midday will be fine,' Rashid said. 'We shall expect you then.'

Gunwharf Lane was part of a small new industrial development on the west bank of the River Itchen, one of the tributaries that fed into the Solent. The Georgian factories that had made cannons for the old man-o'-war sailing ships had long since disappeared, but a number of the waterside jetties still remained. Sleek Lego-like modern offices and warehouses inside neat chain-link compounds had replaced their old brick and slate counterparts.

'It's all very new,' Christy observed. 'This used to be my patch, before I transferred to Swinthorpe.'

We were gathered in a supermarket car park a mile or so away. On the way there, we had stopped off in the Swinthorpe suburbs to pick up a little Smart car that belonged to Jane Christy's mother, whose daughter had sweet-talked her into lending to us. So our transport now comprised Duffy's old green van, Christy's black Saab and a sawn-off roller skate.

Christy extracted the two radio mikes from her tote bag. 'You two may not be keen, but this will be crucial to the evidence.'

Ravi shrugged. 'There's no reason why they should suddenly distrust us. We've earned their respect.'

I recalled the killing of Steve Cranford and the attempted lorry hijack that we'd thwarted for the gang. 'Ravi's got a good point. I think we need to wire-up, otherwise all our efforts could still be for nothing.'

The relief on Christy's face was obvious. With expertly deft fingers, she fitted the mini-mikes to the inside of our shirts. The separate battery transmitters, which were dummied-up as cigarette packets, fitted easily into a trouser pocket.

'Latest radio technology,' she explained. 'Mike to transmitter has a same-room range of some fifteen feet. Range from transmitter to base – that'll be Brian and me – up to three miles. But in reality we'll be lucky to get more than a mile.'

Now set, we closed in on Gunwharf Lane. I drove Christy's Saab with Ravi in the passenger seat, she followed up in her mum's Smart car and Duffy in his green van.

I selected a deserted side street that had no parking restrictions and pulled in. We gave the radios a test, then Ravi and I set off in the Saab, checking the radio reception with Christy all the way. By the time we got to the edge of the industrial estate on the bank of the River Itchen, the reception was still good, but not brilliant.

Here businesses, large and small, clustered around the waterside in a confusion of narrow lanes. Mobile cranes moved noisily like devouring robots amid a giant scrap-metal yard, alongside boatyards and dry stack facilities. There were also restaurants and smart marinas with pontoon jetties that reached out into the river, where millions of pounds' worth of yacht bucked gently on the swell.

The place we were looking for backed directly onto the river. At first sight the compound appeared abandoned and unused, surrounded by a rusting twelve-foot steel fence. The compound was anonymous, devoid of signage at the gate or on the building within it. There was no clue as to whether it was a just a retail or storage facility, or if it housed offices or a workshop. Any vehicles must have been parked around the back by the waterside, and out of sight from the street.

As I climbed out of the driver's seat and peered through the chain-link fencing, I noticed a couple of the CCTV cameras jerk suddenly into action. They, at least, looked to be

newly installed. Our arrival hadn't gone unnoticed and someone was watching us.

I spotted two things then, lying amid debris on the inside
of the wire. A commercial estate agent's SOLD sign and a
larger, more faded board with the hand-painted legend
'Seahorse Chandlery'. I mentioned my find aloud, so that it
could be picked up by my secret microphone and maybe
help DC Christy trace the new current owners.

It took me by surprise when the gate suddenly swung open
of its own accord. It was electronically controlled – expensive
and very unnerving. I climbed back into the Saab and drove
in, parking by the main reception door of the building. The
cameras followed us like live, modern-day gargoyles.

'They might want our advice on site security,' Ravi said, as
we opened the car doors, 'but they haven't wasted any time
in making a start.'

Rashid appeared at the front door of the office. 'It is good
to see you again,' he said, but without much warmth. 'I am
concerned when you do not answer your mobile phone.'

'I explained,' I said. 'We had a routine security check.
Changing all our numbers. It is something your own organisation must learn to do regularly.'

Rashid smiled slyly. 'So it is not just that your battery is flat?'

I shared his little joke. 'No, and we didn't run out of credit
either.'

The gang leader took a step back and inclined his head.
'Please, come through.'

We stepped into the corridor. It had the typical look of
abandoned commercial properties, bare fitted carpets strewn

with papers and cardboard cups, and magnolia walls pock-marked with smudges of Blu-Tack and ghostly squares of space where pictures had once hung.

To our right, the only piece of furniture remaining in the room was a large fitted reception desk.

'So you've just moved in?' I guessed.

'Yes, it was a chandlery,' Rashid said boredly. 'Selling bits and pieces for ships. They went bankrupt and we just bought this for a good price. We will do better, maybe we do interior fittings.'

I was *sure* they'd do better – importing heroin direct from Afghanistan. My mind was racing. 'Stripping out fancy yacht interiors and refurbing?' I asked.

Rashid nodded. 'We have many wealthy contacts across the Arab world.' Of course, I realised, the perfect cover for importing heroin. Customs rummage crews can't go around tearing apart luxury yachts unless they have very accurate intelligence because of the cost of getting it wrong.

Rashid continued, 'We have already installed CCTV, but my new boss Masood Babur will appreciate your advice on all security features. Fencing, anti-surveillance equipment . . .'

'Understood,' Ravi cut in. 'And training of discreet armed personnel, I imagine.'

Rashid allowed himself a slight smile. 'Exactly that.'

We had passed two large rooms where gang members, some of whom I recognised, were erecting storage racking, tools and electric drills lying all over the floor. It was like a master class in IKEA assembly. Now we arrived at a back office, a plain door, on which Rashid knocked respectfully.

The voice that answered was strong and commanding. For a moment I hardly recognised it as belonging to Dr Zam-Zama's second-in-command, Masood Babur.

He was seated behind a teak flat-pack desk which, judging from the packaging and instructions on the floor, had only just been assembled. His slender body seemed to grow taller in stature each time I saw him. Perhaps it was his growing self-confidence now that he had been in charge in the UK for a while. He still wore the neat toothbrush moustache but had ventured into a barber's shop to give his short black hair a modern spiky look. What really took me by surprise was the distinctive embroidered waistcoat he wore over a simple collarless white shirt and black trousers. That waistcoat had belonged to the murdered British infiltrator Jooma Khan. Babur was wearing it proudly like some sort of trophy from the man he had ordered to be put to death.

'Your arrival is good timing, Britishers,' he said in stilted English.

Mullah Siraj Chadhar was seated at one end of the desk, where the two of them had obviously been poring over papers together. 'In fact it could not have been better if you had been sent by Allah himself.'

'Perhaps we have,' I said. 'He moves in mysterious ways.'

His tiny blue eyes blinked behind the gold glasses. I don't think he knew the Christian expression. 'Quite so,' he replied, sounding confused.

'We have a VIP arriving this afternoon,' Babur cut in, seemingly anxious to get on.

'Your first customer?' Ravi suggested.

A hint of a smile passed over Babur's thin lips. 'In a manner of speaking. He has been my chief in Afghanistan, my tribal leader. He comes here by motor yacht. Very expensive, very beautiful.'

Ravi said quickly, 'Does this yacht have a name?' I suddenly remembered we were radio-wired; Ravi obviously hadn't.

'It is the *Gully Nargas*,' Babur replied. He shook his head, and I wasn't quite sure if it was in disbelief, envy or wonder. 'I have been on board once, at the marina in Karachi, where he purchased her a year ago. She is a most beautiful creature of the sea. Sixty metres long with luxuries.'

'And what does *Gully Nargas* mean?' I asked.

Babur's eyebrows raised in surprise at my interest. 'It is a small native flower of my country. Often worn at funerals.'

Ravi nodded. 'I've seen it, too many times. Yellow and white, tucked behind the ear or pinned to the lapel.'

'And the yacht is mooring here?' I asked.

'Yes, see,' Babur replied, pushing back his chair and walking across to the panoramic window with its view of the building's car park and the River Itchen beyond.

As I followed him I noticed a number of weapons laid out on a trestle table; it looked as though someone, I guessed Rashid, had been in the middle of sorting them out with corresponding ammunition. The gang's collection appeared to be expanding rapidly. I was surprised to see a couple of machine pistols and a sniper rifle.

Babur pointed through the grubby glass of the window. 'You see, on the other side of the office car park, we have our own jetty for our customers to moor their boats. At all tides. That is good for business, I think.'

I nodded, knowing sod all about yachts and yachting. But I could see the metal-railed jetty running flush to the river-side car park and realised that couldn't be a bad thing.

'But your chief isn't coming here to have a refit for his yacht?' Ravi guessed.

'No,' Babur replied. 'He is coming to inspect his entire UK operation.'

It occurred to me that there might be a huge stash of heroin on board. 'And will he be bringing in some – er – product?'

I just caught the look Rashid gave me – as if he thought I was a complete idiot. 'Of course not. A man like him will never arrive with *product*, as you call it. Men like him make a point of being out of the country whenever product arrives.'

Ravi came to the point. 'So what exactly do you want us to do?'

Masood Babur turned sideways to face us directly. 'This man, my tribal leader, has betrayed his peoples. He has betrayed all the men who work for him over here. That includes Mullah Chadhar and young Rashid and his follow-ers in the Swords. He takes all the money from this operation for himself, not for the foundation.'

'The foundation?' I asked.

'Al-Qaeda,' Chadhar said helpfully. 'That is the literal meaning of the word. The foundation, the cause.'

'Now we will take it back,' Rashid hissed, his voice low with anger and his eyes dark and fierce.

'It will not be easy,' Babur said. 'He is ruthless and his crew are armed and trained by his friends in Pakistani intelligence. That is why we need your help.'

I don't know why I bothered to ask the question. I think I just *had* to hear that name again. Needed the confirmation. Needed to know that I'd come full circle.

Babur said it like he had a particularly nasty taste in his mouth. 'Dr Zam-Zama.'

# Thirty-Five

It still came as a shock. Hearing that name again. Two years earlier, it seemed to be the only name we ever heard at special forces' HQ in our area of Afghanistan. Dr Zam-Zama was the enemy, a bête noire, the devil incarnate. He was the evil magician who could conjure up ambushes, shootings and some IED explosions on command, leaving blood and gore and ruined lives in his wake.

We'd wanted him then, and now we wanted him again. Fate had flipped us the other side of the same coin. Bizarrely, this day al-Qaeda and I would be on the same side, facing a common enemy.

From Egor Baran's research, we knew that the orders Ravi and I would now be following from Babur came directly from Abu Ahmed al-Kuwaiti. And al-Kuwaiti was of course the personal courier of Osama bin Laden himself.

I felt suddenly calm. My pulse slowed and I could swear I could feel the blood icing up in my veins. 'You want him dead?' I asked directly.

Mullah Chadhar looked flustered. 'Er, discreetly indisposed—'

'Yes,' Masood Babur interrupted abruptly. 'Exactly that.'

It was time for business. 'Are you in radio contact with the *Gully Nargas*?' I asked.

Rashid answered. 'By satellite telephone. With one of my men in the other office. To see if there is any problems with the port authority, or customs.'

'What is the procedure?' Ravi asked.

'The *Gully Nargas* is Karachi-registered at present,' Rashid replied. 'She entered EU waters ten days ago, flying the yellow flag.'

'Where?' I asked.

'Marseilles,' came the reply.

I had to smile. Dr Zam-Zama had sauntered into the European Union through possibly the slackest and most world-weary seaport on the continent. It was recognised as a hotbed of drug- and people-trafficking, gun-running and smuggling in general. It was said that many officials' pockets were bursting with bung money and they were cross-eyed with permanently looking the other way. Once the yacht had officially cleared immigration and customs, she was free. Free to lower her yellow flag and sail on to anywhere else she liked in Europe. In this case, it was Southampton Water and the River Itchen. Was it surprising that the country was awash with drugs and illegal immigrants, I asked myself?

'So no need to inform the port authorities?' I guessed.

Rashid smiled slyly. 'Technically, no. Apart from some hand weapons that can be quickly hidden, we are told that the yacht is clean, you understand? So, especially as the yacht is still registered in Karachi, we play the good guys and inform of the arrival. We are a new business and want to establish a good reputation with the authorities. You understand?'

I understood perfectly. The Swords' 'cover' business was eager to get in the good books of both customs and immigration from the start, for when clients in the future arrived with less innocent cargoes.

'And what,' I asked, 'was their response to the yacht's request for clearance?'

Rashid shrugged happily. 'For no crew to leave the ship until three o'clock this afternoon. If customs have not arrived by then, everyone is free to go. The man on the radio suggested as it is a private yacht and inbound from Marseilles it will be a low priority. Apparently, they are stretched just now.'

I considered all this for a moment and wondered what Jane Christy might be making of this at the other end of my covert radio transmission. 'Do you know how many crew are on board?' I asked. 'How many bodyguards?'

The Swords' leader shrugged. 'No idea.'

'Then find out,' I suggested in response to his sloppy attitude.

'Maybe Zam-Zama will become suspicious if we ask too many questions.'

I said, 'Then tell them you have a welcome lunch for them. You need to know numbers for food, and plates and glasses from the local restaurant.'

Ravi added, 'Try and get a list of names. Just first names will be fine. Sort out important people who will join Masood Babur here and Mullah Chadhar. That will probably include any bodyguards, but not crew and engineers. Sort the wheat from the chaff.'

Rashid hesitated. 'I am not sure this is a good idea . . .'

'We are running out of time. I'll do it for you,' Ravi snapped. 'Lead on. I speak Pashto.'

As they left the room, I turned back to Babur. 'Where was the yacht built?'

Babur shrugged. 'I would not know.'

I pointed at the laptop on his desk. 'Is that Internet-connected?'

'Yes.'

'Then, sir, I suggest we get googling. Try the yacht name or a yachting website.'

Ten minutes of web-surfing found various sites including one listing luxury yachts and their details. It transpired that the *Gully Nargas* had actually been constructed in Florida. We downloaded photographs and a basic set of technical diagrams, which I spread out on the table.

I was beginning to study this when Ravi returned from the other room. He looked pleased with himself. 'I spoke to the skipper. Nice as pie and speaks excellent English. He's actually a Danish national, Mikkel Jepsen. I gather he's been around the block a few times and doesn't ask too many questions of his masters – as long as the money's good.'

Ravi glanced down at his notepad, and continued, 'He liked the idea of a welcome party. I told him immigration might want to see passports and so on, so he happily gave names and ranks for all the crew. Total of nineteen. Zam-Zama has a wife or mistress called Basma. There is also an important guest and friend of Zam-Zama's on board called Nagi . . . I recall that name. I'm sure he's a big-shot lawyer. Well in with the ruling elite in Kabul. And I think the next three may be bodyguards, but I can't be certain. I've got family names of Mir, Davi and Lak. That's the top of the party list. After that, there is a couple who work for him. Remember Reza and Asifa? Believe it or not, they are still his housekeepers.'

It took a second for me to recall the names. Then I remembered with a shock that they were the couple who had been duped by Ravi's recce party before the meeting over two years' ago. Zam-Zama had made Reza play Russian roulette, with a pistol at his wife's head, as punishment. 'Something odd there,' I murmured.

'Maybe Zam-Zama has some hold over them?' Ravi suggested, then continued, 'the rest of the crew comprise three deckhands, a chief engineer and his grease monkey. There is a chef and two assistants. Then a waiter and barman.'

I shrugged. 'Anyway, do we have an accurate ETA?'

'Jepsen said two o'clock,' Ravi replied. 'Pretty much on the nose.'

It was now twelve forty-five. 'We don't have much time.'

While Ravi had read out the list, I pencilled in the likely location of everyone on the yacht as best I could: skipper and a crewman on the bridge. Maybe Zam-Zama in the stateroom with his VIP mate. Chef in the kitchen and engineers below deck . . . It was clearly never going to be better than fifty per cent accurate at best.

'Then we've got to get Zam-Zama ashore,' I decided aloud. 'Try and separate him from the rest of them.'

Ravi shook his head. 'You'll never do it. The most you can hope for is to split the party in two. Tell them that most of the crew should stay aboard until immigration arrives. We'll take them sandwiches. Tell Zam-Zama we have a buffet for him in the office.'

I could see what Ravi was getting at. 'So he'll come ashore with his wife, Basma, and this VIP mate of his, Nagi. Maybe the skipper, too.'

'And his bodyguards?' I asked the unanswerable question.

'I reckon yes,' Ravi replied. 'He's bound to be nervous, tense. If I was him, I'd make sure I had my armed muscle guarding my back.'

Half to myself, I said, 'At least we'll have some of the crew left on board, out of harm's way.'

'That'll pitch the two of us against Zam-Zama's three heavies.'

'Unless he and his mate are armed, too,' I added thoughtfully.

Rashid had walked back in and been listening carefully. 'But they will be totally outnumbered by my men.'

I blinked. God, I'd forgotten Rashid might have his own ideas about going down in a blaze of glory. That's the trouble with martyrs.

I said politely, 'That's probably not a good idea.'

'But *you* have trained us!' he retorted defiantly.

I smiled. 'Er, yes, but only up to a point.'

The man looked offended. 'What do you mean?'

Searching for the right words, I told myself, 'Look, your men are getting better, but they're not good enough yet. This is going to be a tricky operation. If all your men are armed and things get tricky, it could be like the old Wild West. And the last thing you need is anyone getting injured or even killed.'

At least Babur was listening. 'You are right, Mr Aston. Do you have a course of action to recommend?'

'How does this sound?' I replied. 'When the yacht moors up, you greet Dr Zam-Zama and his party, and invite them ashore. Only Ravi and I will be armed. When they come into the office here for their welcome buffet, Ravi and I will surprise and disarm any of them who are carrying weapons. Then we are in control.' I added, 'What happens after that is up to you.'

'We can take the yacht back out to sea?' Babur asked.

'If that's what you want,' I answered.

Babur said with quiet menace, 'And when we return, Dr Zam-Zama will no longer be with us.'

I understood. 'Accidents often happen at sea,' I said.

Rashid appeared satisfied, but something clearly troubled him. He turned to Babur. 'I understand Mr Aston's worries about my men. But I do believe that I at least, trusted leader of your loyal Swords, should also be armed. For your own safety, sir.'

Babur thought for a moment and nodded. 'Of course, that would be wise.'

Ravi and I looked at each other and I think we both realised it would be counter-productive to argue against it.

I said, 'OK, but can we get that display of guns covered up before the port authorities arrive. And also, is there somewhere we can get some buffet food and sandwiches for the arrival?'

Rashid nodded. 'There is a restaurant nearby. We already have a good relationship with them. I shall send someone.'

It seemed that everything was set. The armoury of weapons at the back of the office was covered with a tarpaulin, but not before Ravi and I had selected three handguns. We picked two sturdy 9mm Smith & Wesson 469 automatics with ultra smooth lines that reduced the likelihood of accidental snagging on clothing. I chose a small Beretta for Rashid on the basis that it was a bit of a 'lady's' gun. Although, truth be told, it could still make a nasty hole in someone.

Selection completed, Ravi joined me outside the office while I lit up a rollie and we went over our plan. During it I had a one-way conversation with DC Christy, asking her to call my mobile if any action was about to be sanctioned by the authorities that I was not expecting. I left my phone on vibrate mode.

The buffet meal arrived and was spread out on the reception desk along with packs of sandwiches made up by the local restaurant.

At five minutes to two, we gathered with Babur, Mullah Chadhar and Rashid at the far end of the car park by the jetty beside the dark flow of the Itchen. Three of us were armed. It was a tense few minutes' wait for the eventual appearance of the *Gully Nargas*.

She was worth the wait. The canvas of dismal grey tones, water and industrial shoreline, was lit up by the stunning white emergence of the yacht through the rolling mist. It was as though a shaft of winter sun had lit her dazzling white hull under a stage spotlight.

Her foghorn sounded, no doubt causing heads to turn. As she began a wide turn to bring her around to our jetty, I saw her sleek silhouette for the first time. There were three decks, topped with an open 'fair weather' bridge above the wheel-house and a plethora of communication aerials. From the plans I'd seen, I knew that a section of her elegant staggered stern could rise up on hydraulic legs to provide a helicopter-landing platform. As the engine note slowed to the deep throb of reverse gear and her bow came closer, there was sudden activity from the deckhands. Fenders were tipped over the rails and two crewmen waited, holding shorelines at the ready. As she closed, I could make out the elegant callig-raphy of her name, illustrated by a hand-painted representation of the dainty white and yellow flower after which she'd been named.

It was left to me to step forward as the crewman hurled the rope from the foredeck. I grabbed it and waited as Ravi followed my lead and caught the second rope that was thrown from the stern. Together we eased the yacht in the last few feet until the fenders rubbed against the edge of the jetty.

Looking up as I secured the lines I noticed more figures beneath an awning on the aft deck.

There was no mistaking Dr Zam-Zama. The flowing lines of his traditional Afghan robes could not hide his massive physique. And, even though his wild hair had been somewhat tamed and trimmed, the large, blunt facial features remained unforgettable.

The slender woman beside him was dwarfed by his pres-ence. She was dressed in long blue robes and a matching headdress. It framed a delicate, attractive face highlighted with heavy make-up. I guessed that this must be Basma, either his wife or mistress. Ravi had told me that the name meant 'smile', although there was no smile on her face today. She looked very apprehensive.

On the other side of her, looking down at us on the small quayside was the man I took to be Nagi, an important associate of Zam-Zama. He looked cool in a yellow open-necked shirt and blue mohair suit. He was slim, verging on skinny, with neatly cropped, jet-black hair and a thin top lip moustache. If I'd had to guess I'd have said he'd had a military background, probably the Pakistani Army.

Not one of them looked particularly pleased to have arrived, and it was Babur who blinked first and waved with a glistening white smile. 'Welcome, doctor! Welcome to the shores of England! Your people are all here to welcome you!'

Zam-Zama barely acknowledged him. With a slight nod of the head, the doctor turned away. As he disappeared from sight on his way down to the lower deck Nagi and then Basma dutifully followed.

The three heavies appeared first. They burst out of the stateroom door, one after the other in quick succession. With their designer wrap-around dark glasses, they might have been three blind men. However, they clearly weren't, as each glanced around, grim-faced, looking for possible sources of danger. There was a conspicuous bulge at the armpit of each man, where a shoulder holster obviously secreted a handgun. They'd either been cloned or were identical triplets. Their mother would have had a painful birth as each stood over six feet and was built like a prize bull. They all had shaven faces and bullet heads and no necks to speak of.

Thankfully they wore slightly different shiny suits, otherwise I could never have told them apart. Dark blue weave was Mir, pale grey was Davi, and Lak had gone for plain black.

Mir turned right towards the stern and Davi went left towards the bow. Lak stayed by the door, looking keen and mean, as Dr Zam-Zama stepped out onto the main deck. He was followed by Nagi, and then the delicately blue-clad Basma.

One of the crewmen had opened up the gate in the ship's rail and lowered a short plankway. Zam-Zama pushed his way forward, leaving Nagi to help the woman down the plank onto dry land. Babur scurried forward to greet the man who had been his boss and leader for many years.

'Welcome, doctor. We have a small reception buffet for you.'

Zam-Zama appeared not to hear. Given his stature he was able to look over Babur's head and take in the surroundings, his new acquisition: the car park, the offices and works area. Only then he looked at the small group of us in the welcoming party.

His eyes fixed on me first. 'Do I know you?'

It had been over two years ago and I'd only been one face in a room. 'I doubt it, sir.'

'You are English?' It sounded like an accusation.

Babur intervened. 'He is a mercenary. He is working for me now. He has passed our loyalty test, doctor.'

The man inclined his head. He understood, and so did I.

But it was really Ravi who had passed the test on my behalf. And Steve Cranford had paid the price.

Zam-Zama quickly lost interest. 'You've done well, Masood. I can see how this place will work well for us.'

Babur gave a little bobbing curtsy. Despite the fact he was about to take on his leader, he still clearly swooned at the big man's few crumbs of praise.

'So you have some lunch for us?' Zam-Zama said, suddenly changing tack. 'I have not eaten English food for a lot of time. I look forward to that.' He laughed deeply, like the deep rumbling of a volcano about to erupt. 'I just hope it has improved.'

'You will keep the crew members aboard, doctor?' Babur asked anxiously. 'Just in case immigration needs to speak to them.'

Zam-Zama nodded. 'Of course, the captain had your message. We three will come ashore, just with my protection people. The others will wait. Captain Jepsen will take care of all official matters.'

'Then, if you'd care to come with me, doctor,' Babur invited, and turned to walk back towards the office. Mir and Lak fell smoothly in beside them, whilst the rest of us in the welcoming party followed. Without a word, the third bodyguard, Davi, took up the rear, scanning his new surroundings with professional wariness.

As we crossed the pockmarked tarmac of the car park, my heart began to thud. I glanced sideways at Ravi, who caught my eye and gave a tight smile. Seconds were ebbing away before the moment when we'd have to strike.

Babur swung in through the glass door and into the reception area that had been laid out with plates full of rather exotic canapés. Rashid ordered one of his minions to take some separate sandwich packs out to the yacht for the crew.

As the door swung closed behind them and we were left alone, the arrival party visibly relaxed.

Babur pointed to the rows of tumblers, bottles and jugs of liquid lined up on the reception desk. 'Pomegranate, doctor, I know used to be your favourite. There is mango and orange juice. Also your old *medicinal* orange juice.'

The bodyguard Mir laughed at that. Davi and Lak caught his mood. All three men smiled, their tense shoulders dropped.

Rashid glanced at me anxiously. He was not smiling. I saw his right hand move towards the open front of his jacket.

I checked with Ravi. He inclined his head.

Zam-Zama held out a tumbler to be filled by Babur.

The Smith & Wesson was out of my pocket. I shouted at the top of my voice. 'FREEZE! HANDS UP!' The snout of my automatic pointed directly at Mir's chest.

Mullah Chadhar and Nagi turned abruptly. The slender Basma gasped.

Zam-Zama dropped his tumbler. It smashed on the floor. 'What is happening?' he demanded.

'For you, sir,' Babur said triumphantly, 'it is all over.'

Mir had raised his hands, and now stood motionless. Lak, too, put his hands above his head as Ravi's pistol was pushed against his temple.

It was then that Rashid's Beretta discharged. He was trying to cover Davi when it snagged in the lining of his jacket, causing him to put accidental pressure on the trigger. The sudden, deafening sound brought us all up short.

I heard the distinctive *ping* of the ricochet on the tiled floor and the loud curse from Babur as he fell. He'd been hit in the knee.

Basma screamed. Quickly recovering she dropped to his side, instinctively wanting to help him.

Ravi called aloud, 'One man down.'

I then realised that was for the benefit of DC Christy, who was still presumably listening in as events unfolded.

Confusion had allowed Davi to recover and yank a large Russian pistol from his jacket. It wasn't best suited for the job, being big and cumbersome, but it was a seriously lethal weapon. If its bullet struck your arm, it would probably take it off. Davi's two-handed aim swung indecisively back and forth between Ravi and me.

The mobile phone in my pocket began vibrating.

For a moment we were all in a frozen tableau of surprise, a sort of Mexican stand-off. Babur lay on the floor in front of us, groaning, but no one took any notice of him.

It was then we heard the voice on the megaphone outside. 'WE ARE ARMED POLICE! REPEAT! WE ARE ARMED POLICE! YOU ARE SURROUNDED! THROW DOWN YOUR WEAPONS AND COME OUT!'

# Thirty-Six

The booming voice over the police megaphone was followed instantly by a sound of crashing metal. Through the window I saw a mechanical digger being driven through the front gate of the compound. Behind it followed armed cops in body armour and NATO-style helmets.

Suddenly I foresaw the small reception area turning into a scene of panic and carnage. 'Everyone keep calm!' I commanded loudly. 'No one needs to get hurt.'

Davi snarled at me in menacing silence, and his Russian automatic decided my face was a better target than Ravi's.

A gang member appeared in the corridor outside reception. He looked petrified. 'Rashid, there are police everywhere outside! What do we do, die as martyrs?'

'No,' Rashid replied with remarkable calm. 'As you can see, we have a few problems. Go back and tell everyone to stay put and keep calm until you receive further instruction from me. Please do that . . . *Allahu Akbar.*'

The man acknowledged this with a little bow from the waist and disappeared.

Then the telephone rang, its jangling noise having an effect like an electric shock.

I waved my pistol at Zam-Zama. 'Answer it. One false move and *you* will be dead – no matter what else happens.'

The big man glowered at me as he snatched up the receiver from the reception desk. 'Yes?' he demanded.

He listened without a word, an expression of extreme distaste on his face. After a moment, he held the receiver to me at arm's length. 'It is some woman.'

'Police?' I asked.

'Yes. She asks to speak to someone called *Aston*.'

He was frowning at me and I suddenly wondered if he was trying to recall where he'd seen me before.

I edged closer to the counter and snatched the receiver from him with my left hand. With my right I waved the Smith & Wesson, making him back up against a wall.

I was still staring down the barrel of Davi's automatic as I cleared my throat. 'Jane?'

'Dave?' She sounded anxious. 'Are you all right?'

'Yes,' I replied.

'Thank God for that!' she breathed.

'*Except*,' I added. 'I do have a gun pointed at my head. Both sides in here are armed. For God's sake, don't let that firearms unit come in here. There'll be a massacre. We've already got one man injured.'

'Seriously?'

'Bad enough. He needs medical attention asap.'

'Understood,' she replied. 'Can we negotiate?'

'You can try.'

Then she said quickly, 'I'm sorry about the change of plan, Dave.' She sounded genuinely apologetic. 'When I realised what was going to happen and that weapons were involved, I had to act and contact Inspector Ryan. From then on matters were out of my control.'

'Sure,' I said stiffly.

'Can we send in a negotiator?' she asked again.

'Wait a minute,' I replied and turned to Zam-Zama. 'Listen, doctor, as you realise, we're surrounded by armed police. If they are forced to storm the place, we may *all* end up dead. They are suggesting sending in someone to talk, to agree things – with you, with us.'

Zam-Zama frowned. After a thoughtful pause, he said, 'Is there an option?'

I said, 'There's not a better one.' I pointed to Babur, whom Basma had helped to sit more comfortably with his back against the wall. 'And your man here needs urgent medical treatment.'

'Him?' The doctor glared. 'You, Babur, are a traitor. After everything I have done for you.'

Babur stared up at the big man. 'Everything you have done for me, you have done for yourself! For years, I was blinded to what you were doing. It was not for your country, the Taliban or our al-Qaeda brothers. Or even for Almighty Allah. All the time it is for *you*. Only you.'

'You talk rubbish like a woman,' the warlord scolded.

'Like your housekeeper Asifa?' Babur spat back. 'Who you keep in permanent punishment with her husband. To give herself to you and your friends when it suits you, for your amusement. All in fear of her husband being killed if she disobeys you. What in the Holy Koran gives you that right?'

'Nothing!' Mullah Chadhar declared, eyes bright amongst the confusion of wild white hair and beard. 'If this is true, Dr Zam-Zama, then you are indeed as evil as Masood Babur suggests!'

Basma looked up from attending to the wounded man. There was no light in her dark, unloving eyes.

'Shut up, holy man!' Zam-Zama snarled. 'What do you know about anything? Keep your nose in your scriptures and holy books, and out of my affairs!'

I interrupted. 'I am going to tell the police to send in paramedics to pick up Masood Babur. If anyone tries to interfere, Zam-Zama will be the *first* dead man.'

Placing the receiver back to my ear, I said, 'OK, Jane. Send in the two medics. But no one armed and no tricks. It's too volatile in here.'

'Roger that,' she replied softly. 'And I'll send the negotiator in with them.'

I announced to the crowded little room what was about to happen. Unsure glances were exchanged, pointed guns wavered as muscles began to tire.

Ravi spoke, echoing my thoughts. 'Look, everyone, let's relax. If any one of us shoots, the chances are we'll all get killed or wounded. Let's keep the peace. So shall we just lower our guns? Stay calm, eh?'

His words did the trick and you could feel the tension in the air begin to evaporate.

Through the window, I saw two paramedics approaching, pushing a stretcher trolley. A third man was behind them, hidden from my view. 'Here they come,' I warned. Then, seconds later, they cautiously entered the room.

'He's over there,' I said. 'A bullet wound to the right knee.'

I watched as they hurriedly manoeuvred him onto the stretcher, the two medics not keen to hang around in a room full of guns and itchy trigger fingers.

It was only as they started to leave that I noticed the negotiator waiting silently in the doorway.

Chas Houseman stood back to let the medics pass.

Not surprisingly, he was staring straight at Zam-Zama.

It took a moment for the penny to drop. I could see the sense of relief in the doctor's expression, his eyes softening and his muscles relaxing. 'It is Mr Houseman, yes? A long time.'

'A long time indeed,' Houseman answered silkily. 'You are well?'

The big man shrugged his shoulders. 'Not so good just now, as you see . . . Maybe we can end this nonsense. These idiots are trying to kill me, my wife and my friend.'

Houseman folded his arms across his chest. 'I shall see what I can do.' His eyes fixed on Ravi. 'Hello, Ravi, I was surprised to learn you were mixed up in all this.'

'It's a long story,' Ravi replied.

'Then save it for another time,' Houseman retorted. He switched his gaze to me, but said nothing. He just slowly shook his head, as though in despair of someone on whom he'd given up all hope. I got the distinct feeling he thought I was no longer worthy of his attention.

He glanced around the cramped gathering. 'For those of you who don't know me, I am Charles Houseman. I am representing Her Majesty's Foreign Office here today and, as

such, I am speaking on behalf of the British government. So
let me tell you how I read this situation.

'Firstly, we are surrounded by armed police. If anyone
here is shot or injured, there will be an armed assault. That is
what *will* happen. That is how it works. Some or all of us will
probably be killed or maimed. Any survivors may be prosecuted under criminal law for any offences they may have
committed. That may be murder, manslaughter, or drugs or
firearms offences. Only you know if that applies to you. I will
not be able to assist in any way.

'Secondly, none of you will be going anywhere, any time
soon. Unless it is with *my* agreement.'

He paused, knowing he had everyone's attention. 'So the
smart thing is for us all to put down our weapons, for a start.
Then we can talk, see how I might be able to assist all or
some of you. I have more power than you might expect to
influence events.' He saw the glances exchanged between
Mullah Chadhar and Rashid, Zam-Zama and Nagi and their
three bodyguards. Sensing he was on a winning streak, he
added, 'Don't worry, I can promise you there will be *no*
assault, if you follow my instructions. So let us put down our
arms. Who shall be first?'

Self-preservation kicked in and the bodyguard Davi was
the first to drop his weapon. It clattered loudly on the floor,
joined by the guns of Mir and Lak as they followed his example. Then Rashid gave up the fight. Now it was down to Ravi
and me. My friend went first and I followed, tossing the
Smith & Wesson onto the top of the small pile of gunmetal in
the middle of the floor.

'Excellent,' Houseman murmured. He could scarcely keep the tone of self-congratulation from his voice; I don't think he could believe his own luck.

'What happens now?' Zam-Zama demanded.

'Now I *can* help you,' Houseman said. 'All of you. Because that will be in the national interest of my country, this country.'

I could smell the fear on Rashid, and see it in his eyes. 'I will be arrested?' he asked.

Houseman smiled. 'Let us see. Only if you have done something wrong. To begin with, I understand there may be more weapons in this building, apart from these on the floor.'

'In the back office,' I said. 'Quite a stash.'

'Thank you, Dave.' His eyes narrowed. 'So pleased to see you being helpful for a change.'

It was Babur's turn. 'You will arrest us for the guns?'

The SIS man shrugged. 'I'll have this place sealed off overnight. Our colleagues in internal security – that's MI5 – will send in their "bin men" if I ask them nicely. Perhaps no weapons will be found here in the morning.'

'And the drugs?' Ravi asked sharply.

'My dear friend,' Houseman asked. 'What drugs are these?'

Ravi's mouth formed into a thin twist of contempt, but he said nothing.

Houseman looked directly at Masood Babur. 'When I leave here shortly, you will have ten minutes before the police come in. Use the time wisely. Telephone friends and family, and business associates – including meat-packaging firms.

Dawn raids normally come at dawn, if you understand me? I cannot help you if you have broken the law. But then it is perfectly possible that you haven't broken any laws. Or at least, not left any evidence as such.'

The crafty bastard, I thought. From holding no cards at all a few days ago, he now seemed to be holding a full house.

Relief dawned on Babur's face. 'I will not be prosecuted?'

Houseman lifted his index finger. 'Just one condition.'

'Just tell me, sir.'

The intelligence officer took a step back and indicated Babur to follow him into the hallway behind me.

Although Houseman had lowered his voice, I could just determine most of his conversation. 'I know you are working on the orders of Osama bin Laden. Those orders are delivered to you by a man called Abu Ahmed al-Kuwaiti. He is your leader's personal courier. His latest contact details are all I need. In return I promise you, you have total immunity for any acts of crime you have conducted in this country.'

'I have committed no such acts.'

Houseman's cheeks pulsed momentarily. 'Try ordering the murder of a man called Steven Cranford. That's a minimum twenty-year stretch.'

Babur stared at him long and hard, his tongue edging nervously over his lips. 'Email addresses, phone numbers, Skype?' he asked.

'I think we understand each other, Masood.'

With that sort of prize to offer our American cousins, I couldn't see Charles Houseman being in line for anyone's firing squad at MI6 for long. He'd be bringing home the

Golden Fleece. Find al-Kuwaiti and he would inevitably lead you to Osama bin Laden himself. It was just a matter of time.

'The information will be with you, sir.'

With a look of satisfaction on his face, Houseman turned to Zam-Zama. 'My dear doctor, you and I must talk in private.'

The big Afghan could barely conceal his anger. 'Indeed, we must, Mr Houseman. We have a deal—'

Houseman raised his hand. 'I said to talk in private. Perhaps back on your fine yacht?'

Zam-Zama nodded, then indicated to his wife Basma and the man called Nagi to go with them.

As they headed out of the door, Houseman paused and turned to me. 'I remember you used to be good, Aston. Bring one of those guns, will you? I need someone to watch my back.'

I was astounded he even thought I was worth talking to. Intrigued, I picked up the Smith & Wesson and stuck it in the waistband of my trousers.

Ravi looked unhappy. 'Be careful, Dave. Don't trust him.'

I inclined my head and followed Houseman and the others out of the door and into the car park. All around I could see the dark blue-clad figures of the firearms unit; some crouched behind the front of parked cars, others on high vantage points of the boat dry-stack next door.

The *Gully Nargas* was rising and falling gently on the swell as we approached. Its crew and the skipper were gathered by the rail, watching anxiously. Their welcome packs of sandwiches had been left on the deck, unopened.

'What has happened, sir?' Captain Jepsen asked as Zam-Zama strode on board.

'Nothing to worry about,' the doctor replied snappily. 'I need to talk urgently with Mr Houseman here. We will go to the aft deck.'

'Er, may I suggest,' Houseman said, 'that we cast off. Maybe go down to the Solent, make sure we are not interrupted by the police or anyone else.'

Zam-Zama nodded. 'See to it, Jepsen, immediately. And send Reza and Asifa to the aft deck with some refreshments.'

'Consider it done,' Jepsen replied and beckoned his crew members. If I read his expression correctly, he didn't relish staying any longer in a place swarming with armed police.

Before I went inside, the last thing I saw was DC Christy running into the car park alongside DI Ryan. Behind them, I could just make out Bernie Bramshaw and Brian Duffy trying to catch up.

I knew that the yacht was expensive and classy, but nothing could have prepared me for its sheer, stunning opulence. I stepped into a stateroom of gilt and walnut veneer panelling with huge clusters of crystal glass chandeliers dripping from the ceiling. The carpet was deep-piled and the gleaming banquet table, with its fine marquetry and inlaid mother-of-pearl, would have comfortably seated twenty guests.

On my way through to the aft deck, the vessel suddenly began to tremble as its engines kicked into life. I could scarcely believe the speed at which things were starting to happen. The *Gully Nargas* clearly had a superbly trained crew, as well as a captain who was anxious to be well away from the shore.

I passed bedrooms with en-suite onyx baths and Jacuzzis and gold-plated taps before stepping down to the open aft deck where I joined Houseman, Zam-Zama and the others.

Already we had cast off. The canvas sun awning above our heads began flapping wildly as we moved out to midstream and picked up the brisk offshore breeze.

There was a polished drinks cabinet and a table being laid out with glasses and pitchers of both water and fruit juice. It took a moment for me to recognise the diminutive steward dressed in all black trousers, shirt and waistcoat. It was Reza, the housekeeper whom Zam-Zama had so humiliated with his wife all that time ago. He clearly didn't recognise me. Why should he? He'd had other more compelling thoughts on his mind at that time.

Houseman was on his mobile phone, talking loudly to be heard above the flapping of the awning and noise of the engines. 'Inspector, it's me, Chas. Has the Special Branch element arrived yet?' A pause. 'Excellent. It should be safe for you to go in now. Everyone *seems* to have been persuaded that surrender is the best option. Our man is Ravi Azoor – you can leave him when you take everybody else in for questioning. Now this might sound a bit unorthodox, but I'd like the building to be sealed and left overnight before you begin your formal investigation of the site. Special Branch and the Security Service will need to take a look in the meantime.'

Inspector Ryan clearly didn't like that, as Houseman added, 'I know, Ian, I know, but national security and all that. Always a pain, but that's the way it is ... Meanwhile I'm having a private interview with Dr Zam-Zama on board his yacht. I'll contact you again later when we make landfall.'

As Houseman snapped his mobile closed, I said, 'So by tomorrow, all those guns will have disappeared, eh? And any paperwork linking heroin or the gang to you.'

The man's lips tightened for a moment, but he didn't answer me. Instead he turned to Zam-Zama. 'Doctor, you realise we need to talk.'

Reza stepped forward, dutifully proffering a silver tray with three glasses of fruit juice. Houseman took one, while Zam-Zama ignored him. I shook my head.

'We have a deal, Houseman,' Zam-Zama growled.

'We *had* a deal,' Houseman corrected.

'Nothing is changed.'

'*Everything* is changed,' Houseman replied. 'That was then, this is now. Do you know what your sidekick Masood Babur was about to do back there?'

'Babur, my assistant?'

'He was about to take over your organisation and kill you in the process.'

Zam-Zama protested: 'He would not have dared.'

I said, 'It's true. Babur is al-Qaeda's man. He thinks you've lost your way.'

'And I think he'd be right,' Houseman rejoined. 'That's another reason why our deal is finished. You no longer hold sway in Helmand, are no longer respected within the Taliban. Our deal is finished, that chapter is past.'

As I looked at Houseman, over his shoulder I saw a detachment of armed police move in on the office building.

The door was kicked in and the first two officers entered, followed by others. I could see DC Christy quickly follow them in.

Zam-Zama had remained motionless and silent, weighing up the situation. At last, he reached his decision. 'Listen, Houseman, if the chapter is passed and our deal is finished, then *so* are you. No one cheats on me and gets away with it. That is something you should know by now. It is a matter of honour, of face.'

Houseman's eyes narrowed. 'Meaning?'

'I believe your government will be interested to learn about the deal *you* made with *me*. A deal that, I am sure, was totally unauthorised.'

I just caught Houseman's gentle movement from the corner of my eye. It was a small gun, mostly covered by his hand. My best guess was that it was a dependable, snub-nosed SIG Sauer P228 automatic.

Zam-Zama took a backward step. 'What is this, Englishman? You want to kill me here, in your own country? This is not Afghanistan, you cannot murder and play games with law and justice here.'

Reza stood, gawping and motionless, at the sudden turn of events.

The faint smile on Houseman's face had frozen into something that was starting to resemble a snarl. 'You'd be surprised what games are played in this country, you evil little shit. Accidents happen in every country. Drowning, I'm assured, is one of the more pleasant ways to die. Maybe you'll get to shag your celestial virgin mermaids!'

Much as I might have agreed with his sentiments, this didn't seem like a good idea. 'Put that thing away, Chas!' I demanded. 'Killing him won't solve anything!'

'Keep out of this, Aston!' Houseman came back irritably. 'You're here to protect me, watch my back. Just do that and keep your mouth zipped.'

Something snapped in my head. 'Just who the fuck do you think you are? Back in Afghanistan you sacrificed one innocent, courageous ally to satisfy this bastard's ego – and your own. You sacrificed Abdullah – and to satisfy your personal lust for glory you mounted an illegal mission that got young Andy Smith killed and me wounded. As an indirect result of your actions two of my friends have died here.'

The SIG Sauer kept pointing unwaveringly at Zam-Zama's head. 'They were desperate times, Aston. I doubt even you knew how desperate it was then. Our units were falling apart at the seams. We nearly lost it. I did what I did because I had to, to buy us time. I had to try and make an unwinnable war winnable.'

As I stared at Houseman, behind him on the riverbank I noticed there was someone on the roof of the old chandlery building. The man was big and moved with a familiar shambling sort of gait I'd seen a thousand times before. As he walked, as though trying to select a suitable location, I saw he had a long-barrelled weapon in his hand. For a fleeting moment I thought it was his trusty GPMG, which he legendarily used with pinpoint accuracy. Then I realised it was actually a sniper rifle, probably the one I'd seen in the Swords' armoury.

Repeatedly Duffy glanced across the water towards me. Finally, he stopped and hunkered down. Suddenly I knew. He couldn't break the old habit of looking after me.

Zam-Zama was saying, 'You English should learn from your history. Afghanistan has always been unwinnable, and always will be.'

Houseman snapped back, the veins of anger showing in his neck, 'But even more so with the likes of you poisoning every attempt at peace . . .'

Zam-Zama took a step backward, tripped and fell. The snout of Houseman's automatic followed him unerringly.

It was decision time. Everything about Houseman told me he was building up the moral courage to pull the trigger, his words, the glaring eyes of a madman, and the perspiration breaking out on his face despite the cold wind.

Without warning, I swung and jabbed the point of my left elbow sharply into his bicep. He gasped as the sudden, paralysing pain of the 'knuckle punch' shot down his arm. His finger involuntarily jerked the trigger. There was a whip-crack of noise as the round punched a hole in the wooden decking.

Twisting round, I grabbed Houseman's gun arm with both hands and forced it up into the small of his back. The automatic clattered to the deck and I kicked it out through the rails and into the river.

'You stupid bastard!' I said, pushing him away and whipping out the Smith & Wesson from my waistband. 'Do you really want us both done for murder?'

Zam-Zama looked shaken, his eyes dark and wary as he climbed unsteadily to his feet.

Houseman turned his anger on me. 'He's the fuckin' enemy, Aston, not me.'

I stood my ground. 'Then let's take him back. He is, or has been, a Taliban terrorist leader. And he's a drug trafficker. He can face the music and a trial. Ravi and I know you've got all the evidence you need against him.'

'There's a slight flaw in that plan,' Houseman snapped.

'Yes,' I replied. 'I know. Your illegal involvement.'

It was then that Zam-Zama made his move. The little 9mm Beretta pistol was an ideal weapon of concealment. I just glimpsed the soft leather ankle holster with its Velcro straps as the man reached beneath the hem of his long dish-dasha.

I lifted my own gun, but it was too late. I saw the muzzle flash, bright like lightning, and heard the noise. Immediately I felt the searing sharp pain in my head. The darkness closed in rapidly, the daylight shrinking into a tight little pinprick amid the inky black. Then that, too, went out.

I heard the second round and winced. But I felt nothing. In fact, I think the sound had alerted something in me. I was coming to, back in Afghanistan on the Chinook that took me away after the ambush. Was I dead, was this what being dead felt like? I suddenly remembered that's what I'd thought then. It was what I was thinking now.

But then if I was dead, surely I couldn't be thinking? There was a throbbing drumbeat of pain in my temple. I risked it, and cranked open one eye. My vision was blurred. My face felt warm and wet. I could feel the stuff in my mouth, sweet-ish. Blood, my blood.

I tensed the fingers of my right hand. OK. My left. Then my toes. They moved on command. So was I brain dead or blind? I had no way of knowing. I squeezed my eyes again, hard. The glutinous red stuff began to separate, gradually, like mucus.

I concentrated and tried to focus. Houseman's face was just inches from mine. His mouth was open and unseeing eyes were staring back at me accusingly.

Houseman was dead; I was alive. Get this wrong and I would join him. Any moment Zam-Zama would put a second bullet in me.

I gradually moved into a half-sitting position. Now I realised I was soaked in blood. Zam-Zama's bullet had gouged a track across my temple, shaving a groove in my skull.

I could hear the man talking, moved my head until I could see him jabbering on his cell phone, the Beretta in his right hand.

In desperation I glanced around for my Smith & Wesson. There was no sign.

Zam-Zama snapped his phone closed and replaced it in his pocket. That's when our eyes met and he smiled. It was the smile of the victor, the man who'd won his last battle, the only one that ever really mattered in a war.

He lifted his Beretta. This time there would be no mistake.

I felt the wind rush on my cheek and heard the ricochet of a bullet on the yacht's metal work. But there was no sound of a discharge. It had been long range.

There could be only one explanation. Brian Duffy, ever looking after me, had fired at Zam-Zama from the shore.

Duffy never missed. Today, when it had never mattered more, he did.

The Afghan had noticed it, too. Puzzled, he hesitated for a second. Then he refocused on me, steadied his aim.

The shot took his legs from under him. He just went down instantly in a deflated heap.

To one side, standing by the drinks cabinet, the diminutive Reza looked pale and terrified. In his right hand he held my Smith & Wesson. Smoke trailed from its barrel.

The Afghan blinked like someone coming out of years of darkness into daylight, and he proffered me the gun. 'I am sorry, sir, I think I may have killed him.'

# Epilogue

'I missed him.' Brian Duffy still couldn't believe it.

'So you cocked up,' I said lightly. It was good to see Duffy on the wrong end of a wind-up for once. 'Get over it.'

He shook his head of shaggy grey hair. 'No, serious, boss. I never misses. You knows that.'

I replied, 'It wasn't your weapon, Brian, you hadn't zero'd it yourself. The point is your shot made Zam-Zama hesitate before killing me and gave Reza time to react.'

He grinned, a mischievous twinkle in the pale-blue eyes. 'So I *did* save your life – *again*.'

It was a month since the events aboard the *Gully Nargas*. Duffy, Ravi and I had met up at the cafe having received a triumphal invitation from Bernie Bramshaw to join him one damp and misty Sunday morning. Andreas was open to cash in on the extra pre-Christmas shopping hours.

I said, 'No, Brian, it was Reza who saved my life. It might have been you if you hadn't gone cross-eyed in your old age. Like the TV ad says, you should've gone to Specsavers.'

At that moment Gem emerged from inside the cafe, carrying a tray. The flashing coloured lights on her toy reindeer antlers were quite distracting. 'Coffee and mince pies,' she announced.

I thought how she seemed to be looking more radiant the

more her pregnancy showed. And although she had occasionally talked about Steve Cranford, his name had been mentioned less and less.

'I love all this Christmassy stuff,' Ravi declared.

'Surely not the weather?' Duffy challenged. 'You's got Sri Lankan blood in you.'

'I've spent so much time in Northern Ireland, Brian, down here in Swinthorpe is like the tropics to me.'

While I'd been recovering from my battle wounds, Ravi and I had been staying at Gem's house and we took it upon ourselves to redecorate the place from top to bottom. The two of us worked well together and enjoyed each other's company. I think we were at a loss as to what to do with the rest of our lives outside of the army.

Events of the past few months had been an unpleasant and scary diversion. Yet for me, the attempt to avenge Jock and Ginger's cruel deaths had proved to be cathartic. For a short time, it had given me a tangible purpose and a goal. I'd been back with old friends. It was almost like being on an op. In the past few weeks I'd felt much more settled and the bad dreams had virtually stopped.

It had also helped, I think, that I'd been out for a drink with Jane Christy a couple of times. We'd been getting on well. Inspector Ryan had been as mad as hell with her for backing my mission with Ravi to infiltrate the Swords – especially when she realised she had to call in an armed response unit to sort things out. But there wasn't too much Ryan could do about it by way of punishment, as she had already decided to leave the police service.

Chas Houseman's presence had confused and muddied the waters. I learned that his superiors had been quick to move in, sanitise the location and brush everything under the carpet as far as possible.

The morning after the shooting, the *Gully Nargas* had left British waters with her crew and passengers. I saw and read nothing in the news about the death of either Zam-Zama or Houseman. It was as though they'd been airbrushed out of history.

Gem pulled up a spare chair and lit a cigarette.

'Naughty girl,' Duffy scolded.

'This really is my last one, promise.' She inhaled deeply. 'By the way, have you seen anything of Lady Penelope lately?'

I shook my head. 'Last time I saw her that madman from Serbia seemed to have taken a shine to her.'

Gem pulled a face. 'I hope she's all right. She hasn't dropped in here for a good three weeks.'

Duffy suddenly said, 'Hey, boss, isn't that your new girl-friend?'

Christy waved as she crossed the bridge and recognised us through the mist over the water. Although wearing her signature trilby hat, she was dressed less formally than normal in a long black skirt and high grey suede boots.

'Classy bit of totty that,' Duffy added. 'And you know what they say about policewomen?'

'What do they say about policewomen?' Gem asked innocently.

I smiled thinly. 'No doubt it's something to do with hand-cuffs and truncheons.'

'Well, she can arrest me any time,' Ravi added. 'In a uniform or without.'

'Hi, boys and gals, how goes it?' Christy greeted, and kissed me briefly on the lips. 'No sign of Bernie yet?'

'He's on his way down from London.' I tapped my mobile phone on the table. 'He called me just fifteen minutes ago from the train. He was at Andover then.'

She was carrying a huge leather Kangaroo shopping bag. 'I've bought half a dozen editions of the *Sunday News*. Haven't read them yet, just had a glance. I'm hoping Bernie might sign them.'

'You'll make a fortune on eBay,' Duffy decided.

Gem stood up. 'Coffee, Jane?'

'I'd die for one. White, no sugar.'

'And a mince pie. My recipe.'

'Love one.'

As Gem disappeared through the glass door, Ravi asked, 'So how much more time before you're a new jobless statistic, young police person?'

'I'm done,' Christy replied. 'I finished on Friday. I'm just soaking up unused leave until early January.'

'What's happening about the Swords?' I asked.

'Interesting that,' Christy said. 'Nothing much, it seems. We've interviewed them all and raided their homes, and that meat-packing plant, but there's no evidence at all. Of course, the firm's computers might yet turn up something. But I wouldn't hold my breath.' Gem returned with her coffee. 'No weapons were found at the chandlery and no drugs. Zilch.'

Ravi shook his head in disbelief. 'And that's *it*?'

'Well, Mullah Chadhar has taken himself off to a new mosque in Birmingham,' Christy replied, 'and Rashid has relocated back to his family in Yorkshire. The gang members have pretty much all been dispersed. Individually I think they've all had their cards marked by Special Branch.'

'Maybe some have even been turned,' Ravi suggested thoughtfully. 'That's what I'd think about doing.'

Duffy grunted. 'Once a spook, always a spook.'

I said, 'And you told me that Inspector Ryan has put in for a transfer?'

Christy nodded. 'Back to Northern Ireland. With a new DI, Sergeant Butler, hoping he'll be given the narcotics remit. Sam hates the drugs game. Things will be different here if he gets the job. If it becomes his patch, the Chip Shop Boys had better watch out ... and the Swords certainly won't be making any comeback.'

'And you?' I asked.

'Something completely different,' she said. 'Maybe breaking in horses.'

I was truly surprised. 'You?'

'Yeah, I ride. I also fancy a smallholding. Chickens and rare pigs.'

I shook my head. 'But you're a vegetarian.'

She poked her tongue out at me. 'I want to grow them, not eat them.'

Duffy leaned forward. 'Wouldn't you miss the excitement of fighting crime, young supercop?'

Christy laughed lightly. 'Well, in truth, I probably would.'

'You could be a private eye,' Ravi suggested. 'I've always fancied that.'

She looked directly at him. 'Being a gumshoe? D'you know what, Ravi, I *have* seriously thought of that. But I couldn't do it all on my own.'

'You and Ravi could work together,' Duffy added helpfully, as he slurped his coffee. 'And my ex-boss has got bugger all better to do. Might keep him on the straight and narrow for five minutes.'

I elbowed him in the ribs.

'It would need more capital than I've got,' Christy said. 'Rents around here are horrendous.'

Gem stubbed out her last ever cigarette. 'Is that Bernie?' she asked.

All eyes turned, as the rotund figure scurried towards us, the tail of his raincoat trailing behind him. He was clutching a big carrier bag stuffed full of newspapers.

'God! Sorry I'm late!' he gasped breathlessly. 'Why do they always do bloody engineering works over the weekend?!'

He fell into the chair that Gem had pulled out for him. 'Here we are! First editions!' he said triumphantly, spilling copies of the *Sunday News* onto the table. Then he saw that Christy had already put a small pile of them on the adjoining table.

Duffy said, 'Thinks we've got the whole print run.'

Christy said, 'Thanks, Bernie. I just had a glimpse. Looks great!'

Bramshaw looked relieved. 'Doesn't it just, Jane! Front page, and a centre four page supplement.' He suddenly looked coy. 'Of course, your ones down here are second edition. A few changes. MI5 was breathing down poor old Russ Carver's neck. He buckled under the heat in the end.'

'Was Houseman mentioned?' I asked.

'Oh, yes, but not by name.' Bramshaw took a deep breath. 'The story is factual enough, as far as we know it. You're all in it. But Russ just had to take names out. And we couldn't identify Swinthorpe as such. Had to turn original factual assertions into beliefs and hearsays – all that sort of libel protection rubbish. Russ wanted to use real names, but MI5 had him by the balls. If he hadn't gone along with them he'd be bankrupt tomorrow.'

I could see the disappointment in his eyes. I said, 'I'm sorry, Bernie. I know you worked so hard on this.'

'Thanks, Dave. That means a lot to me.' He rubbed his eyes roughly with the back of his hand and took a deep breath. 'The good news is, Russ has invited me back as a sort of *special* features editor. Maybe four big stories a year. Not staff, freelance. But then times are hard. You can't have everything.'

He spread out a copy on the table so that we could all see the *TEA WITH THE TALIBAN – Britain's Secret Mission* headline. Turning the pages he came to the four-page centre section and the last article. I read the headline aloud, ' "The Saffron Solution"? What's that?'

Bramshaw thumbed his glasses more securely on the bridge of his nose as he explained, 'Something Houseman never mentioned. I only picked up on it with my own research. Apparently Houseman had the idea of substituting the growing of heroin poppies with the saffron crocus. Saffron is a bloody expensive spice and apparently the best of it is grown in Kashmir. Perfect climate, see? It would provide a big alternative part of their deal and a part-solution to the Afghan problem.'

'That wasn't mentioned on the video of the meeting between him and Zam-Zama,' Ravi interjected.

'Ah!' Bramshaw said in triumph. 'That's because Houseman turned the camera off for a short time while they discussed it. If you study the footage *really* closely you can spot the joins. Houseman saw that project as his baby. Trouble was, he knew if the video was viewed without that element it would seem pretty damning – him pleading with the Taliban and offering a heroin concession to the UK.'

'So what happened to the alternative saffron idea?' I asked.

Bramshaw removed his spectacles and began cleaning the lenses with a paper napkin. He said thoughtfully, 'Put simply, the macho Afghan tribesmen just thought it all too sissy and unfamiliar for them. I think Zam-Zama pretty much thought the same. They all preferred to stick with what they knew. Opium.'

So Houseman had genuinely tried to pull off a masterstroke to help end the war. 'That's crazy,' I murmured.

'Crazy but true,' Bramshaw rejoined. 'But then life often is, don't you find?' He paused for a moment. 'Anyway, does anyone fancy a proper celebration down the pub? First round on me.'

'Bloody good idea,' Duffy said with feeling.

Bramshaw was on his feet. 'But no ordering doubles, mind.'

We began to make a move, settling our bills with Gem, when an old lady in a red woollen hat and driving a very elaborate electric wheelchair, zoomed up to our tables.

'Edwina!' I said, surprised. Trying hard to keep up behind her was her new Serbian friend, Manni.

Gem looked delighted. 'Oh, Edwina, how *are* you? Where have you been? We've been starting to get so worried about you. Nobody on the street seemed to know where you were.'

Edwina patted her hand. 'Dear child, hardly know where I've been myself. Had an ulcer on my leg and got taken into hospital. Then some dreadful infection; at one point they thought they might have to amputate. Manni's been brilliant, looking after me.'

Gem was horrified. 'Edwina, you can't go back on the street! You must stay with me.'

The old lady beamed. 'Thank you, dear child, but no need. None of you will know, of course, but remember that ad in the *Journal*, the one you saved for me? It was some solicitors trying to contact me. All about the estate of my late step-uncle Augustus. Came from a very wealthy family. Apparently he was a talented artist and a gambling wastrel. I only remember him from when I was a child, a charming and white-bearded man who seemed to adore me. My father stopped his visits because of his penchant for kissing me on my bottom.'

Christy was taken aback. 'What!'

'I was only three or something,' Edwina said with a shrug. 'They thought he was some sort of perv.'

'Perhaps he was,' Bramshaw observed, suddenly showing an interest.

'But a nice one,' Edwina returned. 'He died recently. And he's left me his estate. A family pile, not far from here. Some tumbled-down manor, very pretty, and a few acres. A bit of money and not too much debt.'

'Fantastic,' I said. 'I'm so pleased for you.'

'Manni's going to look after me,' she assured. 'It won't be easy to make the place pay for itself. It's got some thirty bedrooms. Manni suggested turning part of it into a business centre, maybe serviced offices. Could do well in this area.'

Duffy said, 'There you go, boss. Perfect for your detective agency.'

My eyes met Christy's across the table. 'Ever get the feeling you're under pressure?' I asked.

Bramshaw began herding everyone along. He called to Christy and me, 'We're going to the Riverside, OK?'

Gem promised to join everybody as her shift was coming to an end.

I waved back. 'See you later. Mine's a pint.'

Now alone with me Christy asked, 'I wondered what you're doing for Christmas?'

'I don't know yet. I haven't really thought.'

'It's only a couple of weeks away.'

I shrugged. 'And you?'

'I'll be seeing my parents. They always look forward so much to me being with them. They never did like my ex. But now they worry I'll never find anyone new.'

I leaned forward. 'And will you?'

Her eyes softened. 'I don't know. Will I?'

I said, 'I think that's very possible.'

'So you'll spend Christmas Day at Gem's?'

I shook my head at all the mind-blowing complications of the average family's arrangements over the festive season. If that were a computer circuit it would simply explode in confusion. 'Ravi's going back to his family in the Midlands and Gem's mum is coming to her.'

'And you?' Christy asked again.

I think I'd been deliberately avoiding thinking about the subject. I said, 'I had promised Daisy.'

'Your daughter.'

I nodded.

'Is she like you?'

'I like to think so. But luckily she *looks* more like her mother.'

Christy smiled. 'I'm sure Daisy will be looking forward to seeing you again.'

I nodded. 'I love the way her face lights up on Christmas morning.'

She indicated the small pile of newspapers on her table. 'Will you ask Bernie to sign them for me?'

'Sure.'

'I'd better be off. Will I see you in the new year?'

I suddenly couldn't bear the idea of her going. I said, 'How about *over* New Year?'

'Now that's a thought.' She reached forward and kissed me on the lips. 'A lovely thought. We can have a drink and think about an office together at Edwina's manorhouse.'

I said, 'Christy, I think I love you.'

She pressed her index finger to my lips. 'Let's do deeds,

not talk. But, for the record, I think maybe I fell in love with you the moment I first saw you . . . Happy Christmas. *Ciao*.'

Moments later a callow youth skulked past me, yet spared me an embarrassed smile. He entered the cafe, passing Gem on her way out. Between us we had managed to get Aaron his first-ever temporary job, making sandwiches. He was absolute rubbish.

Gem waved. 'See you at the pub, Dave.'

'See you in ten,' I called.

I was alone now outside the cafe. I lit another roll-up and watched the river of humanity passing back and forth in front of me. There were bright young girls with tinsel in their hair and laughing blokes with baseball caps and hoodies; white guys as well as black, Asians and east Europeans, males and females. Then pensioners, bent with the weight of age and worry, and with little to look forward to.

When I thought about it, the world had changed so much since I first went away to war as a young man.

I realised then that for all that time I'd been fighting and risking my life for a brave new world that, in the end, would never be quite what we had hoped for.

I had done the same thing that our fathers and grand-fathers had done before us.

Picking up my mobile, I keyed the number. 'Hi, Daisy.'

'Dad!'

'Hi, darling. Will you tell Mum I'm coming home for Christmas.'

# Acknowledgements

I should like to thank a number of people, friends and associates, for their help, advice and interest in the preparation of this book.

They include Colonel Alan Jones of the hugely respected SSAFA charity (Soldiers, Sailors, Airmen & Families Association) at Warminster. Despite their magnificent efforts and the work of other charities, and strong regimental support groups, many individuals still slip through the net. All too frequently our fallen heroes still end up on the streets or in our prisons.

*Of those who have seen combat, it is said that there is no such thing as an unwounded warrior.*

I am also indebted to Barney and others from the front line in Afghanistan.

Inspirational Sally Eyres, ex of the blues and twos; former soldier and dear pal 'Big Brian' Mullett; motor maniac Oggy; lifelong seafarer Maurice Husband for setting me on a straight course, and young cybernaut Alex White for bringing me up to speed.

And I reserve a special thank you to my dear friend Jim Speirs for his understanding in allowing me to share and replicate his personal experiences in fictional terms.

It will be increasingly vital in the coming years that we all fully understand the personal legacy of war that is left with many of the individuals who fought on our behalf. Not all will be able to cope.

They will need us, as much as we needed them.

Terence Strong, London 2012